Musical Muse

Wives and Lovers of the Great Composers

by Arthur McMaster

foreword by Dr. Roger Vogel

Orchard Park Press
Greenville, SC

For Mac and Rita,
they knew something about inspiration

Musical Muse, Wives and Lovers of the Great Composers. © 2007 by Arthur McMaster. All rights reserved. No part of this book may be used or reproduced in any manner without written permission, except in the case of brief quotations embodied in critical articles and reviews.

For information contact Orchard Park Press, Suite M, PO Box 1711, Taylors SC 29687.

This OPP edition published by arrangement with
Catawba Publishing Company,
5945 Orr Rd., Ste. F. Charlotte, NC 28213
Charlotte NC 28213.

Cover art a illustrations by Jan Haire, Greenville SC

McMaster, Arthur.
    Musical muse : wives and lovers of the great
    composers / by Arthur McMaster ; foreword by Roger
    Vogel. -- 1st ed. pbk.
    p. cm.
    Includes bibliographical references and index.
    LCCN 2007935741
    ISBN-13: 978-0-9628594-9-6
    ISBN-10: 0-9628594-9-4

    1. Composers--Biography. 2. Composers' spouses--
    Biography. 3. Mistresses--Biography. 4. Inspiration.
    I. Title.

    ML390.M33 2007   780'.92'2
        QBI07-600255

Musical Muse

Wives and Lovers of the Great Composers

by Arthur McMaster

*"A maid of twenty and not yet a wife,
A man of thirty who is but a lover,
Are losing fast, and may never recover,
The spring of life.*

Robert Schumann to Clara Wieck (1839)

Contents

CHAPTER ONE	BACH, Johann Sebastian,	5
CHAPTER TWO	BARTÓK, Béla	14
CHAPTER THREE	BEETHOVEN, Ludwig van	22
CHAPTER FOUR	BERLIOZ, Hector	32
CHAPTER FIVE	BIZET, Georges	43
CHAPTER SIX	BRAHMS Johannes	51
CHAPTER SEVEN	CHOPIN, Frédéric	61
CHAPTER EIGHT	ELGAR, Edward	73
CHAPTER NINE	HAYDN, Franz Josef	87
CHAPTER TEN	LISZT, Franz	96
CHAPTER ELEVEN	MAHLER, Gustav	109
CHAPTER TWELVE	MOZART, Wolfgang Amadeus	123
CHAPTER THIRTEEN	PUCCINI, Giacomo	141
CHAPTER FOURTEEN	SCHUBERT, Franz Peter	151
CHAPTER FIFTEEN	SCHUMANN, Robert	159
CHAPTER SIXTEEN	STRAUSS, Richard	175
CHAPTER SEVENTEEN	STRAVINSKY, Igor	185
CHAPTER EIGHTEEN	TCHAIKOVSKY, Pyotr Ilyich	200
CHAPTER NINETEEN	VERDI, Giuseppe	206
CHAPTER TWENTY	WAGNER, Wilhelm Richard	221
CHAPTER TWENTY-ONE	Others: Baroque; Classical	239
CHAPTER TWENTY-TWO	Others: Romantic; Early Modern	253
AFTERWORD & APPENDIX		267
APPENDIX		269
RESOURCE NOTES		277
AUTHOR'S BIOGRAPHY		301

Arthur McMaster

Acknowledgments:

I must recognize some colleagues, friends, musicologists, and a few loved ones who have given me their time, ideas, critical faculty, and encouragement in my bold pursuit of over one hundred women who inspired some of the world's best classical music.

My debt to Ms. Robena Cornwell is enormous. Robena is the University of Florida Music Library's Senior Librarian. She not only helped me to complete two years of research at Florida but gave me some particularly insightful ideas about what institutions had what additional primary source material.

As for expertise in music biography, Mark Mitchell, the brilliant author of *Virtuosi*, (Indiana University Press, 2000) offered a close reading of parts of my book while the work was still looking for direction. Mark helped me to see that it was then too academic – a fault no doubt of this author's having spent so many years in graduate schools and on academic research. Finding my audience was critical, and Mark gets credit for whatever positive results accrue.

I extend my profound thanks, as well, to Dr. Roger C. Vogel, professor and chairman of music theory and composition at the University of Georgia, who offers a Foreword to the book. I am grateful to his wife Ellen Ritchey for her close reading of parts of the manuscript. Ellen, a fine soprano, evidently shares with me a keen interest in Mozart's motets. Thanks, as well, to Noel Scott, at the Library of Congress, for his feedback. Noel is a long-time friend, and a valuable Wagner man.

Some of my best help came from abroad. That should not be surprising, since every one of my so-called "great composers" is European. My dear friend Hans Müller-Borchert, in Rheine, Germany, was helpful to me in my work on Mozart and Wagner, especially so on some tricky translations of Wagner's letters and his biography. I felt I had to check on some previous interpretations, and his recommendations were invaluable. Hans even helped me to locate the lakeside villa of Maiernigg, in Austria, where Mahler successfully courted Alma Schindler. I thank Brian Newbould, Professor Emeritus of Music at the University of Hull, for his steady support of my work on Robert Schubert – his expertise, my passion.

Closer to home, I am grateful for the support and confidence I got from French horn instructor and my colleague, Ericka Tyner, Professor of Music at Converse College, in Spartanburg. Evidently horn players gravitate to Richard Strauss, which turned out to be a boon for me. My good friend Dr. Tom Schott read parts of the manuscript at the half way point, egged me on, gave me some invaluable research advice, and chided me into making a few changes in style. His close editing was invaluable.

I had to have something of a muse too. My wife Sue, with the patience of Job, read nearly every line of the book, pointed out typos, transpositions, redundancies, and logical fallacies, and proved to be my font of strength when I needed an extra glass of ruby Syrah to keep going. My web-designing daughter Kellie read the Mozart chapter – probably not one of her favorite musicians – and asked a few penetrating questions that proved essential for me in my exploration of the Masonic connection in Wolfgang's bizarre story of a brotherhood betrayed. To these people and to so many other fellow music lovers I say thank you, and I hope you will enjoy this book. You helped to make it a reality.

Arthur McMaster

Foreword

Since the beginning of recorded history love has been the inspiration for poetry, for art, and for music. So it is that the lives and loves of musicians and composers have been the subject of so many novels, plays, and motion pictures. Now one book, impressively researched and richly detailed, brings much of that complex history into focus.

Even as early as the fourteenth century, when composers' names were just beginning to be identified with music in Europe, there is a well documented-relationship between Guillaume de Machaut (then in his 60's) and a rather madcap teenage French girl named Peronne. Although conducted primarily by correspondence, over a period of several years, from about 1362 to 1365, the "affair" resulted in over 9000 lines of poetry and eight musical compositions by du Machaut.

What is not generally known is that the creation of a work of art requires a great deal more than just inspiration. It is hard work. One need only look at the revised manuscripts of Beethoven to see how he labored over each note, revising passages many times. For Frédéric Chopin, as well, the ideas came fairly easily; but it was with difficulty that he crafted the complete work. As a composer, I know from experience that many, many hours go into the completion of a substantial musical work. A miniature the size of a popular song (about a minute, without repeating the verses) might be crafted in a single afternoon, but a symphony, a concerto, or a sonata takes months or even years.

Of course love, for all its splendor, is not the only source for inspiration. A classical composer may be motivated to create a work by world events, by a commission, an intriguing idea, or a request for a composition by someone with whom there is no known amatory relationship.

That said, the most intriguing source of inspiration in art remains the romantic one. A book that provides a great deal of information about the most well-known composers of Western art music, and their loves, whether the attachments were legitimate or otherwise, is Arthur McMaster's *Musical Muse*. This book will surely be of interest to classical music devotees everywhere.

Roger C. Vogel, PhD
Professor of Music
The University of Georgia

Arthur McMaster

Introduction

The inspirational role that one person may play in another's genius is not a new theme. Francis Scott Fitzgerald had his spirited, dreamy, reckless Zelda. Señor Pablo Picasso was Fitzgerald's contemporary in more ways than one, and the painter's many Muses were as outlandish as any collection this side of Ursa Major. Among a vast array of Picasso's lovers, male and female, there was the tall, winsome, and strikingly beautiful French model Fernande Olivier, who got Pablo through the funk of his Blue Period. Fernande was supplanted by the rakish poet Guilliame Apollinaire, whose childhood Norman Mailer described as "even more uprooted, grand, debased, cockeyed, and bi-valued than Picasso's." Artists of every time, dimension and description need a spark – maybe sometimes even a salacious jolt.

So it has always been with musicians. For many of them the muse was a girl who seemed to share a common chemistry, perhaps a beautiful and blazing kindred spirit, sometimes it was even a wife. Men like Franz Liszt, Gustav Mahler, and Richard Wagner required a succession of them. For the emotionally-charged Pyotr Tchaikovsky the catalyst was neither obvious nor, to his bourgeois thinking, was it socially satisfactory. Frequently, one's object of affection is not only out of reach, by social standards, but also out of bounds. Convention, of course, has no place and less merit in the world of the muse.

In this volume, I offer the stories of 100 women and a few men behind the scenes and the opera screens, at the piano benches, singing and cavorting in the concert halls, and not a few poised upon the feather beds of twenty-eight of the world's great classical music composers, performers, and conductors. Twenty composers get their own chapters. I include here not only the muses of predominantly heterosexual men, but the compositions, longings and musings of a few gay and bi-sexual composers as well. After all, what sense does it make to assign a greater inspiration to one kind of sexuality over another?

Musical Muse: Wives and Lovers of the Great Composers

The subject of Musical Muse cries out for our attention, as I know of no other consideration of muse-inspired compositions. Their vital work comes to us through musical histories, letters and memoirs, and quite a few woefully dry biographies. Because I had to put this work into some larger context, these twenty-two chapters also serve to present a sampling of many other compositional efforts. It would be quite impossible to do a decent job of naming and defining all the works of these so-called "great composers" and this book is not intended to serve as a full treatment of the oeuvre of any one man or woman. Rather, it is about how their muses came to matter. I offer my apologies to any of the men and women of our rich classical music past if I have misrepresented any of their words, talents, motives, or persuasions. An appendix links the principals and their compositions to their many muses.

Here's an historical appetizer: Immediately out of school, in 1713, the young Giuseppe Tartini eloped with the young ward of his master, a Cardinal of the church. Unfortunate for us, historians have misplaced the lady's name. Knowing he was in a spot of hot holy oil Giuseppe, never one to overlook an obvious escape route, left town dressed as a monk and entered a monastery in Assisi. He remained there incognito for a number of years while he studied the violin. When the heat was off, Tartini came out of seclusion and lived openly with the young woman in the sanctuary of Vienna. We don't know what she did to amuse herself while Giuseppe was at Matins, or while doing his devotions and learning his craft as a violin composer and virtuoso. Whatever she did or did not do to inspire the fiddler, something fine did come of it all.

This Baroque master's best known piece is the violin sonata "The Devil's Trill," which he supposedly wrote upon waking from a dream. Could the Trill be called something of a catharsis? Many of the works linked here with a specific muse were exactly that, a way to come to grips with something out of reach, denied, something that might have been. Muses tend to urge and to inflame; they inspire.

My purpose for researching and writing this book is two-fold. As a poet and classical music lover I have long been intrigued by what force of nature inspires creative work of the highest order. The number of times in which composers worked with female poets has not been sufficiently assessed, for that matter. Brahms, Liszt, Schumann, Wagner, Mahler, and especially Elgar all used poetry in their compositions. Wagner's lover Mathilde Wesendonck is a good example of poet-muse. We would not have *Tristan und Isolde* without Frau Wesendonck's tender verses offered to Richard when he was supposed to be tending to his brilliant and equally willful wife. There are hundreds more examples considered here. The tools of the muse are varied. Not surprisingly, they often involve another art form.

Beginning, as I had to, with Johann Sebastian Bach offered me the greatest challenge. Poor fellow had practically no love life whatsoever. Before or beyond the two women he married we find no evidence of any girlfriends. Bach seems to have had no flings. He found room for the two wives in his life only in the most perfunctory sense, for together the three of them made many little Bachs – twenty in fact. But Sebastian Bach's women seemed to offer him little "muse-ical" inspiration. I have attempted to show where there may have been some; but in truth I could not relegate him to Chapter 21, with the "Other Baroque and Classical Masters" because he was simply too important to music. Besides which his name comes at just such a place along the alphabetic continuum that I could not finesse the result. So the one man least likely to elucidate the role of the muse in classical music starts us off. Another hard worker, Bartók had a bit more luck. By the time we get to Beethoven and Berlioz, I trust the reader will be on board with me in my mission – to champion the remarkable, sometimes almost chimerical and often unheralded women in the lives of many of the world's great composers.

I came to this project after discovering the existence of one Magdalena Hofdemel, Mozart's final, and very nearly his fatal, girl friend. I also felt the need to locate the source of a few of his piano concertos, which have been my own specialty, my own fixation. You will find the elusive and desirable Magdalena in Chapter Twelve.

There were other incentives. I have long been a student of classical music, especially so some of the late-classical Germans. Robert Schumann's life was the focus of some of my better poetry. I studied piano for many years, and having given up playing I am content to study, to teach, and to listen. Perhaps more importantly, I am an inquisitive kind of fellow who wants to better understand the raw intangibles of creativity. Now I can share with you my findings.

Here are a couple of more teasers: Did you ever wonder about the motivation behind such pieces as Liszt's *Liebesträume*, or Puccini's *Turandot*? They are here. We even find, not surprisingly, that Ravel's *Bolero* was written for a certain special someone. In fact, for any man or woman who would truly understand the human dimension of classical composition, the romantic, heart-searing, worry-all-night-about-her kind of stuff, this is your book.

The word "muse" comes from the Greek; *Mousa*. According to mythology, one of the nine daughters of Mnemosyne (memory) and Zeus each preside over a different art or science. The Muse of epic poetry is Calliope. Euterpe is the muse of music and lyric poetry. Erato is muse of the poetry of love. They often work and play together in that quixotic place where poetry, music, and romantic love conspire to entangle the lives of those men and women who intrigue us for their peculiar genius. The influence of the muse demands and deserves to be recognized. I think signore Giuseppe Tartini would agree.

Arthur McMaster
Greer, S.C.
2007

CHAPTER ONE

BACH, Johann Sebastian, (1685 – 1750), German

" Ceaseless work, analysis, reflection, writing much, endless self-correction, that is my secret." (Bach)

By all definitions a serious fellow, J.S. Bach started with little and lived frugally for the rest of his days. That is a fairly standard observation about Bach, but it allows the reader to understand something truly fundamental about this musician. Sebastian's was a life of moderation, measure, and proportion. In fact, as to proportion: "... in his life, wine and women have always come a long way after song in [the] great composer's consciousness."[1]

This sober assessment illuminates the particularly difficult work of the musical muse in one man's life. Bach did not have as many lovers, or in any fashion as many "flings," as did most of the men who would follow him in a career of music and musical genius. But he seemed to do all right with the two he did have, if a progeny of twenty children and an enormous body of superb work is any measure. The Baroque master himself laid down the law: ceaseless work! Let's say he came from serious stock.

Bach was born to music, as were countless of his cousins and arguably most of his children. There had been Bach musicians of some note for generations. As a child he took to music much as he took to the rest of his studies, with seriousness and purpose. Born in Eisenach, on 21 March 1685, learned the organ from his older brother, a church musician. This was Johann Christoph, who had studied with the estimable Johann Pachelbel. All of Bach's brothers were also named Johann, so usually he was identified as "Sebastian." The boy came under his brother's care at age nine when both parents passed, leaving him with little money and few prospects, besides a prodigious musical family history. By the time Sebastian was fifteen, Christoph's own family had grown large enough that the younger sibling found it necessary to find other accommodations. Sebastian Bach was placed with the masters of a school for poor boys in Lüneberg, south of Hamburg. He was on his way to greatness, but for a few years he would have to sing for his supper.

Sebastian earned his tuition by singing in the choir. Fortunate for the boy, the Michaelisschule offered free room and tuition to children with good voices. Bach qualified as both needy and talented.[2] He left Lüneberg in 1702, completing his studies but financially unable to go on to a university education. Still, having prepared himself well in voice and organ lessons, Bach was considered for a position at the Jacobiskirche in Sangerhausen, near Halle, where his contemporary George Frideric Handel was born and grew up. He nearly landed a job, at seventeen, when the Duke of Weissenfels personally intervened and placed a crony of his into the position. Undeterred, Sebastian was hired at the Weimar court as violinist, but only briefly so. He made his way in 1703 to Arnstadt securing an even better post as organist at the New Church, or *Neue Kirche*.

Here the young man began what would be a career of forty-seven years in music. He was eighteen years old, and under the terms of his contract Bach was expected to accompany the services of the *Neue Kirche* on Sundays, feast days, and other occasions of public worship. Bach's contract made no mention of any obligation to provide the church with figural music, that is, more advanced choral music, usually with instruments. Indeed, "performance of any vocal music more complicated than chorales and simple motets was virtually ruled out by the poor quality of the ... students ... and the situation was aggravated by Bach's inability to maintain good discipline among them."[3] Soon a young lady would complicate matters more. No muse; she did shake things up for Bach.

As with many first jobs Bach, too, was driven desire to do more, to create and succeed. That said, the urge "to move on" was also great. Here fate offered a way: Bach had a great falling out with the church fathers fairly early in his tenure. It seems he'd brought a young girl into the choir loft to spark the choir boys' enthusiasm. Bach thought they needed a stimulus. Girls were not allowed! This maneuver apparently scandalized the elders and opened the door for his mutually agreed exit.

Some suggest the girl was his distant cousin Maria Barbara, whom he would soon marry. To this day, however, we cannot be certain who she actually was. In any event, a chastised young Bach had let his enthusiasm overwhelm is discretion. He had been in Arnstadt all of three years, and it was time to move on. Marie Barbara can now make a proper entrance.

Passing through yet another disappointing job as church organist, Bach came to Mülhausen in June 1707 where he composed a great number of choral variations, fugues, and fantasies for clavier.Sebastian's compositional career truly began here at Mülhausen. There was more to the Arnstadt imbroglio; Bach was perhaps too innovative. The church elders complained of over-elaboration , uncomfortable with "the virtuoso organist inside the young man – the heir to Buxtehude and Böhm."[4] Among the compositions firmly dated in his Mülhausen era include Martin Luther's famous Easter work *Christ lag in Todes Banden* (BMV 4), and a magnificent funeral piece.

Meanwhile, the young man had become close to Maria Barbara, daughter of his father's cousin Michael Bach. They wanted to marry, and after Sebastian secured a new position, in Mülhausen, they arranged for a wedding at the village church in Dornheim, near Arnstadt, on October 17, 1707.[5] There were certainly a lot of Bachs present, from many branches of the tree. There must have been some special considerations given to the young couple, as apparently the fees for the church service were waived or returned. Bach wrote some original music for the nuptials. Never one to let an occasion for work go by, "[t]here are two wedding pieces by Bach that may have been written around the time of his own wedding: the cantata *'Der Herr denkt an uns'* (BWV 196) … suitable for the small Dornheim church … and a Quodlibet, or makeshift musical melody, (BWV 524) … including references to Bach's circle of family and friends."[6] Some of this remains speculative, however, as detailed records are incomplete or lost. Did Bach find a Muse? Maybe.

Maria Barbara not only did not get to change the last letter of her name upon marriage, but she kept the same surname too. She was nineteen-years old when they met and all of twenty when she married her cousin, Sebastian. Music had always been a part of Maria Barbara's life – a nice fit for them both. We tend to know more of her children with Johann Sebastian than we do of her.

Four of their six children lived, and two came to be first-rate musicians, Carl Philipp Emmanuel, born in 1714, perhaps especially so. Still, "Sebastian and Barbara were of approximately the same age; both had been reared in homes where music was considered of paramount importance; and both were orphans drifting along without strong personal ties. Each could lighten the other's solitude and provide in each other's lives the anchorage they both needed. No wonder the two young people were so irresistibly drawn to each other, and 'The Golden Crown' [the court] witnessed an idyllic love affair."[7] Barbara thus becomes our first Muse, though she was hardly dynamic or flamboyant in the part. The more bold and audacious ones will appear in subsequent chapters.

The young Bach couple made a happy life together; he was in charge of the music, she of the babies and looking after her husband's creative needs. Evidently they were successful in their division of labor, as this was a time of significant composition. Bach stayed busy with his church music assignments: weddings, funerals, and other special occasions. Even without these otherwise unplanned churchly celebrations, Sebastian Bach was responsible for the music of six services during a normal week.[8] What mattered at least as much to him was, here at Mülhausen, he had opportunities to compose for weddings, funerals and other such special services; and he was making a good bit more money than he had in Arnstadt. His compositions included the grand cantata "*Gott ist mein Koenig*" (BMV 71), and two other vocal works where Bach showed significant structural variation from what had come before. He was entering a highly "experimental time" in his life. "The cantata BMV 71 put Bach on the map, so to speak: it was published well ahead of comparable work by his contemporaries Telemann [four years older] and [his exact contemporary] Handel."[9]

Ever the peripatetic artist, Bach was soon looking for opportunity. A short eight months after their autumn marriage the Bachs were relocating again. In June of 1708 Sebastian traveled to Weimar, at the request of the court. He was lured away by the prospects of a better position, more pay, higher prestige and a massive organ renovation that must have appealed to his aesthetic senses. Sebastian Bach's biographers suspect that, as the health of the court organist Johann Effler began to fail, the reputation of the young man in Mülhausen became stronger and more appealing. Bach accepted an offer that tripled the Arnstadt salary. Bigger changes were forthcoming.

Maria Barbara learned she was pregnant. The money would be especially important. Besides the fiscal practicality of the move, Bach knew that he would be exposed to musicians and opportunities in Weimar that would not be available to him in the provinces.

We learn of a passage in Bach's resignation letter that sheds light on his overall musical plans. He writes that he acquired, at some cost, a good store of the choicest church compositions, suggesting "his self-directed manner of learning," enabling the young composer to examine a broad range of music.[10] This Sebastian Bach was diligent.

Years later, Maria Barbara and Sebastian's third son, Johann Gottfried Bernhard Bach, was appointed organist at neighboring St. Mary's church. Only his sense of position in the hierarchy of the Weimar Court *kappele*, or band, could have caused the twenty-three year old man to question whether he was moving up fast enough. Bach was number three of twelve full-time court musicians, ranking behind Johann Samuel Drese the Kapellmeister and his son Johann Wilhelm Drese, the Vice-Kapellmeister. Perhaps more importantly, Bach was clearly a favorite of Duke Ernst August of Saxe-Weimar. He continued to write church music and to stay out of the way of the raging dispute among religious factions as to what kind of music was orthodox and what was leaning toward heresy. Still, Bach's musical functions at Weimar were not exclusively liturgical. Playing at the "divine services was of central importance, but this task was essentially limited to accompanying hymns and providing introductory chorale preludes." He needed and would pursue broader opportunituues.[11] Fortunate for him, royalty liked diversions.

Bach played for the entertainment of the ducal family and they tended to show him off to visiting dignitaries. In so doing he presumably played some of the Italian music then coming into favor, but we get the idea that Bach was somehow distrusted by certain members of the court. In his splendid little volume on Bach's life the French musicologist André Pirro offers the extent to which Bach had a better grasp of French and Italian music, perhaps again ahead of his contemporaries, because of his deeply-seated inquisitiveness, his determination to find such music, and to master it. From his access to the music libraries of the great churches where he worked, Sebastian would have found Monteverdi's written music, and he came to an interest in the French influence through his association with his early teacher Georg Böhm. Bach, then, may have made less gifted musicians around him made to feel even more vulnerable for his pronounced and far-reaching talents. It would be reasonable to suggest that this love of learning and musical discoveryalso predisposed Sebastian Bach to continue to search for the ideal appointment. He was a highly accomplished organ and clavier player, but he chafed at the restrictions of narrowly defined jobs. Being the Weimar court organist and its "chamber musician," allowed him time to continue to work on his own violin technique. Although we tend to think of him today as a church-music composer, he sought every opportunity to work outside of the church's well regulated needs.

As an example, Bach did not write the so-called *Hunt Cantata* (BMV 208) until about March of 1716. This was to celebrate a favorite duke's birthday. It is his first known secular cantata and his first work of truly large-scale proportions.[12] When further advancement at Weimar seemed in doubt – actually Telemann had been offered and declined the post of Kapellmeister when it opened –Bach again began to think of moving on from the court. The good Maria Barbara supported him at every turn. He'd always been able to find an increased salary with each move. Could he do it again? This time there were further complications.

Because of their internal jealousies and suspicions Sebastian had lost favor with the Saxe-Weimar court, and he with them. Then, in January 1717, he was offered and accepted the position of *Kapellmeister* at Cöthen, some sixty miles to the north. The money was an important consideration, and here he earned 400 thalers per annum, nearly a third again what he was being paid at Weimar. Not surprisingly, Bach was not allowed to leave Weimar graciously, and he may have even been briefly jailed for what his peevish boss, Duke Wilhelm, saw as a lack of loyalty in Herr Bach. The young musician had enjoyed composing and playing for Wilhelm's brother, Franz August, who admired the Italian style, particularly concertos, which became a common bond between these men. When Wilhelm preferred Telemann over Bach the message was clear. It was once again time to move on.

By now the composer and Maria Barbara had four children at home. Their last child together was born in 1718, Leopold Augustus, who lived but one year. Twins born five years earlier in 1713 had died in infancy. Barbara's unmarried sister Friedelena had come to join the family, and to help with the children, but she also became another source of comfort to her younger sister.

Quite apart from personal tragedies, Sebastian's professional time with the court in Cöthen was a happy and productive time. The town was small and provincial, yet it was distinctly Calvinist, meaning Bach would have fewer liturgical compositions due. He was not required to be the church organist and could turn to instrumental music. Bach stayed six years, apparently admiring the musical talent of his patron Prince Leopold, and creating "a profusion of work," including "the suites for orchestra and the *Brandenburg Concertos* – [which] reflect the exuberance of an artist discovering new means of expression, and the peace of mind of a composer who had found real understanding."[13] The extent to which Maria Barbara coaxed or inspired her husband is unreported. The most we can say is that, like a true midwife, she was there at the creation.

Things went well for the family for about three years. The oldest child, Johann Friedemann, was showing his innate musical talent. Quickly, his father became the boy's tutor, designing a "clavier book" for his instruction. In May 1720, Sebastian agreed to accompany Prince Leopold to Carlsbad, today known as Karlovy Vary, in the Czech Republic, on a sojourn of chamber music and the healing properties of the Bohemian spa town. When they returned in July, having been gone barely three months, he received the shock of his young life – Maria Barbara was dead and buried. Only thirty-five years old, this wife, mother of four, this ever-so loving partner and Muse had been in perfectly good health. Bach was devastated.

No biographer seems to have discovered what killed the woman, although it has In any event, Sebastian, in one of the rare occasions that he wrote music specifically for her, "… intended *the D-minor partita* (BWV 1004), and the chaconne in particular, as a musical epitaph to his deceased wife."[14] Barbara had been the practical, the necessary Muse. Where and to whom would Sebastian turn next to keep him going, to urge and cajole him?

Bach's children were now ages twelve, ten, six, and five. Maia Barbara's sister Friedelena was not up to, or was unable to, serve as nursemaid after her sister passed away, but she did stay with her brother-in-law until she died in 1729. Bach remained unattached for eighteen months before he took his next wife. This one seems to have been more suited to the role of Musical Muse. For this woman he'd write some of his best loved music.

By the time Bach re-married – the young lady was twenty; he was thirty-five – the composer's career was solid, if not yet spectacular. Her name was Anna Magdalena Wülken, or Wilcken. Her surname has been variously recorded, but these are the two most common spellings. They married on 3 December 1721, beginning a romance that had some chance to mature. Like Barbara before her, Anna Magdalena was a musician, but much more so than the first Frau Bach had been. Apparently, she was also a gifted soprano. Anna Magdalena, like her husband, had been employed by the Cöthen court.

Here we get a good sense of the woman's importance to Bach and his work: Magdalena may well have been more interested in operatic music than was her husband, but she was able to appreciate Sebastian's greatness and young enough to adapt to his new interests. Magdalena may have been leery of her new responsibilities, which included looking after four stepchildren, the oldest only seven years her junior. With her "husband she succeeded in creating a cheerful, comfortable home…. Magdalena knew the secret of enjoying the simplest pleasures with all her heart…" This disposition helped her a great deal in a life that was "filled to the brim with the duties of running a large household most thriftily, a life in which she had to go through the ordeal of child-bearing thirteen times, and seven times saw a child of hers carried to the grave. How Sebastian on such occasions tried to instill courage into her suffering heart is revealed in Magdalena's music book, which he presented to her in 1725." There is one further insight: "Three times he wrote into a different version of his aria, based on Paul Gerhardt's hymn: 'Fret not, my soul, on God rely,' meant to lift her out of the day's turmoil with simple and deeply felt music."[15]

This well-known book contains the famous and much loved song, based on his poem beginning, *Bist du bei mir* (If thou be near…)[16] Magdalena was in every regard a helpmate and loving wife and mother. She had to endure the hardship of her older stepchildren's lack of affection for her. Recognizing this strain, Bach devised for his Anna her own small music book, not intended as an instructional but considered a "collection of musical declarations of love, not one that incessantly alludes to yearning, affection, and kissing but one dedicated to mutual feelings and experiences, one that is far richer and more comprehensive."[17] His love for the woman cannot be doubted.

By all accounts the composer was not particularly affectionate or emotive, but his young wife encouraged him to reach deeper, to expand his musical talents. It's now impossible to evaluate how successful she was in inspiring her husband, for it seems the politics of court favor, which Bach needed in order to have time to write, were not on his side. Magdalena could only do so much to facilitate his work. Things began to sour for Sebastian in Cöthen when his young friend and patron Prince Leopold married a young woman with no interest in music.

Bach told Anna that he felt "neglected and superfluous." His thoughts turned to the future for his growing family and for his art. Leipzig was calling; he was restless. Bach wondered, however, if he would be likely to find the same personal satisfaction he had enjoyed at Cöthen. What should he do? Where could he go; how would another move impact his wife and family?

Although Bach would be taking what seemed a salary cut, there would be more money to be made in incidental and occasional work. Magdalena, however, would lose her position as court singer, where she had made 200 thalers per year. That would hurt. What about his responsibilities as family provider? Bach hated to see his wife lose her job, which she enjoyed. Amazing as this seems now, it was not done for a woman to sing solo music in the churches of the time. "Thus, to the young singer the removal to Leipzig would mean the renunciation of any professional activity of her own."[18] Simply put, Anna Magdalena was willing to sacrifice her career for her husband's.

For his part, Bach was looking for a step up and out; the idyll of Cöthen was over. Ever the practical fellow, he had to think of the larger the family. The Bach children would soon be considered for a university education, and Sebastian had to consider their futures. He and Anna knew that the Cöthen school system offered them little. A move to a bigger city, with an intellectual, commercial and cultural vibrancy, would likely offer everyone more opportunity, except perhaps the good wife Anna – Anna the sacrificer. For Bach, surely there was more prestige in the Leipzig position, though perhaps less comfort. In the end, his sense of work and fiscal responsibility won out. They moved to Leipzig in spring of 1723, Sebastian taking his official post on the first of June as St. Thomas Cantor and music director over five churches. He had never had more responsibility, more opportunity.

Sebastian would also have to add certain teaching responsibilities, including Latin – which he often delegated – but he was determined to make a go of the job. Indeed, he did just that. In fact, he held the job until his death in 1750. The St. Thomas appointment was the longest he "enjoyed" anywhere. Some musicologists have suggested that Bach was also eager to return to sacred composition, perhaps engendered in part by the death of his loving Maria Barbara.

Bach wrote some beautiful liturgical music at just this time. His *St. John's* and *St. Matthew's Passions* are magnificent. The *St. Matthew* was first performed at St. Thomas church, the largest of the five, on Good Friday, in 1729. This is a massive work, which he accommodated to the rest of the liturgy on this special holy day, along with other motets and hymns, some of which were original.

"Of cantatas alone he supplied, according to [Bach's first biographer Johann Nikolaus] Forkel's statement, five complete sets for the entire ecclesiastical year, 295 different works in all […] Bach composed one cantata per month up to 1744."[19]

Oddly, little more is said about the young wife that facilitated so much of her husband's career. Anna Magdalena became the principal recorder, or scribe, of Bach's music. In the year 1740 Sebastian's eyesight began to fail and his health was no longer robust. When his writing slowed he settled into more teaching responsibilities, eventually taking over the position as director of the town Colegium Musicum. Perhaps the man with the life-long, enormous work ethic knew that his career had finally reached a kind of plateau.

In 1747 the aging genius who had helped to define the dramatic Baroque period, marked for a deliberate moving away from the Renaissance period, was invited to visit his King, Frederick "the Great," at his palace in Potsdam. It was the kind of recognition he had always aspired to, and it was doubly sweeter for sharing it with his son. Carl Philipp Emmanuel had been in the King's service as clavichord accompanist since 1740. Now such a reunion was surely a great success. Bach was asked to return the next day and to play again, which he did. Bach soon completed a piece of music he'd improvised for Frederick. Sebastian dedicated it to his new benefactor.

The composer's instrumental music, his small chamber works, and his larger scores mark him as a master of 18th century music. But it is his church music that seems the more glorious. Somehow, Bach had always managed to accommodate the distinctions in musical preference, or demand, of the ruling Lutherans or Calvinists. He worked to accommodate whoever was paying the bills. One has to wonder if he had not taken on such broad and diverse work would we have ever seen the majesty of his two great passions, or his epochal sacred work, his *Mass in B-Minor*, with its dominant choral fugues, dating to 1733, but which he worked on until the year before his death.

During the last years of his life, as his eyesight continued to fail, the man grew weaker, and on 28 July 1750, he suffered a stroke and died. In his last hours he was working with one of his sons-in-law on a hymn that he called *Vor deinen Thron tret'ich heimit*, which translates to "I will appear before they throne."[20] Bach had a premonition of his last working days.

Anna Magdalena, thirty-nine when her husband died, lived another ten years, though not in any comfort – all but ignored by her husband's children with his first wife. There was nothing Bach could do to turn that situation around. The children simply did not take to her. As for Sebastian and his Magdalena, surely they were very much in love; she made much of his success possible. Why did Bach not write more music for her or dedicate more to her? We have, of course, Magdalena's music book. Certainly that collection of music for his wife is a testament to her contributions to the man's work. An answer to the larger question may be found within Bach himself, and perhaps more so in the time in which the couple lived. The same problem exists in trying to tie Domenico Scarlatti's music to either of his wives. Let's say that it was a matter of the convention of the times, complicated by incomplete research material.

Sebastian Bach may have had some romantic inclinations, and even intentions, as a musician, but the milieu was not conducive. Though there were exceptions, the musical styles were largely inappropriate to personal emotion. Put another way, the music focus Bach knew and composed was not compatible with the sweeping, lovely melodies that would seem much easier to write only a few decades later, when women were celebrated openly for their inspiration.

Whatever music style or form the principal composers of the day worked in they took some inspiration from loved ones. In early music, however, the Muse often worked without much recognition. In short, religious music: fugues, canons, motets, and masses, is less likely to be inspired by another's love and romance than are playful songs, grand suites and operas, and majestic symphonic works.

Coming shortly after Bach and Handel were two men with more obvious Muses; Franz Joseph Haydn, who was eighteen-years old when Bach died, and Wolfgang Amadeus Mozart, born three years after Handel's death. With the coming of these composers, and the birth of the Classical era that they divined and brought to the western world, we find the beginnings of music that was more readily dedicated to a loving companion. Only a few years later, for example, Haydn's affection for Luigia Polzelli, followed much later in his life by that for Rebecca Schroter, represent near-ideal examples of how musicians honor and celebrate "the Muse." Papa Haydn occupies Chapter Nine. Herr Mozart is at home in Chapter Twelve.

CHAPTER TWO

BARTÓK, Béla (1881 – 1945) Hungarian

"Of the three musicians who dominated the musical scene during the first half of the twentieth century – Stravinsky, Schoenberg, and Bartók – it is the Hungarian master who, despite his immense intellectual control, remainednearest to the instinctual, the irrational in music, and thus to the Dionysian spirit in art."[1]

Béla Bartók once told an interviewer that he felt he had been born not once but twice. This was not some religious, fundamentalist awakening. His epiphany had to do only with finding the kind of music that would delight him and, indirectly, make him one of the best-known musicians of his generation.

Hungarian folk music constituted something nearly sacred to the teenager. He'd first heard such music sung by a servant in his house.[2] The singer, an unidentified young girl, was a catalyst, if not a certified Muse; but the she led the impressionable Béla to his distinctive place in European music. Many would follow, as we find that a number of women inspired Bartók in his essential compositions, and frequently in his creation of nationalist music.

Bartók was born in the Hungarian village of Nagyszentmiklós, near the Romanian border, on 25 March 1881, to a couple totally dedicated to this child. Béla's father, a fine amateur musician, died when the boy was seven. His mother quickly became responsible for his early education, and she was also Bartók's first piano teacher. The woman saw an enormous talent in her son and did whatever was necessary to foster his perceived advantage. A quick learner, he also had an ear for native music. What Bartók found from listening to this one servant girl's folk songs, and then to those in her "region," was revelatory. Bartók saw this as music composed and sung from the heart, music so emotionally strong, from that day forth he came to love what he called "peasant music."

Composing simple piano pieces at the age of nine, the boy was drawn in his teens to the national idiom and consciousness of Hungarian and other folk melodies. Such early focus or clarity of purpose – such consciousness – would prove to be his strong suit.

That said, there were those who criticized him for his under-appreciation of the prevalent German academic Romanticism. Fortunately, this bit of narrow-mindedness on the part of certain of his elders did not prevent Béla Bartók from becoming a unique composer and a genius among the merely also-talented.

Piano lessons, practice, and early composition marked his late-teen years. So, too, did a generally weak physical constitution. Mrs. Bartók took a leave of absence from her teaching position, and mother and son traveled to Meran, in the South Tyrol, where Béla was advised by his local doctor to avoid the piano. How could he realistically be expected to do that? This young man lived for music.

To follow such instructions would not be easy for young Béla, who convinced his mother that he must return to practice after showing some return to health. When fully ambulatory, Bartók returned to the music academy and that fall capably performed Liszt's *Piano Sonata*. "The glowing press review in the *Budapesti Naplo*, noted of Bartók's performance that "[a] year and a half ago he was so weak the doctors sent him to Meran ... and now he thunders on the piano like a little Jupiter."[3] Maybe Bartok had something to prove.

Entering the winter of 1902, Béla said he was ready to concentrate on Hungarian folk music. He was stylistically influenced somewhat by Johannes Brahms, but he was also captivated by the forward-looking and exciting work of Richard Strauss, especially in his fascination with Strauss's superb counterpoint exposition of *Zarathustra*. They were innovative composers, yes; but Béla would not be content to follow. He began to sense another influence. Bartók soon met the first in a series of young women who would captivate and, frankly, torment him. She was Stefania Geyer, a violinist of remarkable talent. Young Bartok's piano accompaniment of this fourteen-year old violin-prodigy's performance, at an evening concert in early March, gained him even further recognition and perhaps contributed to his desire to teach piano.[4] Béla felt as if he were intoxicated. Who was this incredible young woman? Truly, he needed some romantic inspiration.

Immediately after the concert, Stefi left Budapest for an international tour. Bartók said he had to know more about her, this girl who might have touched his heart; she had no doubt left an impression on his imagination. Fortunately for this composer, and all who would come to love his music, Stefi would be back. Meanwhile, the ever-surprising force we call Fate had been offered, and had accepted, a big part in the man's life.

It was Béla's teaching that led him to his first romantic love, and arguably to his first musical Muse. Bartók became infatuated with sixteen year-old Adrienne (Adila) Aranyi, herself a violin prodigy and then a student with Jenő Hubay, who also instructed young Miss Geyer.

Adila and Béla had met socially, abetted by the gregarious Mrs. Emma Gruber, later to become Mrs. Zoltán Kodály. Emma Gruber's salon provided the meeting place for serious young musicians, academicians, and the upwardly mobile social artists of Budapest. She was also a quintessential matchmaker.

By November, Béla was smitten; he wrote to his mother that he loved Adila. In fact, he wrote Adila at least sixty-five postcards, each containing a unique musical score. According to one biographer, "[o]ne postcard, dated 29 November, contains the first page of Bartók's composition for violin and piano, signed by the composer and headed, '1902, Nov 23, *emlékeré* (in remembrance).'"[5] Adila certainly liked young Bartók well enough, but she seems to have had no romantic convictions of her own, and after something of a trial romance, largely unrequited, Bartók returned in earnest to the composition of his *Four Pieces for Piano*, dedicating the *Fantasy # 1* to the busy match-maker Emma Gruber.

In May of '03 the young man completed his study with his composition teacher, János Koessler, performing the Liszt *Spanish Rhapsody* with such technical skill that he was exempted from the year-end composition examination. Now, his work would become even more nationalistic, even as Béla's career as an international concert pianist would begin in earnest.

Ironically, it was the path of piano teacher not composer or impresario that brought him back to Stefi Geyer. In December of 1906 Bartók succeeded another of his teachers, the ailing Mr. István Thomán, at the Academy of Music, in Budapest. At the first of the year he "took over the advanced piano class, whose objectives were to provide students with theoretical and practical instruction leading to a performer's career and the award of a state diploma."[6] In May, Bartok attended an Academy concert to enjoy the work of former students, which he was delighted to find would include "the beautiful 19-year old violinist Stefi Geyer, with whom Bartók had [this time] fallen hopelessly in love."[7]

Shortly thereafter, Béla traveled to the tiny town of Jászberény, near Budapest, ostensibly to collect folk music for his grant-in-aid summer project. Here he joined Stefi and her brother at the home of Geyer's relatives. Bartók was now twenty-six. He presented himself wearing a highly affected mustache, short beard and pince-nez eyeglasses. While Stefi was amused, Béla was attempting to locate not only his style but his future, and perhaps in more ways than one. He was ostensibly there to gather Hungarian folk music. Stefi's recollection, however, is that "'Bartók joined us under the pretext of collecting songs. It was obvious that he was following me, because there isn't much to be collected in Jászberény and he hardly found anything.'"[8] Did Béla's act work?

Sensing that the young lady was not yet won over, Bartók redoubled his efforts. At least for now Béla was not taking no for an answer. Stefi agreed to correspond with him while he continued his objective fieldwork. The agreement, she said, would have to be good enough. Fresh from this apparent advance in attempting to gain her heart, Bartók devised innovations and permutations on Hungarian folk music for his *Second Suite* that, specifically in the fourth movement, "represents the first adaptation of Hungarian peasant music peculiarities for a new style of composition.[9] Mr. Bartok was innovative in more ways than one. He also soon found an outlet for his broader compositional skills.

Although Béla had been channeling his talent to the melodies and transcriptions of Hungarian music, something he would return to for most of his life, it was his abiding infatuation with Stefi that "prompted a return to German romanticism that persisted until she broke off their relationship toward the end of February 1908, and he vented his anguish by composing the *First Elegy for Piano* immediately thereafter."[10] Could he compose without her? He'd have to learn to do so. We'll see in a moment how the infatuated young composer actually brought on the final rift between them.

During the rest of this decade Bartók completed and dedicated numerous short pieces for his absent Muse Stefi, including the second movement for his *Concerto no 1 for Violin and Orchestra*. Why did they fail as a couple? Religion and politics separate many who might otherwise be close. Their falling out came sharply with Bartók's frank diatribe against the Roman Catholic Church, a church she loved; and with his incautious belittling of Geyer's persistent faith. When Bartok declared himself in his letters to her to be a confident and honest atheist, he injudiciously added that he was appalled that she should accept the "clumsy fable about the Holy Trinity." Béla said he could not believe that she had chosen to be "a slave to such notions." With that hurtful admonition he figuratively cut himself from her trust and her affection once and for all.

In subsequent letters, Bartók reflected that he had worked on the concerto, and done so "as a confession [of love] to you." In Stefi's response of 13 February 1908, she requested that they end it now and that Béla kindly present her the manuscript as a parting gift. He agreed.

With Stefi effectively out of his future, if not his thoughts, Béla Bartók the very next year would meet another young woman – his student Marta Ziegler. Never slow to come to the point, he promptly asked her to marry him. Marta accepted! Now Béla had real work to do. He needed the love of a good woman. Could it truly be Marta? Would she be inspirational? One big domestic drama resolved for now, Bartók was not long deterred from getting back to the business of composing music.

Béla was eager to pursue his new found fascination for "peasant music," which included such representative instruments as the peasant flute, bagpipes, and the *Drâmbă*, or Jew's Harp. His first musical composition with such odd combinations lead, in September '09, to his delightful *Two Romanian Dances*, op 8a, no. 1. Did Marta have something to do with it? Apparently so. She proved to be a good listener, as well.

The composer was vexed by what he saw as the ravages of loves lost and found. In a letter dated 4 February 1909, Bartók wrote to Marta: "I strongly believe and profess that every true art is produced through the influence of impressions we gather within ourselves from the outer world of 'experiences.' He who paints a landscape only to paint a landscape, or writes a symphony only to write a symphony, is at best nothing but a craftsman. I am unable to imagine products of art otherwise than as manifestations of the creator's boundless enthusiasm, regret, fury, revenge, distorting ridicule, or sarcasm. In the past I did not believe, until I experienced it myself, that a man's works designate the events, the guiding passions of his life more exactly than his biography."[11]

To what extent his young wife Marta continued to influence his composition or his play is less clear. We know she did yeoman work as transcriptionist and attendant to his notes and ideas. The next year they had a son, whom they named Béla. The boy's birth gave the young father some much needed stability. Marta was often ill and, as we know from Bartók's letters to friends and sponsors, this was a difficult time for them. Béla tried his hand at conducting only once, in Berlin, and found it unsatisfying and by all accounts perhaps unsuccessful. He never tried it again.

Béla also tried an opera, and by most assessments it was successful. In 1911, when he was thirty, Bartók composed *Duke Bluebird's Castle*. It has been called one of the most remarkable operas of the new century. What can be made of any female or romantic influence here? The work is moody, extravagantly romantic, and steeped in the verisimilitudes of love. In short, the Duke escorts his "new" wife, Judith, to and through magical doors that open, metaphysically speaking, into revelations. Maybe they are levels of consciousness. Determined to bring light and beauty to the creepy old castle, the lady demands access to the locked doors. The first few rooms are bloody – either having been places of torture or weapons lockers. The third door is more promising, where mountains of jewels and gold loom, but they too are covered with blood.

The young wife has more work to do. The fourth door leads to flowers, bathed in a blue-green light, but the soil is bloody. Can Judith save the Duke from symbolic heartbreak and tragedy? When she opens the fifth door, everything seems to be in splendor. The central hall of the castle is now bathed in light, just as Judith promised. Was it because of her love and devotion? Here, all is perfect; the Duke loves her. But the woman is driven to find more, and she presses on. This is where the composer locates his ambivalent feelings.

Judith demands to open the final two doors, although the Duke bids her not to do so. Such opulence should be enough. What might we learn here about the need to seek and have more? The parable is clear. Predictably, with the opening of the sixth door, the light begins to fade. Judith wants to know whom the Duke loved before her. He does not want to be put into this situation, but Judith has demands it be so. Upon passing through the final door Judith finds herself among the prodigious Duke's other bejeweled wives – there are three, and none, seemingly, were content to leave well enough alone. Defeated by her own curiosity, fair Judith takes her place among the others, and the castle passes back into darkness. No one's lot, least of all the Duke's, is improved for the woman's relentless pursuit of total disclosure. Duke Bluebeard reluctantly tells Judith to accommodate herself to whatever place has been kept for her by the other women. Thus is the grim fairy-tale told.

What shall we make of this story?

Perhaps Béla was compensating, rationalizing. If that is the case, one has to wonder which door or doors he invented for those who brought him the most tears. Was Judith supposed to be his own Marta, fated by melodrama to learn something more about her own Duke's past? Or was she the wife that never was, the love that had eluded Béla? Bluebird was not his only autobiographical opera.

If one can make a case for Bartók's finding compensation for his lost loves in the fate of the Duke, what more can be said of *The Miraculous Mandarin?* This is a story of seduction, brutally played out, but not until the Mandarin had satisfied himself in the embrace of the seductress. Using a rising and falling, positive - negative musical theme Béla found successful in *Two Portraits*, in 1908, and which Bartok dedicated to the decline of his relationship with Stefi Geyer; here he suggests more of a progressive excitement, danger and agitation, followed by resolution, as the Mandarin achieves his fated goal. Few composers were as persistently self-revelatory as Béla Bartók.

In November of 1923, and with his relationship with Marta now under great strain, the composer seems to have reached an important musical plateau with the premiere of *Dance Suite for Major Orchestra*, in Budapest. As quickly as that chapter closed, romance was back. Béla and Marta divorced and he promptly fell in love with another one of his students, Ditta Pásztory, whom he promptly married. Béla and Ditta had a child in 1924. They named him Peter. Bartók had again secured the home front.

But Béla did not stop redefining himself only by taking a second wife. He found he needed to reshape and perhaps reenergize his spiritual life, as well. Shortly thereafter he converted to the Unitarian faith, which his son Béla Jr. suggested was more in keeping with his father's sense of religion, one needing to be "free and humanistic." Promptly, Bartók composed the Slovak folk-song cycle entitled *Five Village Scenes*. Designed to showcase the work he had done in his years gathering what may be described as essentially tribal music, he dedicated the piece to his exciting new Muse, Ditta Pásztory.

Bartók was particularly active in 1926, composing some of his most profound and stylistically interesting piano music, including *Nine Small Pieces for Piano,* and his *First Piano Concerto*. He also composed the rudiments of his *Mikokosmos* series. These are 150 small pieces for piano, arranged by technical difficulty, which he worked on for over ten years. He supposedly wrote these as studies for his son Peter's piano lessons.

The composer had finally reached a more contented and productive place in his life, and not surprisingly Béla Bartók entered what some critics have called the height of his compositional career. Béla and Ditta came to America for a concert tour in 1928, following an ambivalent acceptance of his *Miraculous Mandarin,* in Cologne. Why journey to America? For one thing, his *String Quartet no 3* had won the Philadelphia Prize. He wanted to be where his music was appreciated. The relocation did wonders for all concerned.

It was during this period that "Bartók's compositions showed a marked increase in power;[12] he composed prolifically and successfully, including…" the *First* and *Second Rhapsody for Violin and Piano; Twenty Hungarian Folk Songs for Violin and Piano accompaniment;* and the *Cantata Profana*. During the next dozen or so years Bartók turned his compositional skills to more demanding works for strings. In '38 he wrote his *String Quartets no 4 and 5*, as well as *Contrasts*, trios for clarinet, violin and piano. The next year he produced his acclaimed *Divertimento for String*, and the *String Quartet no 6*. If Bartók could not have accomplished all this without support and inspiration, it would not be difficult to locate and credit the likely source.

Ditta was an accomplished pianist, and she accompanied her husband on tours of many European cities. Bartók wrote to his former student and friend, Wilhelmine Creel, about how well Ditta played in her role as second piano. The couple apparently made their premiere performance in such a duo role in Basle, Switzerland, in the fall of 1938, even as European politics were becoming ever more difficult and frightening. We get the sense from the tone of his letters that Ditta's willingness to travel and perform with Béla helped him to keep his mind on music and off the coming war. The man was frightened of the war's implications for their personal freedom.

An energetic letter writer, Bartók told his friend and former student, Mrs. Dorothy Parrish, on 8 February 1939, that he was much distressed with the German *Anschluss* with Austria – a most lugubrious political event – and he "fear[ed] that Germany may exert a fatal influence" in Hungary, becoming "quite a German colony," as had happened in Czechoslovakia. Ditta and attention to his work together took his mind of the Nazis.

Béla was happy in his music, and best; he reported that he was "… frequently playing concerto compositions for two pianos with my wife." He told Mrs. Parrish they had played in Basle, London, Amsterdam, Brussels, Luxembourg, and of course in Budapest. Soon they would leave for Paris.[13] Béla Bartók was finally content.

Entering the 1940s, and what would be the final few years of his life, Bartók spent a great deal of time in New York City. That spring Columbia University offered him an honorary degree and a position to arrange its huge collection of Yugoslav folk music. He was eager for the task. For a while he also tried to honor the now tiresome and wearying commitments that had kept him touring, but the onset of his leukemia in '42 forced him to curtail much of these assignments. On the other hand, much as he loved New York, the on-going war in Europe was keeping him a virtual exile from Hungary. Such worry took a toll on the man's weakened condition.

Friends and loved ones provided an occasional elixir. A visit from the conductor Serge Koussevitzky, who came to see him on his sick bed in New York, roused him from his lethargy.[14] It was owing to this visit and some much needed encouragement that Béla managed to complete his first major work in America, the *Concerto for Orchestra*. He was sixty-two years old and fighting to stay engaged in all he loved. His latest Muse had a bit more work ahead, as well.

It is fitting that Ditta would prove to be the spark that Bartók needed to compose his final work, the *Third Piano Concerto*. He'd intended it to be a birthday surprise for her. The composer had asked son Peter not to tell her what he had prepared; he wanted to present the piece to dear Ditta. Sadly, the composer, so in love with homeland, with its peasant music, and with this one woman, did not live to finish the last few measures. Béla Bartók died on 26 September 1945, his wife and their son Peter at his side.

Béla Jr., the elected lay-president of the Hungarian Unitarian Church, arranged to have his father's remains sent home to Budapest. Bartók had written his final work and written it for the only woman he was certain had ever truly loved him. There were no more scary rooms to enter. No pretense. No war. No unfinished work. The frequently anxious, weary, and much traveled Béla Bartók had completed his final journey.

CHAPTER THREE

BEETHOVEN, Ludwig van, (1770 - 1827), German

" My angel, my all, my self – only a few words today… why this deep grief, where necessity speaks – can our love exist but by sacrifices (?)

[from Beethoven's letter to Antonie Brentano; his **Immortal Beloved**]

Beethoven inherited both copious talent and huge expectations. Like Bach some fifty-five years before him, Ludwig van Beethoven's talent and his productivity outstripped that of all his family members. Unlike Bach, however, and more so unlike Mozart, his father Johann cared little about the boy's ultimate musical development, except for what he might earn from little Ludwig's youthful celebrity. Clearly, Ludwig's father actually did more to handicap the young man than to help. "Those that were nearest him in blood were furthest from him in spirit, and there can be no doubt that the hardships of his youth nurtured the seeds of the eccentricity and moodiness which marked him later on and estranged many of his friends."[1]

What makes any of this awkwardness relevant to our examination of female inspiration is that Beethoven seemed to be even more awkward and uncomfortable with the fairer sex than he was at home. Yet, the five or six women in his mature life made an enormous influence on his music. He never married any of them, or any other woman for that matter. Truly, Beethoven may have been more unlucky in love than any of the other twenty-eight composers considered in this book. Considering the history of Johannes Brahms who followed him both in birth years, and was seen by many as his heir, that is no small distinction.

Beethoven's actual birth date is obscure, being either 15 or 16 December 1770. His baptism was recorded the 17th which, by church tradition, would suggest that he was born the day before. Ludwig had little general education, a fact that always bothered him. His mother, Mary Magdalena, had no known musical talent, but she was nevertheless important in shaping her son's disposition. Married once before and widowed at nineteen, she was pious and serious-minded, and one biographer says "her earnestness rubbed off on Beethoven's music, which was observed by contemporaries as more serious than normal."[2] He was devoted to her.

Ludwig's father Johann was employed, initially under his own father, the Kapellmeister (Director of Court Music), as a tenor; though he also gave voice and piano lessons. Apparently the man also taught violin. When he felt his son Ludwig was ready for broader exposure he passed him on to other court musicians. With great good fortune the lad fell under the instruction of Christian Gottlob Neefe, a near-exact contemporary of Wolfgang Mozart. Young Ludwig prospered under Neefe's tutelage, and at the age of fourteen "Beethoven's contribution to the musical life of the court was officially recognized when he became a salaried member of the retinue."[3] Beethoven also learned from Neefe the concept that music can and should convey a sense of the times, an awareness of politics, popular culture, and personal freedom. These notions would be particularly relevant in Beethoven's maturation as a composer. We'll see this focus; some would say this purpose, repeatedly in his larger compositions.

Music pedagogy can be fascinating: Carl Czerny was one of Beethoven's prized pupils; he passed along such extra-musical training as the importance of politics on music to his own students. One of them was Hector Berlioz, whose music takes its meaning from time and place as much, or more, than does any other early nineteenth-century composer.

Neefe also served as Ludwig's composition teacher and in some sense as his sponsor, helping the young Beethoven to secure precious funding for his continued musical study. Neefe told the financial administrators at court that the eleven year old, who had just completed *Nine Variations for Piano on a March,* deserved financial assistance for this accomplishment alone.[4] Ludwig would prosper if he might travel and study abroad. Neefe told the court that this young fellow, showing so much promise, would certainly become a second Mozart if he were encouraged to carry on as he had begun.[5] No one can say what the impact on his music might have been had he done so.

We know that as a boy and then as a young man Mozart had been given every opportunity to travel broadly in Europe. His father was self-sacrificing, albeit highly controlling. Beethoven realized none of that. True, he did get one trip to Holland with his mother, playing at the Royal Court in Rotterdam. We learn that he was well treated there, but Ludwig was not much impressed with the rest of what he found in the city. He journeyed to Berlin and to Prague when he was twenty-six, but thereafter Beethoven was seldom given to travel, and in his maturity he did as little as possible, also forgoing relocation to London.[6] With the onset of deafness a few years later Ludwig's travel would have been nearly impossible anyway.

Returning to the *Variations on a March*; this composition seems to have been written as a funeral piece to commemorate the passing of Ludwig's second cousin, his good friend and violin teacher Franz Rovantini, who the year before had died at the age of twenty-four. Beethoven and his cousin Franz were closer than most brothers, and even as a youth Ludwig demonstrated a tendency to dedicate music to those closest to him. His next composition seems linked to one person in his life, and it foreshadows more that were more obviously written for that certain someone. This was his *Description of a Maiden* (Schilderung des Mädchens), also published in 1783. *Mädchens* was followed by a sprightly *Rondo in C for Piano*. Ludwig that year was in high spirits. We'll return in a moment to who that *mädchen* likely was. Eventually, of course, Beethoven would write a great deal of music to and for his many Muses. Before he could contemplate his love life, however, he had to address more immediate and more troubling affairs.

At home, Ludwig's father was mistreating him, beating him, and regularly getting drunk. The young composer turned his attentions away from these domestic horrors and concentrated on a world not of his family's making. This was also the time when Beethoven seems to have fallen under the spell of the intellectual and learned communities of Bonn, attracted first to the Order of the Illuminati, and subsequently by freemasonry. Stimulated by Classical literature, this was a period of Ludwig's great intellectual growth, or at least of curiosity, for such subjects.

Next he found well-to-do and influential patrons, leading him to his first piano students Eleonore von Breuning, and her brother Lorenz. It is entirely feasible that he remembered Eleonore, one year younger, in his *Mädchen* song. Her nickname was "Lorchen," and she remained his friend well after their brief attraction ended.

When Elector Maximilian Friedrich died in 1784 his successor Maximilian Franz provided jobs as court organists for both Ludwig and teacher Christian Neefe. This altruism gave the young Beethoven the opportunity to earn a decent income and enough time to work on his own compositions. Elector Franz was a true patron of the arts, and he particularly enjoyed instrumental music, which was a boon to Beethoven who was moving ever more in that direction and away from the church music associated with the Baroque period and the work of his hero, Johann Sebastian Bach.

A new and expressive style began to flourish in Bonn at this time; encouraged by the Elector, who was an accomplished viola player.[7] Beethoven now had the proverbial friend in court. Though yet a teen-ager, his future must have looked promising. In 1787 Ludwig decided to go to Vienna – just a short trip. There the young man met Mozart and chanced to play one of his host's piano concertos. We learn that Mozart then played something Beethoven subsequently improvised upon, and "a torrent of astounding music filled the room." Mozart remarked: "Keep an eye on this man – the world will hear of him some day!" Anything seemed possible. But the occasion was ruined by alarming, personal news back in Bonn.[8]

It was his mother's failing health. Beethoven's friend Franz Ries, a violinist and sometime teacher, came to his aid financially, after Ludwig was recalled to Bonn by his father to attend the terminally ill woman. After she died, and as father Johann's capacity to deal with the most pressing family matters failed, Ludwig emerged as the de facto head of household and the primary bread winner. Taking time from his court organ duties and other functions he began to give more private lessons. Keyboard lessons have often led to some fine romances, and Beethoven's experience would be no different.

Looking back on such lessons, it becomes more likely that Beethoven wrote the *Schilderung des Mädchens* with Eleonore in mind, though it could just as well have been "Jeanette d' Honrath, [a young lady] from Cologne who used to visit the Breuning family."[9] Jeanette was a friend of Eleonore. She met the young teacher Ludwig van Beethoven under these somewhat formal circumstances, as Beethoven often provided his services to the well-to-do. The odds were that he'd have well healed students; they were the ones whose parents could afford to have such a talented musician teaching their children.

Jeanette had a "pleasant voice;" she bewitched Ludwig thoroughly, still the young peoples' relationship apparently went nowhere. Beyond Eleonore, and if not Jeanette, who else captured Ludwig's young heart? There were many, and not a few of them proved to be powerful Muses.

We know that he had another girlfriend at this time, and one for whom he wrote music. In 1786, Ludwig composed a *Trio in G for Piano*, autographing it to the family of Count Friedrich von Westerholt, one of the Elector's key retainers. But it was not the Westerholt family that the young man pined for; it was daughter Maria Anna, whose father had also arranged for her to take lessons from Beethoven. The composer-teacher fell in love with her, risking his heart on a girl whom he must have known to be too far above his social station for anything good to come of it. In fact, all of Ludwig's affairs of the heart seem to have been directed to the aristocratic girls. Ironically, it was Franz Wegeler, van Beethoven's friend and early biographer, and who himself married Lorchen Breuning, and who years later described Beethoven's attraction to Maria Anna von Westerholt as a '*werther lieb*,' an unhappy love. Wegeler also noted that most of the women Beethoven tended to go for were of a higher social rank than he was. Some biographers think this was done consciously to keep the relationships tentative, poignant and intense. Although Ludwig van Beethoven never married, he did manage to make a couple of strong offers, as we will soon see.

Shortly after this one-sided affair, Ludwig began work on a *Trio for piano, flute, bassoon and orchestra*, marked in part '*Romance Canticle.*' This *Romance*, scored in E minor, was Beethoven's most ambitious work up to that time. Little of the manuscript survives, though it seems certain that it was completed, revised, and played on a number of occasions in Bonn. We know little more of Maria Anna von Westerholt, the teenaged piano student and tentative owner of young Ludwig's heart, but we celebrate any influence she managed in engendering "a major milestone in Beethoven's compositional development."[10]

More importantly, Beethoven was now working with Franz Josef Haydn, who had taken on personal responsibility for the development of the twenty-one year old. They worked together for nearly three years in Vienna, until Haydn went to London – he had wanted Beethoven to go with him. Beethoven considered it but could not bring himself to abandon what he took to be his ever-growing responsibilities.

Mozart had now been dead for nearly a year, and many expected that Beethoven would succeed him as Vienna's preeminent musician. What a preposterous obligation this was to lay at the foot of a man so young. Did he have the will, the talent; did he have the determination to become a national music hero? Ludwig's expectations were less; he told his friends that he would go to Vienna to study and make some money. Instead, Ludwig made a life there.

Lorchen Breuning wrote in Beethoven's autograph book a short verse that promised eternal friendship, wherever he might go. Her brother Christoph wrote that "his [Ludwig's] song would echo victoriously." It must have seemed that everything was now possible, and everyone wished him well. After his relocation to Vienna, Ludwig frequently looked back on his early, perhaps idyllic days in Bonn. Mozart had virtually anointed him upon Ludwig's first visit to Vienna. Now he would have to prove himself well away from the place of his youth, ensconced in this city that had so great an influence on nearly all of 18th century music.

The move from Bonn was complicated, though why he left is easy to figure out. Beethoven wanted challenges that Bonn and the surrounding region could not offer. Whether or not Josef Haydn encouraged or coaxed Beethoven to Vienna and in so doing speeded the young composer's self-sufficiency, there were big changes ahead. These were changes that made Beethoven reconsider what a life in music meant to him. More personal drama would be found just ahead.

When the young composer's father died suddenly, his brothers in Bonn found they had no caregiver. After all, Ludwig was now nearly six hundred miles away in Vienna. Maximilian Franz agreed to provide some legacy funding for the boys from their father's court salary. But when Franz and many of his retainers were themselves compelled to relocate, because of the pressures of European political intrigue, things became even more unsettled for the Beethoven family. With Maximilian's court in trouble, and Ludwig's stipend running out, the young composer made arrangements to bring his brothers to Vienna. He even helped Karl to find work, which tended to stabilize family requirements. That quickly, Beethoven's remaining door back to Bonn was closed. Ludwig never returned to the city of his birth. While dealing with added responsibilities and with whatever emotions he had following the loss of his father, a difficult man and a bully, things were not running smoothly in his new home.

For one thing there was the difficult situation with Haydn as principle teacher. "He had come to Vienna with great expectations, honorably greedy for knowledge and hoping at last to be able to complete his musical equipment, but he was bitterly disillusioned. Haydn's lessons fell far short of his hopes… nor did [Haydn] teach the theory of music with the accuracy which Beethoven desired…[and] as soon as he realized mistakes were being passed over in his work he began to look for other teachers."[11]

This is not to suggest that Ludwig didn't learn a great deal, nor profit from his days with Haydn. In fact, under his tutelage Beethoven wrote some extraordinary music, including two cantatas, one on the death of Emperor Joseph II, and a set of variations for violin and piano based on Mozart's *The Marriage of Figaro*. He also wrote the music he called *Se vuol Ballare,* designating it his Oeuvre 1, which he dedicated to his past love, Eleonore "Lorchen" von Breuning. When his few years with Haydn ended Beethoven began a successful association with Johann Albrechtsberger, an accomplished musical theorist and composer. He also spent some time with Antonio Salieri, best known for his operatic work, and somewhat notoriously as no friend to the late Viennese demi-god Wolfgang Mozart. For all that, Beethoven was not idle when it came to garnering social support. The young composer learned how to win some influential friends and sponsors and soon had the courage to try again in romance, something at which he had had little success to date.

"The best proof of Beethoven's self-confidence and trust in his own future at this period is the fact that in 1795 he made a proposal of marriage to a former colleague in Bonn. She was Magdalena Willman, now famous in Vienna as a singer. Her refusal – ostensibly because she considered Ludwig too ugly – does not appear to have caused him any real grief… He realized that his star was ascendant and that nothing could bar is triumphal way."[12] Ludwig van Beethoven was keeping his focus.

Unlike his affairs with most girls for whom he had strong feelings there is no evidence of his having written any music specifically for Miss Magdalena Willman. Here, the lad showed some perspective, given that she thought so little of him. Moreover, he likely thought that time was on his side, and there were many women yet ahead. To the next couple of them, in recognition of their inspiration, he would dedicate some of his best-loved music.

Beethoven deliberately withheld from publishing some of his compositions because Vienna was slow to accept, to warm to, any real innovation. Every age is known for its innovation and well as its intransigence. Vienna was no exception, and Ludwig felt the intrinsic stubbornness of Vienna at the dawn of the nineteenth century. As a result, and making use of cultural convention, Beethoven tended to showcase several of his works at the homes of influential patrons before attempting to go public. "Thus his opus 1, three [piano] trios dedicated to [his patron] Prince Lichnowsky, did not appear until 1795… quickly followed by further works which … had been kept back – [including his *Piano Concerto #2 in B flat*]."[13] His friend Albrechtsberger may have also reawakened in Beethoven an interest in broader musical themes; and the next few years found Ludwig energized, writing a number of piano sonatas, a cello sonata, and a good bit of string music.

He had another awakening. His *Piano Sonata in E flat* [1797] is dedicated to one of his students, the fair Countess Babette von Keglevics, or Keglevich, as it is sometimes recorded. Babette was said to be a particularly gifted student, and Ludwig would receive the young lady for her lessons in a state of dress suggesting some degree of familiarity – in fact, wearing his bedroom slippers! Little more is known of her relationship with the young man, then twenty-seven years old. Babette might have had real possibilities, but then, again, she was from that patrician group Beethoven could not realistically hope to join. Perhaps it was just as well. To the extent that Fate was involved, Ludwig's serious romances were still ahead.

Musical Muse: Wives and Lovers of the Great Composers

In 1798 Beethoven wrote the beguiling *Twelve Variations for Piano and Cello* (opus 66) for a woman he called *Ein Mädchen*. Although she is not identified, we sense that one young lady was continuing to work on his head. Returning to church music, Beethoven wrote the oratorio *Mount of Olives,* followed by his *third piano concerto,* in 1800. Ludwig then also wrote his *Symphony #1, in C major,* at the age of thirty. The next year he seems to have stopped pining for Magdalena, or "Lorchen," or Babette. Why? We surmise it was because he was captivated by, totally in love with, his most recent student, the Countess Giulietta Guicciardi. He wrote for her the sublime piece of music that came to be called *The Moonlight Sonata*. As fate would have it, she married another man within eighteen months and moved to Italy. Nonplussed, Beethoven wrote to his friend Anton Schindler: "I was loved by her, and more than her husband ever was. Yet he was more her lover than I …"[14] Ludwig's tone also may have suggested that he didn't feel he had the tools or the time to marry. Suddenly he was too busy. He now came to an even more monumental crisis in his life than the disappointments of an unfulfilled love. This time the implications were truly dire and long-term. By 1802 the composer began to sense that his greatest fear was coming true; he was going deaf.

Beethoven had suffered symptoms of hearing loss for ten years, taking various cures as prescribed by the doctors and practitioners he depended upon. We learn a good deal about his fears and expectations through a document written to his brothers called the Heiligenstadt Will. In his 28th year, he wrote that he was "in despair," forced, he said, to become a philosopher. This was a particularly intense time for Beethoven creatively, and he persevered with his music composition through shear determination. The next year he began work on another symphony, itself highly dramatic, which has come to us as the *Eroica*. This was a breakthrough symphony, highly emotional, and much more a step into the nineteenth century. The symphony in E-flat major was his to be Ludwig's paean to Napoleon, until Bonaparte had himself proclaimed Emperor, thereby showing himself no less vain and self-exalted than the Bourbons he would replace. Beethoven struck the little general's name from the score. When he assigned a name to his music, a personal tribute, it carried great weight. Napoleon had shown he no longer deserved such honor.

Next Beethoven attempted to complete an opera, a major work with which he had struggled for a numbers of years, vexed by delays and disputes. One thing seems clear, however, that his inspiration for *Léonore,* which would become the opening of his *Fidelio* opera, was inspired by his love for a specific woman. As in the past, she was a high-born countess and realistically not in his social circle. The French libretto that attracted him was "*Léonore, ou l'amour conjugal*; it was a text by Jean Nicolas Bouilly. The ideal love theme of *Léonore* complemented Beethoven's needs, and certainly spoke to his out-of-reach aspirations for marriage, brought on no doubt by his deep affection for the Countess Josephine Deym (née Brusnvik).[15] We'll soon see how this one fits in to the long line of Beethoven's disappointments.

Josephine, his Léonore, was perfect for Ludwig, as he had come to fashion his love interests. She was beautiful, the source of tremendous inspiration, and she was impossibly out of reach for him. That should have made it easy. There'd be no further complications. Would not his work sustain him? The opera *Fidelio*, completed in 1814, is surely one of his major works. Would it have had the same force if not derived from one of Beethoven's many unfulfilled loves? After all, the musical Muses for Ludwig van Beethoven were many, they were intense, and they were – each one – uncompromisingly disappointing. It must be said that there was more to Ludwig's relationship with Josephine than with some of his earlier women. Three female members of the aristocratic Brunsvik family took piano lessons from Beethoven, including Josephine, nine years younger than Ludwig. Josephine first met the composer, her teacher, in 1799. Perhaps his most cherished student at the time, she was then twenty-years old.

After the premature death of her husband, in 1804, Josephine and Beethoven began a courtship, of sorts; apparently there was a mutual love and high expectation from both parties. Their affair was most intense during the period up to 1807, as evidenced by their letters; but their relationship faltered sometime shortly thereafter, and she married another in 1810. Josephine, too, was eventually too distracted by social obligations. The reasons likely involved "class" and its facile expectations. As we know, such social conventions had done in Ludwig on a number of previous occasions. In truth, there had been some speculation that Josephine was actually Ludwig's much celebrated and misidentified "immortal beloved," but most musicologists and biographers have now identified another more likely candidate for that role. I will return shortly to the case for her, for Ludwig's IB.

Just because Josephine chose to marry another, after a ten-year "relationship," with the composer, was no reason for Ludwig to opt for celibacy. He was still teaching piano to the wealthy and the gifted, and regularly so to those young *mädchens* who might find a bit of romance above or below the white and black keys. Almost immediately love got another chance, fashioned from Vienna's elite, young music circle. For a number of years Beethoven's' primary physician had been one Giovanni Malfatti. Some time in early 1810 Ludwig fell in love with Dr. Malfatti's daughter, also his student; her name was Therese. Beethoven intended to propose marriage to her that April. As on so many such occasions, however, something happened and nothing came of it. Well, on second thought some of his best known music came of it.

There is an amusing story as to how Ludwig came to write and dedicate his piano bagatelle *Fur Elise*. It seems that the well-to-do Malfattis invited a number of their friends and social equals to a soiree at their home, asking Ludwig to play one of his short piano pieces, which he had just composed, and which he had planned to present to his fair Therese. He would play it for her that evening. He intended to follow up his performance and the dedication with a bold marriage proposal to Therese. It was all a bit high risk, but it was also quite romantic. According to one of the guests, Baron Ignatz von Gleichenstein, Beethoven's friend, patron, and sometime secretary, the good doctor Malfatti served a strong punch and Beethoven got horribly drunk. In fact, Ludwig was barely able to play the piece and "was in no condition to ask her [Therese] anything of such importance."[16] Therese, however, acknowledging that the music had been written for her, asked that he inscribe her name onto the title page. Beethoven wrote in a barely legible hand, *Für Therese,* and the young lady kept it all her life. The original manuscript was found after her death in 1851, when the publisher who asked for it recognized Beethoven's hand, if not his lettering. He published it, appropriately, under the classification of bagatelle but misread the inscription, which he annotated on the copy for the public "*Für Elise*," and one of Beethoven's best loved and most easily recognized musical scores has been known by that name to this day.

In fact, Beethoven was writing a great deal of piano music at this time, including the so-called *Emperor*, his *Piano Concerto #5*. The previous year he had also completed his *Symphony #6*, the *Pastoral*. Ludwig was not ready to give up on composition or to give up on romance. Within another year the composer, now forty-one years old, would fall harder for one woman than he had for any in his youth or his early maturity. Her name was Mrs. Antonie Brentano, married to a man fifteen years her senior. She was also the mother of four. The Brentanos had moved to Vienna from Frankfurt so she could be nearer her ailing father. Born Antonie von Birkenstock, in Vienna, on 28 May 1780, she was ten years younger than Ludwig and was considered quite a beauty. She met the composer through her sister-in-law, and within a short period of time Antonie and Ludwig were much in love with each other. True to form, she was not exactly available, being inconveniently married. What we know of their affair, documented by some of the leading Beethoven scholars, clearly traces their romance to certain times and specific places, and seems to be corroborated in the so-called Immortal Beloved Letters. Let's say the existence of their relationship is well confirmed.

In no place does Ludwig call her by name in these letters, which were found in his desk by his secretary shortly after he died on 25 March 1827. Rather, he addresses her: "My angel, my all, my very self ..." Like the Heiligenstadt Testament, poignant indeed, which announced his deafness, the letters are not expressly addressed. The former were intended implicitly for his brothers, of course. But they speak to a larger readership. Although the Immortal Beloved letters are not addressed we have many clues in the lettering and allusions to places Ludwig and Antonie had been seen together. Nor was the set of three letters ever sent. So why write them at all? Was Ludwig sublimating something he found difficult to deal with directly?

The observation that they were written as catharsis is appealing but not wholly satisfactory. Beethoven may well have meant to send them to Antonie, but he likely changed his mind when he realized the hopelessness of the situation. After all, she was not only married but she would be in Vienna for only as long as it took her and her cuckolded husband to reconcile some personal, family business. He wrote the letters near the end of their affair, likely in the summer of 1812. Without a doubt, Beethoven had learned to be circumspect about his romances. There were further complications. During their year or so of living in close proximity, and as their friendship grew to love, Antonie was frequently ill. Whether or not she was truly ill we cannot know. Ludwig did travel to her home and played music for her. They had a few days together in Karlsbad in July of 1812, shortly before she and her family moved back to Frankfurt. After that, they never saw each other again.

Beethoven wrote some beautiful music for Antonie, and he dedicated a good bit more. She had been a heady inspiration in his music, as he wrote for her the song *"An die Geliebte,"* (To the Beloved), his Opus 238, in December, 1811. The original text has Antonie's note "Requested by me from the author on March 2, 1812."[17] Ludwig also dedicated to her the enigmatic *Diabelli Variations on a Waltz, Op 120,* only completed for the woman whom Maynard Solomon calls "his intimate friend"[17] some twelve years later, when he was fifty-three years old. Could Antonie have ever truly left him? Not in his music.

In her own diaries the woman wrote of "elective affinities," where some few people understand each other spiritually and emotionally as if they had always been one. Antonie was the *sine qua non* of musical Muses, and the most powerful one of the many Beethoven was fortunate enough to have. Of course, to be completely honest, Beethoven's music transcends all these romantic hullabaloos. The significant emotional detail is compelling, but Ludwig wrote for himself, too. He wrote for others who had encouraged and moved him. Beethoven composed because he listened to, and responded to, whatever was central to his genius. His many women helped all they could, or might.

Beethoven had many loves, many Muses, and at least as many shatteringly lost romances. But his music is bigger than the poignancy of a half-dozen affairs. Still, the ones we know about, where they impact his music, are compelling to the music lover. Their names resonate in his music: Lorchen; Therese; Josephine; and Antonie – his "Immortal Beloved."

Beethoven lived only to the age of fifty-six. Cirrhosis of the liver actually killed him. Antonie Brentano outlived Ludwig by more than three decades, keeping his memory alive. We suspect that he did not outlive his memory of her.

One further story is told about Beethoven and his ill-fated love life. Ludwig might have had an affair with his sister-in-law, Johanna, the wife of brother Kaspar. After his brother's death, in 1816, Ludwig adopted their son Karl. All this followed a bitter court battle in which Beethoven accused Johanna of being unfit. Winning the legal battle, Beethoven raised Karl, the mother objecting ever so little. Ludwig claimed a natural father's right to the boy, calling him "my bodily son." In Beethoven's *Conversation Book*, where the deaf composer wrote and received much of his daily discourse, the composer records that the boy Karl was studious. He was a decent piano student, sometimes willful, and he tended to melancholy. We learn that in despair, Karl tried to take his own life in 1826. Still, the boy was like a son to Beethoven, and we suspect that he may have actually been the composer's son. Certainly it would fit the pattern.

According to Beethoven's long time friend and early biographer, Ferdinand Ries, Johanna also had a second child, in 1820. This was a girl, and she was unquestionably illegitimate. After all, her husband Kaspar had died four years earlier. Johanna had not remarried. We know the child's name was Ludwika, which is an unusual name. While Ludwika seems an unlikely name for the widow to give her child, it might have been given to her to recall some one, extraordinary, relationship. Or, given all we know of Ludwig van Beethoven's history of misplaced love, was it surprising at all?

CHAPTER FOUR

BERLIOZ, Hector (1803 - 1869), French

" In his creative world, Berlioz journeyed down the familiar path of imitation, aggressive experimentation, and arrival at a comfortable, detached classicism. "[1]

Poet Delmore Schwartz once observed that children and dogs are Shakespearean. So was Hector Berlioz; but what was Schwartz's real message? Surely he was going for some sense of both comedy and tragedy at work in one's life. For Berlioz, to be Shakespearean meant a great deal more. No doubt "the bard" influenced him, as did no other literary figure. Like many a dramatic figure, Berlioz was unlucky in love – unlucky by Shakespearean dimensions.

Critics, biographers, and his contemporaries struggled to find "the real Berlioz," the man who wanted to "be remembered for his all-encompassing love of art and for a commitment to high ideals that both dominate and unite his work as composer, conductor, and critic."[2] The question of a "real Berlioz" is grounded in his dual and often opposing temperaments – the impetuous, short-tempered Frenchman who learned to conduct in order to preserve the precision of his compositions, and the misty-eyed, moody Romantic who would readily weep hearing the most passionate piano work of his idol, Ludwig van Beethoven.

Is it even a serious question – this notion of a "real Berlioz?" Probably. This is a man who, for inspiration and surcease from a harried work schedule, kept a mistress for years as his first marriage disintegrated – a love and union that he had worked so hard to make work. Yet he boldly cheated. Nor is it an easy to portray the real Berlioz as apolitical, which he claimed to be, while he followed revolutionary sentiments in France. His biographers seem to agree that Louis-Hector Berlioz was truly a revolutionary in music, and that he challenged and changed the temperament of music in nineteenth-century France.

Berlioz was the oldest child, and he outlived all of his siblings, two of whom died before the age of twelve. Fondness for his sisters, named Nanci and Adèle, "evolved into an affection for women in general; he was always at ease in the company of women and quick to enjoy an affair of the heart."[3] Given such a pre-disposition, Muses would come to play an extraordinary roll in the man's career.

Berlioz grew up in a turbulent time, his country, such as it was, was at war throughout his most of his formative years. Napoleon, and to some extent his republican successors, dominated France and shaped the intellectual life of Hector Berlioz. As a result, he tended to see the music being written and performed in the foreground of all this political chaos as, quite simply, either relevant to such unsettled conditions or not. Music that had a strong sense of the spirit of the times had to be captured in art – in all art. In this regard he shared something fundamental with Beethoven, born some thirty-three years earlier.

Berlioz, like Beethoven, would capture such drama in music. He also came to lead a vanguard in the metamorphosis of serious French music. The young people with whom Hector chose to spend time talking, drinking, and making sense of the world shared his excitement of the new order. While national politics were inspirational, Berlioz tried to remain apolitical. He may have tried to so in part to protect his income from being on the wrong side of an argument. He did not keep his feelings entirely private, even so. Pecuniary considerations aside, and like Franz Liszt who would play such a strong role in his life, Berlioz was also drawn seriously to art, to literature and to scholarship. If he would be true to his art he would be true to his sense of ethos. We'll return to his politics. What of the young man's introduction to music? What, for that matter, of his musical Muses? As in Beethoven's life there were many.

In the truest sense Berlioz was largely self-taught, as was Richard Wagner. Contrary to the usual path to classical greatness, Berlioz did not learn harmony, composition, or even his scales on the piano. He never learned to play the instrument in any accomplished manner. At age twelve Berlioz played tunes on the family flageolet, a small, simple flute. The next year his father bought him a real flute and he later played and gave instruction on the guitar. Eventually, Hector learned percussion and had some familiarity with strings. He even took voice lessons, becoming quite a good singer. Curiously, he never mastered the piano, usually the bedrock instrument for composition.

Ever alive to where music might be heading, Hector championed the introduction of the saxophone, which the gentry of music resisted. But then almost everything Berlioz did in the world of classical music was in some sense a "road not taken." Moreover, he was not a prodigy in the sense that his good friend Mendelssohn, or Mozart before, had been. Fortunately for him, and for all who cherish his classical, often outré output, Hector's work ethic was as strong as that of any classical composer.

Berlioz's musical interests were highly eclectic, and encompassed everything from peasant music to opera. Often it was the simple forces of nature that shaped his ideas. As a young man he spent time in the fields and forests near home, at the edge of the French Alps. Berlioz has been called a pantheist, for his love of the divine spirit in nature.[4] Not surprisingly, then, nature seems to have been the setting for his first awakening to the opposite sex. Moreover, an unplanned encounter with a young woman may have given Hector the insight he needed to find his musical center. Her name was Estelle Deboeuf.

Young Hector met Estelle, a daughter of a family friend, in the summer of 1815. He recalled what the attractive, self-confidant, and perhaps a bit flirty eighteen-year old wore at that chance meeting, even remembering the color of her boots. "She seems the embodiment of [the poet] Florian's *Estelle*, a pastoral romance that had shortly before spoken directly to his budding sexuality."[5] They saw each other for a few years after that August day, and his fascination for Estelle contributed directly to his *idée fixe* about a man's desire for a woman, a desire that seemed unattainable, always perfection out of reach. Such thematic purpose would work consistently in his music.

The Estelle fantasy may well have played directly into his tortuous need for the love of the singer Harriet Smithson, a dozen years later. When Berlioz became infatuated with the more mature woman, she was also out of reach. Or at least she was initially. In fact, they could not easily communicate because she spoke no French. Hector did have passable English language writing skills. At age twenty, however, when he wrote the music to the small opera, *Estelle et Némorin*, the first young woman's countenance still burned brightly in his reverie. We know that she also became the prime mover for the music of his best-known composition the *Symphonie fantastique*.[6]

Berlioz struggled mightily to find his way in a career roundly devalued and opposed by his parents, especially his father. Determined, he taught himself to read music after experimenting with the flute, at home. He bought or borrowed music to study it more carefully, comparing what he was hearing with the notes of the composer. They did not always track. Studious approach to music lead Hector to a collateral career as a music critic and reviewer, which began for him in 1823. For many years the composer made his way financially by writing music critiques. He so loved writing music, however, that when he received his baccalaureate degree in 1821 he made a pact with his father that he would continue his medical studies in Paris, but only while trying to make a success of music. His father, slow to recognize Hector's genius, withheld most sustenance money, perhaps as a way of showing his distrust of the whole "performing" world. Berlioz had the grit to persevere.

As a youth Hector was drawn to nearly every variety of music, including Glück's opera, the classical music of Haydn, Mozart, and then to simple folk melodies. Of course, there was always church music, and he would soon discover and champion the still-underappreciated symphonic music of Beethoven. Self-taught, none of these forms seemed out of bounds to him.

His first compositions, we learn, were solid enough to engage some local musicians who found his music difficult – not bad or immature, but unsettlingly new. At the age of twelve, Berlioz had composed for small, local chamber groups. He enjoyed and learned a great deal from the rigor of religious music, particularly motets, and he advanced his compositional ideas with friends and acquaintances of the family.

Many of his earliest pieces are lost, but as a young man and well into his adulthood, Berlioz tended to compose in the flush of inspiration, and then revise. His youthful compositions were well received, but Berlioz was drawn to a more complex form of music. Nature and the church gave him ready subject matter, and his first so-called full composition was a mass, the *Messe Solenelle,* in 1825. Berlioz knew he could, and that he must, write music beyond these staid and safe forms. He was destined for opera and for sweeping symphonies. Ten years in the future lay his *Messe des Morts,* the Requiem; to many it would be his most highly regarded sacred music.

Hector was constantly tinkering with and salvaging parts of music which he would put aside and then return to, sometimes years later. Immediately after enrolling in the Paris *Conservatoire,* for composition, in 1826, he began writing scores for international competitions. He did this in part in order to convince his father that he was serious about being a successful musician. Winning a major composition prize would establish him as a viable composer, and would perhaps prompt his father to increase Hector's paltry stipend. As a minimum, he would establish a reputation to attract more students and secure commissions for music criticism. Might such fame appeal to a young woman? Perhaps the work would open a few more doors.

Harriet Smithson, an Irish singer working with a British Shakespeare troop, would come to Hector Berlioz through a tragic drama. *Hamlet* must have had many parallels that Berlioz was deeply drawn to. But then Berlioz was always drawn to what Harold Bloom called "the theater of the world," which *Hamlet* and Goethe's *Faust,* another work that fascinated Berlioz, certainly are. "Shakespeare," Berlioz wrote in his *Memoirs,* came upon him "unawares, struck me like a thunderbolt. The lightning flash of that discovery revealed to me at a stroke the whole heaven of art, illuminating it to its remotest corners. I recognized the meaning of grandeur, beauty, dramatic truth… I saw, I understood, I felt … that I was alive and that I must arise"[7]

Miss Smithson came to Paris in 1827 with her unhappy chaperones, her mother and her hunchback sister. Berlioz fell deeply in love almost at first sight, not with the sister, and he confessed his love to Harriet almost immediately. What true level of talent Smithson had is not agreed. Initially, she seems to have been more an emotional Ophelia than a technically accurate one, although on at least one occasion her interpretation, her hysterics, may have worked in her favor. On one occasion in singing her role in *Hamlet* she froze up, lost her place in the score, skipped a significant number of lines and brutalized the blocking. The audience loved it. With this grand faux pas she was a huge success and the woman was thought to have given a brilliant performance.[8] Upon such melodrama great romances begin, and sometimes they end.

For at least a while, in Paris, Harriet all but owned the part of Ophelia. Smithson also played the role of Juliet, perhaps toying with Hector's sense of just to what extent he was fated to play the suffering Romeo – denied his own true love. His father was not about to entertain the idea of a singer, and a foreign singer at that, in the Berlioz home. Yet Hector knew he must somehow have her. He continued to write impassioned letters, but Ms. Smithson shied away from him for his zany antics and oaths. Berlioz is reported to have run from the theater wailing in tears one evening when he saw her, as Juliet, in the arms of another man. It is no real stretch to find that the *Romeo and Juliet* symphony, which he wrote some ten years later, was conceived in this awakening to what he saw as his absurd destiny.

Posit that every artist should have a center of gravity, some inspirational source. For Hector Berlioz it was romance. His light and power came from women – not just women alone, but the love of women, and more exactly the love of women he could not have. While he seems to have had fewer than many of his famous contemporaries and musical compatriots, the ones he did have proved to be his musical wellspring. Hector apparently did not believe in casual love-making or bed sport. Making love for Berlioz was more about love than sex. He had no need for dalliances. German writer E.T.A. Hoffmann said that the core of romanticism was "infinite longing." Hoffman could have been describing the heart and mind of Louis-Hector Berlioz.

At the age of twenty-seven, Berlioz finished his cathartic *Symphonie fantastique,* which allowed him to come to grips with his *idée fixe,* his obsession, his forlorn love for Harriet. His biographers note the recurring themes and antecedents in some of the more spectacular parts of this symphony. The fourth movement, *March to the Scaffold,* owes its key ideas to a fragment of one of his earlier operas. Berlioz ,"believing that Harriet Smithson was interested in him after all, felt a surge of confidence in his powers " 'Oph's love has multiplied my capabilities a hundredfold' [and] in such an exalted state of mind he could well have sat up all night composing."[9] This was wishful thinking, of course, but the inspiration of Harriet has never been in doubt.

No sooner had Berlioz reconciled himself to an incomplete relationship with Smithson, but he met the woman who would teach him about real, tangible, physical, love – and subsequently of loss. Enter Camille (Marie) Moke. "Hers was a gift that makes artfulness assist and not replace nature. She was a siren as well as an extraordinarily good musician and vivacious companion. By the end of April [1830] he was done with Harriet."[10] Of course, he wasn't done with her at all, and we will return shortly to the idea of who was done with whom, and why.

While it lasted – they were in love by 1830 – his relationship with Camille was somehow sharper, perhaps because it seemed to him the more credible. Apparently, she did love him. In the spirited, graceful Camille, Berlioz saw the fairy spirit Ariel, Prospero's servant in *The Tempest*. In a letter written to his friend Humbert Ferrand from Paris, in October of that year, he wrote: "My poetic ideas turned towards the drama of *The Tempest* and inspired me to write a gigantic overture of an entirely new kind for orchestra, chorus, four players at two pianos, and harmonica. I offered it to the director of the Opéra, who agreed to put it on as a part of a large, spectacular event…. It's entirely new. My adoring thanks go to my blessed Camille for having inspired this composition."[11]

Still, Berlioz had difficulty separating his feelings for Harriet and Camille. Whatever lay unresolved with Harriet Smithson, Hector and Camille were making marriage plans. Undeterred by his family's intransigence, burning with the thrill of romance and aching to prove himself a man, Berlioz gave free rein to his compositional genius. In 1830 he won the *Prix de Rome*, having twice been runner up, or passed by. Previously presented with Berlioz's superior work, the judges were just not up to his innovative level. In 1829 Hector finished something the judges could better understand. This was "*The Death of Sardanapalus*," a theme he took from two Romantic bastions, Byron and Delacroix. For Berlioz, the Prix de Rome had become "a matter of tactics."

Berlioz arrived early in March in the city of Rome to claim his prize and take up lodgings with the other winners. He did not much care for Italy, at least at first, nor was he fond of things Italian, including most music. He missed his young fiancé; he puzzled over why she did not write to him. Increasingly distraught, Berlioz considered leaving the city and forsaking his prize. Then the letter arrived that all men who are away from a loved one most dread, and it did not even come straight from her but rather from the girl's mother. Camille had decided that she would marry M. Camille Pleyel, a much older, accommodating gentleman musician. Berlioz was beside himself. He is said to have contemplated taking her life, then his own – he had harbored suicide attempts before – and then decided better of it all and returned to composition.[12] Hector had learned a difficult life lesson.

What of this man who took her away, this Camille Pleyel? "It did not last: the female Camille earned a reputation for her scandalous reputation with men, and Pleyel left her four years later, in 1835."[13] Did this shocking and hurtful turn of events inspire Berlioz? Perhaps. It's hard to say. Maybe he calculated he would move on by rethinking his abhorrence for quick flings, and a few escapades on the beach at Nice proved a needed resuscitative. Done with Camille, Berlioz was a free man again, though deep down he discovered he was still aching for the elusive Harriet Smithson.

The year 1831 was one of the busiest composition times in his life, his unnamed Muse, or Muses, were extraordinarily adept. Back in Rome he "remembered these days as the happiest of his life. Hector returned spontaneously to composition, completing sketches for his next major work, an overture after Shakespeare called *Le Roi Lear*. Quickly he began to rough out a second overture, this one taking Walter Scott's *Rob Roy* as a title. He contemplated further refinements of the "new" *Symphonie fantastique*."[14]

The revised and, for now, complete *fantastique* was performed on 9 December 1832. Hector had worried and worked at the theme for four years, more if we count as its genesis the *idée fixe,* the obsession which became his essential purpose to write it.

By some irony no Romantic could fail to enjoy, Harriet Smithson attended the performance, along with Frédéric Chopin and his outlandish paramour George Sand; Liszt; and Hiller. They were there to support their friend. Hector had not invited Harriet but they talked after the performance and agreed to meet the next day. Her own career was failing, the premiere roles she once had were now behind her. Moreover, her English Shakespeare troop was going bankrupt. Ms. Smithson now found herself drawn to this young, attractive, bright, energetic man who had once so spiritedly wooed her. That the program music was all about his infatuation for her could not have failed to appeal to Smithson. She rethought her future. Perhaps the timing and circumstances of their meeting would be propitious for all.

Hector wrote to Liszt. The big discovery was that he loved Harriet still. By the next month, February 1833, Berlioz decided to end all anxious vacillations and offer her immediate marriage. "She accepted his reckless proposal; given her plight and his situation, his offer could only mean absolute devotion."[15] The wedding still lay eight months in the future. The man's parents still objected strenuously to Harriett, and her misfortune of breaking her leg getting out of a horse carriage only caused more complications. When they did wed the marriage did not turn out to be what either of them would have hoped. Maybe there were too many complications. Her career collapsed while his reached new zeniths. After 1831, Hector Berlioz began to see his life as "a Romantic novel." Indeed it was, and the reasons should be obvious. If serious music must be born of human drama, all these players had mastered their lines and blocking.

"The *Symphonie fantastique* is the first major composition to test Berlioz's notions of imitative dramatic music on a large scale, the first of four primarily orchestral works – the others being *Harold en Italie, Roméo et Juliette,* and *La Damnation de Faust* – to address the question. His rhetoric, to be viable, required that instrumental music deal directly with human situations – the love, for example, that develops between two strangers as if by fate."[16]

Hector and Harriet had a child in 1834. Louis was the light of the twenty-one year old composer's life; but before long the couple's relationship began to weaken. Her career, gradually ebbing, was now in freefall. Her health continued to fail as well. The couple considered and rejected a tour in the United States. Berlioz appealed to his friend, the playwright Georges Sand, to write something to help Harriett. Would she, could she create a part for a woman to sing a few lines? Sorry, he added, there could be no French required. Harriet knew almost none. Sand said she would try, but it was a fool's errand. Hector still loved his wife; she provided the emotional center to the life he had so long needed. Smithson was now becoming more than needy.

This brings us to the composition Berlioz told a friend he would save if all others were to be lost. He had been considering writing a large-scale sacred work describing Judgment Day; and in the spring of 1837 he got his chance when the French government commissioned Berlioz to write a mass for the nation's fallen heroes. Finally performed in December 1837, the mass was grand indeed, designed for a massive orchestra and a chorus of 400, all to be sung in Latin.

The conductor, a semi-competent government employee known for less than inspired work, nearly lost his place in the score when he put down his baton and decided to take a pinch of snuff just as the brass section was to take over the theme. Berlioz had anticipated just such a cavalier attitude. He was ready to jump in and take over the baton and did exactly that, conducting through the remainder of the piece. The performance was a great success. His preparation paid off – another significant lesson learned.

But Berlioz could not save the loss of what had been a tumultuous romance and marriage. By 1840 his marriage existed in name only. Harriet began to drink heavily and accused Berlioz of having affairs. No doubt there was cause for Harriet's jealousy. On his first trip out of France since the Italian journey, "Berlioz was accompanied by a young, attractive French-Spanish singer, Marie Recio, who thirteen years later became his second wife. The Berlioz first marriage was not yet wholly destroyed. It died hard; the agony lasting from 1841 to the final separation in the autumn of 1844."[17]

Berlioz defended his actions: "By dint of being accused and tortured in countless ways, always unjustly, I could find no peace or rest at home," he wrote. "In the end I came, by accident, to enjoy in actual fact the position wrongly imputed to me, and my life was transformed."[18] The infatuation with Miss Recio had more to do with his need for a woman than his potential to embrace and sponsor a young singer. She presumably saw it as both. Hector took Ms. Recio on successive concert tours, to Belgium and later to Germany. Soon, he was introducing her in select social circles as his wife. Their twelve-month period together, before the first Berlioz marriage began its final decline, was a time of "important musical activity." Hector completed his *Funeral and Triumphal* symphony and dedicated it to the recently deceased Duke of Orleans. Between concert tours Berlioz took leave of Marie Recio and returned to his family in Paris. There he worked on his breakthrough *Treatise upon Modern Instrumentation and Orchestration*, espousing his concepts of the origins of types of music. Berlioz had previously published much of the work in short articles. He added quotes and illustrations taken from the published work of the masters, adding his own ideas on the "science of music," something he believed in strongly and which was influenced by his study of the medical arts.

Marie continued to assist and inspire. Initially as clever socially as she had been musically, she became more awkward and socially injudicious later in her life, often embarrassing her husband. By most accounts, however, she was a fine music manager for her Hector, a task she came to willingly as her own career withered. Indeed, by 1844, as her voice would not sustain her any longer, Berlioz was on the cusp of writing some of his best, or at least best-appreciated, music. By this time Hector was also getting some recognition as a conductor, a field he had entered only because his music was sufficiently different and demanding, and often on such a grand scale, that otherwise accomplished men were mishandling it. Recall that such experience was magnified by the lesson he learned from the near failure of his *Requiem* in 1837.

Berlioz continued touring during the years 1845-47 and was usually accompanied by Marie. At first she attempted a few small singing parts as a mezzo-soprano in his operas. By 1847, however, he was anxious that she not sing, and according to one biographer, he was somewhat embarrassed when she did. Still, his passion for her had not dimmed and they married when Harriet died in 1854, having suffered a series of strokes. Marie had been his mistress and in every sense his Muse for the best part of thirteen years, but she apparently never lit the artistic fire in him that Harriet Smithson had. One wonders if perhaps Marie had seemed somehow too available. His love for Harriet had been a quest; she represented that unattainable prize that Hector Berlioz first came to seek in his youth. Inspiration requires a bit of drama; Hector needed lots of it.

Once they were actually married Berlioz found to his dismay that Marie's charms were more illusory than real. In an ironic role reversal the woman came to cherish him, she obsessed over him, and her jealousy and nearly mad behavior underscored the condition. Yet, while Hector and Marie, along with her able mother, made a life together for twenty years, his "Ophelia" never died. Ophelia was Harriet. There were other, less tractable, concerns.

The Berlioz couple understood how to best weather the coming revolutions of 1848. In fact, Hector and Marie were in London much of the time of crisis, living the life of exiles. On his return to Paris the composer enjoyed the unexpected company of Richard Wagner, who had been politically injudicious in Dresden and was subsequently living as an exile in Switzerland, then in Paris. With revolution still in the air, Hector's music seemed to reach a new level of accomplishment, even in the eyes of his most ardent critics, as the reception of the *Damnation of Faust* would prove. After that he wrote little until the oratorio *L'Enfance du Christ*. This was a piece he had worked on for nearly four years, beginning in 1850. Like so many men whose creative lives are recalled here, Berlioz derived a great deal of satisfaction from periodic work in sacred music. What drew him back to the spiritual is unclear. Maybe he knew Marie was unwell.

Berlioz's second wife died of a heart attack at the age of forty-eight, on Friday the 13th of June, 1862. They had been spending the day with friends in the countryside, near Paris. Marie had been experiencing symptoms for some time, and that quickly, among close colleagues, she went out of his life as dramatically as she had come in. Marie's mother lived on with Hector, each apparently helping the other to understand what had befallen and to get on with living.

Berlioz wrote to friends that he was ill-fated to romance. There were too many tragedies in his love life. Hector felt fate had been cruel. M. Berlioz was, after all, the Romantic who had his hero proclaim in the opera *Beatrice and Benedict*, earlier that year:

> *Tis better, after all, to be fools than clods*
> *Let us adore, whatever says the world,*
> *Let us taste the folly for a day, let us love.*[19]

After this music, a weary Berlioz said he was ready to "cut the bonds that attach me to art." He found he could write no more music. Yet against all odds, that summer, while visiting the grave of his second wife, Berlioz met another woman and quickly fell in love again. Her name was Amélie, and she was twenty-six years old, roughly half of Hector's age. Not surprisingly, this was a romance even more ill-fated for Berlioz than the two that had preceded it. In March of 1863 he wrote to his friend Ferrand the following note: "The matter in question is one of love, a love which came to me wreathed in smiles, which I didn't seek out and which for some time I tried to resist. But the isolation I live in and the inexorable need for affection which is killing me were too strong. I allowed myself to fall in love."[20] He also talked himself out of it, perhaps realizing that this romance made no sense on any sane level.

We know little about the young lady except for her Christian name and what Berlioz tells of her in his many letters. In August, September, and October of 1864, in three letters to Princess Carolyne von Sayn-Wittgenstein, Liszt's famous paramour, Berlioz made clear what he felt and what had become of the girl. This is how Berlioz remembered the terrible surprise of finding her for the last time: "May I take you into my confidence once more? I'll merely tell you that my favourite walk, especially when it's raining, when the heavens open, is in the Montmartre cemetery, near where I live. I go there often, I have many connections there." He continued, "Recently I even discovered there a grave of whose opening and closing I had been unaware. She had been dead for six months and no one had thought or been able to tell me that she was dying; she was twenty-six years old, she was beautiful, and she wrote like an angel. I had, we had, agreed it was wiser not to see each other, not to write … It was not easy. We caught sight of each other in the distance in the theater one night… She was already dying and I didn't know it. Six weeks later she was dead. I didn't know that either."[21]

In 1864, the twice-married, twice-widowed Berlioz was sixty-one years old. He would live four more years, enough for one more journey of the heart. Hector began visiting and writing the woman who had always remained fresh and perhaps foremost in his reverie, his Estelle. She was now Madame Fornier, living in Lyon. Eager to see her, he wrote her in September 1864, asking to let him visit. She assented. Her own son was about to be married.

What would she remember of him? Think of him? Estelle had little actual recollection of Hector, of those charmed days they seemed to care for each other. Later he wrote to Carolyne, again telling her that his heart was truly broken, that he went "from one misery to another." He summed up what his life had come to: "She has no vivid memories and she thinks as you do that my imagination is largely responsible, and no doubt she knows as well as you do that the imagination tells lies … I shall be as cautious as possible, and perhaps one day she will find herself saying, in the recesses of her heart, 'It would be a pity not to be loved like this.'"[22]

Though not composing he still wanted to show the world his music, and in 1866 Berlioz made one last trip to Vienna, to conduct his *Damnation of Faust*. His colleague Eduard Hanslick records his reception as "rapturous," and that it was as much the man as the music that delighted the masses.

Hector Berlioz's music was always better received in other European capitals than in his homeland, yet he almost single-handedly changed the face of music in France. Considered by many to be an eccentric, his music nonetheless became immortal. He had founded no school; even his ideas for grand composition were reputed in the advent of a German neo-classical revival.

What had this man's life come to? Toward the end of his life Hector Berlioz was revered by promising young Russian composers, men such as Borodin and Mussorgsky, whom he had championed. Mussorgsky's *Night on Bald Mountain* (1867) seems to owe a debt to the Faustian elements of the *Fantastique*. That same year Berlioz, already familiar with Glinka, and given his fondness for the Russian folk melodies, met the twenty-seven year old Tchaikovsky. In some ways Berlioz seems to have been an inspiration to this new breed of composers. He journeyed to Moscow and St. Petersburg to direct three concerts in January and February 1868; then he fell ill in Nice, in March.

Berlioz cut back on his travel but he accepted the job as curator of the instrument collection at the Paris *Conservatoire* that summer. His final, small, musical triumph was presiding over a choral festival in Grenoble that August, so near to where he had been born almost sixty-five years before. His health deteriorated in the winter of the new year.

Hector Berlioz suffered from a series of strokes and was nearly paralyzed in early March, 1869. Then, on March 8, in the arms of Marie Recio Berlioz's mother, Hector fell into a coma and died. His music was done, an era closed too soon. Berlioz was nothing if not a romantic, even in the nature of his burial. The man who had needed so much the inspiration of women in his life and in his music asked to be laid to rest in the same cemetery of Montmartre where his beloved Harriet and the inspirational Marie already lie. The three of them, with a little help from their friends, had made some of the world's most memorable music together.

CHAPTER FIVE

BIZET, Georges, (1838-1875), French

" *He never wanted to be a heave- stormer, and preferred Apollo to Dionysius.* "
(Harold Schoenberg)

    Alexandre César Leopold Bizet was born in Paris on 25 October 1838, to a pianist and a hairdresser. The mother was the pianist, by the way. His father also gave singing lessons. As for amusing family histories and senior-citizen chutzpah, the child's godfather had difficulty with the given names, especially César, and immediately began calling him Georges; and thus was the child baptized.

    Coming from a musically-talented family the boy had the predictable advantage of early exposure to music and "at the age of four he learned his notes from his mother at the same time as his letters."[1] His father gave private voice lessons in an adjoining room as Georges listened at the door of his bedroom. We can almost see the little fellow vicariously playing along, struggling to identify the notes. We sense he was precocious. Adolph and Aimée Bizet had only one child and he consumed their time and affection. Such beginnings often encourage the advent of genius. Adolph also taught his young son the piano and simple harmony, encouraging the boy to attempt some simple composition.

    We discover that Bizet could play Mozart's piano sonatas "with taste and affection" when he was nine, and by age ten he was admitted with a special exemption into the Paris Conservatoire. Here the young man studied with Pierre Zimmerman, a student of Cherubini; and with Charles Gounod, who was twenty years Georges' senior but would exert an influence on Bizet all his life. The careful instruction, listening into the instruction of others, and a great deal of practice paid off. When he was eleven Georges won his first notable prize in music. This was the *Prix de Solfège*. He took prizes in piano and organ play for three of the next five years. By 1856, the young Bizet was writing his one and only true symphony, the *C Major*. Georges was now seventeen, and ironically this music would not be much heard until he was long dead – in 1935, in fact. At the same time the lad had decided that he was ready to compete in musical composition for the *Prix de Rome*, which his countryman Hector Berlioz had won in 1830. This prize was given annually to five artists, saving always one for music. As had happened in years past, and to Berlioz as well, the judges refused to give a first prize that year. Georges took the second and came back the next year to win the first with the cantata *Clovis et Clotilde*. This prize carried with it a five-year scholarship, or grant, with a two year sabbatical in Rome, sharing the Villa Medici with other laureates.

There was ample opportunity to travel and to take in other *kultur,* which a young man, even a Parisian, would likely not get to see. Would such a sojourn to nature, to "poetry, painting and scenery" not benefit him? Such an experience certainly had influenced other young composers. In fact, "To men of a like nature a residence in Rome is likely to stimulate the imagination and strengthen the soul," one biographer has observed. His time in Italy would be "an aesthetic advantage, in a real but also in the widest sense…" In fact, "the modest muses inhabit waste places that know not the stir and chatter of boulevards… Most musicians need all this as a challenge to their wits, or as a daily spiritual food."[2] The grand language is a bit over the top, but his point is unassailable. Rome would be a breakthrough.

The opportunity worked to Bizet's advantage, and he wrote to his father in May, "the more I see of Rome the more I am enraptured." This observation had little to do with the prevalent music, however; as he also observed that here "anyone who could strike a chord with two hands was considered a great artist." Italy might be a land of song but not of great music. In fact he wrote to his teacher Gounod in Paris in September 1858 that nine months without hearing a note of good music left him unable to judge his own work. Redoubling his efforts while "in splendid exile," as he called it, Bizet wrote some pieces of particular interest. His "assigned" compositions proved more valuable than the young man might have expected or hoped. "The three obligatory works… were *Don Procopio*, an *opera bouffe* [along with some comic opera sketches taken from Molière]; *Vasca da Gama,* a symphonic ode with chorus; and a funeral march."[3]

He was particularly delighted with his first opera. The story came to him from a book he found at one of the small bookshops he frequented – Georges was teaching himself Italian. He wrote the opera as a substitute for the required sacred music, a mass, deliverable to the Académie des Beaux Arts in Paris. Predictably, he was applauded for his efforts and chided for not following the rules. Bizet wrote home to share his elation over how well his comic opera had been received, including the quote from the Académie "… this work is distinguished by an easy and brilliant touch, a youthful and bold style, precious qualities for the genre of comedy toward which the composer has shown a marked propensity… M. Bizet will not forget the obligation he has undertaken as much to himself as to us."[4] It would remain to be seen just how much such light and comic fare would become Bizet's strength.

He left Rome to return home in July 1860, planning to take his time and enjoy more of the countryside. He had recently written to his mother of an idea he had for a symphony on four cities. Rome, which was recognizably Europe's city of lights, would be the subject of his first movement; Florence would be the scherzo; Naples the finale. By the time he got to Venice, however, bad news awaited him. A letter from his mother, writing from her hospital, frightened Georges and expedited his direct return to Paris. The woman rallied briefly as her son arrived home, but she was dead within a few days. "Thus just at the outset of his career, when his mercurial nature most needed guidance, he was deprived of that being whom he believed most fitted to give it."[5] Parallels to Beethoven's first visit to Vienna, learning of the death of his mother in Bonn, are not only remarkable but a bit eerie. Monsieur Bizet proved resilient.

Georges soon found solace in the ample bosom of his mother's maid. While he was known to frequent the ladies of easy morals Bizet also enjoyed a fling with conveniently close Mme Marie Reiter, a winsome domestic in the employ of the family. When Marie became pregnant in 1861 there was an effort to deflect the parentage to Bizet's lonely dad, Adolphe. In fact little Jean was Georges's child with Marie. They raised him as a "little cousin" and only with the composer's untimely and early death did Marie, who dutifully stayed on to help around the place, disclose that indeed her papa was, indeed, the then twenty-two year old composer.[6] Did she inspire any music? Marie was likely too busy to be his Muse.

In fact, to what extent anyone can show a trail of musical inspiration from Bizet's surprisingly bountiful affair with the Marie, two years older, is problematic. Most assuredly his musical production took a sharp upturn in the years 1861-65, including the operas *The Pearl Fishers*; *Ivan the Terrible*, which he withdrew; and a couple of years later with his *Young Maid of Perth*.

While Bizet's music was often brilliant the composer suffered early for having selected uninspired librettos. The French loved the exotic locales; *Fishers* was set in Ceylon, and that was engaging to the theatre patron. But when the paying crowds thought the libretto was boring they simply walked out. Naturally, the music itself then had no chance at all. Georges learned this lesson well, and he situated his *Carmen* in Spain, which the French generally looked upon as being a somehow exotic.[7] Interestingly, Chabrier, Debussy, and Ravel all offered operas set in Spain. Maybe it was just the extra mouth to feed that drove Georges to go for the sure win.

Meanwhile, with Marie having gone back to her native Alsace to give birth to "Cousin Jean," Georges Bizet found himself in dire straits financially. He wrote to his publisher in the autumn of 1862 asking for assistance, for 1800 francs, in fact, detailing what vast compositional work he had in mind. Some work was to be transcription and some was arranging other men's music, but he also had in mind writing, "… polkas, dance-hall pieces, quadrilles, proof-correcting, transpositions, signed or unsigned, arrangements… and scores for two flutes, two trombones, two cornets, even two pianos." Bizet was ambitious. "I give you my word," he wrote," that we will make a good thing of this for both of us."[8] Arguably, Marie and little Jean were making their presence felt.

The 1860's were a difficult time for opera in Paris. Government subsidies, so important to Berlioz a generation earlier, were now harder to find. Bankruptcies were common. The opera managers also wanted a sure thing, and new or young composers were anything but "sure." Besides, the city's theatergoers were set in their ways, they had their favorites and they were not much interested in grappling with something fresh. "The same works, or replicas of them, were performed hundreds of times before the same bourgeois family audiences, who were more interested in each other and their match-making than in operas they ostensibly came to see and hear."[9] As Bizet had found, much to his frustration, a composer had to be something of a venture capitalist to have his music performed, or he must find a generous benefactor.

Even then, new works were likely to be resented or ignored. Mina Curtiss captures a correspondence between Camille Saint-Säens and Georges Bizet in her superb biography, <u>Bizet and His World</u>. She records their letters thusly: "'Since they don't want us in their theatre,' I used to often say to Georges Bizet, 'let us take refuge in the concert-hall.' 'That is all right for you,' he would reply, 'but I am not made for the symphony. I need theatre. Without it I don't exist.'"[10] Bizet had clearly staked out, at least for the time being, his purpose as a composer.

Bizet did not necessarily stay wedded to this view, turning frequently to works for piano and orchestra in the mid- to late- 1860s. Still, even though Bizet had the occasion to question its success financially, his first real opera was well received by those whose opinion he valued. At the age of twenty-four he found himself on stage with the performers of *The Pearl Fishers*, enjoying their obvious delight with the performance. Some of the more hide-bound critics thought he had overstepped his proper place, spontaneously accepting praise as if he were "somebody." But Hector Berlioz, like Gounod, whom Bizet lionized, thought the score and performance were superb and said so in his review, proclaiming it a "… real success … full of fire and rich [in] coloring."[11]

About this time Bizet's father bought some land in Le Vésinet, just twelve miles from Paris, and here he built two small cottages. Adolphe took one of them, the one with a kitchen; Georges took the other. This was the cottage with room, though barely, for a fine piano. The two men shared a vegetable garden where they cared for asparagus and strawberries. Bizet continued work on his score for his much-delayed and ultimately unsuccessful opera *Ivan the Terrible*,[12] which he salvaged as the grist for a number of other compositions. But it was the young composer, not the fruit and vegetables, that proved to be the big attraction that late summer of 1865, for soon they had an interesting new neighbor. Her name was Mme la Comtesse Moreton de Chabrillan. She was beautiful, inquisitive, and in search of something more tangible than asparagus. Finally, George Bizet would be meeting his first real Muse. A late starter; he finished strong.

The Comtesse was no common "royal." "Born in 1824, Céleste Vénard, the daughter of a so-called "loose mother and an unknown soldier," had fled from home in her teens in order to escape the attentions of her mother's lover, and in the course of a remarkable career had been by turns prostitute, actress [her stage name was Céleste Mogador], circus rider, novelist, dramatist, and author of a volume of memoirs." She even got to star, in 1864, in one of her own plays."[13] In other words she was a perfect fit.

Georges took to her immediately. Was it her totally outrageous personal history? Whatever the nature of the physical chemistry that welded the two of them, something about her made a clear impact on Bizet's music. They were not intellectual equals, but "… he spent much time in her company, often working for hours on end in a room, complete with piano and music paper. According to her account, she was the only woman he invited to the small musical gatherings in his bungalow, at one of which he played through the whole score of *La Joile Fille de Perth*."[14]

The breezy Céleste is also considered to have been the source of his greatest, or best loved, musical accomplishment. In fact, "[c]ritics have suggested that Céleste was a model for Carmen, especially because of her vivid self-characterization: "My character was formed early. I loved passionately or hated furiously…Moderation is no part of my nature. Joy, affection, resentment, laziness, work – I have overdone them all. My life has been one long excess."[15] George, against all counsel, could not get enough of her.

We learn, in an examination of Bizet's opera, "Carmen clearly belongs to this category of women. She is known to the men in the community as available – albeit [as she makes clear in the *Habañera*] on her own terms."[16] Their attraction, again, was essentially physical, as so many of Bizet's short liaisons had been. Was he finally to find his center, someone to give him a sense of who he might be as an artist? By and large, Céleste was more a libidinous fancy than a true soul mate or life love. She may have cleared the way, it seems, for Georges Bizet to find another – the one woman who would in most ways complete him.

In October of 1867 Georges wrote to his one-time student and good friend Edmond Galabert that he was happy, content with his writing, in love with *Jolie Fille (The Fair Maid of Perth)*, and now determined "… to climb, climb, always climb. No more evening parties! No more fits and starts! No more mistresses!" He promised "All that is finished!"[17] Could even Georges have believed it to be so?

The composer told his friend Galabert that all that was behind him because he had met "… an adorable girl whom I love." He announced that he intended to marry her. This was, of course, Geneviève Halévy, daughter of his beloved teacher. It took Geneviève a while to get past the scandal that seemed to attend Georges' liaison with Céleste, but eventually the betrothal was on track and they were married in June 1869. Bizet's work over the next few years was frantic. Theirs seemed the ideal marriage for a composer. Working now with both the Théâtre-Lyric as well as the Opéra-Comique, Bizet started three operas, though none were finished and performed in his lifetime. The former theater went temporarily bankrupt as the

Franco-Prussian war (1870-71) took its toll on the arts, as well as on the thousands of hopeful young men carrying their flags of battle.

Nevertheless, he was sufficiently taken by two librettos to begin some broad musical sketches. One is based on an epic poem by the Provençal poet Mistral. The other was to be based on pieces by Sardou and Phillipe Gille. Georges Bizet found the operatic potential of these works appealing, but he had already begun as many as six other operas that remained incomplete. Then, "[i]n June, 1870, Bizet and his wife went to Barbizon for the summer, and he set work on both libretti at once. Disappointingly, he did not have any luck with the politicians, and he was soon overwhelmed by greater events that menaced the very existence of France."[18]

Napoleon III and French Forces attacked and were summarily defeated by Bismarck. Unexpectedly, the thirty-one year old Bizet volunteered to fight in the National Guard, as had his friend Camille Saint Säens. Jules Massenet served briefly with the infantry troops. None of these men seemed to have had to do any actual fighting, though Georges did draw sentry duty and had to spend time, at least during the day, with his fellow soldiers. At home, young Geneviève was not well, unused to having her husband away. Putting his music again on hold, he wrote to her: "My dearest love, I can't see you this morning. I am on sentry-duty at 11 o'clock – and haven't even time to grab a bite to eat on the run. But I shall come back for dinner. I don't know just what time. In any case, have dinner ready at six o'clock. I love you, my love, with all my soul."[19] Of such sacrifice is true French soldering made!

In any event, the Prussian victory was complete by the end of winter, though the worst of the violence was to come in the early spring of 1871. The emperor was jailed and civil war raged, tearing the city apart. The Bizets made for the little village of Le Véisnet, where he had met and wooed the beguiling Céleste just six years earlier. Geneviève's health gradually improved, though she remained nervous about her mother's incessant nagging, and eventually Georges was again able to think about work. Then, in July, Geneviève gave birth to the child who would be their one and only. Jacques no doubt added to Bizet's sense of need for things to return to some kind of normalcy, some source of income, for that matter.

His proposed comic opera *Djamileh* was, while no stand-alone success in 1871, perhaps the stylistic breakthrough Bizet had been searching for. He again wrote to Galabert that he had "found his path – with a gaiety that permits style." Indeed, this inauspicious beginning was the genesis of his best known and most highly regarded opera, *Carmen*. We recall that the inspiration for the heroine was his outrageous "countess."

Bizet returned to other projects he had put on hold, and soon new commissions arrived. Would Georges be interested in writing incidental music to a play? The request came from his old friend Leon Carvalho, the director of the Théâtre-Lyrique. Bizet agreed to write the music for Alphone Daudet's play *L'Arlésienne*. The melodrama was not an instant hit, but it did get a few supporting, critical reviews. By November, with better billing and preparation, the work had become a big success, and as we know it has survived as a mainstay of contemporary program music. *L'Arlésienne* proved to be Bizet's second masterpiece and demonstrates the breath of compositional genius of a composer who had seen so many of his operas go unexpectedly flat.

Back home, Geneviève was busy with the baby and with finding what she could do to keep Georges content and focused on his work. By early 1873 Bizet began work on the ambitious five-act opera *Don Rodrique*. He wrote the entire score over the summer and autumn, intending to work on revisions after getting the broad construction in his mind. Bizet asked Gabriel Fauré to listen to what he had and to give him his ideas. Fauré was another innovator in French music, known primarily for his keyboard brilliance and organ compositions. But Bizet could never seem to focus on one project at one time. Soon thereafter he returned to work on the first act of *Carmen*. Predictably, *Don Rodrique* would never see the light of the stage. *Carmen*, as we know, would become his most celebrated work, though it did not come together in the course of a few weeks, as had his *Rodrique*, or even the perky *L'Arlésienne*. In fact, along the way Bizet became fascinated with writing a score for his cherished wife. This was an oratorio to be called *Geneviève de Paris*. We'll return shortly to how Bizet came to design and complete his tribute to his Muse-wife.

Bizet was not alone in often attempting too many projects at once – a sign perhaps of genius in need of some discipline. Or maybe he needed some time to set aside, albeit temporarily, the bold operatic work he knew would be his finest.

Bizet finished the weighty *Carmen* score in August of 1874, having set it aside time and again, not once because of illness. He must have thought perhaps he had waited too long. He was tired and his health, never robust, was worrisome. Georges complained of angina; he was overweight. But what truly slowed him down was a long-lasting throat infection, reported as abscesses, which only worsened as he aged. In January of '75 Bizet sold the score of *Carmen* to his publisher for 25,000 francs and pronounced himself well pleased. He told a friend that he had "… written a work that is all clarity and vivacity, full of color and melody." Bizet told his business partner "[I]t will be amusing…"[20] But he could not let go of the project, like a poem that is never quite finished, rather is temporarily completed.

Now he worried about such matters as the number of female voices in Carmen's Act I. The opera opened on March 3rd, and on that day Bizet was awarded the title of chevalier of the Legion of Honor. What more could the man hope for? The answer was, surely, general acceptance of his art and labor. But the conservative Paris audience found the whole proposition too déclassé, and there was as much criticism for the story line of loose women as those who found it, in certain parts, "brilliant." One review said Bizet was a "ferociously intransigent Wagnerian." Another spoke of its erotic fury, but pronounced it undramatic. One even pronounced his *Carmen* obscene. This was not the result he the ailing thirty-seven-year old Bizet had foreseen.

To be Wagnerian, in such a context, was a near insult. Bizet had been hearing it for years and he resented it, thinking his work as cutting edge. The Wagner implications suggested that he had no ideas of his own. After all, critics said, French music should be more than what the nutty German was doing. Bizet was despondent. He would not have wanted to be called Wagnerian, for that matter, for any reason that had to do with honesty or moral character. More on this remarkable story follows in the Wagner chapter.

It is ironic that it was his untimely death that kept the opera running as long as it did. The *Carmen* curtain went up forty-five times that year, more than any other work at that opera house. But what propelled it to such popular fascination seems to have been less the reports of its bawdiness, but rather the shock of its composer's unexpected passing on the night of *Carmen's* thirty-first performance. Thereafter, a macabre fascination with what strange new creation the young and now surprisingly deceased Bizet had wrought worked to keep the people coming. Superb irony! All the while the opera was in gestation it had proven to be a source of enormous anxiety and mixed emotions for the composer, though he never lost faith in his work. Now Bizet and his fated *Carmen* were all the rage.

In fact, *Carmen* proved to be one of the most successful of late 19th century French music. Allegedly, Peter Tchaikovsky, just two years younger than Bizet, "prophesied that within ten years it would be one of the most popular operas in the world." And so it came to be, by "…engaging nearly all the controversial themes of the late nineteenth-century culture simultaneously, its scandal and eventual success were virtually assured."[21] What happened to the fellow that he faded so fast?

His last days were said to be melancholy. Bizet's heart was not strong. And we surmise that the business of being called a "Wagnerian" took a great toll. Georges told his wife Geneviève he had to get out of the city, and on the 31st they left. He wrote to his long time friend Ernest Guiraud at this time that he was "feeling quite done in."

The last piece of music he seems to have worked on was again that tribute to his Muse, his wife. This was *Geneviève de Paris*, based on a poem popular at the time. It is fascinating to review the material Bizet was thinking about in his final efforts. In Act I Geneviève is a child, receiving a sacred blessing; in Act II she triumphs over evil. In Act III Geneviève is in Attila's camp, and in Act IV she heroically leads a salvation effort to a beleaguered and starving Paris. The composer found it fitting that, in the final act; the woman is triumphant, defeating the scourge Attila "solely by the efficacy of prayer."[22]

What makes all this a bit remarkable is that Bizet had long proclaimed his own studied indifference to the church and to her ways. But his wife was not an agnostic, as her husband perhaps was; she was a believer. So at the end of the little composer's life his Geneviève seems to have given Bizet a look at eternity that he had not foreseen, and likely never expected.

Georges Bizet died on 3 June 1875, apparently of a throat infection that spread to his weakened heart. Or did he die, as those who knew him best have suggested, of the heartbreakingly tepid reception of his remarkable work? At his funeral on June 5th the organist played musical variations on excerpts from Bizet's compositions, notably *The Fair Maid of Perth*, *Carmen*, and *L'Arlésienne*, along with Chopin's *funeral march*. That night, the special performance of *Carmen* was unbearably moving; and the press which had so damned the opera three months before … [now] proclaimed it a masterpiece.[23]

CHAPTER SIX

BRAHMS Johannes: (1833 – 1897); German

"Music and love were, for Brahms, very closely allied – the women he loved were musicians; musical creation competed with his emotional life; love was sometimes sublimated into composition."[1]

Johannes Brahms the man, as much as the musician, proves to be one of the more difficult of the classical masters to define. Hailed as the last of the great Romantic composers, he nevertheless inspired a number of the big reformers, including Arnold Schoenberg. Caring deeply for his reputation, he toured extensively giving concerts well into his forties. Yet he told his close friend and first biographer Max Kalbeck that praise made him uneasy. Women seemed to make him even more uneasy. There were more than a few that helped shape his preeminent music. Similar to the awkward circumstances surrounding Beethoven's adventures with the Muses, Brahms never made one of them a life-mate or a wife. Clara Schumann, when we get to her, was the nearest miss.

The composer's father, Johann Jakob Brahms, made a living playing various instruments, including flute and most of the strings, in Hamburg's taverns and dance halls. Jakob played the double bass well enough to provide for his young wife and small family. Johannes was the first-born son, his birth date was 7 May 1833; and he entered the world with what most every genius needs to get started, dedicated parents. The boy began to show an early interest in church music, perhaps because the Reverend Johann Geffcken was a family friend. He taught young Johannes numerous Lutheran chorales. The true beginning of the boy's musical interests came with his father's instruction in violin and cello, although Johannes showed more interested in piano.

His youth was remarkable only in that he was a true child prodigy, and not unlike the expectations Leopold Mozart had for his son, Brahms' father also encouraged his son to be paid for showing off his precocious talents. While Jakob made something of a living in music, the income it brought never seemed to be enough. By the time there were three children the family's precarious arrangements had come apart. Poverty has always been a family affair, of course, so when Johannes was able to do so, at about ten years of age, he was doing what he could to add to the family's bank account. Like his father, Johann began "to take engagements playing the piano in the many drinking and wenching dives of the notorious St. Pauli area, near the harbor."[2] It was this early exposure to the seedier side of man's nature that contributed to Brahms' later difficulty in relations with women. "At a very early age, he could have few romantic illusions about the opposite sex, let alone about his own."[3]

Studying and taking his music lessons by day, working late in the bordellos, the young man's strength began to wane. On some nights he was so tired he could barely walk home. A wealthy friend of the family, Adolph Giesemann, invited Johannes to spend several weeks with him and his family at Winsen an der Lühe, in the country. Accepting, Brahms soon recovered his health and developed a great love for the natural world. Perhaps of equal importance, he was fated to meet a young woman, not surprisingly, a piano student. This was Adolph's young daughter Lieschen, one year younger than Johannes, a girl who became much taken with her teacher, and he with her. They became quite close and she later came to stay at the Brahms' home, getting to know Johannes better. She may have been the metaphorical wellspring for the young man's decision to compose.

Lieschen was Johannes first real girlfriend, and whether or not the young lady had anything directly to do with it, that summer, in 1847, when Johannes was fourteen-years old, he began to write some part-songs for the Winsen Choral Society. From this experiment, young Brahms began to take a serious interest in composition. Even his master teacher, Eduard Marksen, who had wanted him to concentrate on his playing and practice, encouraged the pianist-composer to press on with his original works, which were largely fantasies and short piano pieces. We know little more of Lieschen, but she seems to have encouraged in Brahms the thrill of composition that would initially complement his talent as a performer.

There were a number of young ladies that would yet inspire Johannes in his music, but before them a few male acquaintances would also play a role in shaping his career, not as teacher and provincial musician but as a widely acclaimed artist. Two internationally recognized violinists, Joseph Joachim, and his friend, the Hungarian Eduard Reményi, encouraged Brahms to begin to tour. Travel and touring came naturally to him, and soon he was traveling widely. Johannes found opportunities in their distinguished company that he would not have found on his own – first in Hanover, then in Weimar, as well as other principal cities of great music. Their sponsorship led the young man to meet and play for Liszt, who was then perhaps the best known piano virtuoso in Europe, though his biographers record that Brahms did not much care for Liszt's style. Johannes found his play undisciplined.

Although it seems preposterous now, Brahms considered Liszt's composition flimsy for "woeful lack of consecutive thought and constructive power [...] which no amount of superficial brilliance could hide."[4] Whatever he may have thought about Liszt the performer he had more serious, personal concerns. Likely some of what troubled him was family finances. His friend Joachim recognized a deep melancholy in Brahms and encouraged him to awaken to his own potential, to continue his travel, to overcome his reticence, and to meet more of Europe's musical luminaries. The advice was sound. The next visit would be perhaps the most important in Brahms' young life. Robert and Clara Schumann were waiting in Düsseldorf.

We move ahead now to the year 1853; the nearly twenty-year old Brahms was immediately and deeply attracted to Clara. He respected the older Robert, twenty-three years his senior; but Brahms was infatuated with Clara, who was also apparently attracted to the good-looking and brilliant young Johannes. To what extent Robert's manic moods and approaching suicidal madness worked to move Clara and Brahms together we cannot be certain. We have every reason to believe they were each a Muse to the other, and more so after Robert's decline.

In her recollections, Clara writes of Brahms "Yesterday [16 July 1853] I was with Brahms from noon until eleven at night without interruption. He was in excellent spirits. We had our swim in the sea together, and again found much amusement in diving for little red pebbles." She continues to reflect on their interlude, "After the mid-day dinner Brahms was lying in my room, in the hammock which I had secured between window and door, while I read to him…"[5] Clara writes that later their conversation took a more serious turn, and he confessed to her "with touching warmth," about how he regretted that to be married and have a son was now impossible.[6] He does not actually say *married to each other*, but the connotation is strong. Was Clara inspirational in Brahms work? In every sense of the word she was.

Malcolm MacDonald discusses the symbol-system the young composer learned from Robert Schumann, and which he later developed from his feelings for Clara: "This symbolism, now widely recognized in Schumann's music, was a private affair known only to the Schumann circle. But Brahms, entering that circle, was initiated into it, and was thus able to recognize it and use it [most significantly the prime Clara symbol, and for much the same reasons as Schumann] in his own works. 'I speak in my music,' he once wrote to Clara Schumann; he was stating the literal and the Romantic truth."[7]

Truly, the details of any romance between the much younger Brahms and Clara, especially while Robert lie wasting away in the insane asylum at Endenich, remain sketchy. Another highly regarded biographer, however, writes of the traumatic period between Robert's attempted suicide in 1854 and his eventual death two and a half years later, at the age of forty-six. Brahms spent the two years totally devoted to Clara and her family. Brahms acted as "a husband," and took care of Clara and the household, even keeping the financial accounting records. Schumann may have actually encouraged something more between them. He liked Johannes and certainly knew how close the young man and his wife had become.

By January of 1855 Robert was intent on starving himself to death. His demons still working on his mind, but he cared deeply about the two people closest to him and how they felt for each other. If he were to die, something he contemplated regularly, surely Johannes would "watch over Clara and the children. She could be muse," suggests Jan Swafford, "to this young genius as she had been for Robert in his great years."[8]

"Schumann had proclaimed Johannes the Fair his successor in music. Now perhaps he retired from the scene to let the young man be successor in him home and in his bed."[9] For her part, Frau Schumann did as much as she could to further Brahms' career, and while Brahms wrote little original music during these difficult years, Clara was championing the composer's work in all her travels, in all quarters, "spreading Johannes's work like a sacred calling."[10]

Robert Schumann died in July 1856, at which time Clara moved with her children to her mother's home in Berlin. Her good friend Brahms took her to Switzerland the next year, chaperoned by his sister Elise. The succession, as Robert Schumann seems to have seen it, was simply not realistic. Soon the time came for Johannes and Clara to move on from their impossible relationship. After all, the widow Schumann was forty years old; the young composer was just past twenty-five. Brahms may have been intimidated by the choices. Could he stay on with Clara? What did she need? Perhaps he needed the love and at least as much the inspiration of a woman closer to his age and temperament. Another factor was more visceral: how to pay the bills? Brahms needed a job; teaching looked like the way ahead. Here it seems Johannes was thinking dispassionately.

He was still a young man, still unproven in his calling. Gainful, steady employment would lead to the Brahms's true independence and maturity. Teaching piano to the progeny of Hanover's, and later of Hamburg's, aristocracy Brahms could continue to look for work as a serious musician. Perhaps he'd find the right position as conductor. Nothing came of his plan.

If he had difficulty finding his way, getting the recognition he sought and the sobriety he needed, it was perhaps his lingering thoughts of what he and Clara might have had that kept him unfulfilled. The fateful relationship with Clara "engendered feelings of guilt, responsibility, and obligation."[11] Torn between uncertain options, he began to think that a younger woman, a less encumbered spirit, might show him how to move ahead.

As if the outcome were scripted, in the summer of 1858, while in Göttingen with Clara, Johannes fell in love with his student Agathe. Miss von Siebold, a young singer, was the daughter of a university professor. We know little of their success as student and teacher, but the couple's passion moved them to act in haste. Johannes asked for her hand in marriage. Still much in the picture, when Clara Schumann got word of this she became irate and wrote to Johannes saying, "I spent difficult days in Cassel, and thought of Agathe and a great many things kept haunting me… O dear Johannes, if only you had not allowed things to go that far."[12] Had things gone that far?

We must ask if this response caused Brahms to reconsider his future with the young, likely more naïve singer. One would likely think so. After all, Johannes was still in love with Clara, and no doubt she with him. Brahms seemed to be facing a hopeless situation. The young man wrote to Ms. von Siebold, "I love you and must see you again, but I am incapable of bearing fetters. Please write me again whether I may come again to clasp you in my arms, to kiss you and tell you that I love you."[13] This fetters remark, however, was hard to take in any positive light. She declined to linger in some form of sexual, marital limbo and decided to move on, perhaps surprising the impetuous, heartsick Johannes with her strength of will.

Brahms was left to ponder his own decision, for Agathe married soon thereafter. "Brahms never saw her again, but he confirmed immortality on her by [some years later] encoding her name in the *String Sextet in G Major*, op 36." Not surprisingly, given how it had ended, "six years later they were still pining for each other."[14] But fetters are not the stuff of blissful matrimony, and we can only deduce that Brahms wanted his freedom more than the love of this one woman. "[I]n the Sextet, which he wrote in 1864-5, he repeatedly calls her name – in the nearest 'spelling' musical annotation allows. The passage where the first and second violins play A – G – A – D – E was explained by Brahms to his friend Josef Gänsbacher, "At this point I freed myself from my final love affair."[15] The young woman, if seeming to offer him only fetters, instead inspired deep feelings and one of Brahms' most searching musical pieces.

One cannot help but assume that after the so-called Siebold affair, Johannes was determined to pursue a series of essentially tenuous, liminal relationships with women. Why not? Clara was now certainly beyond his reach; yet no other woman would be so permanently in his mind. The women he favored after 1859 remained somewhere between friendly, platonic fellow travelers on one extreme, and women of "easy virtue" on the other. Many were musically gifted; otherwise it is doubtful if Brahms would have been much interested. Most were young singers. The first of these, and there were four in a row who may have influenced his music and served in some sense as a Muse, was Bertha Porubsky.

Brahms returned to Hamburg to find something of a ground swell of interest in his music, and particularly for his *D Minor Piano Concerto*, just performed by the Hamburg Philharmonic. In fact, his concert performance in March quickly sold out, creating even more interest in the young man. Some few months thereafter some members of the choir agreed to sing for him, selecting from Brahms own *Ave Maria*, composed the previous year. The evening proved so successful and engaging for all that another performance was agreed, Brahms leading the ladies of the *Akademie* in his new set of pieces, the first two parts of his *Marienlieder*, folktales of the virgin, as it has been called. We can only speculate as to whether or not Brahms was enjoying some heightened word play.

"A solo quartet of women worked further with him," we learn, and "naturally he developed crushes on several of these young women, and they of course the same with him."[16] This is where Bertha Porubsky arrives in his life. She was visiting from Vienna. When Johannes saw her he begged his hostess for an introduction. Herr Brahms was immediately captured by Bertha's charm and grace, her disposition, so different from the starchy, North German propriety and manner. Brahms still had an eye on some of the other young women, as well, perhaps most especially on Laura Garbe, of whom he joked to his sister that this was her "future sister-in law."

Marriage, of course, was not a realistic option for Brahms – not to Bertha, not to Laura; truly not to anyone. Why? The composer was concerned now with making his mark upon the highest circle of music. He had too much work to do to get married. Besides, he found the business of romance to be always a bit awkward. A flirtation would be welcome, an inspiration divine. The acts that followed were messy. A bit of playful wink and wonder was not too much to hope for, was it?

Soon Brahms began writing choral music with his delighted singers helping him to perfect the music. Some of his creations would have included the *13th Psalm*, for three-part women's chorus and organ, Op 12. He also wrote a *Funeral Hymn* for mixed chorus and wind orchestra, Op 13, while under the influence, so to speak, of this young, adoring *Frauenchor*. It was during this interlude that he began working on *Twelve Songs and Romances*, Op 44. "Besides his own pieces, which the girls copied into part-books decorated with elaborate drawings, he indulged his passion for older music. In their three years under his direction the women sang music by Bach, Handle, William Byrd … and other Baroque masters."[17]

Here Brahms' biographers are unconvinced as to whether or not Johannes may have had true, sexual affairs with one or more of these girls. If so, there is nothing recorded in anyone's diary or memoirs to so state. He tended to vent his lustier humors with the prostitutes he later came to frequent so easily. "He fell in love with virgins real or imagined; he bedded the whores. If there were exceptions to that, he managed to obliterate them from the record as effectively as his rejected pieces."[18]

Brahms' affection for Bertha, however, remained a pitch above the mundane rhythms of the Platonic heart. He wrote her regularly and included little songs he had composed especially for her, all the while her Hamburg aunt keeping an eye on the relationship. The next year, Bertha returned to her home in Vienna, her destiny as Muse demurely fulfilled. This was another example of a love interest gone but not forgotten. Perhaps he would see her again? He tried. In 1862 Brahms was in Vienna, ostensibly to observe first hand the nature of Europe's long regarded great city of music – the city of Mozart, Beethoven and Schubert. Come to that, since he was here, perhaps he might renew an old acquaintance. Johannes went to find Bertha. Ms. Porubsky, however, was inconveniently now engaged to be married.

Such a turn of events was not his biggest disappointment. Brahms had been expecting to hear that he'd been named to lead the Hamburg Philharmonic. It was not to be. The job was offered to his friend Julius Stockhausen. Brahms had always known his destiny was to be Kapellmeister in his hometown. How could this reversal of fortune be true? Perhaps, he thought, his family's socially embarrassed circumstances may have impacted the decision to go with Stockhausen. Whatever the motive or reason, the twenty-one year old was forced to make a new plan. Would he assume the role of the rejected and expelled, or might he turn this disappointment into opportunity? Brahms wrote his closest confidant, Clara Schumann, telling her that the news of this lost position represents a "much sadder event for me than you can imagine or perhaps grasp." He told her that if he could not even secure such a job in his native town, what could he expect elsewhere? He would not choose to "flit about in the wilderness of the world," but rather "one wants to be bound, and to acquire everything that makes life worth living." Brahms told Clara that he was afraid of solitude, needed "the happiness of a family circle."[19] He was hurt, angry, and resentful. Gradually the man was able to gain some perspective. Showing considerable maturity, he reconsidered his options. Why not move on? Although he could not have seen it clearly then, the Hamburg setback allowed Brahms to find the rest of his life's work in Vienna. If not Hamburg, Vienna would do nicely. Vienna was better, but he soon found he truly missed someone.

Was Bertha really out of his life? Shortly after Brahms settled in to his new home he found that Miss Porubsky had indeed become Mrs. Arthur Faber. Yes, she was out of his life. This was a disappointment he had to somehow put behind him. Certainly his career must now be his only focus. He would concentrate on work, not women. Could he do it? Distractions aside, opportunities soon presented themselves. His hero Johann Sebastian Bach had made the same choice, but then his temperament was much different from that of Johannes.

Brahms was invited to present what would be his first important performance in the city. This was his *G Minor Quartet,* written the previous year. The composer took the piano part himself. His friends, in an extra effort to make him feel welcome, invited soprano Luise Dustmann, a carefree divorcee, to participate as well. Johannes was delighted with the favor. Brahms had met Luise in Hamburg, where she had been flirtatious, calling him by the very familiar "Hansi." Not in the least shy, the young woman responded to his complements on her performance in Beethoven's *Fidelio* by "suggesting a rendezvous the very next day."[20] Maybe the straight and narrow path he had vowed to find would be easier to talk about than to travel. The reasons were complicated.

Brahms was now particularly vulnerable, needing friends, needing the affection of those he knew and respected. But was Luise, or *Fidelio* as she called herself when they were together, the right girl? She may have done more for him than flatter his ego. Michael Musgrave, in his recent biography, says that Luise Dustmann, who taught at the Vienna Conservatoire, actually encouraged Brahms to settle in Vienna.[21] It is unlikely that Johannes needed much overt encouragement, as there was so much history and opportunity calling to him here. Still, her midwifery is praiseworthy. Their romance fizzled, but she had done for Johannes the important work the fates had given her to do.

We move ahead to the year 1874, where we find the composer visiting friends in Leipzig. The culture mavens of the old city, once home to the immortal Bach and much more recently to Mendelssohn, had made the Gewandhaus one of the premier orchestras in the world. These men, these power brokers, had invited Brahms to be the guest of the city for what they offered as "Brahms Week." This was an ego boost! Mendelssohn was now gone from the city for twenty-seven years, but Brahms was eager to test his skills and reputation, even against such impressive musical forbears. His host was Heinrich von Herzogenberg, a well-regarded composer of mostly chamber music and choral works. Heinrich was not alone in welcoming the composer. Brahms was delighted, as well, to renew his acquaintance with the man's wife, Elisabet, whom Johannes knew as the young daughter of his rival von Stockhausen. He did not know it yet, but the Muse was back.

Elisabet won his heart once. In fact, Brahms had had to shuffle her off to another piano teacher, so keen was his fascination with her beauty and charm. Elisabet could be quite a distraction. She attracted her young friend, the underappreciated British composer, Ethel Mary Smyth, as well. Maybe now that Elisabet was married Johannes figured he could be more at ease. Or could he? Apparently Brahms was still somewhat smitten, though the three shared broad musical interests and got along well enough, considering the awkwardness of it all for Johannes.

It seems "Clara Schumann, who knew and liked the Herzogenbergs, felt an occasional pang of jealousy over this 'beautiful blond aristocrat.' But Brahms basked in Elisabet's approbation. A considerable musical circle gathered around 'Lisl' in Leipzig…"[22] Just when he thought it was again safe to journey into the company of women, Brahms found his heart at risk again. Even as much as four years later, Brahms was working on the opus 92 *Quartets*, the earliest of which dates to 1877, "celebrating Brahms's amicable passion for Elisabet von Herzogenberg."[23] Surely this is the inspiration he had hoped to find following the end of his intense relationship with Clara.

Here, at last, was another first-class Muse. Consider *O Schöne Nacht*. Here Brahms weaves a sumptuous nocturne, a scene of bliss and harmony that only belied his own awkward and uncomfortable situation. Eventually, of course, the interlude ended, at least in a temporal sense, and Johannes returned to Vienna. Likely he was never able to put the beguiling Lisl von Herzogenberg out of his mind. Fate rumbled in to the picture about that time.

When Heinrich took ill in 1888 and the couple moved to Berlin, perhaps for necessary medical help, the long Lisl – Johannes affair of the heart waned, "but it never snapped, and Elisabet's death in 1892 was a profound grief for the composer. For long her photograph had stood in his room; and there it remained, almost to the end."[24] Only Clara Schumann would prove to be a greater source of love and inspiration to Brahms than his Lisl. That rigor and discipline he said he must have proved elusive, harder to find that he might have thought. Soon he had other women on his mind.

One young lady brought some combination of temptation and musical inspiration to Johannes's romantically unsettled world. Her name was Hermine Spies, and her all too brief passing in and out of Brahms's life was nearly as devastating as any that had gone before. A consideration of their time together should help the reader to understand why.

As we know, Brahms's music profited enormously through his need for criticism. For most of his creative life he trusted men and women who had earned his respect; he listened to that criticism. The von Herzogenbergs were particularly valuable in this manner. We know that he remained ever in search of feedback from his friend Hans von Bülow, as well as from his teacher Eduard Marxsen, to whom he dedicated his *Second Piano Concerto*. It was through shear good fortune, through the voice teacher and his close friend Julius Stockhausen, champion of Brahms's *Lieder*, that he would meet the lovely and distracting Hermine Spies. When he did so, in 1882, Johannes Brahms was nearing fifty years of age. He must have thought, albeit mistakenly, "well now I am passed all that business with romance."

Likely, Hermine was the last "female acquaintance to attract him seriously."[25] It appears that they became such a public couple, in fact, that their engagement to wed was "expected in Viennese circles." [26] He met her at the home of his friend Rudolf von der Leyen, in the small town of Krefeld, near Leipzig. So attracted was Johannes to Hermine Spies that he returned to Krefeld to spend time with her that summer. He also needed a place where he could think, to write, and here Brahms completed his *Third Symphony*. She seemed to settle his nerves. Hermine, as a minimum, must be credited with "an assist" for this major work.

Beyond her beauty, talent, and charm Brahms was also delighted that she was so dedicated to him and to his compositions, particularly to the songs. She told one friend that she plays Brahms 'the livelong day,' enjoying a kind of respite from her work as a professional singer. Brahms had his *Lieder* copied for Hermine and presented them to her as a Christmas gift. But his heart was not safe. Just as it seemed Johannes had a new lease on life, tragedy struck – perhaps as it had done in his life, again and again. In January 1892, Elisabet von Herzogenberg died of heart failure. Her death was a great loss. No woman besides Clara Schumann had been closer or more important to Brahms, and truly he was no longer as close to Clara as he had been, or once thought he should be. Further tragedy was awaiting.

Later that year his sister Elise died. Such ill-fortune comes in threes, for "then in 1893 death carried off the merry and invigorating Hermine Spies … at the age of thirty six. [27] Johannes was devastated. How could he accommodate himself to so much personal loss? As he had learned to do, ever the stoic, he would work his way through the grief. Hermine, it seems, left Brahms with one more inspiration; was once more the Muse he needed. Just after he met her, and off and on for the next four years, Brahms wrote a series of songs, including *Six Songs and Romances,* Op 93a, and at the age of fifty-three he wrote three sets titled *Five Songs,* Op 105-107, which seem "other-worldly calm." Opus 105, number 2, is called *Immer leiser wird mein Schlummer, or* Ever fainter grows my slumber. It is a song about a dying girl. With infinite pathos it recalls, as if in a dream, the main theme of the slow movement of the *B flat Piano Concerto.*" Actually, "*Immer leiser* grew directly out of the ageless Brahms' romantic friendship with the young singer, Hermine Spies."[28]

It is interesting that he had also written a symphonic cantata in 1892 for Lisl, as a memorial to her and their friendship, but the work bogged down until his supreme source of inspiration, Clara Schumann, intervened and pushed Brahms to finish it, which he did in 1896. We know the work as *Vier ernste Gesänge* (Four Serious Songs). It was the last music he ever wrote. He had been ill for a year or more. Johannes Brahms died on the 3rd day in April the next year, suffering from cancer and liver failure.

Ironically, none of his women outlived him; not the younger ones, not even the indestructible Clara, the one whom he loved above all. Clara Schumann had died nearly one year before him, at the age of seventy-seven. Surely, no one did more than Clara to inspire Brahms as a musician. No one was more Muse and alter-ego to the artist. In all likelihood, it was also the reality that he could not have Clara for his wife that kept him from any truly serious relationship with any other women, no matter what confused feelings he may have had for Clara, or for that matter she for him.

To equivocate just a bit, confusion for Brahms may have played the most consistent part in his life. Beyond the nearly impossible relationship he had with Robert Schumann's wife, certainly his teenage experience working in the dance hall-brothels did not do him any psychological good when it came to love, romance, and sex. Johannes Brahms had many romantic friendships, and perhaps he enjoyed the splendor of some true loves. These Elysian moments proved highly inspirational in his music, but it cannot be said that he ever got what he felt he truly needed, as in all likelihood Brahms never really understood what that might mean. Johannes Brahms, we must gather, never did know what he needed. He was not the only composer remembered in this book to be so troubled.

The Hamburg piano player was said by many to be the successor to Beethoven, dead six years when Brahms was born. The role of Beethoven's successor was a mantle claimed by few, aspired to by many, and not necessarily earned by any one. Brahms may have come the closest. Not unlike the master before him, Brahms never did resolve his conflicted sense of what he truly wanted from the fairer sex, except to know that quite a few of them, certainly Louise, Lisl, Hermine, and most especially so Clara, were profoundly important to the remarkable timbre of the man's music.

CHAPTER SEVEN

CHOPIN, Frédéric: (1810 – 1849), Polish

He could be witty, malicious, suspicious, ill-tempered, charming. There was something feline about Chopin. (Harold Schoenberg)

Much like Bartók some seventy years later, Frédéric Chopin was a champion of "national music." Poland's history was glorified in her art. One biographer suggests that Chopin's "thoroughly Polish masterpieces – these first civilized mazurkas, adapted for the piano, became the bridge between Polish folk music and classical music."[2] Who was this proud European, half-French by blood, who chose to live apart from his beloved Polish homeland most of his life? Why he chose to do so had much to do with the role five women played in shaping Frédéric's distinctive musical output.

Born to French - Polish parents, Chopin was three months older than Robert Schumann, and would live almost exactly the same number of months as his immediate contemporary Otto Nicolai, himself born three days after Schumann. In fact, 1810 was a bountiful time for musicians. Mendelssohn was born the year before; Liszt arrived the year after. These men influenced each other enormously. Robert Schumann adored Chopin and his music, though Chopin never could warm to Herr Schumann. Both Chopin and Nicolai left home at the age of sixteen to study; Chopin went to Warsaw – not so far away. He left Poland for Vienna when he turned nineteen. Nicolai took up his studies in Berlin. Both are best known for their funeral marches. Good things seem to come in clusters, perhaps especially so in the world of classical music.

Chopin's father Nicholas, whose French family was nervous about Napoleon's ambition, moved to Poland at the age of sixteen and took up the trade of music tutor to one high-society family. Apparently, Nicholas was well regarded for his talent as a teacher. But his on-again, off-again position with Countess Skarbek's household suffered from the malaise of their constant economic stress. Theirs was a family with aristocratic pretensions feeling the effects of a bankrupt economy. The woman who would become Frédéric's mother was employed there too, as the family housekeeper.

Justyna provided Nicholas Chopin with four children, Frédéric Francizek being the second born and the only boy. His was not the only musical talent in the house, however. "Both parents were musical. Justyna played the piano, Nicholas the flute and violin, and chamber music lent added joys to the conviviality of family life."[3] Already at age four, Frédéric was working with his mother and older sister at the piano. At seven he had outgrown their knowledge and skill and began to take formal lessons from the Bohemian tutor Adalbert Zywny. The next year Chopin wrote his first piece of music for a woman – actually for one of the young Countesses. More on this effort in a moment, but surely little Frédéric was doing all he could to keep the family contract in place. He had already attempted to write some simple scores.

Chopin had actually taken to composition for piano at the precocious age of six. The lad had been playing many of the masters, but was drawn especially to Bach and to Mozart. This was an attraction the young man never abandoned; and during the height of the so-called Romantic era Chopin remained essentially a classical composer. As a youngster he enjoyed improvising and innovating from the original works, "with Zywny carefully noting down tunes and accompaniment, Nicholas [Frédéric's father] lending a hand with copying." Young Chopin decided, however, to note his own improvisations, learning how to properly mark the requisite notes and staves. How or why he decided to write for one of the girls is unknown, unless he had a crush on her. "One day in 1817, Zywny walked into the Chopin family's drawing-room and produced a sheet of music. It was a Polish dance, a *Polonaise in G-minor*, which Frédéric had recently composed and dedicated in the mandatory French to one of the younger Skarbek countesses."[4] Had the eight-year-old Frédéric Chopin felt the first stirrings of the musical Muse?

The boy quickly outgrew Mr. Zywny and the Chopins placed the boy, then eleven, with Joseph Elsner, pianist, composer, and director of the Warsaw Conservatoire. Serving also as the director of the national opera, he was considered a master music teacher. Chopin found with his mentor access to the most influential of Polish music circles. First, however, Chopin had to learn to discipline himself even beyond his own strict work ethic, following Elsner's guidance in counterpoint and musical theory. After all, much of his early training had been largely anecdotal and imitative. He worked at least six hours a day, usually more, often working himself to exhaustion. His native genius and hard work paid off, but at some cost to his health. The teen-aged "Chopin was rapidly discovering his own true voice as a composer,"[5] though even as a youth his health was never robust, and he frequently complained of weaknesses.

Nothing of his own experience with illness, however, could prepare him for the loss of his closest sister Emilia, in April of 1827. She was fourteen years old. Beethoven, in every sense a hero, had died one month earlier. The effects of these two loses on young Chopin were enormous, thought to have inspired his composition of the *Nocturne in E minor*, "perhaps the most emotionally compelling piece to arise from his middle teen years."[6]

The loss of his sister had shaken his sense of place, and soon Chopin became fascinated with the idea of foreign travel. In fact, "what he wanted above all at this stage was to go abroad, throw himself into the mainstream of European music… Paris, Berlin, Vienna, now it was all available to him. His father had already promised to take him to Vienna during the [next] summer holidays."[7] Chopin was disappointed when the trip did not materialize, but a family friend, Dr. Jarocki, convinced the family that Frédéric should accompany him to Berlin for an international congress of scientists that September. Such an experience would be an opening to the rest of the world. There the young man attended many concerts and declared the city of Berlin to be "wonderful." Returning home the draw of Vienna, until recently the home of the great Beethoven, also remained strong. He gave the matter a good deal of thought. Vienna was centre stage.

By the time he left Warsaw, he had earned tremendous acclaim for his music. He had some important people yet to meet however here in Poland. We don't want to get ahead of the story, however, for Frédéric was on the cusp of a brief but poignant romance.

It would be unfair to all parties, and most certainly to Chopin himself, if we did not credit his first Muse as being his boyhood friend Titus Woyciechowski. His fellow student was a big, handsome, musically gifted lad to whom Frédéric wrote the most heart-felt letters of devotion. Evidently, "the virile Woyciechowski had an empathy with Chopin's delicate music, and in his presence inspiration would come more readily than in the musical gatherings at Warsaw's genteel drawing rooms."[8] There is nothing to suggest that the boys ever actually shared any physical intimacies, through Frédéric often wrote to Titus on how he would lavish kisses upon him. While no letters from Titus to Frédéric remain, there seems no doubt that they shared a special bond. That said, at least one biographer takes the view that "From early childhood, Chopin felt at home in female company. Women, more than men, held out to him the promise of solicitude and strength which his nature craved."[9] We know that there were a half-dozen Muses yet to come in Chopin's brief life, but his friend Titus enjoys the privilege of being the first to have Chopin's music specifically dedicated to him. This was the *Variations*, "the first fruits of his orchestral labours, because he felt Titus was the only one to understand the innermost meaning of his music."[10]

Such affairs are seldom uncomplicated. We cannot know how Chopin's deep feelings for Titus affected his thinking about women, but Frédéric Chopin was now on the verge of his first heterosexual romance. Frédéric had toyed with the idea of more travel, a brief excursion with friends to Vienna and Prague having proven exciting and successful in broadening his musical horizons. He was still unfulfilled, and we suspect that he was lonely. Timing was important now.

Still in Warsaw, the hometown girl Constantia Gladowska won his heart, seemingly without any effort or intention on her part. Constantia was an attractive mezzo-soprano, also studying at the Warsaw Conservatoire. She was nineteen years old and she possessed a certain mystery that felled the vulnerable young composer.

Constantia was the daughter of a Warsaw theatrical producer. She was said to posses a grace, "both physical and musical, which went straight to the young Chopin's heart. She became his first intense experience of sexual infatuation, and on the evidence it seems safe to assume that he was as much in love with the conditions as with the girl."[11]

Chopin had been obsessed with her for six months when he wrote to Titus that she was his "ideal." For her part, she carried out her vital function as Muse even though she could hardly know his feelings, for Frédéric was too flummoxed to speak to her of his romantic angst. Oddly, Chopin's love letters about her were sent to the stoic Titus, as if somehow he could or would manage the affair of his friend from afar. Chopin wrote the *Adagio* of his 1829 *Concerto No 2, in F minor, op 21,* for Constantia. He then wrote what he termed "a little waltz" in her honor. This was, of course, his *Waltz No 10, op 69*. As for what Titus thought his role in the whole affair should be we know nothing at all.

Chopin did make one fairly bold gesture to Constantia, and that was to convince her to accompany him in the performance of his only other piano concerto, this work in *E minor. op 11*. The concert was given in Warsaw on 11 October 1830, just before he left for Vienna. Meanwhile, while they shared time at the Conservatoire, he had begun composing a series of songs for her to sing, which is interesting because Chopin had shown no interest in such compositions before. Now they captivated him and together they practiced the music in her singing rooms. When Constantia finally suspected his true feelings for her she "may have been inclined to reciprocate them; but since Frédéric could not bring himself to speak of his love, and she was not a girl to be forward, nothing was said."[12] This was an opportunity Chopin could never reclaim, and Constantia may never have understood what she had meant to him. Perhaps, too, Chopin's lingering feelings for Titus made the move to Constantia all the more difficult. In retrospect, we can be grateful to the young woman having influenced his only concerto. She married in 1831, her own career never truly coming to its expected maturity, her potential somehow unfulfilled. Constantia outlived Chopin by some forty years.

Papa Nicholas Chopin now weighs in with his own brand of inspiration, telling his son it is time for him to take his place in the work of serious music. That place was not located in Warsaw. By the next summer, with performances at the National Theater further making him a national celebrity, Chopin wrote to Titus that he could stay in Warsaw no longer; his uncomfortable romantic longings for Mlle. Gladowska were making things worse. What could he do?

That autumn Frédéric and Titus left for Vienna, having made their plans to journey together. Frédéric had been considering it for years. After all, Chopin was now a graduate of the Warsaw Conservatoire, and he wanted to test his mettle as a serious musician against the world's known best. His friend quickly made other plans. With all the turmoil and political unrest around them, it was little wonder that Titus was swept up in the call of Polish nationalism. He returned just six days after their arrival in Vienna to join in the Warsaw uprising, leaving Frédéric to decide if this was truly the city for him.

No doubt Vienna lost some of its appeal with his loving friend gone off to serve; and within months Chopin was certain this venture had been a mistake. He wanted out; he wanted Paris. Goodbye to Vienna. After much intrigue over travel documents, Frédéric left the Austrian city on July 20, 1831, "on a leisurely journey en route to Paris."[13] The man may not have known his heart but he knew that Vienna was not for him.

Actually, he had a fine time in Munich along the way, ostensibly waiting for his funds to catch up. Here he met his contemporary Felix Mendelssohn, also passing through the Bavarian capital. Chopin even found time to perform his *Fantasia on Polish Airs* to a receptive Munich house, and at least to one important critic. We know that the French capital had been in political and economic revolt for a year and writers and musicians were waging their own brand of social and cultural warfare, as well, in the heady spirit of Romanticism. "Chopin appeared on the scene at the perfect time to catch the cresting wave."[14]

Owing to a range of circumstances, not the least being all the revolutionary discord roiling across the continent, and perhaps because Chopin was legally in Paris in a temporary capacity, on a Russian passport, he began to prepare for French citizenship. His desire was granted on August 1, 1835, nearly four years after his arrival. A proud Pole, this bit of Russian suzerainty was likely uncomfortable for him. Besides which, as a French citizen he considered himself less at risk by the vagaries of international politics. Settling in to a community of geniuses, that December he wrote Woyciechowski in Warsaw that Paris is "whatever you care to make of it."[15] Chopin was sure this time; he made Paris his permanent home.

Frédéric and Franz Liszt had now become close friends, if not necessarily kindred spirits, in their approach to music. Chopin often spoke, perhaps injudiciously, about Liszt's showy vulgarity. The former was a composer first; the latter was brilliant in writing music, but he piano virtuoso above all else. While they differed in style they were much alike emotionally, and this fact accounts for why they cared so deeply for each other's friendship. Both suffered from manic-depressive moods. Liszt "had a major nervous breakdown after the collapse of an ardent adolescent love affair…"[16] Chopin had avoided such high drama so far. The lost love in Franz Liszt's life, of course, was Caroline de Saint Circq, whose family disapproved of the highly unorthodox young Hungarian and did what they had to in order to scotch their budding relationship. Liszt, who would later blaze quite a libidinous trail of his own, had to be hospitalized for her loss, and some thought he had actually perished from the experience. Franz Liszt was perhaps more melodramatic than his Polish friend Frédéric.

With Titus and Constantia out of the picture, Chopin felt a void. Did he need someone to care for; to write music for; to love him? The aches and anxieties of uncertain love, something almost all people have experienced, were now heading directly for Frédéric Chopin. We can put a name to the heartaches. Delphina.

The young lady was an aristocrat. So many classical musicians were drawn to these kind of women. The couple had first met in Dresden; she was then in the company of her parents. Now, in 1831, whatever the tone of his resumed relationship with the Countess Delphina Potocka, Chopin was getting plenty of inspiration from the woman who would be the next major Muse in his life. There is no doubt that he loved her. There is a great deal of disagreement, however, about the kind of relationship they had. One reason that the biographers do not agree is that there may have been some fabricated evidence, in the way of personal letters, that make their fling seem more heated than perhaps it was. If we take even a cautious approach, it does seem certain he loved her deeply, even though she willfully had other dalliances while they were together. Delphina Potocka was audacious, to say the last. Maybe that is exactly why she was such an inspiration to Frédéric.

Truth be told, Chopin had already been wounded by love's games in a more temporal way; he contracted gonorrhea from a prostitute named Teresa, likely in Munich. Chopin called such working girls "ladies of mercy," and he called their close encounters together "duets." But unlike the similar experiences of Beethoven and Brahms, such interludes or escapes into adult entertainment were not his habit or in his comfort zone. His looks and charm made up for all that. All Chopin had to do was to look interested.

Somehow, women were drawn to him, although he did not play a broad field. "Love, friendship, and the support of women, always there for him, were the backbone of Chopin's existence ... and when he embarked upon the conquest of Paris it was [another] woman who became one of his most devoted."[17]

The Countess Potocka was beautiful, musically talented, and separated from her husband, who apparently was a big philanderer. Learning where he had settled in Paris, and then avoiding that part of town, she took the initiative to invite Chopin to dinner, and they quickly became nearly inseparable on the Paris scene, making music together. "When Frédéric's *Concerto no. 2 in F minor* for piano and orchestra was published in Paris in 1836, he dedicated it to her."[18] He dedicated a good bit more to Mlle Potocka.

Whatever the truth may be regarding the nature and passion of their relationship, most biographers now agree that Chopin was not overtly a sexual man. His was simply not a physical nature. He was romantic, it is true, but he was not particularly hot blooded, as was his friend Liszt. Stating it somewhat ambivalently, he could have still been a virgin at the age of twenty,[19] the duet with Teresa perhaps having written *finis* to that chapter. In any event, his relationships with women, at least until he met Aurore Dupin, better known by her writing name George Sand, were perhaps more platonic than Dionysian.

This one was different. Delphina Potocka had a major impact when Monsieur Chopin was most impressionable. Beyond her musical talents, one big attraction for him was that she, too, was Polish. She had a reputation of living life at the higher registers, and one friend called her "Don Juan in petticoats." Clearly she made a lifelong impact on the composer. Delphina was five years older than Frédéric, and she was eons wiser. Much later, when their need for each other cooled, they remained close friends.

Chopin may have been hurt by her many flirtations and digressions, commonly held at her lakeside villa outside Paris. He seems to have accommodated himself, in any event, to this state of affairs. In one of his letters to her he wrote: "You yourself told me I could say it with music rather than in writing. I wish I could write you beautiful and poetic letters because I know you like such things, but as much as I love you, you must not expect such an accomplishment from a mere piano player."[20]

While she was away, and apparently this was frequent, he wrote music for her. "He was discovering in himself what was to become a fundamental element in his creative process." During such periods, when he was not blocked from getting the notes down, he was engrossed in his *Etudes*. He wrote her such music as the *Nocturne in G Minor (op 15, no 3)*, and the *Mazurka in C Minor*, as well as whimsical sketches that are now lost, or else he had them destroyed. Frédéric decided that enforced absence sometimes worked to his benefit, because he was putting his creative energy into music and not, as he had said, into her.

Frédéric told Delphina that "desiring her passionately, there's a way towards creativity. When I long for you musical ideas come rushing into my head."[21] She inspired him perhaps at least as much when they were having trouble. One biographer tells it thusly: "The history of the Etude in E-flat major is also interesting. According to Chopin's letters this Etude was based on the motives of the "reconciliation improvisation" which he played to Delphine [sic] Potocka." She continues: "[Mlle] Potocka, though she was an accomplished pianist, never noted down Chopin's improvisations. We know only from Chopin's letters to her that the Etude in E-flat major originated in a programmatic improvisation set against the background of a quarrel with his mistress."[22] Such energy as comes from quarrels can generate fine music.

This work perhaps suggests that even when their romance had cooled she continued to inspire in Frédéric some of his most sublime music. The storms eventually out numbered the more peaceful times together, and by early in the year 1836 Chopin had had enough of her wandering ways. Still, he needed a woman in his life; he wanted love, a true and committed love. His next infatuation was waiting for him, and this time, the lady was in Germany, in Dresden.

Recall that Chopin had obtained his French passport in the summer of 1835. He had had it in his mind to travel, and now he learned that his parents would take a holiday in the Bohemian spa town of Karlovy Vary. Frédéric was still fascinated by what music was being made in other cultured cities of Europe. He met up with his parents, spent some time getting reacquainted and catching up on his remaining sister's growing family, perhaps only making him all the more interested in the settled life. Parting with his parents for the final time he headed back home, stopping on the way in Dresden, where he made the happy discovery that the Wodzinski family, old friends, was now living there, having recently quit Geneva. The boys had been close friends in the early 1820s.

Chopin's imagination, however, was stuck on young Marie Wodzińska, something of a protégé, being both an accomplished pianist and artist. She was also quite beautiful and won many hearts, but the first heart we know she won was that of the vulnerable Frédéric Chopin. The twenty-five year old composer had been her teacher, years before, but now this young lady surprised him with her wit, charm, and beauty. Apparently, Chopin spent about a month with the family, enough time for Frédéric and Marie, nine years his junior, to fall in love with each other. Still, even as he was making his plans to leave Dresden, Chopin was too timid or introspective to say anything about how he felt, much as he had done, or not done, in the company of Constantia just a few years before.

Recall that Frédéric could never find his bearings with Mlle Gladowska. He was a good bit older now and past that disappointment. Would he have the courage to speak to a girl he loved? It would not be easy. The young man struggled; he suffered so with anxiety. Marie may have seemed too perfect, and predictably he missed his chance, at least for now. In late September Chopin left to return to Paris, feeling somehow failed and empty. Muses, of course, can be patient and they do what they can, when they can.

"He left Marie with two musical mementos of their days together: One was a *waltz in A flat*… the other a fragment, the opening bars of which were to become his most popular nocturne, the one in *E flat, op 9, no. 2*."[23] The piece has been described as dream-sweet melancholy, and he inscribed it to Marie with the French *'Soyez heureuse'* – be happy. Against all probabilities, his tongue-tied ways did not spell the end of their nascent romance.

Chopin returned to Poland, still recovering from the ravages of a decimating illness that had swept through Paris. He was not well and needed "a companion to look after him and love him. It was time to consider marriage," He returned to Marienbad [Karlovy Vary] where he knew the Wodzinskas [sic] were staying. "They were alarmed at his state… Marie took advantage of his having to rest by sketching him."[24] When the family returned to Dresden he followed; asking for her hand in marriage. Was this the same fellow? Marie was flattered, but ironically social class considerations would now ruin the composer's chances, much as they had done for Beethoven's romance with the ladies of the gentry and aristocracy. We recall especially the German composer's ill-fated attempt to win Maria Anna Westerholt, forty years earlier.

Chopin plaintively made his case, even as Marie's mother explained that such things must be given time. The pretense of their social incompatibility seemed to anger Chopin. He kept all the letters he had saved from the Wodzinskis, binding them into a packet, which he kept until his death, calling the affair *Moje Bieda*, or "my misery." "It would seem to be no coincidence that the *Funeral March*, which was to become his most famous composition, as the heart of his *B flat minor Sonata*, was composed at around this time."[25] Frédéric followed up this sublime work with another engendered by his loss of the fair Marie. This was his *B major Nocturne, op 32, no. 1*, "a musical parable of love and loss whose surprise tragic ending is as powerful, in its way, as anything he ever wrote."[26] Marie and her mother would not yield. The romance was doomed.

Chopin was in bad spirits and ill health. He turned to his male friends for companionship and understanding, and this is how, in a visit to Liszt and Liszt's paramour Marie d'Agoult, in Paris, he found the one woman he would spend most of the rest of his life with. Her married name was Mme Aurore Dupin Dudevant, but as a highly regarded author of erotic novels she was better known as George Sand. Sand – the woman who said, "my profession is to be free."

At first she repulsed him, her baggy attire and smelly cigars, but there was an energy that appealed to him on a new and exciting plane. One biographer makes the observation: "I have always thought that Chopin saw Titus in George Sand; and his homosexual tendency, which he clearly had, as well as his love for women, now seemed to come together in the masculine female, George Sand."[27]

Sand's impact on Frédéric's music is uncertain, a theme we will shortly return to. On the personal level, however, she quickly took a liking to Chopin, which may have instinctively brought him closer to her. No doubt he admired her intellect and flair, though it also seems to have made him uncomfortable in equal measure. By February 1837, Sand was professing her own adoration for the composer. Would this one stay?

One apparent vulnerability may have been a plus. Women liked to mother him, and Sand was just crazy enough to see their sexual relationship as somehow incestuous. They took adjoining apartments in Paris and began a nine-year relationship, played out during the first years about half in France and half in Majorca, then in 1839 they tried Marseilles. Still, while Sand turned up her own libido with Balzac and the Impressionist painter Delacroix, Chopin's health was still failing. To make things worse, his emotional health was in jeopardy. Of course he was jealous of Sand's broadly arrayed affections, but as he dwelt on it more and more he began to rethink his previous relationships. Was Countess Potocka still interested? This was an impossible situation made worse by Delphina's professional singing engagement in Paris late in 1842, rekindling both his confusion about and his passion for the woman who would not leave his mind.

Apparently his resumed longing for Mlle Potocka did something for his music that Sand had not done recently. Chopin wrote music for a woman again, perhaps finding some satisfaction in the special musical bond they once shared. His *Polonaise in F sharp, op 44,* was dedicated to Delphina. "He wrote a love letter to her saying that he longed for her as a dying man longed for the last rites and the guarantee of heaven."[28] This relationship was never going to be heated again. They did come to love each other, perhaps, but only as friends. Maybe Delphina Potochka helped Frédéric in another manner, one that has lived on well past their unsatisfying, temporal existence.

Chopin finally found his footing with Sand. For the lady in question, this meant that her extant lover, one Félicien Mallefille, must be summarily dismissed. She was cleaning house, so to speak, writing to a confidant that "the little person," she also called him "the boy," had a frightening effect on her. No doubt she relished the effect she had on Frédéric. Few musical Muses were as studiedly outlandish as our George Sand.

The sex was intoxicating, but Frédéric's health was not good and his attention to his music waned, especially so in 1838 on the island of Majorca. Weirdness rarely works well for long, and soon Chopin began to loath the place, as well. Worse, by now the couple was sharing time and accommodations with Sand's two teenage children, which must have made Chopin even more uncomfortable. To further complicate things, the piano he had requested, and which he greatly needed in order to do much real work, was slow in arriving. Chopin settled into a funk.

He wrote his friend Julian Fontana, besides complaining of his illness, his *Preludes* were not coming together as he had planned. He promised to complete this work as well as the *Ballades*, op 38, "shortly."[29] His work had not stopped, of course, but a combination of things worked to make this one of Chopin's least productive years. He did finish the 24 *Preludes* that winter, which stand among his finest works.

The couple left for the mainland as quickly as they could make the necessary arrangements in the spring, and as if the change in locale were prescriptive his health began to improve. Frédéric may have willed it that he would be well again on French soil. Mme Sand now became more instrumental in the care of Chopin than at any time before. Soon they were spending all the time they could at her chateau in Nohant, not far from Paris, but far enough away from the city to feel a sense of tranquility. The passion of their first months together now gave way to something more comfortable. Yet, for all the impact that George Sand had on his psyche, and no doubt on Frédéric's sense of self and his self-confidence, he never dedicated any of his work to her.

Truth be told, their relationship was often strained, made more so by the antics of Sand's daughter Solange, who tended to flirt with her mother's man. As time passed, Chopin grew more affectionate toward Solange.

Suddenly things turned around creatively. Sand was inspirational after all. Was Solange? As his health took a turn for the better, Chopin entered what would be among the most creative periods of his short life. He fought back from weakness to the height of his powers. "To the next few years would belong the majority of his finest works: the two great Sonatas, the *A flat and F minor Ballades*, the *F minor Fantasy*, the *A flat Polonaise*, the *Barcarolle and Berceuse*, the *Polonaise-Fantasie*, the late nocturnes, and numerous mazurkas of prophetic originality."[30] George Sand may have had a sense of what ministrations worked best. Frédéric may not have dedicated works to her, but she clearly made a huge difference in his work.

Whatever her role was in preparing Chopin to get back to composing, Sand seems to have found the right touch. They stayed together through the worst of his violent mood swings, until Chopin discovered that Sand's libido too had moved on. After all, how long could this virago remain asexual? George Sand had taken up with a young journalist; we know him as "Bouli," about the same time that Chopin took eighteen-year old Solange's side over that of her mother in a major family dispute. Then, Bouli moved into the quarters at Nohant, creating an impossible situation for the now thirty-five year old, nervous, anxious, and consumptive composer.

Early in the winter months of 1846 Frédéric returned to Paris. Chopin began to give piano lessons again, perhaps sensing that his life with Sand was gone. The couple tried to patch things up, but the next year they decided to call it quits. He would never again return to Nohant, "to the house and the countryside where he had composed some of his most magnificent music during the seven extraordinary summers Chopin spent with George Sand. Nearly one half of his lifetime's musical creation was born in Nohant, thirty of his sixty-eight opus numbers."[31]

Whatever else she did to or for Frédéric, she did what she had to in order to help him to be productive. The love of the free-spirited Muse had been strong, and she had done a great deal to contribute to Chopin's storied success. They split up because everyone was going nuts, exacerbated by tensions in the bizarre household where young Solange had brought her new husband home to add to the emotional battles. Then too, Sand may have thought that Chopin was in love with Solange. The authoress became obsessive and cruel, pushing Chopin away. Finally, their time together was over. Maybe Frédéric thought he could use the rest.

It happened in the wake of France's 1848 revolution, the beginnings of a Republic that Sand had written and agitated for. Chopin was too tired for politics. He had witnessed most of the action this time from his sick bed. Meanwhile, the composer had no students and no prospects in Paris. Now he needed something to give him a spark. Chopin decided to try England and Scotland; maybe he'd make some money. Frédéric's urge to be somewhere else was again strong. The idea had merit; after all, Chopin always did find renewal in travel. Here, incredibly yet another Muse awaited him, and she was not a moment too late.

"Given the state of his health it may have been a foolish decision, but it opened the door for the entry into his life of a new, full-time female presence."[32] The moneyed and influential Scotswoman Jane Stirling had an ear for music, and she played the piano passably. She had been Chopin's student, and she had been pining for him since 1832 when she first met him on the continent. Miss Sterling told Frédéric that she was devoted to him. Jane spoke fluent French and had spent a good deal of time in France, apparently staying in touch with the composer by mail, ever since their first association as student and teacher.

Stirling could be of practical help, too. She acted as Chopin's agent and laid much of the groundwork for his travel to and around Great Britain. She even tried to arrange a permanent position for him in London. Chopin seemed willing to reconsider a long-term relocation, and asked his doctor to advise him on how to best take care of himself in making such a journey. After a week of settling in, Frédéric was optimistic and, finding many Polish expatriates in the city, he agreed to his first public performance there. Chopin performed a Mozart duet with Julius Benedict at the mansion of the Duchess of Gainsborough, rekindling ties to some exiled French royalty.

He soon found himself deeply engaged in London Theater and the city music scene, coincidently meeting and becoming very fond of Jenny Lind, the Swedish opera singer who was making her own mark on Covent Garden. Jane Stirling continued to play her role as Frédéric's social coordinator, confidant, nursemaid, and loving friend. Likely the two were never lovers, but then that would not have been in Chopin's best interests anyway, physiologically or emotionally. He was truly never quite over George Sand, and likely even less so over Delphina Potocka.

Apparently, the only music Chopin ever wrote for Jane Stirling, or at least what he dedicated to her, was his *Two Nocturnes, op 55*. She was influential in pushing his reputation abroad and specifically getting him to play for British subjects and aristocracy. He turned down the opportunity to play with the London Philharmonic, thinking the orchestra unready and the setting too cavernous for his controlled style. Chopin spent three "summer" months in Scotland, Jane doing all the planning and advance work; but Frédéric could not write there and he certainly could not suffer the cold, wet weather. His spirit was fairly strong, but the man's constitution was weak.

Near the end of his inconvenient sojourn Frédéric was in desperate need of money, and so he accepted an invitation to play before a crowd of 1200 people in Manchester, where midway through his now standard performance of the *Sonata in B flat minor* he seems to have had some kind of hallucination, stopped playing, walked off the stage, and then moments later came back to complete the work. He said he saw demons on the keys. Frédéric wrote to one dear, old Polish friend that Jane and her sister, his managers, were driving him too hard. In November he returned to Paris, through London, eagerly awaiting the warmth of his friends, his comfortable salons. Frédéric wrote to Solange – he was now writing to her regularly – that the London climate was "inconceivable."

Back in France he seemed to rally, but likely it was only the joy of being home. As to his first home, Warsaw, truly he gave no thought to it; though he did write and ask his sister Ludwika to visit him. His money was nearly gone again. At this stage Chopin was too weak or dispirited to teach much. Jane Stirling sent money, but in another bizarre turn of events the concierge who took the money on Chopin's behalf hid it from him.

Other friends were keeping him alive, if not truly solvent. The irrepressible George Sand consistently made inquiries of his health and his well-being, but there would be no physical contact between them again. Sand was too proud, and perhaps too jealous of the warmth that was clearly shared by her daughter and the quickly failing composer. Sand told a mutual acquaintance that it would be impossible for her to visit Chopin now, "the result of inescapable destiny."[33] She was, after all, a weaver of human drama.

As Frédéric lie dying, that 12th day of October, 1847, Delphina Potocka arrived. Chopin, elated, asked if she would sing something for him. Of course she would. Was it not somewhat ironic that she chose Stradella's "*Hymn to the Virgin?*" He asked for more music and someone played Mozart. Chopin said he loved Mozart better than any other composer. The man was beginning to find closure, holding ever closer what he most cherished.

Frederic Chopin died five days later, surrounded by a few friends, including his last pupil, Adolph Guttman, by his sister Ludwika, as well as dear Solange, "who sat with him, his hand in hers."[34] The man's funeral was like that of a deceased monarch. At Chopin's request the Mozart *Requiem* was integrated into the Catholic mass he had carefully sculpted; it had been unheard in the city for nearly ten years. Then the orchestra played Chopin's own storied *Funeral March* from the *B flat minor Sonata*, during the Offertory, along with two *Preludes*. Three thousand people jammed the great Church of the Madeleine, where Napoleon had been buried nearby, some twenty-eight years earlier. Chopin's casket, draped in black velvet, simply bore the initials F.C.

Once more the great composer for piano would be found in the care of a loving lady. The enormous expenses for his service and interment were defrayed by his long-faithful and loving attendant Jane Stirling, the final Muse to the man who best captured Poland in Paris.

Arthur McMaster

CHAPTER EIGHT

ELGAR, Edward (1857 – 1934) English

"You think it horrible that lust and rage
Should dance attention upon my old age;
They were not such a plague when I was young:
What else have I to spur me into song? (W.B. Yeats)

Few classical composers had as many outright Muses as did Sir Edward Elgar. Perhaps only Liszt and Verdi before him seemed as keen for the inspiration of the ladies as was the man recognized as England's greatest composer, or at least as her greatest Romantic composer. Elgar's emotional and physical draw to women did not start early, as it did for Berlioz, for example. Once he found inspiration in such partnerships, however, he could not bear to be without them. The last, and perhaps the most fascinating of such liaisons, bloomed when the composer was seventy-one years old. By that time he had much soured on his place in the world of music, vowing to write no more, but Elgar came to a change of heart. Come to that, if not for his "V.H." we would not have his *Symphony #3*, which remained unfinished at the time of his death in 1934.

His father was a pianist and for a while he made his living as a piano tuner. The Dowager Queen Adelaide, William IV's queen and widow, must have taken a liking to him because William Elgar was fortunate enough to gain a commission from the royal family in 1843, as "court piano tuner;" so there was some income and prestige, though little enough of the former. Later, William also sold sheet music and instruments.

The Elgars lived above their modest store at 10 High Street in Worcester. Anne liked poetry, and especially Longfellow. It was a taste her son would come to share. In fact, little Edward began to write his own poetry as a pre-teen and by the age of fourteen he was also setting his verse to music. He enjoyed concocting musical scores. Self-taught, Edward was strongly encouraged by his father.

Even in his youth, Edward Elgar could be both highly innovative and tenacious in getting the written work to fit the musical score. Sometimes his modifications affected the content of the source poem, forcing an adjustment to the verse. "With each stanza Edward's music became more complex... Faced with the choice between verbal and musical interests, the boy's loyalty went all to music."[1] The first dedication of a piece he was obviously well pleased with went to his sister Lucy, five years older than Edward. He dedicated it thusly:

> THE LANGUAGE OF FLOWERS
>   Poetry by PERCIVAL
> The Music composed and dedicated to his sister Lucy
>   by Edward W. Elgar, May 29, 1872[2]

Actually, Elgar was also the poet. He later identified himself to Lucy as "Percival," probably not wanting to detract from what he wished to claim as the main effort, the music. The dedication to his sister suggests the boy's sense of family closeness and no doubt his need to show affection. Eventually he would dedicate music to his many Muses, but his early years were marked with much emotional uncertainty.

Tragically, of the first three sons born to William and Anne Elgar, Edward alone survived to manhood, loosing older brother Harry and then Joe, two years younger than Edward. Elgar was nine years old when Joe died. His sisters always held a special place in his heart. But the deaths of his brothers informed and shaped his early music as much as the thrill of romantic poetry inspired him later in life. Biographic research is clear that, for much of his life, Edward Elgar was fixated on death, perhaps less so as he aged, but as a boy this fixation was strong. His mother read him passages from the poem "The Better Land," suggesting that eternity would offer a sweetness not found in this life.[3] Arguably, his greatest musical composition, *The Dream of Gerontius*, is the tale of just such a quest. Gerontius was a mystical poem written by Cardinal John Henry Newman. We'll return shortly to the curious history of Elgar and that piece of music.

Edward found his early musical training close to home. His father played violin and his Uncle Henry played viola in a makeshift band that the city fathers cobbled together to support the Three Choirs Festival. This was a group that came to Worcester every three years. One year, Beethoven's *Mass in C* was on the program. Hearing it seems to have been some kind of epiphany for young Edward. Excited about being able to see the orchestra, he decided he would like to write such music to "... make it [the orchestra] play whatever I liked."[4] The size and complexity of the orchestra alone appealed to him, and he began then to think in terms of extemporizing music – what poets following the advice of America's Ezra Pound would call "making it new."

Edward's father had also been an organist at nearby St. George's, a Roman Catholic Church, although William and Anne, for now at least, were Anglicans. Years later Edward would become church organist there, as well. Anne converted to Catholicism after the birth of her first two children; William eventually followed. Edward, then, had the opportunity not only to experience church music at an impressionable age, but also the added benefit of seeing his father's direct hand in it. "His formal musical education in both composition and playing was [almost] non-existent, yet six weeks after his fifteenth birthday he was playing the organ at Mass at St. George's for the first time."[5] His life-long friend Hubert Leicester recalled that Edward missed a good bit of school, not that he was "a truant," but rather that "Elgar, being a genius, was far from wasting his time [while] he was out in the countryside reading scores, trying to gain inspiration to write music of his own."[6] Edward probably surmised even then that inspiration rarely comes from rote learning.

Edward took some piano lessons while a youngster at the Dame school. Living above a music shop as he did, Elgar had ready access to nearly all the instruments; his father lead him from piano to organ, to strings and provided some limited exposure to trombone and bassoon. He played at the age of twenty with a local chamber ensemble, composing a good deal of what the group played. Clearly he had the gifts, but Edward was frustrated by his lack of any major support.

Elgar resented his father's inability to provide a formal music education. He longed to be great, but the family could not hand him an express ticket, which he seemed to think he might in other circumstances have found, perhaps been entitled to. His lack of a formal music education was the first of many great frustrations in the life of this most introspective man. "It took Elgar a long time to accept that great music does not write itself but has to be struggled for, and as a child he may have felt he had musical gifts trapped within him which he was somehow unable to express."[7] Moreover, beyond the small amounts of money he made as church organist, giving instruction, and doing the odd benefits, he seemed stuck on how to proceed in any professional fashion as a musician.

After very limited violin study, now twenty-one year of age, Elgar decided he must now become a serious composer. But how was he to break in? Whom did he know to facilitate such entry, and where could he expect to begin? He was still a couple of years away from meeting the first of his many musical Muses, and one in particular that might show him the way.

Edward found two positions in the world of music that gave him the time he needed to devote to composition. Elgar was an early leader and instructor at the Worcester Amateur Instrumental Society – in two years time he would be their conductor. He took the position of Bandmaster with the delightfully unexpected name of the Worcestershire Country Lunatic Asylum. Here Elgar arranged and wrote music for the staff, which seemed to have an early understanding of the role of music in therapy.

About this time he and his younger brother Frank, along with his friends William and Hubert Leicester, along with Frank Exton, merged their talents to form a woodwind ensemble, the Potting Shed Wind Quintet. Besides having an ear for the most bizarrely named organizations and musical ensembles, Elgar was responsible for the group's composition. He also played bassoon with the rest of the Potting Shed boys. Edward's music from this era, lost for nearly a hundred years, was discovered by a British flautist in the manuscript section of the British Library in 1976.

These simple melodies made their twentieth-century première on BBC radio that year.[8] Elgar was making the first steps as a composer – on his way to a greatness he so earnestly sought. Soon, Edward became organist at St. George's, and he immediately began writing original church music. "In 1979 the church celebrated its fiftieth anniversary and Elgar obliged with two liturgical settings, *Domine Salvum Fac* and *Tantum Ergo*. They were repeated a year later and he added a *Salve Regina* for a service, marking the opening of a new chancel; his father played the organ while the young man led the orchestra. Edward had also written an Easter anthem, *Brother for Thee Who Died*, and two hymn tunes, one of which was published in the Westminster hymnal."[9] All of this music, mostly for the church, gave him a necessary confidence. He also knew that he wanted to composer on a far larger scale.

Fresh from these successes, and with some money in his pocket, albeit not enough to enter a serious course of study, Elgar journeyed to Leipzig and the prestigious Gewandhaus. He was eager to learn what he could of Schumann and Wagner; he said he wanted to be swept away with their genius. At least as important, he was also on the verge of finding his first major love. Elgar proclaimed Schumann his ideal composer. This Leipzig excursion, and his exposure to the Gewandhaus, was supposed to be serious business – his future. But fate had taken a seat near his own at the Gewandhaus. Simon Mundy tells it thusly: "Elgar very satisfactorily combined business with pleasure by including an English girl of seventeen called Edith Groveham on his visits to the opera, but he was rather more interested in her friend who was also a student in Leipzig and who preoccupied him for most of 1882 and beyond."[10] Most of the composers he admired had no difficulty in combining business with pleasure. Edward Elgar learned to follow suit.

The young lady was Helen Weaver, an unremarkable girl from his home town of Worcester, though one whom he had likely known through their families and mutual friends. Helen's brother Frank was a friend and was part of Edward's music circle. Her father, who ran a store on High Street, near William Elgar's music shop, died suddenly when Helen was still a young teen. One result of this tragic loss was that she came in to some money, money that allowed her to go to Germany and study. It would have seemed ironic to young Elgar that Helen was doing in Leipzig what Edward most wanted to do – devote himself seriously to music.

Helen was two years younger than Edward. When they came together in Leipzig, under such mutually grand expectations, they shared an immediate infatuation. Surely this was the "most intense relationship" of Elgar's early life. His reaction was not surprising. That spring of 1878, when Helen was seventeen and Edward nineteen, they were in love, and he dedicated the second of his *Harmony Music Wind Quintet* pieces to her. Five years later, the pair was engaged.[11] Edward Elgar had found his first musical Muse, and she would figure prominently in one of his greatest pieces of music, though not for about fifteen years. The Leipzig adventure ended when Edward's funds ran out. The much infatuated couple hated to part – promised to stay in touch. They did.

Out of money and opportunities to extend his own musical or even romantic fortunes, Edward returned home to Worcester to give violin lessons and to work on a score that would be known as *Intermezzo Moresque*, regrettably now lost. He then turned to a more popular theme, a suite for strings he called *In the Olden Time*. This was a series of dance themes that may have recalled his memories of Leipzig. Elgar could not forget his Helen, though now four years had passed. Would Helen wait for him? Elgar wrote to his friend Dr. Charles Buck, an amateur cellist, that he was in love and would soon marry his *"Braut."*[12] This would have been surprising news for Helen. The German word *braut* means wife, but is also used to suggest a fiancée. At best it was wishful thinking. Edward was attempting to keep the girl, but tied to that goal he had to continue to compose, to earn adequate money for a marriage, and to somehow shorten his anxious, long distance relationship. Fate was not moving the couple in the direction Edward would have wanted or could have expected.

In fact, Elgar took another detour enroute to his romantic dream. After a quick visit to Scotland and the Lake Country the young composer wrote a piece of music that he had begun with ambitions of morphing into an orchestral suite. Likely his anxiety and affections for the missing Helen got in the way, and the piece became instead a delightful little polka. He called it, most suitably, *Helcia*. Elgar could not get the distant Muse, Miss Helen Weaver, out of his mind. Actually, Helen had returned briefly to Leipzig, for her course of study, but then had to return to Britain with the serious decline of her mother's health. If there was anything positive in all these interruptions the purpose must have eluded an exasperated Elgar.

Then, in the worst of all scenarios, Mrs. Weaver died and her daughter was now technically an orphan. What could she do what should she do, about her music, about the man she thought she had fallen in love with? Helen began to have second thoughts about marrying a musician of uncertain prospects, and she broke off their shaky engagement in the spring of the next year, leaving Edward heartbroken. As if to write "quit" to the whole affair, Helen soon left on a steamer for New Zealand, heading for a marriage that seemed to offer her more. The twenty-six year old Elgar was devastated.

From such trauma, however, came some restorative and brilliant music. Elgar never forgot Helen Weaver, and her memories would show up for years in his most heart-felt compositions. He realized he'd have to work his way through the loss of this woman. Meanwhile, he also knew that he had the skills to make a career in music. He was certainly smart enough to understand that had a great deal yet to learn; he knew where to put his energies.

Elgar continued frequent train trips to London to hear his favored compositions. Already strongly attracted to Brahms and Wagner, Edward soon became fascinated with Antonin

Dvořak's work. Both Schumann and Dvořak were particularly powerful in their influence on Edward, "two composers whose combination of romantic lyricism and strong rhythmical contrast finds similar expression in the music of Elgar."[13] Hearing Dvořak's *Symphony Number 6* in D Major, written in 1880, constituted some kind of breakthrough for him; Elgar became more ambitious in his writing. About this time he returned to one of his earliest pieces, the *Romance* for violin and piano, written in 1878. He made necessary copy changes and revisions and attempted to interest the Covent Garden Promenade Concerts in his work. Edward also submitted for possible publication *Une Idylle*, a piece "written in 1884 and dedicated to Miss E.E. of Inverness, a 'forgotten romance' of his Scottish holiday in 1884."[14] Was he trying to awaken or rather trying to dampen the hurt of his loss of Helen Weaver?

Over the next few years Elgar wrote some respectable church music. Actually, he worked in many forms, including the composition in 1892 of a short concert overture; the highly regarded *Serenade for Strings*; and he completed another cantata, *The Black Knight*. None of this work established Elgar as a great composer. He did give a number of solo recitals during this time, having resigned the lunatic asylum job, turning his energies instead to teaching. Not uncommonly, a student caught his fancy. In fact, three of them did, but he only managed to marry one of them.

Two young sisters were evidently fine students under his tutelage, they were so remarkable, in fact, and he later dedicated music to them. To Hilda Fitton he dedicated *Pastourelle*, a short work for piano and violin. To her sister Isobel, who studied viola with Elgar, we have Variation VI *(Ysobel)* of his much scrutinized *Enigma Variations*, completed in 1898. Isobel took lessons so as to accompany her friends and family in a small local orchestra. These were not Muses, they were friends. That said, and while there is no suggestion of a romance between them, young Edward must have thought sufficiently highly of these girls to dedicate music to them, especially for Isobel, as all the other "variations" are dedicated to people especially close to him, including the woman who would be his wife. The other clearly known dedication is to his best friend.

The third of his female students was a good bit more mature than the Fitton girls. She was Caroline Alice Roberts, a friend of the Fitton family who, in autumn 1886, and at the age of nearly thirty-eight, decided to further her own music instruction. She and Edward got along well, whatever may be said for her playing technique, as he proposed marriage two years later. While courting, she wrote him love poems and he wrote a small composition from one of her poems, dedicating it to her: his piano piece *Salut d'Amour* which, along with an unidentified work for violin and pianoforte, he sold in London for two guineas.[15] Edward's Muse was back. *Salut* was his first sale!

He and Alice – she preferred her middle name – were married in May of 1889. Interestingly, the Reverend Father Knight, presumed the celebrant of their marriage at St. George's church where Elgar had long been organist, gave them as a wedding gift a copy of John Henry Newman's poem *The Dream of Gerontius*. Elgar already had a copy of the poem and was well acquainted with the theme. Actually, the presentation of the poem deliciously preordained something else that would be truly major in Edward Elgar's life. What of our newly minted Mrs. Elgar?

Alice, an accomplished and published writer of romance stories and poetry, has been portrayed in biographies as something of a "liberated woman." The lady was bright. Meanwhile, thirty-one year old Edward needed a center to his life, and at least as much he needed an intellectual companion. The couple matched wonderfully in this regard. They worked together to overcome his perceived lesser social status, still quite sharp in Britain, as well as the stigma of his Roman Catholic religion, a source of woe and dismay to Alice's Anglican family and haughty social circle. Her parents, quite fortunately for Edward, were both conveniently deceased. At least there would be no drama on that end.

Nine years his senior, Alice wrote him poems that spoke of art and music, and she catered tirelessly to his aspiration to "musical genius." Alice believed in him; she pushed him in his work as she had come to understand the necessities of disciple, growing up the child of a career military man. Alice was a catalyst in his work, someone he trusted on a daily basis. Without her support and devotion he probably would not have become a great composer. But was she his Muse? "While so much of Alice's literary activity after 1886 was inspired by Edward, the inspiration for his music wandered nostalgically and with more than a touch of fantasy around other women who were less practical but more alluring."[16] The assignment of Muse can be difficult; Alice certainly helped her husband; in fact she pushed Edward to make his often enchanting music.

The two were "cocooned in the business of marriage." Did it work? Elgar sold four short pieces in their first year as man and wife, 1889; and now his music was heard at the Crystal Palace, in London. Edward was jubilant! Soon they moved to West Kensington, into the city, to concentrate on the business of his composing and on selling his work. Edward was on the verge of some of his best writing and his first major breakthrough as a composer. Marriage seemed to agree with them. Quickly, Alice was pregnant.

Elgar was working furiously now on his first true concert overture, to be called *Froissart*. The name was taken from the fourteenth century French romantic writer and chronicler Jean Froissart, popular when Edward was a boy. Some biographers credit Elgar with achieving some fine and almost risky orchestration with this piece to "protect the melody," covering his necessary solo ventures with as few instruments as possible, avoiding the "thickness" problem he saw in Schumann, and taking instead much from Dvorak's approach.[17] This was a breakthrough in its own right, a technique he called upon time and again. Moreover, this was the innovation he felt was a gift, and alone it suggested a significant maturation in his work.

As this music was coming together, and he had an offer to publish *Froissart,* Alice gave birth to their only child, a girl, whom they named Carice for her mother's first two names. Edward had already used the name in his dedication of *Salut d'Amour* to Alice. His light *Sevillana Suite* had also been critically well received in London, but the Elgars were struggling to make ends meet financially, especially so now with the baby. Edward returned to teaching, starting a violin concerto and then, for unknown reasons, abandoning it. Suddenly, he found he was losing focus on his work. The close of the nineteenth century in England was a particularly troubled time.

London was expensive, cold and gloomy; the Elgars moved back to the countryside, to Malvern, near Worcester. This made a positive difference in his outlook. There, Elgar returned to Longfellow, the poet his mother loved, and Longfellow's translation of the German poem *Der Schwartze Ritter*, the Black Knight. He wrote the "secular oratorio," for a choral festival, in speed and confidence. It was patterned after the deep, Germanic influence of Handel on English music. The big choral societies loved this kind of music, and they paid well. Elgar had already found someone to produce it at Worcester and he was content to have it published there, his first home. He likely was confident that the *Ritter* oratorio would later return to the capital. For now Elgar had reached a kind of plateau. He took great pleasure in his recent work, including the mellifluous *Serenade for Strings*, which he also wrote in 1892. He rightfully felt he had found some real success in his most recent efforts. Both Alice and Edward needed a break, an inspiration, perhaps a sabbatical, and a trip to the Continent seemed just the ticket.

The couple left for Germany in August in search of "the masters," first visiting Beethoven's Bonn – then on to Bayreuth and Wagner, where they heard *Parsifal*. On the way home they visited Heidelberg and took in Mascagni's recent opera *Cavalleria Rusticana*. They returned loaded with inspiration. Alice wrote poems and Edward made a few musical sketches. They agreed to return to Germany, and they did so for the next three summers. Gradually, they built up between them a heady series of compositions "... which became the *Songs from the Bavarian Highlands* – it was their most complete and lengthy collaboration."[18] Elgar's work was further sustained by his wife's poetry, a frequent contribution of the true Muse.

The composer began working with an organ sonata. He had more starts than finishes, though he found some success with *Scenes from the Saga of King Olaf,* a cantata again taken from Longfellow. In 1896 he wrote the Catholic oratorio *Lux Christi,* followed the next year by *Sea Pictures*, which were five songs for contralto and orchestra. Elgar remembered well the axiom as to where financially successful music comes from. The piece that would make his name world famous lay just another year away. To complete it he would call upon the inspiration of not only his wife and best friends, but of his ex- and distant loves as well.

Elgar completed his *Enigma Variations*, more properly titled, *Variations on an Original Theme (Enigma)*, in 1899. He dedicated the work, in fourteen parts, "to my friends." Biographers and students of Elgar are more fascinated by a couple of the more esoteric, or less forthcoming dedications. Suitably, it seems, he dedicated Variation I to his wife, inscribing it C.A.E., for Caroline Alice Elgar. Most of the rest are inscribed to people he cherished, including Variation IX to his best friend and publisher August Jaeger, whom he called Nimrod, for the Hunter – Jäger in German means hunter. Interestingly, Variation VI, with its solo viola, went to "Ysobel," his nickname for Isobel Fitton, one of his favorite students, of whom he long remained terribly fond.

But it is Variation XIII that has vexed would-be experts for so long. It is subtitled *Romanza*. The dedication has no letters, simply three dots, an ellipsis … Initially the dedication, based on its theme from Mendelssohn's *Calm Sea and Prosperous Voyage*, suggested a lover or close friend who had gone off by sea. Could it be the Lady Mary Lygon, also a woman close to Elgar, but never suggested as an intimate? Or did another woman close to him take a voyage which Elgar would wish to be calm and prosperous? Most certainly so. "One recalls that Helen Weaver sailed for New Zealand in October 1885 … Several devoted Elgarians insist that the *Romanza* is nothing but a poignant memory of his former fiancée. But is it putting too great a weight on this delicate miniature tone-poem to suggest that it carried the burden of lost love, [a moment in time] he still longed for? Perhaps Elgar cast a fleeting glance behind him as he thought of separation by sea and land…The music, in any event, is full of dream-like regret."[19] Dedications are not always, and perhaps not even usually, about romance. This one, Variation XIII, almost certainly was precisely that.

His Variation XIV is to E.D.U., which is the composer himself, sounding out the initials as Edoo, which was Alice's nickname for Edward, and sounded like the French "Eduard." This last and longest of the variations suggests, some have said, a sense of fulfillment. It is interesting that he puts his lost love Helen, if that is who XIII actually represents, closest to him at the end of this signature work. Then, too, the original theme which Elgar selects to repeatedly vary has never been conclusively identified and is the source of even more speculation. Elgar told his Enigma Variation X friend, Mrs. Richard (Dora) Powell – his Dorabella – that she of all people should know what the theme was.[20] But Dora seems not to have known, or she chose not to say. We might like Simon Mundy's assessment of the whole matter: "It is quite possible that it never referred to a musical theme at all or that the origin of the main theme and the feelings of isolation and longing it evoked in Elgar himself represented an enigma."[21] This judgment would seem to cast a light on what Dora Powell might have or should have known, as Edward might have confided in her something he might not share with his wife, Alice.

Whether or not Edward and Dorabella had an intimate or romantic relationship is also open to question. Probably they did not. They met in 1895 when Dora was twenty and Edward, thirty-eight, needing conscientious help with his work. She proved able and willing, over the years remaining friendly with both Edward and Alice and gaining their confidence, even acting as a first-line critic of Elgar's emerging music. Long after his marriage in 1899 to Alice, who frequently said she would prefer to stay at home, Elgar escorted Dorabella out and about and to the theater. The name Dorabella comes from Mozart's opera *Cosi Fan Tuti*. Alice was happy to have her husband content, and to be accompanied by their mutual friend. Where Edward seemed to want or need more, Alice was comfortable with things pretty much as they were. Here, we'd have to say, her limited role as Muse, was beginning to truly stall.

Elgar was eager to take on another kind of work. In January 1900 he began work on the deeply religious, the overtly Catholic, oratorio *The Dream of Gerontius*. Recall that for a wedding gift he and Alice had received a copy of Newman's epic poem. Working quickly, by

March he sent the first completed part to August Jaeger and awaited his reply. "The poem touched all his feelings of faith and also, perhaps more importantly, reached the meditative and deeply sad aspect of his character which he never [before had] allowed himself to express in his music... It expressed a yearning for certainty after doubt and loneliness."[22]

Unfortunately, the fates were unkind, or maybe they were otherwise engaged, but the première was a flop. An ill-prepared Hans Richter badly bungled the conducting job, as did the chorus and soloists at the Birmingham Music Festival even more. The reviews were, at best, uneven. One critic called it "fourth rate" while some few found it rapturous. For most, *Gerontius* suggested greater work to come from this man. Elgar proved them correct a few years later with his oratorio *The Kingdom*. Successive performances of *Gerontius* fared much better, salvaging the work in the eyes of most concert goers and reviewers. In fact, after the debacle at Birmingham, Edward regularly took the baton to conduct his first performances. He enjoyed conducting and soon was looking for opportunities to do more.

Whatever the critics and patrons had to say about it, Elgar was never particularly satisfied with his sacred music. He began with motets and other church music, but he never felt he had done what he could, or might. Eventually, Edward learned to trust his colleagues who advised him to concentrate on his orchestral strengths. "[T]his lesson was not lost on his contemporary juniors. Vaughn Williams, Holst, Walton, even Britten and Tippet, have consciously or unconsciously sown their seeds in the furrow which Elgar ploughed and which he abandoned when he realized that he had exhausted his capacity for inspiration by religious themes."[23]

That autumn he sketched out the music to "his gayest orchestral work, the overture *Cockaigne* which contains a passage where a military procession passes along a street in London." He had been working on a number of marches, "... one of which was intended for a soldier's funeral."[24] This work led him to his best loved or best known work, not at all funereal, and much accepted as England's second national anthem. There is perhaps no single piece of music played more often to commemorate the passage into the working world for adolescents. It is as popular in the U.S. as it is in England.

Edward told Dorabella in May that he had 'a tune that will knock 'em flat;' then he played for her the *D major Pomp and Circumstance March No. 1*. Soon a libretto by Arthur Benson was made to fit the music and *The Land of Hope and Glory* became a smash hit. It remains a standard in the London pop music scene. Elgar's two highly successful pieces earned him knighthood, bestowed in 1904. He was just hitting his compositional stride. It was in 1901 that he began the winsome *Introduction and Allegro for Strings*. The next year he began the epic *Falstaff* symphony, which occupied him for another dozen years. Unhesitatingly trying more and varied work, he returned to sacred music again in 1903 with the highly acclaimed oratorio *The Apostles*, followed by his majestic *Symphony in E flat major*. More important to the man, Elgar had emerged all the stronger for his early uncertainty and knockabouts. Without question, his wife Alice and the couple's close companion Dorabella had lent untold support. What more could Sir Edward want? Maybe it was something both more and less than love?

In his tome <u>Edward Elgar, A Creative Life</u>, Jerrold Northrup Moore carefully presents Mrs. Alice Stuart-Wortley's relationship with Edward without innuendo. Alice Stuart-Wortley was the woman Edward Elgar came to call *Windflower,* and he eventually dedicated significant works to her. Indeed, though their relationship seems to have always been platonic, she would become one of his most powerful Muses.

Alice, the daughter of the painter Millais, and her husband Charles met the Elgars in October, 1902. We find that Mrs. Stuart-Wortley "was a brilliant and deeply sympathetic woman with a fine understanding of artists." She agreed to use her family influence to arrange for *The Dream of Gerontius* to be performed at the "as yet unconsecrated Westminster Cathedral."[25] This was a huge triumph for the strongly Roman Catholic Elgar, both spiritually and professionally. It would not be true or fair to ascribe to their relationship anything that put her above or beyond the love and devotion Edward was enjoying from his wife, and from the dutiful Dorabella. Nonetheless, Alice Stuart-Wortley may have inspired him in a manner that flattered his new found sense of acceptance in a society heretofore out of his range. This new-found sense of place and purpose must have tangibly lifted Edward, a seasoned and accomplished self-doubter. We should remember that at this time he was still two years from being knighted, and from several honorary doctorates. Place and position mattered deeply to the forty-five year old man who, in some ways, was still the boy living above his father's music store. Stuart-Wortley personified much of what Elgar yet aspired to become.

In December of 1909 he wrote her from Italy saying that he would dedicate the sonnet he was writing to her, but it would not rhyme and "would not be good enough for you." Moore finds that he was "left alone with his memories [and found this] intolerable."[26] Apparently he began calling her *Windflower* based on his themes, but also because of the potential confusion and "irritation" of two women close to him, both called Alice. Edward wrote his *Violin Concerto* for her in 1909, telling her he had "been working hard at the Windflower themes, but all stands still until you approve."

Their relationship rested on her sensitive response to Elgar's music and its highly sensitive idiom; he warmed to such appreciation – souls in harmony – without "disloyalty or infidelity to either of the other marriage partners."[27] Again, Alice Elgar frankly seemed to welcome another woman's careful scrutiny and encouragement of Edward's music, as she had done with Dora's interest, recognizing that Alice Stuart-Wortley probably better understood her husband in some ways better than she did. During this time, while he was also working on his *Elegy for Strings*, Elgar wrote the song *The Angelus*, his opus 56, on a theme from his holiday travels in Florence. Edward dedicated it to his *Windflower*. Other music that is recognizably inspired or encouraged by Alice Stuart-Wortley includes sketches for a piano concerto, for which he took time from his *Second Symphony,* and later his 1919 *Cello Concerto*. They corresponded frequently after the Elgars relocated and remained close for many years.

Throughout his mid and late sixties, Elgar tormented himself pondering the extent to which he was appreciated, or not appreciated. By and large, he thought he should have been more highly celebrated. He continued to write many part-songs and incidental music, completing his successful run of *Pomp and Circumstance* Marches with No 5 in 1930. Though Elgar's music owed much to Brahms, Schumann, and to the classical masters he came to consider his compositional personality somehow out of phase with the new century. For instance, he disliked Stravinsky's *The Right of Spring* and the colorful *Petrushka*. He professed to dislike much "of the contemporary composers and the younger school,"[28] though he had an interest in the emerging jazz music in America. What is a bit ironic about this fact is that Stravinsky, whose music he did not like, was an even bigger fan of American jazz. The Russian's music was much influenced by the American idiom. Elgar's was not. Even before reaching this level of estrangement, Edward announced that he was ready to swear off music, telling August Jaeger that "he would rather ride his bicycle & take in the heavenly countryside.... [with] no interest whatsoever in music..."[29] As he had done before he came out of his funk, but now he was tiring.

Actually, Edward may have been insecure working in the larger forms – *The Music Makers*, a choral work completed in 1912, notwithstanding. His most popular works, if not necessarily his most accomplished, came from concert overtures and marches. He managed to complete two symphonies by the time he was fifty, but the slighter pieces came more readily. Elgar, now living comfortably in Hereford, also enjoyed his hobby as an amateur chemist. He rowed on the water and read for enjoyment. Perhaps he was genuinely tired of music. Or perhaps he needed one more spark. Did he have more music ahead?

"By 1912 Elgar had largely achieved all he had set out to do... He was knighted, bemedalled, applauded; the great peaks of his career had been climbed. He had become, at the age of fifty-five, a national institution... [But] the coming years were ones of restlessness and an awareness of the fragility of all he had built... To Elgar there were new and strange forces ... that were making his style out of date."[30] We get a picture of a man who wanted to settle in to retirement and not much more. One gesture that seemed to fit the temperament of a younger Edward Elgar was his delightful number he called "*For Women*," in 1915. This was a vocal piece included in his orchestral collection, "*The Spirit of England.*" Elgar was always full of fits and starts.

By 1917 he was refusing to see visitors. Early the next year something happened to pick up his spirits – hearing his 1909 *Violin Concerto* played for him on recorded disks, some of the first products of this new industry. Elgar began work on a violin sonata, and wrote music for piano and strings, as well as a cello concerto. Could he have found another lease on his fragile musical genius? It is difficult to say what awakened his creative energy, but it would not last.

Upon the death of his beloved and ever-faithful wife Alice on 7 April 1920, Elgar embarked on ten long, nearly empty years. Devastated, he told one friend "'the world no longer exists for me.'" He wrote to another, "All I have done was owing to her and I am at present a sad and broken man."[31] We learn that Elgar had closed off his ties with some of the women to whom he had been so close and needed for his inspiration. Even his dignified friendship with his *Windflower*, Alice Stuart-Wortley, appeared "devoid of any inspirational fire." Edward seemed to have given up. Could there be something, someone, to get him going again? The question brings us to consider the genesis of his final major work, another symphony.

Like so many stories that tell of the magic arising from untapped human emotions, Edward Elgar's story takes another upturn. We move ahead to November of 1931 where there waits a musically talented and sophisticated young woman named Vera Hockman. She was given the opportunity to play her violin with the London Symphony Orchestra in her hometown of Corydon when their band required a few local orchestra members to rehearse *Gerontius*. Vera was sufficiently accomplished to perform with the orchestra, and the rest, as we learn, is history. Elgar was conducting, and for some reason he noticed her, playing dutifully with the second violins. Something about her drew his eye.

An understandably anxious Vera had no way of knowing what awaited her after the rehearsal – a meeting with the maestro himself. She tells it thusly: "I hardly seem to have to look at the music, my heart and soul went out to him because his was a way not to command the orchestra but to implore them to give all the fire and energy and poetry that was in them. You could feel the love and veneration… A few minutes later I was talking to a small group of players – raving about him – when someone touched me on the arm saying, 'Sir Edward Elgar has asked to be introduced to you.'"[32] The fates had intervened again.

Edward took her out for a drink, and she told him that playing for him with the orchestra was the most wonderful experience of her life. They continued to see each other, to discuss their music, to nurture each other's interests. Soon they were both clearly in love. Her early marriage to a prominent barrister had foundered. A gifted musician, Vera had gradually become friendly with Ralph Vaughn Williams, who had by now come into his own kingdom in England. But a particularly strong draw to Elgar, something moving her to a more remarkable destiny, prevailed. For Edward, peering into the second violin section that day, she must have seemed heaven-sent. This woman was the kind of inquisitive, sensitive artist he now needed in his life. "For Elgar needed muses always, that is inescapable,"[33] says Michael Kennedy, in his Foreword to Kevin Allen's splendid story of Vera. We cannot be certain what, besides enormous admiration, drew Vera Hockman to Sir Edward, after all she was nearly forty years his junior. Clearly he needed her. "There can be no doubt that for both partners, her relationship with Elgar was one of the great love affairs, though doomed from the beginning by the burden of the composer's years…"[34]

Virtually all we know of their meeting and the beginning of their relationship comes from Vera's memoir, "The Story of November 7th, 1931." Elgar enjoyed with Vera the last of a series of the romantically-inspired relationships which marked and centered his entire creative life. Vera's inspiration generated the renewed creative impetus which led Elgar to grapple with the *Third Symphony*, the *Piano Concerto,* and *The Spanish Lady*, his first real attempt at opera. What a time to attempt such a massive kind of work! All of these works, of course, remained incomplete at the time of his death, but the *Third Symphony* was very much Vera's, as he clearly marked the second subject of the first movement as "V.H.'s own theme."[35]

Ironically, the unfinished piano concerto he returned to in his last months had begun under inspiration of an earlier Muse, Mrs. Alice Stuart-Wortley, Edward's *Windflower*. The aging composer discovered his strongest soul-mate last. He had long made poetry central to his music, and now he had someone to help him further discover the nexus of the two. We find that "Vera, whose responses to music and literature were as intense and as intuitive as Elgar's, went on to suggest extracts from various poems that she felt to be related to particular passages in his music."[36] Theirs was the pinnacle of creative collaboration.

By April 1933, Elgar was inquiring of Adrian Boult's assistant, Owen Mase, if the BBC would be interested in his new symphony, anticipating its prompt completion. Mase assured Elgar that, should it be compete and ready, they would "put it in our big series of concerts commencing next autumn."[37] Could Elgar assure them, Mase asked, that it would be ready? By the time Edward got the letter he had again fallen ill and taking to his bed. Nevertheless, he assured the BBC fellows that the work would be ready for rehearsals by autumn; he requested nothing be announced until all the "materials" were ready. Elgar would make no promises as to conducting, saying: "we will wait & see." He had other things to do, things to take care of.

In the next few months he did some traveling. He also wanted to do some guest conducting. He visited the teen-aged Yehudi Menuhin in Paris; and then he wanted to drive to the south of France to see Frederick Delius, five years younger than Edward, and by then blind and feeble from syphilis. The two got on famously and they drank champagne to each other's health. To their health; why not? Elgar was now seventy-seven and knew he was gravely ill.

By that winter Elgar was in a nursing home, the pain for his full-blown cancer abetted only by increasing doses of morphine. Toward the end he wanted promises that no one would tinker with his unfinished symphony. "No one would understand," he said. Edward did not say just why no one would understand, but we can intuit his reasons. This was, after all, his final music, his music for Vera. It remains today, in a different sense, the last of his famous enigmas.

Near the end, his daughter Carice convinced the old man that he should forgo his recent determination to be cremated. Yes, he agreed, she was right. Edward should lie next to his wife Alice, who he said had been his all. Edward Elgar died on 23 February 1934. His new friend Frederick Delius, with whom he had recently toasted each other's health, died four months later. His poet-Muse Vera Hockman, not surprisingly, saw Edward through his final, temporal hours.

CHAPTER NINE

HAYDN, Franz Josef, 1732 – 1809, Austrian

"Young people can learn from my example that something can be made out of nothing. What I am is all the result of the direst need."
 Franz Joseph Haydn, as told to his friend Albert Christoph Dies.

Like many of the other thirty or so men whose lives and work are recalled in this volume, Franz Joseph Haydn was born to a family focused primarily on securing the essential necessities of life, but his parents offered something not even well-to-do families might, an abiding love of music. When Franz Joseph was only four years old the child imitated a fiddler he saw performing in the tiny Rohrau village square by scraping a twig along a block of wood. Music was the child's delight, and the Haydn family encouraged his fascination, although his mother still hoped he would someday become a Catholic priest.

Sensing the child's gift they did much more to secure his future. His parents allowed him to leave the household when he was only five years old. He would stay with Anna Maria's brother Franz, living in nearby Hainburg. The town was much larger and the young Haydn could have the opportunity to study his grammar lessons, but also to take some music instruction as well. Uncle Franz was both schoolmaster and choirmaster at the Church of St. Phillip and St. James. The church possessed a grand organ and many string instruments, so Franz Josef was exposed to some decent play and could even experiment on his own. His voice, however, took him the furthest, or at least can be said to have been his proverbial ticket to real music training. At the age of eight he was admitted to the St. Stephen choir school in Vienna. Here, young Franz Josef Haydn would spend the next nine years and enter into a life as a professional musician.

His tenure ended not because he had learned all he could from the musicians and teachers at St. Stephan, although that is likely the case, but because his voice broke as he reached puberty. In a bit of family drama his brother Michael, five years younger, and who had an even more beautiful voice, took his place.

Franz Joseph's experience at the choir school yielded one unexpected result. He developed an interest in composition, perhaps because he was encouraged by his teacher, Adam Gegenbauer, who diffidently taught violin, to "arrange or write variations on the church music he sang."[1] His music education in Vienna, much of it coming only with much personal sacrifice, was keen and plentiful. With few prospects for income, however, Haydn found himself only subsisting by playing and singing in street serenades. His voice had come back, and he was now a highly regarded tenor, but he wanted to compose, not to entertain. "In the end it was a serenade that brought Haydn, at nineteen, his first commission as a composer."[2]

Franz Josef caught the attention of a street impresario who asked him to sketch out some music for a pantomime he was working on. Haydn's on-demand piece was a miniature *opera buffa* for which he received the princely sum of twenty five ducats. The piece, called "The Crooked Devil," was a big hit. Unfortunately the music seems to have been lost.

Master Haydn enjoyed the acclamation and unexpected success in this, his first composition, which only made his interests in continuing to do so all the stronger. But such limited satisfaction would sustain neither his body nor his sense of true capability. To learn as he worked, Franz Joseph composed at night, in his fifth floor garret, but he was aware that he was not properly trained for the work he was attempting. He needed a teacher of music theory. Being self taught is laudable but it has serious limitations, even for the genius.

This was about the time Haydn was studying and playing the counterpoint exercises of C.P.E. Bach. Carl Phillip Bach, a well respected music theorist and "enlightenment" composer, was eighteen years his senior and was now one of the most influential musicians in Europe, certainly so in Haydn's young life. C.P.E. Bach, as much or more than any other, led the way from the polyphony of the Baroque period to the early classical style. Historians point to Haydn's interest in Bach's sonata form as leading directly to the advent of Haydn's own symphonic oeuvre. Haydn's work began to mature, with the help of such indirect instruction and influence, but to put brotchen on the table he still needed to take on students. Putting first things first, Haydn was struggling to make financial ends meet.

Unexpectedly, providence appeared with a kindness. Through a well-placed friend Josef met Nicolás de Martinez, who wanted his ten-year old daughter to take music lessons. Haydn was hired, working with the child for three years, earning his board for the labor. He was finally making enough money to get by. The real payoff came by yet another association. Miss Martinez was also taking voice lessons from Niccolò Porpora, the Italian composer and voice teacher, now making his living in Vienna. The two became quick friends.

Porpora led the way to one Countess Thun, a wealthy and well-connected aristocrat who wanted her own lessons. She took clavier and voice lessons with Haydn in the mid-1750s, and at last Haydn had influential patrons, although we learn that Haydn frequently worked sixteen hour days. Slowly, Franz Joseph was pushing his way into the world of privilege. Now he could concentrate on his own music, his basic needs no longer in jeopardy. At age twenty, in 1759, Haydn wrote his first symphony, which he presented at one wealthy patron's home in Bohemia, the composer conducting from the harpsichord. In attendance was Paul Anton Esterházy, prince of the Holy Roman Empire and Joseph's next boss. What of his lady friends?

Haydn would never again want for work, money, or fame. Now he needed a woman, and what he especially wanted was to be married. His first Muse was as close as the next octave. The one that would truly matter, his Luigia, was still a few years away.

Let's continue to stay in the moment. Among his pupils in Vienna were the daughters of a hairdresser, Johann Peter Keller. Haydn fell in love with young Therese, who predictably could not return the affection. In fact, she entered a convent, taking the name Sister Jospeha. Haydn was so flummoxed by her that he wrote and dedicated his *Organ Concerto no. 1 in C Major* to Therese, or Josepha. He may not have been certain of his own purpose after she made that lifestyle change. One biographer notes, however, that when Haydn was an old man trying to relate the exact composition he had dedicated to Therese – he was twenty-six years old when he wrote it – he may have confused it "with some other composition which he wrote for his first love."[3]

We have a clearer understanding of the other music Haydn wrote expressly for Therese. This is the *Salve Regina in E,* for two sopranos, chorus and organ; a work that shows an influence of Porpora.

Therese was lost to him. Caught up in the confusion, the hurt, and the emotional drama of his first failed relationship, Haydn promptly proposed to and then married Therese's older sister, instead. This rebound maneuver was perhaps Franz Josef's greatest blunder, and no one seems to be able to offer a compelling reason for his actions. Haydn married Maria Anna (née Keller) on 26 November 1760. "The fact that she was three years older than Haydn and not particularly good looking need not have been insurmountable obstacles to a happy marriage, but it was soon evident to the composer that she was ill-natured, totally indifferent to music and quite incapable of providing either a home or children."[4] Whatever made him make such a preposterous decision Haydn would now face some gargantuan obstacles to the success of his music. More problematically, he would have to find love and inspiration elsewhere. Quickly he proved highly adept at doing exactly that. Lady Fate seldom fails to surprise, and musicians are frequently targets for her most surprising antics.

Shortly after his ill-conceived wedding Haydn's job with a Viennese orchestra ended; the group was disbanded. For the composer this was, perhaps, the only good thing that came out of 1761. Prince Anton Esterházy made Haydn an offer. Professionally, this was a perfect job; things were looking up.

Of course, there was still that injudicious marriage. Making such a choice is in itself interesting from another point of view. This sister fixation, and Haydn's decision to marry a member of the rejecting girl's family, foreshadows the actions of Mozart with the Weber sisters some twenty years later. We recall as well the strange decision of Antonin Dvořak to marry "the other Čermakova." Such bizarre echoes in musical history intrigue us even today, though all such lessons must be individually learned.

Meanwhile, in spite of his banal and loveless marriage, Haydn was busy and content with his new position with Prince Anton. For the first time Josef did want for money or esteem. Rather, he enjoyed all the pleasures and emoluments of work at the Esterházy palace. Best, he was free, in most senses of the word, to pursue his work in original composition. Franz Josef was also meeting many of the empire's elite, doing his reputation no harm, as his music soon became better known and celebrated.

In 1766, at the age of thirty-six, Haydn became Kapellmeister to Prince Anton Esterházy, gaining the opportunity for arranging much of the formal and informal palace music. Attentive to the Prince's favorite musical diversions, many celebrated operas were plentiful, including Haydn's own work. Franz Josef worked on more symphonic music than anything else, though he also continued with his splendid church music. Haydn was, in most respects, expected to produce the kind of music the family Esterházy wanted. His work and his time belonged to the royals.

Come to that, Haydn and the other house musicians were feeling a bit reigned in, and most could not even have their families with them while employed in the orchestra. Even "Papa" Haydn, so called because he was a well-liked and effective Kapellmeister, would like to have had more freedom to travel and to perform for the Viennese court, but he made the most of his privileged servitude. After all, he was well kept, well paid, and well respected. His thirteen years at Eszterháza palace also gave him adequate time to work on his own compositions. In fact, he wrote twenty of them from 1761 to 1765. Now what he needed was the simple pleasure of romance. Little had gone right so far.

We find that "[t]he passion and melancholy breaking forth in many compositions of this period were not due to external occurrences, or even to an unhappy love affair. If anything in Haydn's personal life was responsible for these unrestrained outbursts, it was not the excess, but rather the starvation of his emotional life… His wife meant nothing to him… What Haydn needed for full mastery of his art was the inner enrichment of vital human contact."[5] Fortunately for Franz Josef, that woman was nearby, a singer at court, and her name was Luigia Polzelli. Some of Haydn's biographers are convinced that the couple, in love for many years, had at least one child together. No doubt she strongly influenced his music. We'll see how immediately.

One of his better known little operas, written for Eszterháza, is *L'isola disabitata,* which means The Uninhabited Island. He wrote it for the nineteen-year old Luigia, whose husband Antonio was cranky, consumptive, and by all accounts a difficult man to live with. Both were employed in the palace orchestra, she as a mezzo-soprano. It was not her voice, however, that won Haydn's heart. Twenty-eight years younger than Haydn, "[s]he was a typical Italian brunette, with dark vivacious eyes, an oval face, an olive complexion, and a graceful figure. Her marriage with the aged and infirm Antonio was most unhappy… and before long [Haydn's] sympathy grew into a deep passion."[6] The two lovers made no effort to hide their passion from their respective spouses.

They began to correspond in Italian; Haydn had mastered the language in no small part for all his operatic work in the Italian style. When the relationship was ending he wrote to her, in 1791, coincidently the year of Mozart's death, that he would never forget her. Her elderly husband Antonio had died and Franz Josef may have seen the way open for them. Only one thing stood in his way, and Haydn was stymied on that count. He wrote to Luigia: "Perhaps the time will come, for which we have so often wished, when two pairs of eyes will be closed. One pair is shut already. What of the other? Well, be it as God wills."[7] They failed to marry, but for a few years Luigia did what all proper Muses are given to do.

We find one compelling and definitive explanation. "[A]t the time when Haydn was deeply in love, Luigia gave him what he needed and by awakening his emotional life played an important part in his development. It seems doubtful that Haydn could ever have achieved the artistic maturity that his works of the seventeen-eighties reveal so splendidly, had his passion for the Italian singer not opened to him new vistas of life."[8] What did he accomplish during his Luigia days? He wrote Symphonies numbered 63 through 92; ten piano sonatas, seventeen string quartets, twenty seven solo songs, and composed his beloved *Cello Concerto in D major* in 1783. Few muses have ever done more. He even wrote a violin sonata, his only one, in 1790. Haydn wrote his last complete and staged opera at the age of fifty-two. *Armida*, curiously enough, deals with the wiles of a beautiful enchantress. And so she was, his Luigia.

She fell out of love with him first; it would almost certainly be the case. After all, the man was now in his late fifties, and she had two small children. Haydn continued to help them financially, but she no longer saw him in the light he must have seen her. His last year with Luigia was also his last year with his good friend Mozart, and when Haydn set sail for London in December of 1790 it was the last they would see each other – this was something Mozart had eerily prophesized.

Johann Peter Salomon, a citizen of Bonn, was by then a concert promoter in London and he made a generous offer to Haydn. Only three months before Prince Nicholas Esterházy had died, leaving to Haydn in his will the sum of 1000 florins per year in gratitude for his faithful service. The composer's financial needs would never again be in doubt. The castle fell to the nephew Anton, who gave not a wit about music and promptly disbanded the late fellow's prized orchestra. Haydn could stay on as Kapellmeister, but truly he had few duties and little to do. For all intents and purposes Franz Josef was set free. The timing could not be better.

Now he needed a change of scenery. No young man, he still had a great deal of music ahead of him, and he fully intended to have another go at romance. Luigia had been the great love of his life, but he wasn't ready to become celibate just because his paramour no longer wanted him. Arguably, four more women would yet influence his work. The composer's story picks up in London.

En route to England, Haydn resumed corresponding with his friend Marianne von Genzinger, wife of Dr. Peter von Genzinger, the Esterházy family physician. He told her of his brave passage on the seas and what high hopes he had for his concert tour. He told her as well that he had been received as royalty. Such complements suited him. Soon Haydn was making his way in the aristocratic circles of the capital city. Josef Haydn took to London and the city embraced him openly and clamorously. He told von Genzinger he would somehow like to return quickly to Vienna, just to get some work done "for the noise in the street is intolerable."[9]

Meanwhile, Johann Salomon had also been busy. Although the opening concerts had to be postponed, by March of 1791 the first program was in place and Haydn's *Symphony #96 in D*, initially called *The Miracle*, premiered. "The considerable success of this concert at once dispelled the malicious rumours spread by Salomon's enemies that Haydn was now an old man whose powers were declining."[10] In fact, the composer conducted the performance from the harpsichord. The reviews agreed that the concert was an unsurpassed musical treat. He also found enough time and quite, when in the countryside staying with friends, to compose symphonies # 93 in D and 94 in G, "the Surprise." That said, he now may have been too much at peace, and he told Marianne von Genzinger that he lived as if in a monastery. He needed female companionship. His temporal salvation would be provided, again, by way of the royals.

"Haydn continued to be a popular guest among the nobility in London; the ladies in particular seem to have been attracted to him. His genial personality and subtle flattery ensured their friendships. He was on close terms with many of them but with one in particular, Mrs. Rebecca Schroter, the widow of a musician, he seems to have been very friendly. To [his close friend and first biographer] Albert Christoph Dies he confided that if he had been single as the time he would have married her."[11] Recall that Haydn was still married, if in name only, to the truculent Frau Maria Anna. The much younger widow Schroter copied out the composer's work and assisted him in other musical detail work. She too had been a trained musician, so Haydn could trust her to do the work correctly. We learn that Rebecca provided him with love and affection as well. In a letter of 10 June 1792, she wrote him: "I shall be happy to see you to dinner either tomorrow or Tuesday whichever is most convenient for you. I am truly anxious and impatient to see you and I wish to have as much of your company as possible: indeed my Dear Haydn I feel for you the fondest and tenderest [sic] affection the human heart is capable of."[12]

According to what we discern from his letters, he spent many days and nights at the lady's home, at Buckingham Gate, offering her music lessons and whatever else he might, still basking in her praise and worship. Haydn was also maintaining a robust exchange of letters with Luigia, who against type now offered to come to London to visit Haydn. So bizarre an entanglement he did not need and he eventually dissuaded Ms. Polzelli from making the trip, and possibly from scuttling his nascent romance with the effusive Rebecca.

Adding to the drama, Haydn's wife got word of his romantic encounters and began threatening him. Her letters were venomous. After a fairly robust 1791, a year in which Haydn wrote four symphonies, he was able to write but two the next year, also finishing the oratorio *The Storm*. Haydn was getting quite a storm from home. It was a period of *sturm und drang* for Papa Haydn.

One might ponder how all this anxiety would impact his creative work, especially given the pace of his concert schedule. "Fourteen important concerts consisting to a great extent of Haydn's own competitions seem a pretty big program for one season, but by no means did they cover all his appearances in public… His creative activity was not confined to the music for the Salomon concerts and the opera. Other new works owned their origin to … for instance, Anne Hunter. She showed him some of her poems and he set them to charming music."[13] Anne was the wife of a well-to-do Scottish medical doctor. Franz and Anne were not likely romantically involved, but they helped each other with their art forms. Her poetry, including "The Mermaid's Song," and "Fidelity," were set to music by Haydn in his popular canzonettas, in 1794. In the song "Fidelity" the poet addresses an absent lover. Even between Muses Haydn found time to compose for his favorite ladies.

By mid-summer of 1792 Haydn was at the end of his commitments and eager to return home to Vienna. He stopped at Bonn, more exactly at Bad Godesberg, meeting the twenty-two year old Beethoven, who was interested in studying under Haydn. They agreed to meet again, after which Haydn made it back to Vienna on 29 July 1792, virtually unnoticed. No newspaper reported his return from nineteen month encampment in Britain. Not surprisingly, perhaps, his much estranged wife was not among the few who did turn out to great him. Haydn did not care; he had other things on his mind.

For simple respite, understanding, and some degree of female companionship, he turned once again to his young friend Marianne von Genzinger. She was a true and tireless source of comfort to the man, now sixty years of age. He played for her many of his new works, gaining energy for what he would turn to next. Perhaps it seemed nothing was out of reach for him. Inconceivably, Marianne died of a stroke just six months later, leaving Haydn without his closest companion. Her loss, coming so shortly after the passing of his revered friend Mozart, left Haydn bitter, cynical, and confused. He had written a number of sonatas specifically for her, telling Marianne just a year or so earlier: "How I wish I could play only these sonatas once or twice to you; how gladly I would reconcile myself to remaining for a time in my wilderness. I have much to say and to confess to you, from which no one but yourself can absolve me."[14] Whatever he may have thought he needed to have absolved, certainly his "works," as a counterbalance were gaining him merit and credit in this life. We cannot know if Haydn was aware of how much he had changed the face of music with his innovative sonata. Simply put, this was a form of a movement consisting of three sections, the exposition, development, and recapitulation, often followed by a coda. In the manner of C.P.E. Bach, Haydn's sonata remained central to classical composition for generations. The extent that his sonatas are linked with Marianne von Genzinger places her among the finest company of Muses.

With Vienna now so much diminished, Haydn began to make preparations for his return to England, where he had contracted with Salomon to conduct six of his new symphonies. Now the man entered what may be said to be his greatest period of composition, made the more so considering what time he took to finish these works. Returning to the city that had showed him so much respect and affection, which Haydn seemed to need more than ever, he may have once again tried to rekindle his liaison with Rebecca Schroter.

Their reunion was inspirational, and Haydn dedicated a set of Trios to her.[15] This would be his *Op 82, No 1 in G Major, No 2 in F sharp Minor,* and *No 6 in D Major*. At least as importantly, "she was the lady with whom he left the manuscripts to the six symphonies he wrote in the course of his visit."[16] The final six are some of his best known and most highly regarded. The last twelve of course are known collectively as the Salomon symphonies; the last six include *No 100 in G Major, the Military; No 101 in D Major, Clock; No 103 in E flat Major, Drum Roll;* and the final symphony, written in 1795, *No 104 in D Major, the London.*

It is interesting to see how, toward the end of his writing career, Haydn returned to church music. He started his career singing in a church choir. He wrote four masses in the last years of his life, and twelve in all, as well as the oratorio *The Creation*. All such composition began upon his return to Vienna, this time a more celebrated man. Papa Haydn had come home. He was tiring; he needed a slower pace. Even so, his Muse days were hardly at an end.

While still in England, and now in his mid-sixties, Haydn needed, or at least continued to seek out, the comfort and inspiration of women. He was drawn to the musically gifted and spirited ladies, and perhaps equally so to attentive women. His *affair redux* with Rebecca Schroter did not catch on. Haydn's biographers are uncertain as to how the two finally let go of their infatuation. Fittingly, it was an opera that was the backdrop for his last liaison, and not surprisingly the young lady who caught his eye and tempted his imagination was the Italian soloist Brigida Banti. Brigida had been a street singer before coming to London, but she won praise in the highest London circles for her "exquisite taste, enabl[ing] her to sing with more effect, more expression, and more apparent knowledge of her art than many much better professors." Haydn found her faultless and wrote an aria for her which she performed at his concert.[17]

Brigida seems to have been the last credited female inspiration in Josef Haydn's life, if we use one of the standard tests, music written for or about some beloved person. Certainly Haydn wrote music for others, and he wrote, as did all composers, for people with whom he did not have any "romantic" attachment. The last Muse, however, nearly rivaled even Luigia Polzelli. Let's look at how and why.

The aria was "*Non Partir bell'idol mio*." This was no a musical handshake or polite thank you. He saluted Brigida for their passing fancy shared, for a non-dramatic epoch that gave him a lift when he so badly needed one. Now he had other music to write that brought him back to his youth, to the church. He was putting a cap on a career that changed the very structure of modern music. Of Haydn's place in the pantheon of classical music we find: "The attainment of old age by a creative artist focuses attention on the sum of his achievement, work upon work gradually accumulating, until at last men become aware of the mountain standing where none was before, transforming the face of the landscape."[18] Few creative artists stand as high as Haydn in the estimation of their peers.

In his remaining years in Vienna Haydn received many awards and honors, recognition that could not come too soon, as now his health was failing quickly. When invited to functions he could avoid he sent a pre-printed card, *Gone for ever is my strength, Old and weak am I.* Yet he did not want to relinquish his nominal control of the music at Eszterháza. He resigned at last in 1804, turning over his duties to Mozart's one-time friend and student Johann Nepomuk Hummel.

Haydn did find the strength to receive a few favored visitors. These included Admiral Nelson's friends Sir William and Lady Emma Hamilton, who had returned from Naples where Sir William had been Ambassador. "It is said that Lady Hamilton hardly left the composer's side during the whole of her time at Eisenstadt." Charmed by her affection, Haydn had a solo cantata sent to his home which Emma sang to Franz Joseph's accompaniment. They also performed a special Nelson aria, *Lines from the Battle of the Nile.* Later the couple accompanied Haydn to a performance of his *Mass in D minor*, also known as the *Nelson mass*.[19] The lady must have become special, indeed, to Herr Haydn.

The portrait of Lady Emma Nelson (1765-1815), hanging in the National Portrait Gallery in London, does not hide how young and beautiful she was when Haydn made her acquaintance. Found in his room when the great classical composer died, on the last day of May, in 1809, was a chart of the Battle of the Nile. We are left to imagine what, at the age of seventy-seven, the old man made of it, what that representation connoted. His battles were behind him, and mostly all were peerless successes. His many Muses had played a grand role.

There was yet one more friend to connect with in his death. He could not be there in the given sense of the term, but he had always been close and revered. At Haydn's memorial service, on 15 June 1809, those paying a final tribute to Haydn were given the privilege of hearing Mozart's *Requiem Mass*. Likely it was Haydn's final request.

CHAPTER TEN

LISZT, Franz   (1811- 1886); Hungarian

"Liszt was a rake who found religion, an innovator who selflessly championed the work of fellow composers. Yet his originality is overlooked and misunderstood."
   Derek Watson

Frenecz, called Franz, Liszt was a contemporary of Berlioz, of Mendelssohn, Chopin, and Schumann, all of whom he outlived. This is only notable because Franz was so sick as a child that he was actually given last rites when he was three years old. He suffered for years from what his family euphemistically called a general "delicateness." Like Mozart's some sixty years before him, Franz's father, Adam, was possessed by his son's prevenient genius and devoted most of his mature life to seeing Franz not only do well in the competitive world of music, but to excel as none had before him, save perhaps Wolfgang himself. By the age of eight Franz was playing and transposing Sebastian Bach fugues. One other comparison intrigues us.

Like Leopold Mozart before him, Adam Liszt, himself a decent pianist as well as part-time farmer, working for the Esterházy family, was a head-strong man who knew best the boy's appropriate path. Unlike Leopold, Adam was no suitable music teacher for his son, although he did give the boy his first piano lessons. This father's challenge, rather, was to find the right teachers and the best sponsors. Sponsors were important because this family was by no means well off.

Unquestionably, Franz Liszt had enormous talent. He began taking formal lessons at the age of six, encouraged to imitate the masters. Franz began playing Beethoven sonatas so well by the age of nine that he had begun to extemporize on them. In fact, he showed remarkable compositional skill while still a child, again as had master Mozart.

The family spoke only German at home; although Franz's early musical influences were distinctly Hungarian. This cultural dynamic influenced both what Franz liked to listen to and to play, as well as what he would some day compose. His home town of Raiding was close to what is now Budapest, and the prevalent gypsy music distinctly appealed to his sense of place. It was the kind of music he would come back to later in his long and full life. It was during his years as an apprentice, however, that Vienna championed the classical style that would pave the way to Liszt's early success.

Owing to Adam's cajoling, a number of well respected sponsors, largely of the Esterházy court, arranged for some private performances. In fact Franzi, as he was called for most of his youth, gave a private concert in Pressburg, now Bratislava, one month past his ninth birthday. Adam then prevailed upon the aristocratic benefactors to come up with enough money for the family to travel to Vienna, where the boy might take proper musical instruction. The effort was successful; young Liszt was given a sponsorship, a remarkable gift of 600 florins over a six-year timeframe. The family left Raiding with their meager possessions to make their way to the capital city on Franzi's talents and not a little of Adam's chutzpah.

On top of this stroke of great luck, the renowned Bohemian pianist Carl Czerny, known heretofore as Karl Černy, took Franz as a prize pupil, noting in his autobiography: "One morning in the year 1819… a man with a small boy of about eight years approached me with a request to let the youngster play something on the fortepiano. He was a pale, sickly looking child who, while playing, swayed about on the stool as if drunk." Czerny continued: "His playing was also quite irregular, untidy, confused, and he had so little idea of fingering that he threw his fingers quite arbitrarily about the keyboard. But that notwithstanding, I was astonished at the talent which Nature had bestowed on him. He played something which I gave him to sight-read, to be sure, like a pure 'natural'; but for that very reason one saw that Nature herself had formed a pianist."[1]

Soon the young Liszt was ready to expand his pallet; he began composition lessons with the famed Antonio Salieri. It was with Czerny, however, that the boy's natural talents were modified and developed by discipline, by method, and by much practice. As for his storied second teacher; Salieri was a major force in Vienna in the development of classical composition. This teacher had developed quite a list of notables. "…Salieri numbered Beethoven, Schubert, Hummel, Franz Xavier Mozart, Franz Süssmayr, the opera composer Peter von Winter, Meyerbeer, Moscheles, and Czerny among his pupils."[2] It is no wonder that Liszt sought him out. "He [Salieri] rarely charged a fee, except from the wealthy … [Even while] Classicism was giving way to the new Romanticism … Salieri, like Czerny, maintained that the ground rules had to be learned before they were broken…"[3] Liszt was confident he was in good company.

This preparation would serve the lad well, as it had so many to come before him. Salieri said he did not presume to teach the boy to compose, that he said he could not do; but he could guide and he could assure that the compositional theory was clear to Liszt, who then enjoyed devising sparkling interpretations and variations on Salieri's own work. Czerny, meanwhile, pronounced Liszt ready for some limited concert work, as long as the lad stuck to the Classics. No new Romantic silliness, if you please.

It was at such concerts, likely enough, that women began to influence the boy. Or he influenced them. Word spread, and his performances soon became a regular attraction to and with the ladies. "The first soirée was at the residence of Councilor Raphael Georg Kiesewetter, who, as a director of an army education department and a music researcher, organized city musical events. The private concert brought in Franzi's first Viennese fee. This was followed by a soirée at the home of Josef Hohenadel, the military assistant bookkeeper … Among his regular artistes were young opera stars Wilhelmina Schröder, Karoline Unger[4], Beethoven's favorite protégée, and Henrietta Sontag, regarded as the best soprano of her day. Liszt's star was ascendant. The three divas were utterly seduced by Franzi, whom they pampered mercilessly, showered with presents, took to their opera performances, [to] rehearsals, [on] buggy rides round the city, and smothered with hugs and kisses. Franzi had his first real experiences of female adulation."[5]

It would be just the beginning. His first public concert in Vienna took place on 1 December 1822, in the town hall. Franz shared the bill with the violinist Leon de Saint Lubin and with Miss Caroline Unger, whom he had met at Josef Hohenadle's home. Liszt reportedly stole the show; the Leipzig newspaper gave a review of the performance suggesting, "a young virtuoso has dropped from the clouds and compels us to the highest admiration." Liszt played the Hummel *A minor concerto*, and Mlle. Unger sang an aria by Rossini. Franz Liszt also "improvised on a theme from his [Rossini's] new opera *Zelmira,* combining it with the andante theme of Beethoven's *Seventh Symphony*."[6] Beethoven remained a major influence in the young man's musical development. We learn that Beethoven once bestowed upon the latter the *Weihekuss,* or master's kiss of consecration.

What of the co-star, the young lady? Caroline Unger would reappear a few years later in Liszt's life, and would make a big impact on his music. Well before Miss Unger could leave her indelible mark, however, Liszt traveled to Paris in 1828 to take charge of his own life, to do what he so much enjoyed, playing and teaching music. Here the seventeen-year old fell in love much the way most teenagers do. "[H]e had come to know many cultured, upper-class families in the capital who were delighted, whether from a love of music or merely with an eye on the enhancement of their social prestige, to engage him as a tutor, and he moved freely, and profitably, among them,"[7]

Liszt began teaching at 43 rue de Clichy, home of Madame Alix's school for young women. One of his pupils was the sixteen-year old Caroline de Saint-Circq, daughter of the minister of commerce in the cabinet of King Charles X. Theirs was a quick fire romance. Together they would create some of classical music's most engaging history.

Caroline wrote poetry and loved literature, and she introduced Franz to the writing of the poet Victor Hugo, and to other modern writers. He was particularly taken with de Lamartine and Dante. "The poetry of the latter two affected Franzi especially, and his preoccupation eventually gave rise to the symphonic poem after Lamartine, *Les Preludes,* and the 'Dante' Symphony from the *Deuxièmes Année de Pèlerinage.*[8]

Although Franz supposedly got on well with the young lady's mother, their presumed love taking shape before her eyes, her father did not have the same idea of what it takes to make a good match. When Liszt began to pay some critical attention he was quickly replaced as both music teacher and hopeful suitor. Papa married his daughter off to some uninspired Count. Not surprisingly, that marriage was not terribly successful. Regardless of Caroline's misfortune, however, young Franz was dismissed. Eventually he would make a triumphant return with a good many other women.

Liszt went into a near coma in his depression over the loss of this, his second, Caroline. In fact, one French newspaper seems to have gotten the idea that the budding young genius was dead and ran a eulogy for him, likening him in his talent to Mozart, who had died in the city in 1791, some thirty-five years before. This was now twice that his death had been prematurely announced. But no; Liszt was resilient.

Caroline's effect on his music is muted and indirect, the Dante symphony notwithstanding, for he wrote little in the couple of years following their breakup, except a *Grand Fantasy*, based on Auber's opera *La Fiancée*. His own fantasy for a woman to become his fiancée would occur far from Paris. Of course, Saint-Circq stayed in his mind. The graceful young poetess would always be a force in his sense of pure romanticism, and they corresponded for years. She became, for the sensitive composer, the "… perfect love made the more perfect by its cruel destruction."[9] Liszt stayed on with Madame Alix for a sort while, making a little money for himself and contemplating his now less romantically bright future. He gave some thought to entering the church, as the religious life always had a strong calling for him. Liszt eventually worked his way out of the doldrums; he had music to write, if he could only concentrate.

Soon the young man took on entirely different interests. He became socially and politically more aware. After all, he had been vicariously dumped by an aristocrat so his daughter could marry at her proper station. The onset of revolution in France, more so in Paris, was yet another siren song for Franz, now a fiery seventeen-year old. The reactionary world around him was threatened by a new intellectualism, and Liszt rallied to that spirit, that marvelous zeitgeist.

Franz returned to concert performances and began to meet more people who would help him define who he would become as an adult, as a mature musician. The more he read and met with people of like mind the more radicalized it seems he became. With his attention now riveted to the writing of Claude Saint Simon, and his insistence that art must be a serious expression of the soul, not something whimsical and frivolous, Liszt redoubled his efforts to music while reading complementary literature. His music would sing his philosophy.

This was the period that Liszt would become spellbound by Niccolò Paganini, trying to capture on the piano what he saw the virtuoso from Genoa do with the violin. The young Liszt met with Mendelssohn, Chopin, and Berlioz, becoming particularly friendly with the latter and declaring how impressed he was with Berlioz's strong move to such breakout, "wildly" romantic compositions as *Symphonie fantastique*, "…which despite its length and form pointed the way to Liszt's own format for programme music, the Symphonic Poem."[10]

As Berlioz was scandalizing Paris with his outrageous romances, specifically with Camille "Marie" Moke, Liszt was about to reenter a world of love, sex, and scandal on his own. He was particularly good looking, outwardly modest, well-mannered and charming. "Franzi's love life was in meteoric [ascent]. Having discovered the joys of love he never looked back and included its extensive study as part of his total life experience. Affairs came easily to him, and there was no shortage of beautiful women who were ready to give themselves to him, on any basis, from life to an hour."[11]

One such affair in the summer of 1831 intrigues us. She was a woman nearly fourteen years older than the young musician. The thirty-four-year old Adele Laprunarède (often written as de la Prunarède), was the wife of an otherwise pre-occupied count. Adele and Franz spent much of a wintry season at her husband's castle at Marlioz, in the Swiss alps, southwest of Geneva. The couple played and made music together, no doubt in every sense of the word. What lasting music Franz wrote is not clear, but she was influential in the precocious youngster's maturation. The affair, predictably, did not end smoothly. With the coming of spring Franz Liszt moved back to Paris. Adele was left to wait out her hubby the count and noiselessly disappeared into history.

Liszt was still spending more time teaching than composing or playing in anything but the smallest salons. One student who took a great deal of his time and energy was Valérie Boissier, whose mother was something of a composer in her own right. Mom wanted Liszt to instruct her eighteen-year old daughter, admiring his fiery intelligence and "perfect breeding." The charming Liszt, now also full of celebrity, must have inspired awe in the young Valérie. Before their formal instruction period was completed, about five months later, they had become quite friendly, spending hours after music lessons talking about literature. History yields no hint of romance. She seems to have been a Muse of the Platonic order, which likely taught Liszt even more about the real world. Nevertheless, Liszt dedicated his *Fantaisie romantique sur deux mélodies suisses* (S 157) to Valérie. They remained friends and corresponded for years. Often ill fortune lies at the other side of such a pendulum, and Liszt found it.

In 1832, Paris was in the throes of a horrible cholera epidemic. People were hesitant to go anywhere they might become exposed. Liszt remained uninfected, but his friend Felix Mendelssohn was stricken, eventually recovering. Actually, this was also the year in which Liszt and Chopin would become close friends, greatly influencing each others' work. Chopin, though only one year older than Liszt, already had written all of his concerto works and most of his piano mazurkas and nocturnes. Liszt, because he chose to occupy himself with travel and teaching, had not yet come into his own as a composer. Frederic Chopin seemed to understand this need in his friend, calling him one of the foremost pianists of the era, comparable to Paganini and his enchanted violin.

By that winter Liszt was also back in touch with Hector Berlioz, who had been spending time in Italy, away from his romantic complications. Liszt composed a few short pieces during 1832, but it must have seemed to his contemporaries that he was preoccupied, somehow biding his time. The year 1833 changed all that. The young man was still giving concerts and taking on a few select students, especially the progeny of Paris's aristocrats, when he met the woman who would be, unquestionably, the single greatest love of his life. Enter the twenty-seven-year old Comtesse Marie d'Agoult, fresh from an affair with one of the city's countless poets. Marie agreed to accompany the Marquise Le Veyer to an evening of musical entertainment. Wealthy and well-educated, well married, and a self-proclaimed serious student of music, Marie also played piano and organ. More, she had two young children at home. What she did not have was any passion in her life. She was looking.

Marie found Liszt "distracted and restless." She also found him passionate in his ideas of art, music, and literature. Biographers report, "[h]er feminine charms were not lost on Franzi, and he saw in her a serious soul-mate, with whom he could share his suffering as well as thoughts and opinions on all the literary and musical works of the time."[12] Their chemistry was remarkable, as the couple shared a common sense of their own frailty and spirituality. Franz needed someone with an abiding interest in mortality and immortality. She needed someone more stable than she.

Artistic and highly intelligent, Marie could be "introverted." Franz was more outgoing, but only on grounds familiar to him. As their great romance began she encouraged him to talk about, to somehow release, the anxiety and pain of his recent and messy break-up with another married woman, Adèle Laprunarède. Liszt and Marie flirted lavishly and wrote each other notes for a few months, but Liszt, listening to another voice, said he was wary of putting Marie into a "disturbed state." This was likely an excuse Franz offered so that he might continue, in the spring of that year, to occupy his time and whims on a formal concert circuit. The two continued to exchange anxious notes. What might they become together, he asked? The lady was less reticent.

Unannounced to Liszt, the Comtesse purchased a small château at Croissy, in Brie, intending to find time for her own thoughts, her writing, for playing the piano, and no doubt to secure a visit or two from the man so much in her thoughts. She may have had bigger plans for her and Liszt. After all, she had now left her husband of six years to be free to pursue her heart. She also had two children to raise, though how she thought another man might fit into that dynamic is anyone's guess. Marie's timing was marred only by Liszt's sudden introspection and his announced fascination with "holy orders." Let's say it was difficult to get the stars aligned. Or was he frightened of how fast things were moving? Could Franz simply set aside his need and love for Marie?

Liszt was always deeply introspective. As he had done before and would again, the composer felt a spiritual calling. He must have told Marie that he was in no hurry to get married or to be tied down. He had issues! Matters became even more complicated when Liszt turned to a personal confessor, who was also spiritual adviser to Marie. He wanted her; he was called to do something else. Arguably, Liszt spent much of his life finding and losing religion. Would that also mean that he must lose this young woman? As an insight into what was going on in his mind, Liszt told Abbé Deguerry that his transcription of Berlioz' *Symphonie fantastique* was like working on the Holy Scriptures. Franz Liszt was a man of two minds.

But what of Marie? "Six weeks after she bought the Chateau de Croissy, Marie invited Franzi to stay."[13] He was non-committal. Their affair that seemed so promising now began to wane. Marie suggests in her memoirs that Liszt sometimes seemed cold to her, perhaps a reaction to opulence and privilege which the somewhat radicalized, yet ever-bourgeois pianist could never feel comfortable with. One biographer offers "[a]s it had already been with Caroline de Saint Circq and the Countess de la Prunarède, and as it was to be many times again in his life, a social gulf lay between him and the women to whom he was attracted. The more famous he became, and the lower the class barriers grew as the century progressed, the less such a distinction came to matter."[14] Whatever was fogging Liszt's mind suddenly cleared.

For no known reason, any transient estrangement passed and soon the couple was behaving like besotted lovers. Abandoning her own loveless marriage, Marie found with Liszt "a dazzling new light," and liberation. Liszt found the "… sudden, total affection of an enchanting lady…. the peace of mind encouraged by economic security, and the sympathy, intellectual and spiritual, that her years brought with them."[15] Perhaps he had only needed time to find his bearings.

In the spring of 1835 the couple left Paris, settling finally in Geneva, sharing all the joys and secrets of two people on a truly compatible plane intellectually. They were much in love. He trusted her implicitly when it came to music appreciation, and even allowed her to help cast a few of his essays for the *Revue et Gazette Musicale* between 1835-1840. The twenty-three year old Liszt also found significant inspiration, "creative musical energy," from their life together. We find in Marie's memoirs: "He started to compose, and while he was working, my presence was far from unwelcome to him. On the contrary, when I tried discreetly to withdraw, he held me back, saying that he found it difficult to collect his thoughts, and that his ideas were far less coherent, when he did not feel me close to him."[16] Liszt was lucky; here was the near-perfect mate and Muse.

Franz wrote mostly piano fantasies, many on a romantic theme, as well as transcriptions for piano from Rossini and Schubert compositions. He also wrote a popular duo for violin and piano taken from Charles Philippe Lafont's romance, called "*Le Marin.*" This was not an easy time for Marie, separated and then divorced from her husband; the woman was now estranged as well from her two young daughters. Tragically, young Louise, just six years old, died from complications of an illness while her mother and Franz were trying to find their place in a highly suspicious, orthodox, and Calvinistic Geneva. Each had to deal with this untimely loss in his or her own way.

After settling in as well as they could, Liszt returned to teaching. He loved to teach and seemed particularly well suited in temperament. He particularly enjoyed giving piano instruction to the more talented ones. Franz certainly did not need the money, which was the reason he had initially taken up teaching. Liszt remained ambivalent, as well, about his career as a performer, however; and although he and Marie would soon embark on a series of concert tours throughout Europe, Franz tended to resent the idea of playing before the gentry. He told George Sand in one of his letters, "paid by them on a par with a juggler or the performing dog Munito."[17] The man had no problem expressing his ambivalence about his calling.

Liszt and his friend Chopin, was now living with George Sand – her name was originally Aurore Dupin – renewed their friendship during this time. Sand was descended from Polish nobility, so her demeanor and radical outlook must have been something of a refreshing surprise to Franz Liszt, another world-class iconoclast.

The women became friends too, for a while at least. George Sand, who routinely dressed like a man and the well-born Marie were quite different in many ways, though they had an unmistakable intellectual chemistry. Writing about their early association, we learn that for a while Marie was suspicious of Dupin-Sand possibly having amorous designs on her lover Liszt.[17] If that was so, nothing ever surfaced in the press or in rumor to substantiate it. Sand was certainly quirky, however, which likely would have endeared her all the more to Franz. Consider one occasion, during Sand's visit to Geneva, where "she loved to lie under the piano as Liszt played, "enveloped" by [his] music."[18] The pianist may well have read something more into her game, the world of flirtation being so deliciously abstruse.

Franz and Marie, while they never married, did have three children, two girls and a boy. Neither parent was psychologically adept at parenting; relationships came under great strain while the children were young. A wet nurse and then a nanny raised them in their most vulnerable years. Later, they were able to stay with Marie when Franz was off on lengthy tours, and the children did spend some time together with their parents when Franz and Marie were both in Italy. Their most famous child together, of course, was Cosima, their first born; she would prove to be as influential a Muse as was her mother, imperfectly to von Bülow, decidedly so to Richard Wagner. Traveling was another discomfort.

This was a lifestyle that greatly bothered Marie, and she made her anxieties known to her lover. In her memoirs she recalls the bargain that she thought they had struck, where "Liszt plan[s] to dedicate four months of each year to concert tours and to live the rest of the time alone with me."[19] The composer played all over Europe, in London, Hamburg, Weimar, Rome, Russia, and back home again to Hungary, where he was invited to become a court musician. He even managed to do some conducting, though he truly relished the role of being Europe's most notable piano virtuoso. Liszt truly pioneered the concept of the solo recital, and so popular were his performances in the capital cities that no other musician's music was likely to be contemplated. Franz Liszt fed on the acclimation. In this sense, Liszt reminds us of many musicians who had to bring their music to the world; Verdi is another good example of this compulsion.

Liszt made something of a splash, too, in staid Bonn, when another woman briefly entered his life. It would be fair to say that Franz was often tempted by the quick and casual liaison. We learn that on one occasion the infamous "Lola Montez turned up uninvited, broke into a private dinner and danced upon a table."[20] She did it to attract the handsome virtuoso. This kind of notoriety did not hurt the allure of the man already presumed to be a diabolically flamboyant pianist, far beyond any of his near competitors. This kind of splash, however, did nothing for the longevity of Liszt and Marie's strained relationship. She had stood by him, encouraging and forgiving him, for over ten years. How much longer could either stand the strain?

The couple remained together until May, 1844 when Liszt's many trysts and wearisome absences from her took their final toll. No abbess herself, Marie was also said to be enjoying the intimate company of a few gentlemen callers while Franz was away, so there may be a mutual deterioration of affection, and from multiple sources. Rarely at home, Liszt gave twenty-one concerts in Berlin alone in 1842.

Nor did Marie did not stagnate intellectually; she was becoming a writer of some note, using the pen name Daniel Stern. Her melodramas were a thinly disguised story of the couple's own troubled relationship. Without doubt, however, Marie the Muse had made Franz Liszt the confident, sophisticated, erudite kind of man and musician he wanted to become. He owed her a great deal, though it is hard to tell if he ever knew it.

For Liszt the world was never quite large enough. He was still traveling and extending his international reputation when he returned to Hungary, just after his 35th birthday. "During these wanderings Liszt invariably encountered many gypsy musicians and worked on "Magyar" pieces including the first *Hungarian Rhapsodies* as well as finding material for his *Romanian Rhapsody*."[21] The man was compelled to travel.

Liszt left for Russia just into the new year, 1847, as now he and Marie seemed to be finished. Maybe it was his need to always be somewhere else. And so it was in Russia that fate and romance would clobber him yet again. As Liszt's preeminent biographer Alan Walker finds, "no other virtuoso in history had traveled so far, had given so many concerts in so brief a period, had enjoyed such fame with the general public." He was recognizably the greatest pianist, 'the first modern pianist' and then ... 'he simply walked away from it all.'"[22] Some would say he was seduced away from touring. What happened to turn him around?

Liszt performed a charity concert in Kiev on the 2nd of February. Following his playing, one woman offered a generous contribution of 100 rubles. This was the Polish Princess Carolyne von Sayn-Wittgenstein, "and at their meeting the whole of his future was altered at one stroke."[23] He was besotted. Liszt changed his schedule so that he could spend much of the following month with her. Carolyne was estranged from her husband, and Liszt eventually brought her to St. Petersburg with him where they met up with Berlioz. This Russian interlude presaged a change in how Franz Liszt would come back, or could come back, to composition. After his return from the Ukraine, and from concert performances for the Sultan in Constantinople, on the cusp of his 36th birthday, Liszt gave his last paid performance as a virtuoso pianist. He was done with that life.

The musician turned now to the long delayed task of composition, perhaps the only discipline in music he felt he had yet to master. "He did not go to Weimar that winter [as planned] but went into retreat with Carolyne at Woronince [Poland in] late September, 1847. When he emerged it was with new creative ideas and far reaching plans for life."[24] A court appointment at Weimar awaited, as did the next the chapter of another love – Carolyne von Sayn-Wittgenstein.

The princess – her married maiden name was Iwanowska – was born eight years after Liszt, in 1819. She was wed to a man with title and family but little wealth, a man who served as an army officer with no particular distinction. They were separated after only a few years and one daughter, but for years her husband Nicholas would not divorce her because the man did not want to lose his wife's money. Such bureaucratic baggage would haunt her for the rest of her life. Carolyne could have no officially sanctioned life apart from Nicholas, who was close to the Russian czar and under no requirement to do what his wife wanted. Ironically, Nicholas did get a divorce in 1855, for his own romantic needs and purposes, and he remarried the next year. Carolyne and Franz remained ignorant of this fact until 1860 when her relationship with Liszt was coming to its own predictable end.

Carolyne came into Liszt's life at precisely the time he needed a boost, another Muse to follow Marie – one to encourage him in his next grand epoch. Franz told his friend Carl Alexander that it was time to emerge from his "virtuoso's chrysalis and allow my unfettered flight." That would be flight to composition, where "[t]here was a deeper artistic imperative at work within him. He wanted to, he needed to, compose. A number of large-scale orchestral works were already germinating in his mind, but his itinerant life-style prevented them from working them out."[25] He had serious work ahead.

Liszt had been appointed Weimar's honorary Kapellmeister, or Director of Musical Theater, in 1842. He decided, five years later, to make an honest account of it. Liszt was drawn to Weimar for broad-ranging reasons, and saw this appointment, soon made permanent, as a chance to "revive and promote" the early music of Bach and Handel, native sons within the ancient kingdom of Thuringia. We find "[i]n all these activities, Liszt was sustained by his new mistress and companion, Princess Carolyne von Sayn-Wittgenstein, the woman who, for better or worse, was to dominate [the rest of] his life "[26]

The princess proved equally a force in the rekindling of his on-again, off-again Roman Catholic faith, to which she was a near fanatical devotee. All they shared, love for the arts, for music, even for religion proved insufficient, and they did not stay together. Carolyne was quite different from Marie d'Agoult in looks and grace. It is not that Carolyne was uncultured; she was said to be odd, one of the many intangibles she passed on to Marie and Franz's daughter Cosima, who was raised by her de-facto "step-mother." There will be more on Cosima and her force of personality later.

For one thing, Carolyne was said to be a bit mannish. She smoked cigars and in many ways she suffered for her unfavorable comparison with Liszt's former love, during their thirteen years together in Weimar. But what is ironic is that Marie, when she was with Liszt, had also wanted the man to slow down and find his way into serious composition. Marie d'Agoult had a sense of what Liszt must do to advance his art. Maybe he did not appreciate what he had. Why did he move on to the princess Carolyne ten years later? The answer seems to have something to do with how any being intuitively knows what it needs. "She [Carolyne] contained within herself all the forces which Liszt lacked… [H]e quickly found that she shared his views in many things, and in particular those concerning the development of music through a closer relationship with literature and painting."[27] Call them symbiotic. For many years they worked pretty well together, though Franz had trouble staying focused. He always had.

This brings us to the Weimar years, his so-called "Years of Struggle." Likely the largely doomed revolutions shaking much of Europe in 1848 made things more difficult for the couple. There was political and, more specifically, there was bureaucratic intrigue as to who would champion what artistic ventures. The so-called struggle was particularly sharp with a series of complications involving Liszt's three children with Marie, most especially their daughter Cosima. Carolyne was also trying to settle the sale of some of her property.

Liszt compensated somehow for all the turmoil; in fact, he had "reached his peak as an instrumental composer during these periods of greatest personal agitation… At times of outer stress, Liszt invariably composed his way back to inner calm."[28] In a direct sense his Weimar years, or more accurately his summers, were also his Carolyne years. She supported him in his music long past when most sentient women would have packed him up and sent him along; for Liszt went on to have more outrageous affairs of the heart, not all of them after he and Carolyne had parted. A few began before they called it quits. Liszt was always fortunate in love, more so than were his women. Events of the day, so to speak, also influenced what kind of music he wrote.

Following the failed political unrest in Paris, Hungary, and Vienna; and with the advent of a reactionary Pope Pius IX in the Vatican, egalitarianism and "liberal democracy" looked far off, indeed. Liszt began to write more sacred music. He found that he was good at it. After all he, and Carolyne more so, were still captivated by some spiritual, even metaphysical calling. Liszt wrote a good bit of ecclesiastical music in 1850, struggling with what remained in him as a Romantic. It's interesting to note that this is the year of his *Liebesträume*, Love Dreams, arguably his most sensuous piece of piano music. Liszt had another Muse in mind for that one.

His plans and sketches for operas, had begun nearly ten years before, as early as 1841, and were based in part on the Romantic poet Byron. He also considered themes suggested by Goethe and was strongly drawn to Gypsy themes. His strength was not in opera, in fact, but instrumental and choral work. His last known composition is the *Mephiosto Waltz*, following the last of his *Hungarian Rhapsodies* (No. 16-20) This was also at this time that Liszt began a long association with Richard Wagner, a source of so much intrigue. In 1848 he conducted *Tannhäuser* in Weimar, and made a piano transcription of the opera which is said to have delighted Wagner, who needed the attention in Weimar. It would not be unfair to say that Liszt was now leaving the opera compositions to a dear friend, the man who would one day be his son-in-law.

Liszt sheltered Wagner when he was involved in the abortive Dresden uprising the next year. Wagner had been denounced as a member of the abortive revolution and, with a warrant having been issued for his arrest; he eventually had to spend twelve years in exile, mostly in Switzerland. All the while Wagner was making himself scarce; Liszt continued to promote the man's work. Richard Wagner came to owe much to Liszt's innovative tome poem harmonies, essentially showing Wagner how to break out of his formal, stylistic scoring in his four operas of *The Ring*. This collaboration was probably a more significant development for Liszt than for Wagner.

Ahead for Liszt were the twelve magnificent Symphonic poems, a musical form it must be said Liszt created and Richard Strauss mastered. Liszt was generous to his musical colleagues and did not turn from them in their times of troubles. When Robert Schumann had his breakdown Liszt wrote and supported Clara. He also championed the music of his old friend Hector Berlioz, when his work was flagging. Ever aware of talent, Liszt championed the young Hans von Bülow, and in 1853 met and encouraged the twenty year old Johannes Brahms. In Paris, Franz Liszt helped Charles Gounod and the young Bizet, referring to Bizet's piano play as simply "brilliant." The composer got around.

As we know, Liszt continued to have his affairs with women, almost as if somehow he could not help himself. While still contemplating marriage to Carolyne – and this possibility dragged on for years – before the pope personally scotched her annulment; Liszt remained open to the most egregious dalliances. The five years or so he spent with Agnes Street, an English-German woman in Weimar and Brussels, did not put a cap on his infidelities. Nor did these peccadilloes impact his music in any adverse way. In fact, it was while seeing Agnes that Liszt wrote his famous *Liebesträume* nocturnes for piano. It would be difficult to find something more thematically romantic.

Franz wrote his *Faust* and *Dante* symphonies between 1854-57, the years in which they were both performed. About 1860, with a dejected Carolyne now living apart from him in Rome, Liszt came to stay with her briefly. Could they reconcile? Whatever else they discussed, it seems that now there were renewed plans for a wedding. This woman's hope was greater than her common sense, but the Church of Rome's decision went against them. There could be no annulment, though Carolyne kept her faith in the church. This final disappointment, however, seems to have been the *coup de gras* in their lives as a couple. Maybe she had held on to this one hope of keeping him faithful, keeping him just for her. Finished romantically, they remained close, by letter, for years.

Interestingly, Franz now began to renew his fascination with the religious life, still pondering his own potential for a life in a contemplative order. Liszt left Weimar for good in 1861, settling in Rome and writing more religious music, including his *Ave Maria* and in 1862 and the variations on Bach's *B-minor Mass*. In 1865 Liszt became an Abbé of the church, and in the remaining twenty years of his life grew closer still to mother church. There had been something of an epiphany in his life. We can only surmise if it had anything to do with the realization that he would never – could never marry. In the end, Franz Liszt chose the one life that had always remained open to him, had always been seductively attractive to him. The life of a monk did not keep him at home.

The great virtuoso and composer died on 31 July 1886 in Bayreuth, having given his career concert earlier that year for Queen Victoria, at Windsor. In his final year he also gave concerts in Vienna, Paris, and Antwerp. He performed in Luxembourg just weeks before he was taken terminally ill with pneumonia.

Liszt wore himself down in travel. That was apparently how he chose to recharge his boundless spirit. In his final months, on his final tour, the London audiences gave him one the warmest receptions of his career. He delighted the students at the Royal Academy of Music, playing for them after inaugurating a scholarship in his name. Such was the nature of one of the most generous, most complicated men in the history of classical music. Some would say that, never satisfied, he simply worked himself to death.

Tired and worn, but ever the romantic, Liszt had come back to Germany for a friend's wedding, set for 2 July 1886 – one that he never managed to find for himself.

Derek Watson describes Liszt's final days. His daughter Cosima, also his friend Wagner's widow, came to stay. In his final week he sat up in bed to play some of his beloved card game whist.[29] He looked back on all that he was, and perhaps all that he might have been. We might surmise that in those last hours Franz also took in a few special memories. And then he was gone. Too ill, the princess Carolyne was not at his funeral. She died months later, the remarkable and truly inspirational work of his last Muse perhaps never fully appreciated.

Arthur McMaster

CHAPTER ELEVEN

MAHLER, Gustav (1860 – 1911); Austrian

" The symphony must be like the world. It must embrace everything."

Gustav Mahler

Although nearly every era of man seems to have brought chaos and dislocation to Central Europe, Gustav Mahler in his youth was witness to a particularly tumultuous time. The Hapsburg Empire was coming apart; the well-known and largely benign socio-political forces of Vienna were waning, and the little Czech-Austrian-Jew, who in his thirties would become a baptized Roman Catholic, found himself homeless in a world he didn't easily fit into. Nevertheless, Mahler was a survivor, and he accommodated himself as well as he could to a world he saw as precarious. Mahler made up for this uncertainty by driving himself to work harder than the next man, to produce magnificent music – he seldom worked on small projects. Finally he worked simply to succeed. He was also somewhat superstitious, as we'll soon see.

Like his near-exact contemporary Edward Elgar, Mahler was fixated with death and loss. He saw it all around him, but especially in his own family. At the age of fourteen, Gustav's brother Ernst, one year younger, died after a protracted illness. Another brother, Otto, said by some music historians to be nearly as musically gifted, shot himself to death at the age of twenty-two. Clearly, Mahler's highly regarded song cycle *Kindertotenlieder,* commonly translated as *"Songs of Children's Death* (1905) allowed him to come to grips somewhat with such personal torment. Perhaps it permitted some reconciliation.

Although seldom credited for his complementary talent, Mahler was a passably good poet as well, influenced by Goethe, Schiller and the intensely Romantic poet Friedrich Hölderlin.

Some of Mahler's poems became the *lieder* that distinguished many of his compositions written in his late teen and into his early twenties. We have already seen that a number of classical composers were also poets, and more so they were often drawn to women who wrote verse. As we know, for years Robert Schumann thought himself a poet first.

Mahler needed what some biographers have called *Liebende Wirheit,* or "loving communion." The philosopher Rollo May says in his *Love and Will,* that the discovery of our need for the "significant other" empowers us. The search for the loving other, and then for many of them, seems to have been essential to Mahler's precarious hold on his sanity. In his life and music he devised a means to compensate, and in some sense to medicate, his trauma. If quantity has a quality all its own, as the aphorism goes, Mahler was aided and abetted by the numerous *mädchens* that crossed his troubled, brilliant path. We will return to the man's romantic history promptly.

Mahler's music seems to cry out, quiet literally, to be taken as a body of work on "being." His achievement was to find a sense of being, a sense of meaningful existence in a Godless universe.[1] Whatever the source, Mahler's meaning, his very purpose, came from music. His use of poetry, much of it becoming the woof and warp of his splendid *lieder,* give the reader or careful listener some insight into this eternal question. Translated by Gabriel Engle, this Mahler poem became the words to his *Songs of a Wayfarer:*

> The Night looks softly down from distances,
> Eternal with her thousand golden eyes,
> And weary mortals shut their eyes in sleep.
> To know once more some happiness forgotten.
> See you the silent, gloomy wanderer?
> Abandoned is the path he takes, and lonely,
> Unmarked for distance and direction.
> And oh! no star illuminates his way,
> A way so long, so far from guardian spirits!
> And voices versed in soft deceit sound, luring:
> 'When will this long and futile journey end?
> When will the wanderer rest from all his suffering?'
> The Sphinx stares grimly, ominous with question,
> Her stony, blank gray eyes tell nothing, nothing,
> No single, saving sign, no ray of light:
> And if I solve it not, my life is forfeit.

Perhaps Mahler suggests in all of this the existential thinking that creativity and human relationships clarify and substantiate a man's meaning. The composer's personality infuses his work in a way so complete that we feel somehow we know the composer. We find that he was sometimes "… solitary, introspective, nature-intoxicated, [and even] near-suicidal."[2] Adding to his difficulties of making sense of who he was and what mattered, his many romantic arabesques and adventures were often unhappy and unrequited. We find our way to Mahler's music through his women, from the age of twenty until his death, thirty years later, in 1911.

He was attracted to the most eclectic of musical forms and fashions, even to martial music of the passing military elements, certainly to include the swaggering Prussians. Gustav relished folk music, religious themes and hymns and he was drawn to the profane, as well. He is said to have begun his compositional career at age six with a small polka, complemented by a funeral march.[3] Mahler gave his first public recital at the age of ten, in his home town of Iglau, more commonly known as Jihlava, in what is now the Czech Republic.

The story of Gustav Mahler's many Muses begins with Josephine Poisl, daughter of Iglau's telegrapher. In the spring of 1879 Gustav was almost nineteen years old. Here is an excerpt from a letter young Mahler sent to a friend, and we see how smitten he is with Ms. Poisl: "My dear friend, I have gotten myself quite badly entangled in the silken chains of the darling of the gods […The victim] now sighs, now wrings his hands, now groans, now entreats…I have spent most of the time indulging in every kind of bittersweet daydream … My eyes are like a couple of squeezed-out lemons, and there is not a single tear left in them."[4] When his love went unrequited, however, he found a way ahead, soon putting it all into a better perspective. Mahler would often be skilled at soft landings.

We then find "[h]owever intense the pain, no doubt unrequited love in Iglau hurt him just as much as his *Weltschmertz* in Hungary … Mahler compels himself with a strong dose of irony to snap out of it." He found a catharsis in music, and he wrote, then dedicated three songs for Josephine at that time.[5] These simple pieces would have comprised much of his *Klagende Lieder*. No sooner was he over Muse One, Miss Poisl, however, than a soprano came along to rend his tender-most heart. Enter Johanna Richter.

Mahler began composing his *Symphony # 1* in 1884 while employed as the second conductor to the Royal Imperial Theater in Kassel. Many Mahler biographers have made note of his infatuation with Miss Richter. The twenty-four year old Mahler's favorite author was also named Richter, this one Johann, the author of a book that had tremendous influence on the musician. The work was "Titan," the same name Gustav later gave to his first symphony. *Titan* is a multi-part tone poem which Mahler fussed and tinkered with for years. But young Johanna was the inspiration for a great deal of his music that went well beyond *Titan*.

Musicologist Jeffery Gantz finds the origin of what Mahler called *Blumine*, or flowers. This was Mahler's name for Johanna, whom he honored with a short trumpet intermezzo. He also wrote an untitled love serenade with Ms. Richter in mind. This piece emerged, humbly enough, as incidental music in 1884. Mahler, however, was seldom satisfied with his music; he liked to revise and even to reconstruct. His *Blumine* theme, modified and transcribed, became the second movement of the *First Symphony* in 1893, although he subsequently emended the piece to leave out *Blumine*. Gustav had trouble leaving it alone. Still, the *Blumine* theme remains strong in Mahler's *First Symphony*. Next, we find traces and entire sections of it in the second *Gesellen*, or Wayfarer, song. But Gustav did not forget about Johanna after the *First Symphony*. The first four notes of Blumine A variant are the first four notes of the plainchant *Des Irae*. They dominate his *Second Symphony*, as well, called the Resurrection. Then again, the opening phrases of the *Fourth* and the *Fifth Symphony* share the joyful reprise of *Blumine*.[6] Miss Richter proved a persistent Muse.

Mahler could not leave her memory alone. "The trio in the scherzo of the Seventh Symphony finds the French horns and the cellos joining in an affectionate *Blumine* … parody… In the opening movement of Mahler's *Ninth*, [another variant of] *Blumine* precipitates the catastrophic collapses of the exposition… in the first violins." Clearly "Gustav's visions of Johanna haunted him to the end."[7]

The winsome, blond and blue-eyed Johanna Richter gave Mahler inspiration far beyond the short time he was actually in her presence. She had a long physical presence in his music, as well, performing until she took up teaching. Did they ever have a true, physical relationship? Maybe… On the cusp of 1885 they spent an unhappy New Year's Eve together awaiting 1886, supposedly both in tears. When Mahler left Kassel and the court theater for Prague days later he never saw her again. Perhaps he left because of his inability to win her. That analysis seems likely. Either way, she left behind a remarkable legacy. Some Muses are easier on the heart than Johanna was on poor Gustav's.

Let's catch up with Mahler in Prague, where he became the "second conductor" of the German Opera Theater. Shortly, he was successful in presenting Mozart's *Don Giovani*, Beethoven's *Fidelio*, and even some Wagner opera. Even better; he then met a young woman who helped him regain his emotional balance and the ability to focus on his own work. The striking soprano to next take his cautious hand was Betty Frank.

We have this picture: "She sang at the *Deutsches Landestheater* [German Theater], took part in Mahler's triumphant performance of the Beethoven Ninth and, in a concert at a Prague hotel which put her in the music history books, gave the premiere of three early Mahler songs with the composer at the piano. The affair between the two brought so much tongue-wagging that word of it even reached Mahler's acquaintances, and perhaps his family, in Iglau."[8] This was another short-lived affair of the heart, but his infatuation with Betty, certainly helped Gustav to move on, maybe even to get some much needed perspective on quick fire affairs. He had a few more in store.

Mahler figured it was time to get serious about his music. He had it in mind that one day he would take up a prestigious position in Vienna, but there were some necessary stops to make along the way. This was a dream even dearer to him than finding a suitable sweetheart. During his short year in Prague Mahler wrote three songs, although none were written for an elusive love. Gustav left Bohemia uncertain of what lay ahead, professionally or personally.

In 1886 Mahler was offered a job as second conductor to the brilliant Arthur Nikisch in Leipzig. He could not have known the next Muse would be so close at hand. "[O]nce Mahler got to Leipzig he found his hands more than full – with a new flame and perhaps his most dangerous rival so far."[9] While contesting Nikisch for the upper hand in Leipzig, and planning to conduct Wagner's Ring Cycle, Mahler found himself head over heels again; this time the consequences were more dramatic.

"It seemed that love alone, and particularly disappointed love, was the stimulus which, at that time, could induce the young Mahler, [as the composer said] to 'find a way back to my true self' through composing."[10] Sure enough, Mahler was about to embark on another hopeless love affair. This time the object of his affection was married and the mother of four children – again triggering the creative process. Mahler wrote "these emotions had reached such a degree of intensity in me that they burst out in an impetuous stream.'"[11] The lady this time was Baroness Marion von Weber, wife of Carl von Weber, an officer in the Leipzig Regiment. He was also the grandson of Carl Maria von Weber, the father of German Romantic Opera. Some further irony attends this affair.

Mahler seems to have done some of his best compositional work at this time, completing the comic opera *Die drei Pintos,* which Carl's grandfather had sketched many years earlier. Other composers had also had an opportunity to work on his mind and his music. It's likely that Gustav took the happy assignment to finish *Pintos* because of his friendship for the Webers, but at least as much for the obvious opportunity to spend time with Marion. Their affair was injudiciously hot and wild; they even considered eloping, attempting to rendezvous at the railway station where Marion had agreed to meet Mahler. When Carl found out about it he went nearly mad and secured a gun, shooting up a car on the train. Evidently the cuckolded Carl was subdued before he could do any real damage.

A small and fine biography by Gabriel Engel, said to be the first on Mahler in the English language, does not mention the affair. In fact, Engel's treatment of the whole *Three Pintos* episode portrays Mahler working diligently with the luckless Carl, enjoying the Weber children, and simply being "… a stage-conductor of wide practical experience, in short, the right man for the work at hand."[12] Maybe Herr Engel thought the affair was of no particular interest or import. Arguably, it was impetus enough for Mahler to spur his *Three Pintos* work.

The most reliable evidence of how close Mahler and Marion really were came many years later from an unexpected source. In 1907, the Dutch conductor Willem Mengelberg wrote to his wife of a visit he had paid to Marion, by that time a widow and living in Dresden. Mengleberg knew nothing of the Leipzig liaison, but when the talk turned to Mahler he noticed "Marion's eyes became moist and she trembled." To his astonishment, she produced a pile of original manuscripts by Mahler insisting she had shown them to no one else. How many Mahler works Marion really had tucked away is unclear. The manuscripts were later lost, probably during the bombing of Dresden in 1945. One of them, however, was certainly an early version of the First Symphony, including the sentimental Andante movement called *Blumine*, which Mahler later struck out. According to Mengleberg, "Mahler had headed the movement *In Glucklicher Stunde* (In an hour of happiness). At the end he had written a dedication to Marion on her birthday."[13]

Meanwhile in Leipzig, on 20 January 1888, Mahler and his able company staged *The Three Pintos* with enormous success. The love affair had allowed him to emerge from a life on conducting, which he certainly did well enough, to full-score composition, which is what he knew he must do. This would also separate him from Arthur Nikisch, who was a superb conductor but no composer. Gustav put the tragic affair with Marion behind him. He'd gotten used to leaving the girl, or she him. For a while, at least, Mahler had also put his anguish and uncertainty behind him. Prague was done; Leipzig was over. Where would he go next?

The answer was just down the Danube, in Budapest. By the end of 1888 Mahler saw himself one step closer to Vienna, still his professional goal. Gustav agreed to move to Hungary and take up the position of Artistic Director and chief conductor. Perhaps he had quieted some of the devils. What was to be a ten-year contract, or appointment, however, was cut considerably short. The reason was not because Mahler was unsuccessful. He had acquired the level of responsibility he felt he needed, and certainly he had mastery of the most important decisions – the artistic calendar, the distribution of assignments, etc. But he had not counted on being usurped by a popinjay nobleman who soon began to wrest control, and did so in a particularly irritating way.

Fresh and flush from a highly successful staging of the entire *Ring* cycle, sung in Hungarian no less, Mahler declared he was ready to get back to serious composition. He was happy to sustain his physical life support needs with the conducting money but, after all, he was a composer. No sooner did it seem Mahler had made the big breakthrough than tragedy and misfortune hit him hard.

His father passed away in February, and his mother in October. Gustav's twenty-year old sister Justine, called Justi, did what she could to keep the younger members of the family together, but the musician felt compelled to return to Iglau and do what he might to try to normalize family matters. He didn't have the temperament for it. No doubt he was distracted professionally, as well, for at that precise time Mahler was preparing to conduct in Budapest his *Symphony No. 1*, then still called *Symphonic Poem*.

The work was received with mixed results. One critic quipped, "We shall always be pleased to see [Mahler] on the podium, so long as he is not conducting his own compositions."[14] He tinkered with the piece for years, eventually scrapping the emotion-heavy *Blumine* second movement, although as we know he retained much of the melody to use again. Meanwhile, his plans for work on his *Symphony No. 2,* to be called *The Resurrection,* boosted his spirits and gave him a much needed new focus.

The reception of his conducting bothered him. The more he thought about the implications for a long-term Budapest association the less comfortable he was with his contract. Pinning the blame, Mahler came to resent what he thought of as their mediocre, meddlesome management. After all, he was supposed to be the maestro here. Mahler still had eight years to go on his contract but he wanted out. Surprisingly, the city fathers agreed to let him go after only two years and he was even able to finagle a nice severance upon his departure. Germany was next. Mahler was still working his way to Vienna.

We jump ahead to 1893 and find Mahler in Hamburg, working as principal conductor for Bernhard Pollini, director of the Hamburg Municipal Theater. Pollini encouraged Mahler to work harder than ever, staging a breathtaking number of major performances, guest conducting in London, and impressing many established, as well as up and coming, musical luminaries. One man in particular Mahler wanted to impress was Pyotr Tchaikovsky, who had seen his own Eugene Onegin done masterfully. Mahler also got to conduct some of the Russian's larger symphonic works that he was so eager to make his own. The work was arduous, as Pollini had promised it would be. Exhausted, Gustav needed to get away, which he finally was able to do, taking a vacation in the Austrian Alps with his sister Justi and a close family friend named Natalie Bauer-Lechner. Natalie had in her mind to become even closer. She gave it her all for many years, but Gustav would take some convincing.

Natalie may have been the best wife Mahler never married. Two years older than Mahler and a fine viola player, she was drawn to him when he was a student at the Vienna Conservatory. Natalie, in fact, left her professor-husband to make herself available, following "an invitation he had made in passing to a group of Vienna friends which happened to include her… Natalie became almost a member of the family, but not the part she wanted to be [and] Mahler treated her like a sister, not a potential spouse."[15]

He confided in her his method for composition. He allowed, "I often begin in the middle, often at the beginning, sometimes even at the end, and the rest of it gradually falls into place…"[16] He was frustrated about not being able to find the time to compose and he needed to decompress, even while Natalie pined. How to get started again was simple, he decided; he'd go back to the future.

Mahler found a fitting sequel to the work he had begun on his *Todtenfeier* movement, five years earlier in Prague. The piece was based on a poem about a fish. Mahler went to great lengths to explain to Natalie just how he saw the fish behaving. Perhaps the young lady had made a reasonable contribution to his work after all, just by getting him to think about the mechanics.

Natalie Bauer-Lechner was unwilling to give up on Gustav, so she did what she could to be supportive of his work. The next year found the thirty-four year old musician with undeniable success as both composer and conductor. He finished his *Resurrection* symphony and performed it the next year in Berlin. Whatever Natalie thought might happen for her and Gustav, however, was evidently not going to happen, though she was slow to realize it. Likely she simply refused to. She remained near at hand – something of a family friend, biding her time. Perhaps she figured Gustav would be available for sometime. If and when he came around she'd be near.

Gustav was looking elsewhere, and suddenly his timing was propitious. Mahler had Anna von Mildenburg on his mind, at least as tenacious in her expectations as was Natalie. Mahler met Anna in Hamburg when she sang a hopeful part in one of his Wagnerian operas. Quickly their romance, impetuous and non-too-subtle, became the talk of Hamburg, perhaps because

Anna herself was not likely to let others out maneuver her. Surprisingly, it was not Anna but Natalie who got to accompany the composer to Austria, where at the edge of the Höllengebirge the composer found the ideal location for placing his grand new work. This was the town at Steinbach am Attersee, near Salzburg. Mahler wrote to Bruno Walter in July of '96, telling him that he had composed all that was to be found there at the mountain. It was a glorious setting. Mahler was also enjoying the winsome company of a young woman.

In writing the sequence of music, the composer named what the animals tell him, he named and set to music "what the forest tells him," and notably - what love said. Was this the love, perhaps, that he heard from one of these women? Or both? Nature was always capable of capturing Mahler's attention. Natalie did all she could to grab some too. Young Anna, however, was likely ascendant even with Natalie at Mahler's side, inspiring the man's composition of the lengthy piece. We know he wrote it in a rush of sentiment and inspiration. Whoever or whatever else may have been speaking to him of love, including the faithful Natalie; the great love of his life he'd decided was Anna von Mildenburg, a Muse of the first order.

Meanwhile, beyond what she stoically understood to be her man's infatuation *du jour*, Natalie had every intention of staying in the Mahler game for the long haul. For all we know Mahler may have retained some measure of emotion for Natalie. Surely he was moved by her steadfast devotion as he worked his way through musical structure of his next major work, the *Third Symphony*. Anna, Natalie, or both had given Mahler their unconditional love. At the end of the day, there's no doubt that one of them represented the love he said was speaking to him. Either way, Mahler was twice blessed. More bounty and more high romantic drama was coming fast.

Mahler got the call he'd been waiting for – now it would be Vienna.

Finally, Vienna! When Mahler arrived in the city of his dreams it was a capital raw with political, social and cultural unrest. There was even an undercurrent of religious drama. The capital city was dominated by its dynamic Jewish population. Did this fact matter to Mahler? Actually, he considered his affiliation with the right religion to be central to his prospects, and here he was nothing if not malleable.

In 1897, the liberal press and the break-away literary and artistic communities were well represented by Jews. The so-called Secessionists had become something of a life force in old Vienna. This was a loosely constructed band, often looking to the author and journalist Hermann Bahr for direction and ideas. Bahr, ironically enough, eventually married Anna von Mildenburg, the young lady who likely had a strong influence in Mahler's composition of the great *D minor symphony*, "the Third," two years before.

But anti-Semitism was also gaining an ugly presence, a dynamic that would play a major role in the choices Gustav Mahler found himself making that spring. With the retirement of the director and chief conductor of the Vienna Court Opera, Mahler was unexpectedly in the running for the top spot. He had come to town as principal conductor of the municipal theater. Could he be so fortunate as to compete seriously for Vienna's top musical post? Learning something about career-ism from many of his former bosses, Mahler took the necessary instruction in the Church of Rome and converted to Catholicism. In part, this was a bold career move. He would not be painted by the same anti-Semitic brush as had attacked so many of his associates. Mahler even made certain to point out this apt change in faith to those who would review his formal application for the job. He needed a more personal boost, however, to actually secure the top position. Could another woman in his life make a difference? Yes; Rosa Papier – coming through!

Rosa was a mezzo-soprano whom Mahler had met some two years before when she sang for him in his celebrated performance of Mendelssohn's *St. Paul* oratorio, in Kassel. She had retired from singing and was now highly influential in the music world of Vienna. Crediting Mahler with the development of her own former pupil, the winsome Anna von Mildenburg, Rosa used her good office to push for Mahler's ascendancy. Finally, using numerous weighty and persuasive contacts and a friendly press to his best advantage, and underscoring his conversion to Christianity, Mahler got the job. Now that he had the best position in Vienna, what would this portend for his music?

The proverbial mountain would yet come again to Mahler, as in the next year the other top directorial position fell into his lap. He had long wanted to conduct symphonic works. In September, 1898, the leadership of the Philharmonic orchestra asked him to take charge. Mahler's dreams might now be fulfilled twice over. Would so much artistic prestige not prove unmanageable? Certainly, as the Director of the Philharmonic, he could expect to give his own works a hearing. But what of the hundreds of musicians he needed to uphold their end? His long run of good fortune came to an ignoble end. Predictably, his troubles came from demanding too much, and not just of himself.

By May of 1899 the elected representatives of the "musicians union" tried to replace Mahler with the aging Hans Richter, whom Mahler had replaced only the year before. Troubles mounted. Soon he was having trouble with some of his singers. He could always replace the ones who would not put out the effort, but Mahler needed help from another dimension. He needed inspiration to compose with deeper feeling for the music. Recruiting talent, he was also ready for commitment. Soon the word of another great romance was in the wind.

With all of Vienna's music now at his command, Gustav Mahler found he needed someone to share his success – more so to share his life. He did not have far to look, not with so many young female voices in his world. There were many options, many women who found him attractive, or at least appealing. Soon Mahler was linked romantically with Marie Gutheil-Schroder, Rita Milachek, and then, more definitely, with Selma Kurz, described as a brilliant and beautiful soprano. Twenty-four years old, she "… gave the Vienna premiere of some of Mahler's orchestral songs and by Easter 1900 the two were snatching secret meetings together between rehearsals."[17] Soon Mahler was writing her heartfelt mash notes about all that was unique in their relationship. Clearly he needed a great romantic involvement as much as compositional ideas. Now aged forty, Mahler was looking for a life partner. Selma Kurz was fourteen years younger. Was the gap too great? Gustav was willing.

He also demonstrated he had an eye for talent. Clearly, this Muse had her own career expectations. Boldly he asked for her hand. Selma told Gustav she felt marriage would do her career no good. Maybe she was right. Even without marriage, Fräuline Kurz made quite a career for herself. Come to that, Mahler could have been something of a Muse for her – at least as much as she was for him. This is what we know:

Born 14 November 1874, in Austria, one of the youngest of eleven children, Selma first attracted notice from her singing in a synagogue. After studies in Vienna and Paris she made her debut at the Hamburg Opera in Ambroise Thomas' *Mignon*. The following year Miss Kurz came to the Frankfurt Opera, remaining for three years, after which Mahler brought her to the Vienna Imperial Opera, conducting her debut as *Mignon*. Their affair was grand and glorious. Selma Kurz sang in Vienna for another thirty years, until the end of her career in 1929. Under Mahler's guidance she became the leading coloratura soprano of Vienna and one of the best-known singers in Europe.[18] As far as we know they remained on friendly terms for years after their lopsided romance simmered down.

Things took an unexpected turn that winter, as Mahler's health declined. In truth, he was debilitated by a back-breaking schedule. One wonders if he was told to stop to smell the *Blumine*! In any event, Mahler's concert performance of Mozart's *The Magic Flute,* on 24 February 1901, was significant for one reason he did not dare expect. In the audience that evening was Alma Schindler, arguably a most fetching and beautiful young woman, surely the greatest Muse to take up house in his heart.

They did not actually meet on that occasion, but she remembered him well from his "Lucifer-like" performance as conductor. In her autobiography and musings about the man who would become her first husband she recalled she had also been highly put off by the rumblings of all of Mahler's affairs of the heart with his singers. She had no doubt heard of the grand affair with Selma Kurz. But she was intrigued and the fates were diligent. At least those were that signal the arrival of Erato and Caliope.

Alma and Mahler met at a dinner party given on 7 November 1901, given by Mrs. Berta Zuckerkandl. Alma relates in her storied memoirs [19] that Berta had invited Miss Schindler expressly to meet Mahler. She demurred, but her would-be hosts did convince her to come to a postponed dinner where Alma could meet the famous composer and conductor. The attractive young Ms. Schindler was drawn to artists, having already been the lover of the flamboyant, modernist painter Gustav Klimt. Now the Alma-Gustav romance seemed preordained. Two months after the dinner party Mahler and Schindler were engaged.

One question remains: Did the mature, forty-something composer ambitiously court the vivacious, precocious Alma? Or did she pursue him? One wonders how he found time for romance, or any personal life, when his schedule was so taken up with directing two major music houses? We know that his own musical compositions had declined to only *Five Songs* for voice and piano, from Rückert.[20] Likely he had at that time already begun sketches for what would become his next symphony. Whatever the impetus, Mahler knew he was in love. Alma, just twenty-one when she met him, had already been in love, or at least in something much like it, with Klimt. Not that Klimt had been her one and only.

When Mahler came into Alma's life she was involved with an older suitor. Hers was a splashy flirtation with the music composition teacher Alexander von Zemlinsky, who wrote the symphonic poem of fated love *The Mermaid,* in 1902. She must have thought that with such a storied portfolio she was ready to be wooed by Vienna's most powerful musician. Gustav Mahler stepped up.

To put things into perspective, Alma would not likely have made quite the impression she made with Mahler had she not been recognized as a serious musical talent in her own right. Mahler appreciated talent. Miss Schindler was confident beyond her years because of her superb musical preparation, or tutoring under artistic parents. But she also knew the score, so to speak, with Mahler's alleged Don Juan reputation. She wooed him as much with her affected naiveté as with her expressed eagerness to learn from him.

Curiously, though a strong-willed young woman, Alma considered her own musical career as a composer to be negotiable. Quickly, Mahler proposed marriage and she accepted. He made it clear, however, that she was to be his wife and his inspiration; he did not need another composer in the house. Apparently, they each made the necessary accommodation because things then moved rapidly. As Jonathan Carr explains it, alluding to their sexual tryst, on New Years' Day 1902, "By the time they married two months later, Alma was pregnant."[21]

Music and marriage proved a good mix, with some predictable ups and downs. That June, Mahler conducted the first complete performance of his *Third Symphony.* The setting was remote Krefeld, near Düsseldorf. While this complex and demanding work had only been performed in smaller editions, and the musicians had little or no continuity with the music, with Mahler, or even each other, the performance was an enormous success. As we know from having examined its many "tell me-show me" elements, the piece is about "universal love and the wonders of nature."[22] Both concepts appealed to the universally inconstant and mercurial Mahler.

The critics, too, were favorable, seeing a "new stage in the development of German music." Alma reports in her autobiography that she cried with excitement. But Gustav's biggest fan that evening may have been Richard Strauss, whom Mahler had likely seen more as a competitor than as a sponsor. Thereafter, both men supported the other, as Strauss was known as the better composer, while Mahler made his reputation more as the preeminent conductor. Mahler quickly made up ground.

What was Alma's continuing role in all this? The answer lies in Mahler's return to composition. He had completed the fairy-tale like and highly classical *Fourth Symphony,* and he did so at a time when his health was deteriorating. This G major symphony is a composition shorter, though by no means less complex, than those that preceded it. Mahler had been worn down from the pace in Vienna and he now wanted something in his life that would give him peace and surcease. He told himself her name was Alma Mahler.

Musical Muse: Wives and Lovers of the Great Composers

At the Austrian lakeside community of Maiernigg the man found he was more at peace than he had been in years. He composed with confidence and a zestfulness he'd not found in a long time. Gustav returned to the poet Rückert again. During the summer of 1901 he wrote eight songs, seven of them based on Rückert's verse. He had used Rückert before. One of the most playful is *Liebst du um Shönheit* or If You Love for Beauty's Sake, for piano and voice, which he wrote as a love song to Alma. Back to work on his *Fifth Symphony*, Mahler managed to find a place for *Liebst* in the fourth movement Adagietto, for strings and harp. He was not finished finding and writing his love songs to Alma.

Music scholarship yields a full accounting: "The composition of a new symphony, the *Fifth*, finished on the summer of 1902 in the peaceful villa of Maiernigg … proved a mysteriously baffling process to Mahler. He realized he had never before been so contented with life and its prospects. The increasing leisure granted him by the lessening burdens of the opera … the happiness of life with an understanding wife whom he loved – the promise of family of his own soon to be fulfilled – this beautiful summer villa of his dreams, yet somehow he seemed unable to apply to the scoring of this new work the consummate technical equipment [sic] which the experience of four huge symphonic labors had brought him."[23] Nevertheless, it was not until the last year of his life, in 1911, that he told Alma that the *Fifth* was truly finished.

Mahler was a perfectionist and a constant tinkerer. In the same way he had labored over the *Titan Symphony*, uncertain of how to stop revising. Mahler's uncertainty with a finished work goes to self-understanding. He had undergone a kind of "spiritual metamorphosis" that had to find its own manifestation in his music. This was not something Mahler would resolve in a short span of time. Truly, his *Fifth*, *Sixth*, and *Seventh* Symphonies are a kind of unifying trilogy.

The years 1906-07 brought the height of his success and personal happiness, and one of the saddest times as well. His *Eighth*, which he said was the best music he had yet written, was finished in August. Sadly, his daughter Maria, not yet five years old and known to the family as Putzi, died the next summer in Maiernigg from complications of Scarlet Fever. Mahler never got over her loss. The illness had almost killed her younger sister Anna. The only way he knew to get past such tragedy was to work. Even that became difficult.

Mahler was also having trouble with personnel matters at the Opera House and soon he decided to resign in protest. Fittingly, the final performance, on 15 October 1907, was Beethoven's *Fidelio*. Mahler was devastated over the loss of little Maria; his health was failing; and he was sick of Viennese politics and intrigue. He had to get away. Two days later he and Alma took a train to Paris; from there they left from Cherbourg for America. He told his wife he had a great deal of work yet to do. Could he write one more symphony? Would her love and inspiration make a difference?

This question begs the superstitious streak in Mahler. He was aware that God, or some recurring twist of fate, seemed to allow only nine symphonies to a man. Beethoven, Schubert and Bruckner had written nine and died. Schubert's Tenth was unfinished at the time of his death. Mahler called his ninth symphonic work *Das Lied von der Erde*, or Song of the Earth, although it was by every definition a symphony. He went on to score and complete the next, the Ninth, but that was the last one he was given time to complete.

His weakened heart gave out after returning from Paris for prescribed blood work, and he died on 18 May 1911, having once again traveled "home" to Vienna. He must have known he was coming back only to die. Mahler's unfinished *Tenth* was completed by Deryck Cooke, fifty years after Mahler's death, in 1966, from the composer's two nearly-complete movements, along with Mahler's sketches and notes.   The background story of the *Tenth* is interesting. Mahler was fifty years old in 1910, living comfortably in New York with his Alma. As we know, Mahler's health had been poor for a long time; and truly his *Ninth* had not been that well received. He was into his third break-neck season at the Metropolitan Opera House in New York, but after all, he was still a man driven, still on the look out for perfection, never satisfied. He was not sure he fit in here, in this crazy city, or perhaps anywhere. Gustav was nervous.

What did he have on his mind? Not unexpectedly, Mahler, still feeling exhausted, began to get home sick. Europe needed him; Vienna needed him. Did Alma still need him? That may have been the one question he did not want to answer. The able musician could manage the rest of the problems, but he needed his energetic young wife.

They left New York together, though she was at sixes and sevens about the departure. We cannot know to what extent Alma wanted out of New York. She might have figured she had problems here too.

 Shortly after their return to Austria, Alma became interested in Walter Gropius, the architect who would become her second husband. They met while taking what the Europeans call "the cure-rest" that summer near Graz. There was no real romance yet, nothing tangible, but the fire was lit and the young couple agreed to stay in touch.

Gustav was focused elsewhere. As was his nature, Mahler was preoccupied with his fame, his reputation. He conducted his *Second* in Paris that April. Later that year Mahler decided to return to Munich, and to take up the baton once more. This time he'd conduct his outsized, much misconceived *Eighth symphony*. For one reason or another he was staying busy and often staying away from home. Against type and against doctor's orders, he even went back to New York in his final spring – actually in April of 1911. Was there something in Vienna he did not want to face?

Alma was making her own plans, plans for a life after Gustav. Later that summer Gropius came to find the Mahlers at home in Toblach. They were living in temporary quarters. Mahler, now sketching his *Tenth*, knew what Gropius really wanted. Gustav invited him in, saying Alma should make up her mind as to what she wanted. He then went off to read; knowing he would only be in the way. Alma and the bright young architect did not try hard to hide their passionate tryst. Even as Mahler's own life was coming to a certain close, she was preparing for her next. Incredibly, Mahler's worship of Alma only seemed to intensify.

What of his unfinished piece of music? There is certain anguish in this, the final, composition. The summer before Mahler died of cancer he scored his most heart rending music in the dissonance of the *Tenth*. Did the impetus come from the Gropius affair? Certainly there was the power of Alma's love, perhaps now leaking away. What moved him now was the idea of his Alma getting on with her life, looking ahead. What could Mahler make of it all?

He tried to capture his feelings of coming loss in this final music, a theme that possessed his mind and spirit. On the manuscript he inscribed plaintively enough, '*Erbarmen!! O Gott! O Gott! Warmum hast du mich verlassen?*' This translates simply as: Mercy, Oh God, Oh God, why have you forsaken me? Mahler titled the unfinished third movement of this symphony *Purgatorio*.

Whatever he had inscribed on the bottom of the title page seems to have been torn off. Mahler did not return to work on the tortured *Tenth* again, but he left one memento for his wife. Written in the notes of the string section of the original score, as the incomplete work ends, are the words "*Für dich leben! Für dich sterben! Almschi.*" To Live for You! To Die for You! Almschi. [24]

CHAPTER TWELVE

MOZART, Wolfgang Amadeus (1756-1791); Austrian

"Dearest, most beloved little wife of my heart! I am longing for news of you…
I am fully resolved to make as much money as I can here and then return to you
with great joy… I kiss you a thousand times."
    [W.A. Mozart letter to Constanze, Sept 28, 1790]

Wolfgang Amadeus Mozart's complete life in music cannot be captured meaningfully in one chapter of an anthology for a general readership. The man's music is entirely too large for a nominal twenty-page précis. We can, however, capture much of his love life and the connection of his women to his music. Mozart's relationships with the ladies, with the few Muses of his short thirty-five years, make for a pretty good story; though in truth the affairs of his love life were not terribly complicated. While he was arguably the world's greatest musical genius, when it came to women he played in fairly simple scales.

Mozart was a master at getting by, whether it was in the province of finding love or in the on agian, off again anxiety of making money. And he was too often disappointed on all counts.

We'll get to a consideration of romance in a moment. As for the other domain, and not to put too fine a point on it; there was no other "classical" composer so talented who had worse luck in making a living at his singular calling. This was a situation unimproved by marriage, as family finances and prospects so often were in those days. Mozart's sister married well and into the aristocracy. It was not so much a romance as a strategic alliance. Apparently, that is what the ever-controlling Leopold Mozart wanted for his son. It didn't work out that way. Wolfgang married only once, and against family wishes. Constanze Weber Mozart was said to have been impish and childish, with little sense of how to handle the bits of money her husband did earn. Nevertheless, Constanze was among the most powerful Muses ever to impact the life of a musical artist.

We begin, of course, in Salzburg. This is the city on the Salzach that the teenaged Mozart would come to find so limiting. Mozart left Salzburg and her certain security for what he presumed to be the likelihood of expanded horizons and for broad-based acclaim. Right or wrong, he was even more certain that his precocious talent was too large for the provincial city. No one can say what might have been had Mozart stayed and made a life there. As we'll soon find, he had a wonderful opportunity to settle in a number of capital cities, including Paris. Eventually, Vienna claimed him, and then all but ignored him. No one city, no one land, no nation-state nor woman fully appreciated Wolfgang Amadeus Mozart.

Like so many great composers, Mozart came from a musically talented family. Leopold Mozart was, in the winter of 1756, an accomplished musician, violinist, and composer. But the talent of his only son, born in December of that year, was so strong and evident so quickly that Leopold devoted most of his maturity to promoting son Wolfgang. Most would say he exploited him.

History agrees that "child prodigies seldom grow up to live normal lives."[1] Wolfgang Amadeus grew up in the shadow of his father's expectations of what splendors the child would know – what sums he would earn. When the young man separated himself from papa Leopold it was in a dispute over the suitability of a woman. Leopold was furious with the boy's temerity and demonstrated lack of humility before the old man's expressed wishes. For his part, Wolfgang was only trying to make a point – a point about his autonomy. Arguably, Mozart never convinced himself of the maturity of his decision. Amadeus Mozart was the prodigal son who never did return home.

As a child Mozart had perfect pitch and nearly total recall, and thus was able not only to play something he had just heard, but he could offer interpretive variations. As a frame of reference, when the child would have been in the first grade in American schools papa Leopold took him on the road. For a while sister Nannerl accompanied them. "When Mozart played in Paris, shortly before he was seven years old, Baron Friedrich Melchior von Grimm, writing in the journal *Correspondance littéraire,* all but went out of his mind. Young Mozart went through some of the tricks his father had devised for him, such as playing a clavier whose keyboard was covered with a cloth … demonstrating his absolute pitch, and so on."[2] The astonished von Grimm, a respected journalist, likened the shock of his first exposure to Mozart as something similar to Paul's vision on the road to Damascus.

Whatever visions came to the mind of Wolfgang while still a child is anyone's guess, but he tended to be brilliant and flighty, accomplished yet artless. Seldom did he court the companionship of reason and perspective. Perhaps he knew his music was enough. His first compositions, at age six and seven, were sonatas for violin and piano. Mozart wrote ten of them by the time he was eight; when, in 1764, he wrote his first symphony. This is the *E flat Major* work, which we know today as K. 6.

Mozart learned a great deal about music while on tour with his controlling father. The Mozarts traveled for more than three years, from June 1763 through November 1766, their stops including most of Germany, Holland, Belgium and Switzerland. All the while the child was composing, some would say for show, including six more sonatas for violin and piano.

This was not a family to travel inconspicuously. Young Wolfgang made the acquaintance of many well-placed and influential people, any one of which might have later helped him to secure a position or situation that would bring in the money. Alfred Einstein makes the point that travel did not interrupt Mozart's life as a young musician. Rather, he says, travel stimulated his creativity.[3] He finds, "Mozart [was] animated by an inner urge to gain stimulation from a new environment.[4] Even after settling down in Vienna Wolfgang changed addresses remarkably often. People interested him more than locale. Unlike his contemporary Haydn, or Mahler who would follow almost a century later, Mozart was never much interested in composing on themes of nature.

At thirteen years of age he met the pope, Clement XIV, in Italy. The lad was getting plenty of fame, but where was the wealth? We surmise that Leopold pushed his son as hard as he did to compensate for his own limited career, not only as musician and composer but as the modestly paid Vice-Kapellmeister in Salzburg. The senior Mozart felt his official position was both unfair and well beneath his talent. Son Wolfgang held the key to family wealth, adulation, and comfort. Theirs was a case study to underscore the phenomenon of a parent's striving to live and succeed vicariously through the child.

Wolfgang's first female interest was apparently his Augsburg cousin, the daughter of his father's younger brother Franz Alois. This was Maria Thekla Mozart, nicknamed the Bäsle, or little cousin, to whom in 1777 the composer began writing naughty rhymes and puns. Wolfgang was an immature twenty and she a much more knowledgeable nineteen, or so most biographies suggest. After their brief fling, the unlucky Maria was the subject of much gossip. In fact, she was mentioned in unfavorable tones and terms around town, it being suggested that she was involved with certain Salzburg clergyman. Eventually "Bäsle" married one such cleric. Come to that, she was compelled to do so.

Mozart may truly have been drawn to his precocious cousin for her more worldly ways and her wit, which in some ways seemed to be as keen as his. The young man's infatuation with her, if indeed that is what it was, actually went back to when they were pre-teens and the families would gather for celebrations in Augsburg, Leopold's ancestral home. We have no insight into what Maria Thekla thought she was getting from this over-heated endeavor. She is our first Mozart Muse.

Wolfgang wrote his Bäsle quite a few notes and letters with lots of brilliant double entendres. At least one Mozart musicologist also finds that while he was expressing himself in words [Wolfgang] seems to have been thinking in music.[5] His genius was certainly inclusive enough to allow him to compose while doodling about excrement and the urgency of sexual functions. The Bäsle letters have generated much speculation on just how intimate their liaison actually became. Perhaps thinking that he owed her something more comely, he later annotated the solo part of a horn concerto for her.[6] It is disappointing in subsequent review that this piece is not further identified.

During these years of mostly asexual whimsy, Mozart, still in many significant ways a child who had always looked to his father to guide and cajole him, was beginning to consider what he must do to stand on his own. Leopold had a grip on the boy that could not have been healthy to young Mozart's maturation. We find that the father actually became dependent upon his young son for his well being. Economic factors were only the most obvious concerns, for "Leopold's struggle to control his son was a desperate one; [h]e was seeking to preserve not merely the source of his surplus income but the integrity of his personality." Further, being unwilling to surrender his control over Wolfgang, he would thwart his son's every move toward independence and maturity.[7] To suggest the father had a death grip on his son's future is no exaggeration.

It is not evident that Wolfgang ever fully realized how much his father was manipulating him, but in 1777, at age twenty-one, the young man was ready to test his own mettle. What alliances might Wolfgang now make and which ones would he begin to let loose? Apparently, he calculated that the first separation had to be from small town Salzburg. Mozart wanted to put as much distance as possible between his first home and himself. He was also ready for the pleasures of self-sufficiency and independence. One well-planned and fated trip away from home was monumental in importance.

Wolferl, as the family called him, and his mother left Salzburg for Munich, planning to go on to other principal cities in search of career opportunities. The distance from his father served to embolden him. Wolfgang wrote to papa that he was confident of finding sponsors. "It was his first trip without his father, and thus the first touch of independence… An air of bravado can be found in these letters [to Leopold] from Munich, Mannheim, and [the more so] from Paris."[8]

His time in Mannheim was productive. Here, only part way through the fated trip, young Mozart met the star-crossed Weber family. Wolfgang and his mother spent quite a bit of time with their countrymen and likely would have stayed longer if Leopold, stewing back in Salzburg, had not intervened. Wolfgang liked Mannheim, in no small part because of the Weber family with whom they were staying. He was soon to become even fonder of one of the more winsome Weber women.

Since Leopold was underwriting the trip, and because he did not approve of his son's new friends, mother and Wolfgang knew that they must eventually move on to Paris. Wolfgang gave his father more to be concerned about than the timing of their trip and the cost of the whole enterprise, as Mozart described a nascent romantic relationship in letters back to papa. Their serious tone frightened the stoic Leopold. His young son hinted he'd found a woman of exceptional beauty and talent. Mozart's second Muse was more powerful than the squirrelly little cousin. Aloysia Weber would, unwittingly, now cause relationship of the prodigal son and the worried dad to become especially anxious.

Mozart wrote his father on 4 February 1778 that he was making plans to travel to Italy with Aloysia, along with her older sister and with their father, Herr Weber. Mozart said that Josepha, the eldest, would be a good companion. He actually asked that Leopold might use his influence to get a prima donna role lined up for Aloysia, in Verona. Clearly, Wolfgang was falling in love with Aloysia and wrote "as far as her singing is concerned, I will wager that she will bring me renown."[9] The eighteen year old Aloysia infatuated him because of her youth and femininity but also by her gifts as a singer, about which he judged: "'She sings most excellently my aria written for De Amicis… she sings admirably and has a lovely, pure voice.'"[10] The piece Mozart had in mind was the *Lucio Silla*, K135.

The upshot of Mozart's fast rush of feelings for Aloysia meant one thing: this affair led the young man Mozart to lose sight of his immediate task – the search for an significant position in music. Instead be began the most adventurous plans for their future together.[11] He made such bold intentions known to his father, intimating that he also had great respect for the girl's father, Fridolin Weber. This testament was not well received in Salzburg and it would not be the first time Mozart showed a serious lack of timing and an absence of empathy for his father's needs and expectations.

Leopold was all the more despondent. According to the senior Mozart the Webers were not "quality people," and Leopold was anxious over his son's judgment and taste. Leopold wrote back: "Merciful God! Suddenly you strike up a new acquaintance with Herr Weber. Now this family is the most honourable, the most Christian family, and the daughter is to have the leading role in the tragedy to be enacted between your own family and hers… Your proposal has nearly made me lose my reason!"[12] Leopold's slings and arrows response could have been predicted. He always presumed to speak *ex cathedra* when talking to his son. There were no grays in the man's world, and this would not be the only time Leopold asked his son to choose his established family over a woman.

That summer the "affair" continued as if the couple might go on together forever, one smitten composer and one unassuming soprano. Aloysia, for her part, was not so artless, nor was her family, especially so the mother. The plan in the Weber household was for the girl to marry up, and no opportunity should be ignored. Then, as if the little affair were scripted by an opera librettist, fate intervened in two ways. Aloysia was offered a part away from Mannheim that would pay her reasonably well, and would even make allowance for members of her family. She had to take the offer. No questions asked. Wolfgang was out.

Leopold was relieved and insistent that his son and the boy's mother press on to Paris. By the time the Mozarts left Mannheim the young composer's love affair with Aloysia was cooling off, certainly so on her part. After all, what she wanted most was financial security, and not just for herself but for her large family. It's ironic that Aloysia and Wolfgang were each expected to be bread winners based on precocious talent. Yet, in both cases, just such parental expectation worked to keep them apart. Especially for the young lady, romance would be forced to await better prospects. Disappointed but undeterred, and looking to his mother as his chief consoler, Wolfgang left for Paris. They arrived on 23 March 1778.

Sadly, Wolfgang did not get to keep her at his side for long.

Barely three months into their stay in the French capital city, on the 4th of July, Anna Maria Mozart was dead at the age of fifty-seven. His letters reveal that the young man attempted to shelter his father from the full truth, at first writing only to say that the good woman had taken gravely ill. Frau Mozart had tried to be champion, guide, and protective parent for her son. She may have sensed that the relationship of the two men was irrevocably strained. Whatever her actual motive or expectation, the trip was too much for her constitution. Taking ill suddenly, she lingered near death, never recovering. Leopold had written to tell her to "be bled;" then he blamed Wolfgang for not having her bled sooner. For her part, the woman refused to see French doctors, astonishingly enough thinking them to be unfit. Falling into a coma after more than a week in bed with an inflamed throat and a high fever, she passed away two days after receiving the last rites of the Catholic Church. Wolfgang, ever the poker player, supposedly had told her that the cleric had only come by to hear him play. Anna Maria Mozart, whatever she may have dismissed or discerned in her final hour, was buried the next day in Paris.

The twenty-two year old Wolfgang was now fully his own man, or he would be if he could withstand the mounting pressures from papa. The fact that Wolfgang was alone in Paris concerned the father all the more. Leopold told his son that Paris was evil, it was another Sodom; be wary. For his part, Mozart did not particularly like Paris that well, and he liked the Parisians even less. Still, this was a musically vibrant city, not least for the many comic operas the French so loved. Mozart could write those too. Young Wolfgang Amadeus was as curious as he was cautious. He made enquiries.

A range of positions were possible if Mozart might agree to accept something less than actually being appointed Kapellmeister, as was his ambition – or perhaps his father's ambition for him. Wolfgang opined that jobs short of that mark would be too limiting. He wished to write to a broad range of music. If Salzburg was too provincial, where else could the young man go to reach his lofty goals? Munich and Mannheim surely seemed promising. No. Leopold was standing firm. Beside which, Wolfgang's lengthy road trip and his mounting expenses in Paris were too great of a financial hardship. By September Mozart was resigned that he had no choice but to return to father. He was all but beaten.

"The latest stage in a cycle of rebelliousness and submission had terminated in renunciation. It was not merely the hope for a post that he had surrendered, but a portion of his manhood as well, for surrender to his father had forced implications of celibacy… For the time being he had set aside hopes for sexual fulfillment and marriage, slowed the development of his career, and once again tried to pay off a debt – he had yet to realize – could never be fully satisfied."[13] Were both Mozart men deceiving themselves?

The father had been busy making plans for Wolfgang to satisfy Leopold's own needs, but Wolfgang took his time in returning. Only recently had the young man turned down an appointment at Versailles, where he would be named court organist. Embedded in the generous offer he refused, Mozart would be free for six months of the year to work in Paris, be free to compose and give lessons; but of course there was no offer for papa Leopold in this deal, and so Wolfgang convinced himself to turn down the one offer of security he actually most needed.

Mozart's time in the French capital had been less than productive, although he did compose his *Paris Symphony in D*, K 297. Moreover, Mozart was still loath to give up on Aloysia. He wanted to know if there was still a chance for them. We know that he wrote at least one letter to her in Italian, a language he had come to manage, if not master, from his operatic work and study. No letters from her to him have survived, but we know Fräuline Weber was going to do the utilitarian thing no matter who was hurt or left behind. As expected, and after a short courtship, Aloysia married the actor Josef Lange in September of 1780. Mozart accepted the end of their relationship and made plans to gradually make his way back to Salzburg. He frittered his way home, stopping for a pleasant interlude in Strasbourg and again in Munich, eventually managing to get back to Salzburg in the early weeks of 1779.

As predicted, Leopold had found his son a job; Wolfgang would be working for Archbishop Colloredo as court organist and concertmaster. Herr Mozart even suggested that the young man might take over as Vice-Kapellmeister in his father's absence. Just how the two convinced themselves that this was a positive, progressive move had more to do with the psychologies of family systems than with rewards and hierarchies in eighteenth century European music. Regardless, the arrangement was doomed from the start. After all, Wolfgang had been virtually compelled to come home by his clinging father. Before examining the totality of his work in 1780 and 81, while in the archbishop's employ, we should return to Aloysia Lange.

True, she was gone but far from forgotten. In order to get some sense of what she meant to him as musical Muse, consider: Mozart wrote seven magnificent concert arias specifically for Aloysia Weber, most of them after she became Aloysia Lange, including *Alcandro lo confesso*, K 294, which he wrote while still in Mannheim. Mozart wrote it to match her voice. That was in 1778 when perhaps they still had a chance at a life together, which of course is what Mozart had expected, Aloysia had doubted, and papa Leopold had dreaded.

The next year Wolfgang wrote the *Recitative and Aria for Soprano,* K 316. He wrote an additional five concert arias for Aloysia after she was married. In perfect irony, she may have had second thoughts about her marriage shortly after becoming Frau Lange. Mozart described Josef as a jealous fool, but then Lange would have had reason to be nervous with Mozart still clinging to hope of a reunion. In any event, Wolfgang did not finish the work until after the couple's separation. "Perhaps he intended it as sort of 'double bar,' symbolizing the end of his relationship with her."[14] Yet the aria he wrote for her in January of 1783, *Mia speranza adorata,* k 416, which is the grand scene of farewell, suggests that Aloysia was not gone from his heart and mind. The word *"speranza"* means hope, and Mozart must have retained some. "[I]t reveals clearly that neither the voice nor the artistry of Aloysia – and perhaps not even their possessor – had yet become a matter of complete indifference to Mozart."[15]

We now come back to the Salzburg epoch. Mozart was discouraged by the virtual bondage in which he felt Archbishop Hieronymus Colloredo now held him. He felt his pay was too modest, at 500 gulden per year; his freedom to perform apart from the cleric's dictates was curtailed. Mozart could not even travel as he saw fit, his access all but denied to opportunities to write opera, his true compositional joy. Mozart did travel briefly to Munich, on his boss's orders, then on to Vienna. There, as if the fates could not be more meddlesome, was the Weber family again, or what remained of them. Fridolin Weber had died, and of course his Aloysia was gone. Wolfgang moved in as a star border. He found a few developments in the city working in his favor, some certainly not. Mozart's opera *Idomeneo* was a grand success, in 1781, at the Residenz Theater in Munich. Elector Karl Theodor praised him and his talent. Praise was not all he wanted or expected. No one offered young Mozart the so-called keys to the city. The adulation over this small opera actually only hastened his anticipation of moving on with his career. Such acclimation may also have underscored his much delayed, personal need to be apart from his cloying father and what he again saw as the disagreeable tones of his native town.

In May of the same year Mozart and his cranky boss the archbishop had their culminating row, the latter calling the young composer "dreadfully conceited," adding that he was a "knave, a dissolute fellow and a vagabond."[16] Mozart resigned even as the cleric and political leader of Salzburg was making plans to dismiss him. When he left Wolfgang was not so much escaping Colloredo and the restrictions the cleric was placing on Mozart's career as he was escaping the drama with which his father was insisting that he continue to struggle. Now he would give up "his dependency [on] the family [to seek] his place as a creative individual in a distant city."[17] He did not have far to look to regain his optimism and ambition to excel.

Even though Aloysia was out of reach, Mozart had strong feelings for the Weber family; and there were still three daughters at home. Josepha and Sophie were unsuitable for a number of reasons, but eighteen-year old Constanze was available; she was a decent singer, at that. We should also note that Frau Weber was still conniving to suitably place her daughters and, with Fridolin inconveniently dead, financial prospects mattered even more. We find that Maria Cäcilie Weber, now head of the household, had come to think, on taking a closer look, that this young Mozart "showed signs of becoming a celebrity."[18]

Presumably the composer did not move in with the Webers with any clear intention of making Constanze his wife, though he almost certainly had a few short-term plans for her. The longer he stayed at the house, ineffably named *Zum Augen Gottes* (At The Eye of God), the more it seemed apparent that something was going on. Frau Weber had played her hand well, sensing that, as gossip turned to scandal, her now "compromised" daughter would have to be married soon. Uncomfortable with the force of popular opinion in Vienna, Mozart wrote to Leopold that he was again considering marriage, then taunting him with the ambivalent post script "God did not give me my talent to hang it around a woman's neck."[19] We have to wonder exactly what Wolfgang did expect to come of his comfortable proximity to the alluring young woman.

While biding his time and perhaps toying with his father, Wolfgang was composing *The Abduction from the Seraglio*, which has also been translated as "The Elopement from the Harem." His opera the previous year was one of only a few pieces he completed, besides five violin sonatas. The year 1782 promised to be far more productive for Amadeus Mozart, perhaps because he was feeling more settled and was surely more focused, apart from both Colloredo and Leopold. In fact, by the end of the year he would also have completed his highly regarded *Symphony No 35 in D major*, K 385, the Haffner. What seems remarkable about the piece is that he wrote it rather quickly – that summer – and did so at the request of his father to honor a family friend's rise to and celebration of nobility.[20]

Prophetically, 1782 was the year of Mozart's own elopement. As for the reception of *Seraglio*, his first full-length German opera, which opened in July of 1782, it was widely performed and acclaimed. In the first couple of months it played in Prague, Frankfurt, Mannheim, Leipzig, and Bonn. The opera finally made it to Salzburg two years later. For the composer, fawning over a woman he loved, as well as finding the acclaim he needed and deserved, his world was nearly complete. At age twenty-six, Mozart was internationally famous. A few elemental parts of life remained unsettled. Wolfgang had had some awkward business to conclude with his father, who was simply not about to approve of Constanze Weber.

Because we are weighing the relative timbre and import of Muses, the more important question might be: what kind of wife was this woman and how would she impact her husband's music? We find "[t]he composer was at this time deeply enamored with Mlle Constanze Weber, and [it is] this attachment to her that supplied him with subjects of the impassioned airs which his work required."[21] Such straight-forward biography was initially thought to refer to his work on his opera *Idomeneo*, but has been subsequently clarified to pertain to his *Seraglio* opera. We'll see why in a moment.

By December, Wolfgang had convinced himself that he was truly in love and must act on this exciting self knowledge – family be damned. Did Constanze love him? It's a good question to ponder for a moment. Many biographers suggest that, if so, it was not in any mature sense of the word. Constanze was a bit of an odd bird, and even Wolfgang thought her a bit bohemian. But she captivated him; come to that she delighted him. Wolfgang wrote to Leopold that he would marry her. Yes. His mind was made up. The old man's reaction was not surprising, writing that such a move would turn Leopold and Nannerl "into beggars."[22]

Without question, the marriage itself destroyed any remaining family fabric. Leopold had been clear that Mozart must be the family provider. After all, what had Anna Maria died for? Leopold was relentless on this point. How could the young man realistically work with such distractions as a wife would bring? Mozart was never more certain of his decision, and is said to have remarked, "since I could not have one sister, I married the other." Mozart and Aloysia had fallen apart three years before the nuptials with Constanze. This would seem to be a long time to have kept a back up plan, much less a wife, on hold.

The follow on question: Was Constanze a good match for him? Mozart may have been trying to have it both ways – the dutiful and practical son, as well as the smitten romantic, when he wrote to Leopold: "She has no wit, but she has enough common sense to enable her to fulfill her duties as wife and mother… I love her and she loves me with all her heart. Tell me whether I could wish myself a better wife."[23] Not only did papa Mozart not give his blessing he wrote immediately to say that he and Constanze must never expect any financial support from that quarter. He had just disinherited his only son.

Wolfgang Amadeus Mozart and Constanze Weber were married in Vienna at St. Stephen's Cathedral on 4 August 1782. Their first child, Raimund Leopold, was born the next June. Tragically, the child died just two months later. Only two of their six children lived – the last was born the same year as Mozart's death, and the paternity of that last child remains in question. More on this scandalous bit of history shortly.

Constanze's love for the young composer, or surely his for her, had another major impact on the man's music. Mozart made a promise to himself that if he succeeded in getting married, something he was uncertain Leopold would let him pull off, and if he might thus celebrate his maturity and agency as a man he would write a special work of thanksgiving. He did. This would be the glorious *Mass in C minor*, K 427, performed on the 26th of October, 1783, with Constanze singing the soprano part.[24] Wolfgang had his vindication. Biographer Maynard Solomon is clear in his recognition of the meaning of this particular mass. "It is written to glorify Constanze; it is her *Magnificat* … [and] it surely stands as one of the most sublime compositions ever written as a gift to a beloved person."[25]

Now Mozart enters into what is arguably the flood season of his composition. He is happily married, more self-confident than he had perhaps ever been. He takes from Constanze a measure of strength and poise he was denied by his own father, who in his turn had never reconciled with his mother for what she had found to be a poor marriage. For her part, it must be said that Constanze fulfilled as much as any woman ever did the true meaning of Muse. Mozart had his inspiration. Could he keep her?

From the winter of 1782-83 to the spring of 1786 Mozart wrote fourteen piano concertos, mostly for specific engagements. His two symphonic pieces were the so-called *Haffner*, discussed above, and the *Linz* Symphony. He also wrote six String Quartets, their Köchel listings 421, 428, 458, 464 and 465, completing the last of them in January 1785. Wolfgang subsequently dedicated them to his beloved friend Franz Joseph Haydn.

It was a busy time for a composer coming to the height of his powers. Recall that the work that anchored 1782 was *The Abduction from the Seraglio*. This opera was one of his biggest successes, though not financially so. He did make important contacts and fraternal liaisons. The composer wrote "a great deal of Masonic music dating from 1785 [to] round out Mozart's production for these years."[26] The Masonic connection would prove even more important than the offers of gainful work. In a few short years the wife of a brother Mason would turn the composer's comfortable world upside down.

Early in this flood period of composition, Mozart must have felt some lingering obligation to try to repair the damage done to his first family, owing to his much disputed independence. In July of '83 the Mozarts returned briefly to Salzburg to visit Leopold and Nannerl. Neither of them was ever warm to the guileless Constanze, and Nannerl was actually rude to her. Worse, while there the young parents got the horrible news, as reported above, that their infant Raimund had died. The child had been left in the care of a nursemaid.

Perhaps the composer expected to solidify his maturity in the eyes of his father, making whatever peace must be made with the estranged Salzburg Mozarts. But the effort came to naught. Wolfgang and Constanze left Salzburg the next day to make their way home to Vienna, stopping enroute in Linz for three weeks. It would be the last time Mozart would ever see his sister. There was now but one woman in Wolfgang's life.

Returning to his work done to commemorate a special occasion, Mozart wrote his *Symphony No 36 in C*, the Linz, K 425, because he wanted something fresh to give the people of the city. This was the first of his Haydn-like symphonies, prefacing "the first movement with a solemn introduction."[27] The remainder of his symphonies would suggest he had studied what Haydn had to teach.[28] They stayed three weeks in Linz before getting back to Vienna in November.

Vienna was a strange and uncomfortable place, and the Mozarts moved again in January of 1784, into the inner city, as Wolfgang was completing his *Serenade in B flat for Winds*, the so-called *Gran Partita*; immediately to begin his thematic catalogue. In March alone he completed two piano concerti – K 450 and 451 – and the *Quintet in E flat for Piano and Winds*. The next month Mozart wrote another *Concerto for Piano* and the *Sonata in B flat for Keyboard and Violin*, the "*Strinasacchi*," K 454. He wrote the piece for the twenty year old Regina Strinasacchi, from Matua, whom Mozart much respected as a violinist. She was not a Muse; he had no particularly romantic feelings for her. But he respected her talent and he accompanied her in the first performance of the piece that April. This was one of the very few times he dedicated an original composition to any woman with whom he was not at least a bit in love.[29] A point of clarification: musical dedications do not necessarily suggest any strong personal bond. Many composers wrote music and dedicated the works out of respect, sometimes even for political advantage. Mozart's dedications usually suggested something more. When he dedicated he intended to convey something extra, something *mit pradikät* – truly special.

To equivocate just a bit, this does not include the *Concerto in B flat for Piano,* the so-called Paradis, which Mozart wrote for his most remarkable student, the blind mystic we know as Maria Theresa von Paradis. We do not know if Mozart had any special feelings for her, other than tremendous admiration. The music now known as his *Piano Concerto No 18,* K 456, however, is surely one his most sublime compositions. Most of Mozart's pupils were young women. By actual count, thirteen of the known sixteen pupils were women, though Wolfgang is thought to have had an affair with only one, that being his fellow Mason's wife, Magdalena Hofdemel.[30]

We'll return shortly to Frau Hofdemel and her outsized contribution both to Mozart's happiness, to his music, to his angst, and to the confusing last few months of his life.

At least four of the women Wolfgang was tutoring at this time were aristocrats and they tended to provide him some steady income as a teacher. As for how and with whom Mozart tended to fall in love, and would from time to time write or dedicate a composition for one of the young lovelies, we have an interesting assessment. The brother of one piano student said Mozart was always in love with one of his pupils. "We know that one of them, Josephine Auernhammer, was for a time in love with Mozart, but he did not find her physically attractive… [though] he dedicated six violin and piano sonatas to her (K 296, K 376-380)… The woman who was … acknowledged publicly, who inspired the greatest of Mozart's dedicated works, the 14th, 17th and 22nd Piano Concertos, [was] Barbara or Babette, Ployer." [31] Why Babette?

She had talent. Mozart had given her lessons in composition. It is also certain that he did not treat her as he did most of his other gifted and winsome students. Remember that Wolfgang was also drawn to talent, and the nineteen-year old Babette, whose uncle was a functionary of the Salzburg Court in Vienna, was certainly among the most gifted of his piano students. He was also attempting, for now, to be true to his wife. Be that as it may, Mozart wrote two of his most beloved piano concerti for Babette, number 14, in E flat (K 449), and the moody number 17, in G (K 453). Constanze seems to have been something of a fan, too, as she gave Babette a miniature water color portrait of her husband in 1795, four years after the composer's death. Wolfgang derived a lot of satisfaction from writing music for those he cared deeply about. Few men needed a Muse more than Wolfgang Amadeus.

Mozart wrote more music for Constanze, such as the partial sonata, k 404, which was intended to be jokey and a good humored comment on his wife's musical depth – or her lack of it. She was an able singer and could read music well enough, but she had no talent for composition. In all, his ten years with Constanze were mostly happy and highly productive. By most assessments, however, Constanze was never swept off her feet, so to speak, by the composer. She likely married him as much because it was her best chance for a successful marriage than because she loved him deeply. That said, Wolfgang's attraction to her is more complicated and involves the ghosts of the girl's big sister Aloysia, his own parents, and no doubt the romance that comes with a well-satisfied libido, self-confidence, and autonomy.

Back to Constanze: "Only a fool, her mother must have told her, would throw away this golden opportunity. So when finally she found herself married to Wolfgang, the man whom her own talented sister had rejected, she no doubt resolved to do what she could to make him happy."[32] Meanwhile, Mozart worried about money. His *Seraglio*, though a popular success, did not produce the successive appointments he had expected. At this point he was largely supporting himself and Constanze by his earnings from the piano concertos and from teaching. Mozart spent much of 1783 and '84 writing and performing for subscription series in Vienna. They, too, were well attended, but the money never quite added up to what it should. The couple almost always had difficulty making ends meet.

Wolfgang needed other stimuli, both social and professional. Constanze could inspire him only so far. She was not his intellectual equal. Besides the *Mass in C Minor,* with its incomplete Credo and no obligatory *Agnus Dei,* Mozart also wrote and dedicated a series of vocal exercises for her, K 393, as well as the *Sonata for Violin and Piano,* K 403, and the incomplete "joke" sonata mentioned before, also for violin and piano, K 404. He wrote the aria for soprano for her, K 440, the next year. These are all not only light pieces, but by most accounts they are almost inconsequential. By 1784, only two years after they were married, Wolfgang apparently needed more – more vigorous companionship.

Mozart joined the Masonic lodge in Vienna in December of 1784, quickly rising in stature. His next major breakthrough was just ahead, and it was another opera – a well funded opera. The composer began work on *The Marriage of Figaro*. In spite of some dire predictions from papa Leopold, ever the pessimist, this opera was a huge success. There is something about its libretto that seems particularly engaging in a way that, perhaps, reflects on Mozart's thinking about marriage.

"As Michael Levey says in his biography of Mozart," quoting from Carr, "this opera is the 'marriage of so much… a marriage of words and music which makes it probably the most perfect of all [of Mozart's] operas." He continues, "[a] marriage of love is meant to be a marriage of true minds as well."[33] But Wolfgang and Constanze were far from being creative equals. Nevertheless, she continued to be the nearly perfect wife and now mother of their child Karl Thomas, born in September of 1784.

For the time being, the man was able to finesse any shortfalls he felt Constanze may have apart from her evident domestic skills. The couple left for Prague and were warmly received in the Bohemian capital. *Figaro* became a Czech standard for the next year, until Mozart gave the world *Don Giovanni* the next; *Don Giovanni* has played almost continuously in Prague ever since. The Czechs took to Mozart as a native son. Acclimation was nice; the composer needed more.

Three months later they returned to Vienna, richer by some 1000 gulden, and the thirty-one year old composer was more famous than ever. Nothing seemed out if reach. By now his impresario years were behind him. He was his own master, but he had to rely more and more on theatrical producers. His income never seemed quite enough. Then more tragedy; Constanze lost another baby, and then yet another. Wolfgang's father Leopold died in May of 1787. They had never truly reconciled. This was the lowest period in his mature life. Things were about to become far more complicated, however – complicated by another woman.

The composer began to borrow money from his Masonic brother, Michael Puchberg. Why he was so broke is not obvious. Some say Mozart gambled, but there is nothing conclusive on that count. We do know that by late summer of 1788, Constanze was not well. She wanted to take a "cure" at the health resort in Baden, and Mozart had to borrow money again from Puchburg to pay for it. During the year he had asked his friend four times for money. Then, in early 1789, while working on his new opera, which was prophetically named *Cosi Fan Tutte* (K

588), loosely "That's What They All Do," Mozart asked another Mason brother for financial help. The man's name was Franz Hofdemel, whose beautiful and vivacious young wife Magdalena was one of Mozart's students.

Timing is important now. We find some speculation that Constanze may have been straying. Or Mozart thought she was. Mozart chastised her for being "too loose." He wrote her in Baden to say "I do wish sometimes you would not make yourself so cheap. You are too free and easy with ... [the name has been deleted in the letter]. In the same letter Mozart told Constanze that she should not torment herself or him with 'unnecessary jealousy.'"[34]

Constanze was thought to be particularly fond of Franz Xavier Süssmayr, perhaps Mozart's closest and most capable piano and composition student. Could the man Constanze Mozart was too free with, in fact, be the young Süssmayr? In May of the same year Mozart wrote again to ask his wife to consider appearances. Was Baden a romantic get away or only a health spa? Constanze visited there regularly, and it could not have been cost free. Her doctor had recommended a series of such treatments. Meanwhile, Wolfgang was busy sorting out his own problems.

In October of 1790 Mozart followed his new opera to Frankfurt. He had already played Berlin. Frankfurt audiences enjoyed another round of *Figaro*, and Mozart played two of his newer piano concerti.

During this tour his letters home to Constanze took on a more introspective and even a forlorn tone. Wolfgang told her in early October "to me everything is cold – cold as ice. Perhaps if you were with me ... But as it is everything seems so empty."[35] He implored her by letter to "love me half as much as I love you."

When Mozart returned to Vienna in mid-November, Constanze was pregnant again. We find "[Mozart] had been away for seven weeks; Constanze's baby was born on July 26, 1791. Conception, therefore, probably occurred towards the end of October, 1790. In the last week of the month, Mozart left Mannheim and traveled to Munich ... Staying with Constanze at the time was the twenty-year old Süssmayr. The baby was to be named Franz Xavier Wolfgang Mozart."[36] Wolfgang Mozart was nowhere near his wife at the time she would logically have conceived. Of course, any reproductive math we might do now, any interpretation as to who did what to whom, seems a bit tawdry. If there was any question as to who was little Franz's father no Vienna tabloid announced it to the world. The infant was said to have Mozart's ears!

Professionally, the year 1790, one year from his untimely death, was one of Mozart's least productive. Besides the opera *Cosi Fan Tutte* we have only three string pieces. The King of Prussia set, *String Quartets* K 589 and 590, joining one written the year before, were subsequently dedicated to King Friedrich Wilhelm of Berlin. "These are three works originated under the most dreadful spiritual oppression, and yet they rise to the heights of pure felicity.[37] Without question Mozart was combating depression, and it was not only about his finances. Constanze, he realized, was almost certainly having an affair with young Süssmayr.

In his final year Mozart found another creative spark, turning around sharply from his previous off-year. His productivity soared with two more operas, including *La Clemenza de Tito*, first performed September 6th, *and The Magic Flute*, which premiered on September 30th, about two months before his passing. There was a great celebration of *Magic Flute* by all parties. Perhaps Mozart decided that he would not suffer alone. He had cut back on his teaching load, retaining only two students. The one we are interested in was the beautiful Frau Hofdemel. All the while, Constanze Mozart was frequently at Baden, even as her husband grew lonelier, more circumspect. Was he also growing impatient?

Early in 1791, Mozart was working on what would be his final piano concerto, a work in B flat major. We know it as his *Piano Concerto No 27*, k 595. One biographer keenly describes this work: 'The intimate feeling makes almost chamber music of it … It is generally agreed Mozart composed it for his own use, but there is no proof of this, and the existence of cadenzas and its introspective character would lead us to think that it had been produced for a pupil.'"[38] For a pupil? "This concerto is one of the most romantic creations in the whole history of art. It is great night music, inspired by love from the first quiet, seductive notes to the last…"[39] That this concerto was written for Magdalena is, perhaps, just speculation. Wolfgang would probably not have been so bold as to dedicate it to her outright, given that people were aware that Constanze and Süssmayr were now chummy. Richard Osbourne, in his program notes on the *Deutsche Grammophone* label of Clara Haskil's skillful performance of the piece, calls it "intensely personal." He suggests "lurking just below the music's sweetly reasonable surface, there are dissonances as painful as any in tonal music."[40] Music was often Mozart's catharsis.

By mid-July Mozart was writing to his wife asking if she might not want to remain a bit longer in Baden. As his hero Ferrando remarks in the opera *Cosi Fan Tutte*, "[w]hen the heart is nourished with hope and love, no other joy is needed." Thus was Mozart in love with two women. *Che complicazione*! The composer may have thought he had found respite and reconciliation in his love for Magdalena. It could not last. That fast, the opera in which Mozart had taken the lead was over.

Wolfgang Mozart died on 5 December 1791, apparently of liver failure and complications from his repeated bouts of rheumatic fever. His magnificent *Requiem Mass*, K 626, was missing a few necessary parts, including the lacrimosa. Prized student and once-trusted friend Franz Xavier Süssmayr finished the work from Mozart's notes, although Constanze was ambivalent about giving him the work. It is hard to say why. Ironically, no one besides Constanze was closer to the composer than Franz Xavier, unless of course it was Magdalena Hofdemel.

There were more complications as to whatever was going on, and with whom. The day after Mozart's passing, Franz Hofdemel was found dead by his own hand. He had severed his throat, but not before attempting to kill his wife Magdalena, who was badly cut by a razor "about the face, neck, shoulder and arms." Her life was saved; she was in the fifth month of her pregnancy.[41]

Some said the woman was pure trouble. Even Beethoven, who had met Mozart in 1789, gave credence to the affair of Mozart and Magdalena by saying he would not play in her presence, perhaps blaming her for the master's fall.[42]

The Vienna newspapers had little to say directly about any illicit romance, but such news apparently traveled in the inner circles just as well. In closing, we learn that "to Mozart, the ideas of love and betrayal, marriage and infidelity, unfortunately stood in close proximity to one another... Uncertainty was the fuel for what, in the end, became a restive quest. The pattern of an insatiable need meeting an insufficient response never found closure."[43] The epitaph of the greatest musical genius of all time was, perhaps, that he never found closure.

Whatever his confusion, his sadness, his uncertainty, or justification for his own behavior, Mozart gave the world music that has never been surpassed. Unquestionably, the willful, the charming, the enormously gifted and the selfish women in his life had no small part in the glorious results.

Bartok's muse, Stefi Geyer (1907)

Beethoven's muse and possibly his "Immortal Beloved" Antonie Brentano

Clara Schumann, muse to two men, husband Robert and Johannes Brahms.

Harriet Smithson was Hector Berlioz's great muse.

Chopin's infamous Aurore Dupin, known to the world as George Sand.

No muse meant more to a man than Mahler's lovely and beguiling Alma Schindler.

Here's the quirky, flirty Constanze (Weber) Mozart.

Wagner needed many muses: Mathilde Wesendock was both talented and beautiful

Arthur McMaster

CHAPTER THIRTEEN

PUCCINI, Giacomo (1858 – 1924); Italian

"Puccini's …was a splintered, neurotic personality, feminine in many ways and rooted in man's strongest biological urge – sexuality."[1]

Giacomo Antonio Domenico Michele Secondo Maria Puccini was born to a large family in Lucca, Italy, three days before Christmas, in the year his friend Ruggiero Leoncavallo was born. Both would write an opera, would do so, in fact, within one year of each other. They would give their work the name *La Boheme*. But only one *La Boheme* would be a major success, as would only one of the young contemporaries.

The Puccini's of Lucca were a musical family, long on tradition, disturbingly short on longevity. Giacomo's father, Michele, like his father before him, was an organist and composer of, mostly, sacred music. The director of Lucca's Cappella Municipale, he died at the age of fifty-one, leaving the eight year old Giacomo the undisputed man of the house. Giacomo's paternal grandfather, Domenico, had died at the age of forty-four, the vessel of his passing a tainted sorbet. Apparently, Lucca took it for granted that Giacomo would become organist and choirmaster, ready at the appointed time to fill his father Michele's post.[2] Or maybe he would not. In fact, Puccini never did become a particularly distinguished organist, though he played it well enough to be a competent church musician. Giacomo's familiarity with the instrument did help him in his early ecclesiastical compositions. Of course, what is opportunity if not the chance to err? Puccini had many such chances.

His organ play during church services got the eighteen-year old into hot water with some clergy and even more so with his sister, Iginia, who was about to become an Augustinian nun.

It seems that Puccini was chastised for too much, or for inappropriate, improvisation on the sacred music, including snatches from Tuscan folk music.[3]

The young man's siblings – he had four older sisters – were dutiful and helped Mamma Albina; but Giacomo, said to have enjoyed a "restlessness of character." Albina records that her son was "pure music, pure jackass."[4]

Giacomo's Uncle Fortunato was entrusted with the boy's initial musical training. Fortunato, however, did not prove to be particularly fortunate for the boy and promptly gave up on his nephew, pronouncing him untalented. Albina saw the limitation in her brother-in-law, not in her son; she looked elsewhere for suitable help. Giacomo resumed his studies with another local instructor before coming under the care and attention of talented teachers in Milan.

Over the next four years, Giacomo was in and out of formal study programs, taking much of his instruction from Milan's esteemed professor, Amilcare Ponchielli. Unquestionably, opera was Giacomo Puccini's reason to write music, his call to create. When he first heard Verdi's *Aida*, in Pisa, he knew that this would be his life's work. He told his friend Carlo Carignani, who would later become an important arranger of vocal scores, "when I heard Aida I felt that a musical window had opened for me."[5]

The first opera contest Giacomo entered came to little and he won nothing. Undeterred, Giacomo returned to Milan with renewed dedication and set his mind to opera. It took a couple more years, but by 1884 Puccini had finished *Le Willis*, or *Le Villi*, as it is more often known, his first critical acclaim. Verdi heard of the work's reception and added his own complements to the reviews of Italy's most important music critics. Puccini was delighted to find himself being compared to Massenet and to Georges Bizet, twenty years his senior. It was a fine start for a student composer. As soon as he began to find success in opera he wrote virtually nothing else.

Soon he would meet the woman, the one woman in his life, who would factor the most heavily, though not by and large positively, in his career and on his psyche. The young man from Lucca was about to encounter a married woman, someone whom he likely knew even before she was married, someone Giacomo could never quite forget. Enter Elvira (née Bontari) Gemignani.

Exactly how or when he met her we cannot be certain. What seems evident is that Giacomo's relationship with Elvira, indeed his utter fascination with her, seems to have achieved critical mass upon the death of his mother. The young composer had been especially close to Albina – he was her favorite. When she died in July, 1884, Giacomo, perhaps now understanding that he was in every sense on his own, decided to make the young woman he had become so infatuated with his paramour. She already had two children. Theirs would be, for the next sixteen years, a bizarre on-again, off-again relationship. Even after they finally wed it was frequently more "off-again."

We surmise that Giacomo was loath to destroy her marriage. After all, her husband Narciso Gemignani was a Lucca classmate. Puccini could not stay away, even though he often left her to find the peace and quiet to compose. Then they had a child together. It was as if neither cared for society's conventions. What was it about her?

Elvira was, "by all accounts, a woman of striking beauty, tall and full in figure ... a face of classical proportions, dark shining eyes and rich, dark-blond hair... [she] was, in short, a woman of impressive appearance."[6] If it was something other than looks that struck Giacomo so profoundly it was certainly not her counsel or sympathetic manner. Often during their tempestuous relationship, both before and after they finally married, Giacomo found solace and comfort in other women. Elvira was the one constant love of his life, but he had many less than permanent relationships, too. Women were highly attracted to his dark, good looks, and his brooding manner. Yet, there was something about Elvira he found different. They acted like husband and wife for years before they were. It is inconceivable how her husband tolerated such a bizarre and truly emasculating situation.

Giacomo and Elvira began living together when the Gemignani children were still quite young. We wonder if it was the fact that Elvira was not truly available that made her so appealing to the besotted young composer. Too, she did have some musical talent. Could she inspire his work? Only barely. In a manner of speaking, many of his dalliances, however, did so inspire, and most of the fellow's other women did so more than Elvira. Let's examine Puccini's many Muses one at a time.

The affair began innocently enough. Narciso Gemignani wanted his wife to have music lessons, and she agreed to study voice and piano. Her teacher was – no surprise here – Giacomo Puccini. How many love affairs began at the piano bench? More than half of the thirty or so men whose stories are recounted in this book found at least a temporary fascination with a piano student or composition pupil. Genius or talent comes first; then one or the other is charmed by a brilliant smile; a few kindnesses; an unexpected touch. Romance follows apace.

It was a fateful encounter for all parties, but at first the relationship between Giacomo and Elvira was ardent and ripe with inspiration for the composer, although the repercussions in Lucca were uncomfortable. The couple began to live together, openly. "Elvira's elopement with Giacomo obviously created many problems. His family, always somewhat strait-laced, was shocked and outraged. For the rest of his life, Puccini was virtually an exile from Lucca... And most pressingly, he [now] found himself with a family to support"[7] Cut off from his first family, Puccini found himself in tough financial circumstances. He occupied his mind with composition, making more changes to *Le Villi (the Witches)* – making it, in fact, a two-act production, and working, in the new year of 1885 on his second opera, entitled *Edgar*.

The couple's child was named Antonio, no doubt satisfying relatives on all sides, if not the village vicar. Now, with a small family, Giacomo felt compelled to succeed immediately. After all, Giacomo, at thirty years of age, was not getting any younger. *Edgar* opened on Easter Sunday, 21 April 1889. "In those years, Puccini and Elvira lived simply, for the most part in Milan... [and the composer now] pinned all his hopes on *Edgar's* success. They were dashed by the Scala audience's tepid reception of the ambitious new piece."[8] The composer's publisher,

Giulio Ricordi, stood by him. He told Giacomo to stop worrying and get back to work. Puccini did just that, quickly deciding on his next subject. It would be Abbé Prévost's story of another ill-conceived love. Here, a young French woman is beguiled into foregoing her unromantic status quo for a charming, duplicitous Chevalier. As she is proven unlucky in love and devoid of common sense, it is only natural that the duped girl will die, destitute, in strange circumstances. With shades of Charles Dickens's Martin Chuzzlewit, the deluded youth winds up, desperate, in the swamps of Louisiana. Martin, of course, overcomes the mendacity of the locals and makes it back to England. Manon, not so fortunate, dies abroad. But then Italian opera, whatever its genesis, is usually at least as melodramatic as Victorian literature.

Meanwhile, while *Edgar* needed a lot of work, the creative appeal of this new opera intrigued Puccini. Giacomo would divide his time between them, but could he realistically work on both? Perhaps it was the difficult financial situation in which Elvira and her man found themselves. Signor Puccini told his confidants that he needed a breakthrough; he wondered if he could ever win. It was in June of 1890 that Giacomo met with a casual acquaintance, the dramatist, soon to be librettist, Marco Praga. Puccini told Praga what he needed for his next opera. Then, after securing the talent of a well-known Milanese poet, Domenico Oliva, the three worked for months on the music, text, and orchestration of the opera that many still regard as Puccini's best work.

Elvira stayed close by, helping as she could with the early drafts. It was out of her hands, however, when the work fell apart as both collaborators lost heart with all the changes demanded by Puccini. Still tinkering with a revised and much improved *Edgar* in 1892, Puccini turned to his friend Ruggiero Leoncavallo, composer of *Pagliacci*, written the same year. Puccini also enlisted the help of Luigi Illica, to replace the departed Praga and Olivia. Giacomo was still working on revisions to *Edgar*, the opera that had caused him so much frustration. In part, he needed the money as much as he needed respect for artistic achievement he felt was his due.

Puccini prepared for the premiere of *Manon Lescaut* in Turin, in October of that year. Blessedly, *Manon* opened to tremendous reviews. Puccini wrote to Elvira that he already realized, even before the opening night of *Manon*, he'd written something extraordinary. People in the company had 'gone mad' over his music. His triumph complete, he had to share it with her. "For Puccini, his long wait was over, and he had won at last."[9] Puccini and Elvira were now financially well off enough for him to buy a villa in the small town of Torre del Lago – by the lake. He lived here for most of the rest of his life, and when not composing he boated and hunted. But Puccini was a man seldom satisfied with his situation, be it personal or professional. There were too many distractions. Not a few of them were female.

The composer found it difficult to remain true even to this woman with whom he had had such an exhilarating and scandalous relationship. Giacomo had hundreds of affairs of the heart. Was he incapable of fidelity? It would not be hard to build a case that he was so bereft. When Elvira took umbrage at his libidinous wandering, Giacomo wrote to her saying, "Good God! The world is full of such things. All artists cultivate such gardens in order to delude themselves that they are not finished and old and torn by strife."[10] The composer's boastful confession of his garden-tilling is particularly interesting. Puccini explained, quite matter of factly, that as an artist he required the passion of an affair to energize his music. In any event, his publishers complained that he was losing strength to compose by always exercising his libidinous nature. He must have been torn by such a dilemma. Actually, Giacomo could have both.

"The publisher was wrong. Puccini's constant quest for the perfect mistress merely inspired him. [His friend and publisher] Ricordi also tried, with Elvira's collusion, to get Puccini's sisters to intercede, but not even Iginia, who had become a nun, was able to win him back…"[11] In fact, while still with Elvira and their illegitimate son Tonio, as they called the boy, Giacomo's next adventure began with a young woman from Turin. We know her only as Corinna – her last name is unknown. Corinna was evidently a beautiful young schoolteacher. They met in Pisa, in 1900, evidently at the train station where he flirted with her while waiting his train back home. Instantly infatuated, he "took a house for her near Torre. Regretting the onset of old age, he complained [to her] about life with the grim Elvira…During one crisis he even decided to leave Elvira for her because she offered him love and inspiration."[12] Arguably, young Corinna became the source of inspiration for another story of amorous betrayal, and one of Puccini's best loved operas, *Madama Butterfly*. But this part of Puccini's story must wait.

Within three months of the successful opening of *Manon*, Giacomo announced his next major work, and by doing so he lost the friendship of a composer he had grown particularly close to. Leoncavallo was working on a score he, too, would call *La Bohème*. Each accused the other of being "inconsiderate." Who had the idea first? Each composer used his connections with key publicists to advance his claim. Both went forward. Only Puccini's *Bohème*, based on Henry Murger's more complex story, *Scènes de la bohème,* has stood the test of time. Accused of writing a series of what some critics called "little weepers," here, too, a confused young lady named Mimi must die. She perishes theatrically in the shabby flat of a serious but misunderstood and unlucky writer named Rodolpho. Here is a poet made to stand for all misunderstood and undervalued artists. Was Giacomo dispatching his ghosts? "True [to] the beating heart of La Bohème is Paris itself, which Puccini captured onstage by recalling his own memories of "Bohemian Life," his student days in Milan and his home turf, Lucca,"[13] where his relationship with Elvira had caused him to be, in many ways, cast away from so much that was important to him. Of course, he did have the comforts of Torre del Lago. Giacomo had only to be certain not to do anything to put undue strain on his "relations" with these neighbors.

At this point it would be useful to find and analyze some common ground in Puccini's mid-career work, up to and through *Butterfly*. It is equally important to ask: to what extent was his work truly autobiographical? Without a doubt, Puccini is venting his angst over his women. There is something particularly intriguing about Puccini's heroines, born with *Manon*, showing, as he says, certain shared qualities.[14] But the character is no classic heroine. Her demise is due largely to bad luck, not to some sense of duty or honor. Nevertheless, "[a]s Puccini's canon grew, Puccini's characters, in particular his heroines, deepened, though nearly all his heroines maintained that special, pathetic melancholy that is adumbrated [foreshadowed] in Manon and perfected in Mimi." Similarly, "[F]rom a strictly moral point of view, she shares Manon's dismissal of conventional propriety; and she has hardly met Rodolpho before she is coyly seducing him"[15] Puccini, it seems, is expiating, or exorcising, someone special – is it Elvira? Is it Corinna? This is an artist who values his freedom, even while justifying his extraordinary physical license. The letters he wrote to Elvira, explaining and exonerating himself, are the other side of the same coin. Giacomo Puccini sometimes got into serious difficulties undeservedly, or accidentally. By way of example, the next couple of years marked two or perhaps three of the most dramatic events in the composer's life.

In 1902, following a number of successful performances of *Tosca*, and with the money coming in, Giacomo's passion for motor-boats turned to motor-cars. In late February of 1903, Puccini had an appointment in Lucca to see a physician about a persistent sore throat. He was showing symptoms of the cancer that would kill him twenty years later. Their journey would take him from Milan to Lucca – from there they would continue on to Torre.

One account suggests that Giacomo, accompanied by Elvira and son Tonio, had stopped in Lucca to see the seriously ill Narciso Gemignani, perhaps to try to patch things up with his former friend, perhaps to discuss his will; but they met with hostility from relatives. Emotionally drained, they set out for their villa in Torre immediately. As night fell, they suffered a serious auto accident on a small country road. Their driver failed to negotiate a sharp turn and the car plunged down a gully. Elvira, Tonio, and the driver were shaken but unharmed, having been thrown from the car. Giacomo was found unconscious, pinned under the carriage. His recuperation was slow and painful. He never did recover full use of the fractured leg. Ironically, Elvira's husband died the next day. While Giacomo healed, the couple made plans to be married. Finally they'd make their union legal, especially so for the well being of their son. But he had a difficult time withdrawing his affections from Corinna, who was, incredibly, still in the picture. Evidently the young woman had fully expected Puccini to marry her. "Through it all," we are told, "it was evident, not least to Elvira, that Puccini loved Corrinna."[16]

Elvira was no one's fool, and she had a streak of vengeance in her as broad and strong as the Tuscan countryside. Elvira sought legal action against the younger woman, which was withdrawn when Giacomo committed to her alone. After the obligatory waiting period, the emotionally well-traveled couple was married. They had already decided to employ an additional staff member in their home, especially since Giacomo still suffered from limited mobility. Here things become even more complicated.

Doria Manfredi was the young village woman who came to work as a maid for the Puccini couple in Torre del Lago, in 1903. No one should have to put up with what this she was subjected to. Doria, or Dora, as her name is sometimes recorded, suffered for six years the groundless insults and torment of an ever-suspicious Elvira, who accused her of having an affair with wayward hubby Giacomo. Actually, Doria was never physically involved with him, but Elvira was playing the odds that somehow they were. She wrote letters to the girl's parents accusing Doria of adultery. After all, the composer had an active history that would suggest that he would seduce the young girl if given half a chance. He probably would have, if she had been interested in him. She was not.

Doria was sixteen years old when she joined the Puccini household staff. The woman even tried to get the village priest to ex-communicate Doria, as punishment for what Elvira was convinced were her sins with Giacomo. The young girl killed herself following a withering barrage of accusations by the crazed Elvira. She took poison and died three days later. An autopsy proved that the girl was "pure" at the time of her death. Her parents brought suit against Elvira. Mrs. Puccini was actually convicted, but the plaintiffs settled out of court for a tidy sum, all of which apparently drove Giacomo to despair and then promptly and, predictably, on to his next major romance. During the worst of the fiasco Puccini had threatened divorce, impossible; suicide, improbable; and then separation – uncomfortable. Giacomo did like being the man of the house. What's an artist tilling in the garden of inspiration to do?

Enter Sybil Seligman, wealth London socialite. Her husband was a financier with a focus decidedly elsewhere. Giacomo and Sybil met at Covent Gardens, following a performance of Puccini's latest opera, *Madam Butterfly*, the oh-so-heralded work inspired by Corinna. Here again, she was a woman of the arts and money; moreover, she had a faultless pedigree as a student of music.

Puccini's long-time friend and composer of "drawing-room songs," Paolo Tosti, at that time living in London, "had become much sought after as a singing-teacher. Tosti was music master to the Royal Family and one of his favourite pupils was Sybil Seligman, who had a contralto voice of exceptional beauty. She was passionately fond of opera, paid frequent visits to Italy, spoke fluent Italian, and kept open house for visiting Italian artists."[17] The lady had Puccini in her patrician sights.

Giacomo must have thought he had died and gone to heaven.

The composer's principal biographer says that their relationship, from the very beginning, was by no means platonic. Years later, after their big affair cooled, they remained good friends, and Sybil remained as well the one person to whom Giacomo could always turn for sympathy and understanding. He wrote to her regularly, she gave him advice and counsel. "A woman of remarkable intelligence and artistic feeling, Sybil became his mentor and confidant in many private and professional matters; she was his 'Sybil of Cumae' – 'the person who had come closest to understanding my nature,' as Puccini wrote to her."[18]

A Muse of the first order, Sybil began to read deeply into a good bit of literature she thought might be suitable for Puccini's use in opera. He rejected most of them, while apparently at least considering one or more works she suggested from Oscar Wilde, but Puccini already had ideas for the next major work, which would be *La Fanicula* – Belasco's raucous the *Girl of the Golden West*. Sybil Seligman had been on pretty solid ground; after all, as Wilde's *Salome* had recently been embraced by Richard Strauss, in 1905. Apparently, during the pinnacle of Puccini's *Tosca*, which had proven highly successful in 1900, and even before *Butterfly*; the composer was thinking of material that would lead him to the wild West melodrama. He needed some convincing. "In June [1906] Puccini was in London and, according to Vincent Seligman, it was [his mother] Sybil who tipped the scales in favour of the [Belasco] play and who commissioned an Italian translation of it. By the middle of July, Puccini made up his mind to set it to music… with the help of Sybil he at once set about procuring popular American music of the 1850s, as well as authentic Red Indian songs."[19] Puccini needed Sybil's trust, her support, and her caring demeanor, however, as much or more than he needed her as a research assistant. Clearly, she did far more for him in his work as a composer than Elvira ever managed to do.

The Girl of the Golden West opened at the Metropolitan Opera, in New York, when Giacomo was fifty-two years old; his career was at its height. The date was December 10, 1910. Enrico Caruso sang the autobiographical role of the larcenous Dick Johnson, who loves Minnie, the beguiling heroine. The opera hit most of the big houses in America, returning to Europe in the next year. When it opened at Covent Gardens, Giacomo sent a note to Sybil, thanking her for her part in the success, "gladdened by a letter from the gracious lady to whom he had dedicated the *Faniculla*."[20]

Puccini wrote a few smaller operas, if any Italian opera can ever be called small. In 1917, after a ten year hiatus, and while much of Europe again went off to war, he composed *La Rondine*, a work often called one of his least inspired efforts. Perhaps he was looking ahead to the innovative triptych he had wanted to write. Perhaps he was between his many inspirational women. If so, we would have to discount the effect on him of two mistresses.

Arguably the more significant was the German baroness, Josephine von Stengel, (or Stängel): at twenty-six, she was less than half Puccini's age. They met while she was separated from her husband, an army captain. "Their affair lasted at least six years… [even while] the composer was still exchanging love letters with Blanke [Blanka] Lendavi…"[21] Josi and Mucci, as she called him, were particularly close and affectionate. He certainly was finding none of that back home with Elvira; and his relationship with Sybil was now comfortably one of just close friends.[22]

The happy couple frolicked together in Munich and later in Viareggio, a small town near Lucca. Mucci was gambling that he and Josi would not be recognized here. They had already been discovered in Bayreuth by Cosima Wagner, insisting to her husband's friend that she be introduced to the young lady. Ever quick to deflect his peccadilloes from the public, Puccini actually denied to Cosima's face that he was, in fact, the famous Italian composer. It's a shame we don't have her record of their meeting.

When the war started the baroness von Stengel became, by birth and marriage, an enemy alien. That development did not seem to retard their ardor for one another. Josi talked of divorcing her husband, who was waging his own losing war against the allies. The much put upon Elvira was suspicious anyway, but became more so when Giacomo announced that he had to make more business trips to Switzerland. She may have put the authorities at the Italian consul in Lugano onto her husband.[23] From that action, and recognizing that Josi was a German and "a possible spy," Giacomo was denied further visas to Switzerland. Josi von Stengel may have been the one woman of the maestro's select circle to have actually cut her own deal. How so? In 1917 Puccini discovered that the baroness had become the mistress of an Italian army officer. That was the last of Josi. It was also the year of the relatively disappointing *La Rondine*. The next year brought his *Trittico*; it would be Puccini's penultimate work, although he continued to labor with revisions to *Rondine*.

We skip ahead now to the composer's final work, which also brings us to his final days. The great opera, unfinished by Puccini, is *Turandot*. Here, we also find our way back to the one young woman of his life he cared deeply for but with whom he did not have an affair. In her death, she gave him one of his most memorable characters.

Puccini is rightly given credit for having pushed the known boundaries of Italian opera. As the successor to Verdi, he went in directions not conceivable in the late nineteenth century. It was Verdi's *Aida*, which Giacomo saw in Pisa, in 1876, that convinced him his future lie in opera. Verdi, to his credit, worked in broader musical fields than did his recognized successor. But by 1904, Puccini had gone into new and unproven time zones with both *Butterfly*, and its disastrous showcasing at La Scala, and with *Faniculla*, which was, if nothing else, recognition of the coming American classical music scene.

Jürgen Maehder, the German musicologist, states "*Madama Butterfly*, [had] led him towards a new conception of theater, while distancing him from the operatic tradition in which his musical means of expression were firmly rooted."[24] Now *Turandot* was again a new beginning, "instead of aiming at psychological identification with the protagonist of the drama, this dramaturgy favored the intellectual fascination with different theatrical genres.... representing a conscious decision on Puccini's part to embark on a new type of theatricality."[25] Moreover, the opera became the means for the composer to come to closure with some unresolved emotions.

The protagonist in Carlo Gozzi's fable *Turandot* was familiar. Recall that the setting for *Butterfly* is Nagasaki. In this opera cruel Princess Turandot, in ancient China, is troubled by her three enigmas. She announces she would marry the suitor who can help her to unravel her three puzzles. Death to him who tries and fails! One man, one heroic, deposed prince named Calaf, will try. Predictably he has a young girl to help him. She is a humble, worthy slave-girl, a girl in service to a powerful family – her name is Liù – and she will destroy herself to save her master from certain doom. Her sacrifice offers what seems a way around the death edict for the young prince. And so, in a fascinating turn of events, the haughty princess and her lover are directly and safely united. Liù gives her life for their happiness, for their future. Anyone close to the Puccinis could not help but suggest the obvious connection to the ill-fated, pretty young Doria. The maid of Torre del Lago, in fact, lives forever as Liù, the slave-girl who committed suicide for love.

Puccini died of throat cancer in Brussels, where he had been ordered to go for surgery, on 29 November 1924. He was sixty-five years old. Puccini's on-again, off-again friendship with

Arturo Toscanini had been repaired, and Toscanini conducted the world premiere of the opera two years after the composer's death.[26] *Turandot* is for many opera lovers the man's greatest work, yet it remains something of an enigma it its own right. Left incomplete, as in Giacomo's personal life, was the grand duet of triumphal love between the man and the woman who simply did not know how to go about identifying and successfully securing their love.

Arthur McMaster

CHAPTER FOURTEEN

SCHUBERT, Franz Peter (1797 – 1828); Austrian

"If Schubert's contemporaries justly gazed in amazement at his creative power, what must we, who come after him, say, as we incessantly discover new works?"[1]

Beethoven served as his professional model, and no doubt influenced young Schubert in ways that reveal much about his compositional choices. In fact, Ludwig van Beethoven, we learn, was like a god to Franz Schubert, and in some ways their personal lives were nearly as conflicted as the other's. Beyond what we see in the young man from Vienna, recorded in a playful sketch drinking and singing with friends, however, there was a "darker Schubert" whom biographers are only beginning to come to grips with. His failed relationships with two women, women who significantly influenced his music, play no small part in the resultant duality of this most engaging, ill-fated man.

Franz was one of four surviving children from the tormented marriage of Franz Theodore and Elisabeth Schubert. Franz was close to his mother and apparently inherited her contemplative disposition, as his father was often portrayed as more taciturn and, slow to make allowances for the claim of genius.[3]

Franz's father, however, must get the credit for encouraging an interest in music and fostering a sense of family commitment to the art. Franz Theodor played a passable cello and he supported his sons in their interests. Franz's talent was evident to the family's church choirmaster, Michael Holzer, who tutored him in voice and violin for years, preparing him for the competition of 1808 to a prestigious music academy. Schubert won a scholarship to the Imperial and Royal Seminary, the *Stadtkonvikt*. Better than the free position, what Franz earned was a close familiarization with the music of Mozart and Beethoven, leading directly to Schubert's early and overwhelming interest in composition.

Franz Schubert was not particularly comfortable at the seminary, however, and he found it difficult to make close friends. To complicate matters, his father made it known that he did not expect, nor did he wish, for his son to make a life in music. Of Schubert's closest associates, one found him particularly introspective – this was not a surprise – and he wrote: "Even in his boyhood and youth Schubert's life was one of inner, spiritual thought, and was seldom expressed in words but, I would say, almost entirely in music." He added, "Even on walks which the pupils took together he mostly kept apart, walking pensively along with lowered eyes ... playing with his fingers as though on keys, completely lost in his own thoughts."[4]

Schubert's father's expectations notwithstanding, Franz's compositional skill and style were remarkable early. It would be fair to say that Schubert was an adolescent genius, as opposed to a child prodigy, as was Mozart. But when he came into his own as a composer, at the age of thirteen or fourteen, he seems to have had the powers of men twice his age. To the year 1811 belong "the first complete songs, his first orchestral work, an *Overture for Strings in C minor* [D8], a set of minuets for wind band, and a *Fantasie in C* minor for piano..."[5] He wrote a bit of church music in 1813, and then began an on-again, off-again student-teacher relationship with Antonio Salieri, who urged him to find composition models in Italian operas. The lessons were pro-forma, however, and hardly contributed to the remarkable growth Schubert was now able to demonstrate. In fact, as his principal biographer Brian Newbould makes clear, Schubert saw his future in the song potential of Goethe and Schiller, while Salieri' s frame of reference remained both limited and limiting.[6] Schubert knew, or he certainly suspected, he could do more.

Like Ludwig van Beethoven before him, Schubert was opening, or was perhaps deliberately moving, the gates of classical music. Unlike Beethoven, Schubert's direction was to "more vivid flights of fancy [and] the seeds of heart-on-sleeve Romanticism."[7] In his fifth year of study at the *Stadtkonvikt* he took a more definite interest in opera, and here Salieri certainly must have been a factor. According to his friend Josef von Spaun, Schubert was particularly interested in Mozart's opera *Die Zauberflöte*. This does not mean that he thought he was an operatic composer. But he had a good sense of what the challenges were to writing such large scale compositions. As a corollary benefit, Franz came to know and become much taken with young Anna Milder, who had a principal role in Glück's *Iphigenia*, composed in 1813. Fräuline Milder-Hauptmann became an important and influential friend and champion of Schubert's work.

That said, he still had much to learn, not only about musical composition but about the viscidities of everyday life. In 1812, as much of Europe again worried about Napoleon's ambition, Schubert's mother unexpectedly passed away. Her death was reported as "nervous fever," ironically this is the term which would be used only sixteen years later on Schubert's own death certificate.

Shortly thereafter, Franz received an ultimatum that his scholastic work must improve. With this news he opted to leave the *Stadtkonvikt*. To have stayed would have placed too great a demand on his time and energy in trying to pull up his grades in subjects he considered less important than his musical education – his true calling. Schubert was also ready, now at the age of sixteen, for romance.

In the autumn of 1813 Schubert entered the *Normalhauptschule*, though he did not lose any interest in his formal music training. In fact, he seems to have become more prolific. One reason for the spate of creativity seems to have been a soprano by the name of Theresa Grob. Schubert was, in the common use of the term, an avowedly religious man. How would Fräuline Grob affect his sense of piety and place?

The story goes like this: Franz was preparing to compose his first mass, to be written in honor of the centenary of the Liechtental church. But he had some trouble with parts of the early text, finding that the credo did not fit the music. "This [was] an almost inevitable conclusion to be drawn from free editing the mass text…" Supposedly he found the given words "musically unpromising."[8] He worked on the mass for months, finally getting the score together as he knew it must fit. Now he needed six soprano voices. Ms. Grob, whom he apparently had known for years, was offered the first soprano part. Enter dramatically the young lady who is recognized by nearly all of Schubert's biographers as the first and most ardent love of his short life.

The Grob family was friendly with the Schuberts. Theresa, who we know sang the key solo piece in his *Mass in F*, D105, had a voice that was hauntingly beautiful. The young people had worshipped together at the Liechtental church, where most if not all of Schubert's early masses were composed and performed. Theresa and the church came together, then, in a way so as to form a sense of great peace and joy. Until he got into his early twenties the church and this pretty, talented girl formed the center of Schubert's world. Franz was twice blessed for this combination. It would not always be so.

Theresa was two years younger than Franz, now nineteen. As an attractive young woman of seventeen she quickly became quite another kind of force in Franz's life. Theresa indicated that she might be more than a friend; the young composer was utterly infatuated. Theresa, it seems, had grown "from a child to a woman with an attractive high soprano voice. The affair developed over the next two years, and raised serious hopes of marriage."[9] But fate worked against them with Theresa's father's untimely death. Perhaps her mother saw emerging "family circumstances," including the need for a reliable income, as compelling. Their romance was derailed; the emotion, the passion, however, remained strong.

Whatever the source of difficulty, Schubert clung to the idea that there might be hope for them. He wrote on at least one occasion to his close friend Anton Holzapfel about his love for Theresa, making his serious intentions known. Schubert's own circumstances, specifically his limited capital, seemed to doom their union. Biographers recount Schubert's words: "I loved someone very dearly and she loved me too. For three years she hoped I would marry her; but I could not find a position which would have provided for us both."[10] More to the point, Austrian marriage rules on income, at the time, made their union nearly impossible.

Schubert wrote a good bit of music to and for Theresa, and likely even more of his songs, dating to 1816, were written with her inspiration. In fact, during the two years that comprise the height of their infatuation, if that is what it was, Franz was at his most creative – a period said to be "virtually unrivaled in the history of Western music."

Franz took inspiration from the poets Goethe, Klopstock and Stoll, among others. "His first Goethe song produced the extraordinary *Gretchen an Spinnrade* (D 118) first performed on 19 Oct 1814. The song is "remarkable not only for its conjuring up of a spinning wheel and its waves of crescendos but for Schubert's empathetic representation of a woman's feelings"[11] We must wonder how much young Schubert owed to Fräuline Grob for such inspiration. Peter Clive clearly attributes the song as being written for Theresa, and adds that Schubert wrote it "a few days after she had sung in the above-mentioned performance of the Mass D105."[12] Theresa is also thought to be the inspiration for *Stimme der Liebe*, (D187), composed in May, 1815. We do not know of any other *chords of love* young Franz might have then been playing in his head.

The work he turned to next, while its inspirational center is uncertain, offers the enchanting possibility of foreshadowing a life he would want to have with the one woman he loved. In the summer of 1815 Schubert wrote four operettas, including *Fernando* (D220), with its quintessentially romantic plot. It is grand music for theater, and the plot is rich in metaphor. In the storyline, following much struggle and overcoming family obstacles, the troubled couple is united in marriage. Schubert attends to the "intimate emotional focus"[13] of the tale. Franz knew what he needed. Meanwhile, Theresa's mother was not yielding.

Schubert was undeterred by the disagreeable Frau Grob's intransigence, still determined to earn enough money so that he might legally marry Theresa. If nothing else would come of their liaison, Franz recognized the awakening of his own independence and his substantial possibilities as a professional musician. While Schubert continued to work for his father as a staff faculty member he decided to move in with his friend Franz Schrober. This was apparently in the late months of 1816, and there he began such highly celebrated works as *Der Tod das Mädchen*, *Die Forelle*, and *An der Musik*.

Schubert returned to his parental home again shortly thereafter, but he had proven something to himself about self-sufficiency and agency. Finally, when he left for good, it was as much a break from the peculiar demands of teaching, for which he was not particularly well-suited, as it was an acceptance of his "life dedicated to art." The Theresa Grob affair was not over, but by now Franz likely had serious doubts as to its longevity. If so, his intuition was correct. Franz did what he could; he wrote music and earned all the money he might to prove his viability as a husband.

Their affair was doomed, however, and he seemed to sense it, though the real reasons were beyond Schubert's control. It was the "prosperous man" alternative all over again, the same shadowy nemesis that had defeated Mozart and his Aloysia. Predictably, within a few years Theresa dutifully married the a town baker. No doubt plum pastries and *brotchen* seemed a more solid commodity than baleful songs and church music. Absent his love for Theresa, and his determination to build a life for them, Schubert likely would not have written so many songs for popular culture. We must recognize that he had a reputation to consider, and Viennese society could be both fickle and provincial when it came to music appreciation. Moreover, without his plan to satisfy clear financial objectives, we might not have the twelve Goethe songs, as well as the music set to poems by such poets as Holty and Jacobi. Franz tried to be strong, holding on to his reputation even as the romance he craved was defeated.

Schubert's dream of demonstrating financial independence had already been shaken with a failed bid for a permanent post. At this point he must have known he had lost Theresa, even before she married the bread man. To show his undying love, Franz] copied out seventeen songs for her, songs which had special association with their love for each other. He presented them to her as a keepsake.[14] The contents were later bound in an album and kept as a family treasure for generations until it became known that at least three songs had never been previously published.[15] Schubert had no option but to move on with his "life in art." As his life with Theresa came apart, Schubert decided to move back with his parents, if only for a few months. Maybe he could get back on his compositional feet. Perhaps, if the fates were kind, he would find another woman to love.

Schubert's financial situation improved early the next year when he was offered a position that, though only temporary, paid well and suggested a broader exposure to the people who would continue to pay well for his services. The job certainly contributed to his emotional healing. In fact, the situation lead directly to Schubert's second and only other significant heterosexual romance.

Count Johann Carl Esterházy engaged the young composer to teach his two daughters, Marie, age fifteen, and Caroline, age twelve.[16] The young man's initial assignment was to accompany the family to their castle south, on the Gran River, some hundred miles from Vienna. Later, Schubert would return to the capital city with the family. In letters home the composer relates that the children's mother acted a bit haughty, but that all got on well and the children made good progress. He may have been distracted somewhat by the countess's chambermaid, Josefine (Pepi) Pöckelhofer, "and there are hints of an affair between them, although the evidence is slight."[17] It seems that sweet Pepi and Franz had a brief, heated romance that summer in Zseliz.[18] Clearly, nothing good came of this liaison, certainly not for Schubert.

It's highly likely this was the time and manner in which the young composer became infected with the syphilis that would eventually contribute to his death. Likely we will never know where he contracted the venereal disease, so prevalent at that time in Vienna. In any event, whether or not Pepi had any influence on his work or not, the light-hearted love affair with the countess's chambermaid occurred at the same time Schubert wrote three piano duets, used to teach the young countesses (D733, D599, D624). Anything else someone a party to this naughty interlude may have learned is unrecorded.

Schubert was musically active that year. He told his friends he felt particularly pleased with his musical poem in six parts, *Einsamkeit*, (D 620), celebrating the ages of man. The work's near imitation of Beethoven's recent song cycle *An die Ferne Geliebte* is too obvious to ignore. Moreover, Schubert was captivated by the heady gratification of composition, not least of which his composition for voice. This is particularly so when we consider Schubert's sacred music, which is among his most remarkable for its complexity, while written against a backdrop of his own religious ambivalence. His father, we know, was a strict Roman Catholic. His faith suggested a lifestyle he expected to be mirrored in his progeny. Yet, young Franz found himself at the age of twenty-one quite "free of all these things." Schubert was maturing intellectually, becoming a more critical thinker.

Here's a bit of clarification: Schubert's faith in the organized church was less certain than his belief in God, and he had no problem emending and adjusting scripture to satisfy the needs of the musical composition. It's likely that he took a more liberal view of what constitutes praise to the Almighty. Whatever the state of his faith at this juncture, his production of church music in these years was significant. He wrote a *German Requiem* (D 621) and six complete Latin masses, along with his better known smaller sacred pieces, such as the *Ellens Gesang III*, which the world recognizes as the *Ave Maria* (D 839). This magnificent piece, among the best known "church music" in the western world, was written in 1825. We would want to know more of its inspiration, but it seems likely enough that it was simply Holy Mother Church.

The next few summers Schubert spent in Zseliz, teaching piano to the Esterházy girls, and here he presumably wrote his four-hand piano works, the duets offering him a way to compose and teach at the same time. Apparently the maid Pepi was no longer in the picture. That first summer Franz wrote the four-hand *Sonata in B flat* (D 617). He was writing a good bit of instrumental music at this time too, and much of it went unpublished until after his death. Music and young countesses were not his only interest.

In the early 1820's, and certainly by 1822, Schubert was enjoying the company of a liberal-leaning intelligentsia that would gather for readings and libations. This group has come to be called the Schubertiads. The group's interests may have focused as much on the libidinous Franz von Schober – later to become Liszt's secretary – as upon those of Schubert himself. These fellows seem to have been the most artistically influential members. Still, the year 1822 was a poor year for Schubert in terms of production. He was by now disappointed that he'd not composed something with the epic power of Beethoven's symphonic work. Beethoven had written his last great symphony #9, the D minor *Ninth*, just three years before. Schubert attempted to complete his *Symphony no. 8*, in B Minor, by the way, but left it unfinished, perhaps sensing that, beyond the first two movements, he could not sustain such a high level of accomplishment.[19]

So much, just then, must have seemed unfinished to him. It is his only work of real consequence for the year, while he continued his tutorial work for the Esterházy's. Franz Schubert was fast loosing strength, his health failing. Apparently, this was the year he first began to show signs, and fatigue, from his illness, later diagnosed at syphilis. The next spring and into the summer, Schubert spent time in a Vienna hospital getting the most obvious manifestations treated. He could not very well hide his malaise from the public, and the next few years were particularly difficult. Ironically, a young lady he had known for years, seen almost every day, now fascinated him.

When Schubert realized that he was in love with Countess Caroline cannot be known, but 1824 seems likely. She was now eighteen. The Count's friend and Schubert's music promoter Karl von Schönstein records that at this time the composer was possessed of a "poetic flame which sprang up in his heart…[and] continued to burn until his death."[20] At one point Caroline jokingly quizzed the composer as to why he had dedicated so little music to her. "What's the point," he answered. "Everything is dedicated to you anyway."[21] This axiom is only partly true, of course, as Theresa Grob had already inspired a number of the composer's earlier works. Subsequently, and whatever we may choose to make of his confession that everything was for her, Schubert did choose to dedicate the *F minor Fantasy* to Caroline. He was well aware that the romantic love he craved was purely fanciful, was in fact impossible. The young royal was Muse to him in the most literal sense. He needed something more visceral. This was a lesson so many of his contemporaries had learned the hard way; there would be no bridging the barriers of social stratification in 19th Century Vienna. Maybe Schubert had other options.

There has been a great deal of speculation over the past decade about Schubert's sexual orientation. A passing reference to "young peacocks" led the musical biographer Maynard Solomon to conclude that Schubert may have been gay, or bi-sexual. The argument and counter-arguments seem to be largely academic, since there seems to be no demonstrable impact on his music. He'd certainly not be the only bi-sexual composer. One way or the other the reality did not affect his need for the Musical Muse.

Looking back quickly, Franz was once clearly in love with Theresa Grob, and then with Caroline Esterházy. The squabbling about whatever other sexual interests seems tangential.[22] Whatever latitude he, like Chopin, enjoyed in his affection for men and women, however, seems to have little to do with the music each man made and played. Both were geniuses. We could make the same case for Schumann.

Because it was so central to the remainder of Schubert's life we must return to a further consideration of his illness. By the age of twenty-seven he'd become very ill. In that regard, the year 1824 looms large for his production. "Yet such is the resilience of genius – that out of his despair came a whole series of instrumental masterpieces. The first four months were of the most productive in his life."[23] He had finished the opera *Fierabras*, for which he had high hopes, pronouncing it tender and intimate. This opera, like *Alphonso and Estrella*, two years before, has all but disappeared. Ironically, his *Rosamunde*, which was written to accompany von Chezy's play, and which was actually ridiculed upon its opening, lives on – at least the incidental music does.

One Schubert composition of the year 1824 most likely to be heard today is *Death and the Maiden*, the haunting *String Quartet (No 14) in D minor*. Here we find a perfect example of the duality of Schubert and his music, and the piece underscores the much darker Schubert.

We find joy and sorrow, life and death, perhaps even the connotation of sex and disease. There was something richly autobiographical here. Schubert was in and out of hospitals during much of this time, often in despair. Yet he wrote some of his most joyous music then as well. He seemed to understand the ambivalence of an impossible love. Schubert knew more about this condition than he would have hoped or expected to.

Over the final four years of his life, and while he still saw his beloved Caroline regularly, he returned to piano music, composing seven piano sonatas. Franz found unexpected energy in his final year, following the remarkable song cycle *Die Winterreisse*, in 1827, the year of Beethoven's death – a loss that must have shaken him nearly as much as the failure of his romances. This was also the year Schubert composed his *Symphony #9, the Great* – a tenth, of course, remains unfinished – plus his final, major work, *Schwanengesang* (D957). These late vocal works, these large scale narratives, influenced Schumann and Brahms, the latter born just six years later, in 1833.

There is one more composition from Schubert's last year, however, that best tells the story of the man and his own inspiration. In the early months of 1828, Franz Schubert began work on "what is arguably the finest of a long line of his fantasies, the one in *F minor*, for four hands… a unique and wholly satisfying structure which bears witness to the distance he had traveled down the path toward perfection as an instrumental composer." Newbould finds that "so personal and masterly an example of his mature art should only be dedicated to Karoline [sic] Esterházy."[24] Other biographers and musicologists confirm that he loved her to the end of his life. Schubert's friend, the writer Eduard von Bauernfeld, wrote in his diary as late as February of 1828, "Schubert really seems to be in love with the Countess E. I like him for that. He gives her lessons."[25] No doubt she was terribly important to him in this, the last year of his life.

Schubert must have known he had only a short while to live, but he intended to spend as much of it as he could enjoying her time, if not anything more physically intimate. Perhaps this fact helps in understanding why he told his publisher he would dedicate his piano duet (D940) to the countess Caroline Esterházy. Love, after all, has many bounties.

Actually, the work did not appear until March, 1829, when it was published by Anton Diabelli & Co., with the dedication to the Countess. Perhaps more remarkable still is that Caroline appears in a group portrait of Schubert and friends, called <u>A Schubert Evening at Josef von Spaun's</u>. Here, the artist recorded the likeness of a woman who had never been to such a gathering, nor was she known to have ever joined a Schubertiad gathering. The *Fantasia in F Minor*, according to some theories, is also a cipher for Schubert's love of the young noblewoman, much as songs 9 – 11 of his 1823 song cycle, *Die Schöne Müllerin*, telling the story of a young man's love for a young girl, may also have been encoded and "constituted a secret programme, namely a declaration of love."[26]

It was actually typhoid that killed him, on the nineteenth of November. He was thirty-one years old. As he lay dying, Schubert told his brother he wanted to be buried near his "other beloved." Was he being coy? Not at all. Two days later Schubert was laid to rest in the Währing cemetery near the grave of the man whom he most revered, Ludwig van Beethoven.

CHAPTER FIFTEEN

SCHUMANN, Robert (1810 - 1856); German

"If ever a composer was doomed to music it was Robert Schumann. There was something of a Greek tragedy in the way music reached into his cradle, seized him, nourished him, and finally destroyed him."[1]

Unlike most of the men whose stories are retold in this book, Robert Alexander Schumann was not born to a family of musical distinction. In fact, neither of his parents was particularly musical at all. Robert did inherit his father August's love for words, especially for poetry, and the path from verse and prose to music composition proved to be key in forming the distinctive genius that was Schumann.

Born the same year as Chopin, one year after his close friend Felix Mendelssohn, Schumann was a member of a generation shaped by constant Central European political upheaval. His birth year, 1810, marked the zenith of Napoleon's power and influence. In fact, Robert's hometown, Zwickau, reposed precariously on the fast route of warring armies. His childhood was made further precarious by the serious illness of his mother, Johanna Christiane, from whom he was separated for two years while she recovered from typhus, moving in epidemic proportions throughout Saxony. The disease was likely exacerbated by the French soldiers' devastation and destruction of local hospitals and public health organizations. The French army, or what remained of them, was returning from their rout at Moscow. The soldiers spread their misery. The innocents found comfort and sanctuary where they could. For his particular brand of solace Robert took to reading, especially the romantic poets.

While his mother wasted away Robert established deeper emotional ties to his father, who struggled to keep his bookselling business viable. Mama's illness, and the ensuing family dislocation, was ironic in that she was the daughter of a military surgeon.[2] When she returned to the home she worried that Robert had become too much of a dreamer. Johanna valued and trusted the practical side of man, posing something of a conundrum for her gifted boy and the suitability of his the childlike interests.

Schumann's father was a skilled writer, and he translated major works of Lord Byron and Sir Walter Scott into German. "An affectionate father, he supervised the intellectual development of his children, [especially so] the son who seemed destined to realize what in himself had been only a fleeting dream."[3]

Robert began to take piano lessons when he was seven years old, encouraged by papa August, whose temperament the boy clearly shared. In fact, Herr Schumann bought the boy a fine piano as soon as Robert demonstrated any measurable progress. The child quickly took not only to the written musical text but he showed a distinct talent for improvisation. Robert's first known composition is a set of dances now, evidently, lost.

Making use of a grand piano at home, "soon four-handed arrangements of the classics were heard. He occasionally played his own pieces, to the delight of his father. Without a doubt the boy was driven in his art to satisfy his father's expectations. His most ambitious pre-teen composition, which he completed at the age of eleven years, seems to have been a setting of Psalm 150 for voices and instrumental accompaniment."[4] This is the Final Doxology, a liturgical expression of praise, and is the grand finale and completion of the Fifth Book of Psalms.

Until Robert, there had been no professional musicians in the Schumann or Schnabel lines. Both parents were industrious, however, and they worked hard for the betterment of their children. Johanna helped Robert develop his singing voice by working with him on reproducing the notes she would sing to him when he was quite young. Be that as it may, the woman did not see music as a fitting career for her children. Perhaps she could not envision how her gifted boy would make a living in the real world. Fortunate for all, she went along with the idea of Robert taking the necessary preparatory lessons, just in case.

Soon, Johann Kuntsch proved a worthy first piano teacher. Robert "evidently could absorb and quickly assimilate the musical ideas of the few composers whose work was available from scores, manuscripts, and the occasional musical concerts that Kuntsch organized in Zwickau."[5] The boy was allowed, and perhaps encouraged, to participate in some of these concerts. Representative of his astonishing creative abilities, Robert could parody or complement people's mannerisms, as well as their exact tone of voice and personalities, through small musical portraits. It was more than a fine party trick. Robert had an uncanny ability to capture other people's personae in musical notes.

Schumann's first rush of romantic feelings were sparked by Emilie Lorenz, whom his older brother Julius eventually married. He wrote her poems. In fact, for years Robert considered himself to be a poet first and a musician second. Soon thereafter, and declared he'd quite fallen in love with Ida Stölzel, recalling in his autobiography: "We loved each other for two years, quite intimately and childishly…"[6] As a boy Robert was intelligent, precocious and charming, later describing himself in his early diary, as "dutiful, childish, and attractive."[7]

The major affairs of his life, of course, were ahead, but to make sense of his many romances the reader must know something about the complementary talents and proclivities of master Robert Schumann. He had spent hours browsing among his father's books, playing the piano at small gatherings in Zwickau, and composing from time to time. He continued to write poetry and at age thirteen had published a small book of verse. "While still at the Lyceum, Robert's fondness for societies and clubs began to show itself," and actually helped to create two of them. One was dedicated to gymnastics and fencing, the other was a so-called secret literary society, the "Schülverein," which took as its maxim: It is the duty of every cultured man to know his country's literature."[8]

Robert was especially drawn to German romantic literature, and especially that of Jean Paul Richter. He was particularly moved by Jean Paul's *Die Flegeljahre* (The Adolescent Years). Robert seems to have taken from that story the haunting idea of a boy with a split personality, and "Schumann later imagined a double personality for himself: His audacious, manlier self he called "Florestan" and his shy, passive self he called 'Eusebius.'"[9] As a precocious teen, Schumann also began writing his own romantic novels. Much of the credit not specifically given to Jean Paul must go to his father.

No doubt, Robert Schumann entered his teen years quite the budding young Renaissance man. He owed his nascent curiosity and his love for the arts to his parents, one of whom he would too soon lose. But during his final years at the Lyceum he indulged himself totally in literature and music. There he made a special friend. She was Agnes Carus, the lovely, intelligent, and gifted young wife of a Zwickau physician and music-lover.

Robert fell in love with Frau Carus – a woman he could never have. Nor could he ever quite recover from the ordeal. Agnes had a magnificent singing voice. Eight years older than Robert, she encouraged his musical development. He wrote in his diary, "Sitting alone at the piano with her for two hours, it was as if all dormant depths woke up mightily… I will go to bed and dream of her."[10] He remained near her, pining for her, infatuated with her, for five years. The woman's husband, a practicing psychiatrist, liked Robert. He tolerated the boy's flirtations with Agnes and even gave him the nickname "Fridolin," the hero of a ballad by Schiller. With Robert hopelessly stymied in his devotion to the woman, it is surprising that Herr Doctor Eduard Carus actually became young Schumann's first psychiatrist – a venture that must have made for some arresting moments.

Robert's father died suddenly, in 1826. The young man quickly missed his father's artistic flair and natural curiosity. As suggested, the boy's mother was of a more practical mien; she wanted her son to study law. This was not a field of study, much less practice, that Schumann cared much about. Ever the dutiful son, however, Robert went to Leipzig to meet his fate. This parental predilection for study of law over music was not uncommon. Stravinsky, among others, went through the same theatrics with his parents. These two artists truly overcame the well meaning parents' obstacles, but not without high drama.

Back in northern Germany, it was another Doctor Carus, this one named Carl, who with his family proved to be inadvertent match makers. A Dresden court physician, he traveled in fairly elite social and music circles, and it was through an introduction by Carus to Friedrich Wieck, living in Leipzig, that Robert Schumann met the esteemed piano teacher and his daughter Clara. In fact, Clara, then just nine years old, was invited to perform at a party at the Carus home on 31 March 1828. Johann von Goethe, the aging *strum und drang* poet and dramatist, supposedly remarked that she played with the strength of six boys. Robert, too, was asked to play the piano. His performance was no less stunning. Friedrich liked what he saw and heard of the young man. The Wiecks both went away impressed. So did Robert.

Schumann was in Leipzig studying law, or giving it a look, anyway. Soon, Robert could face it no more. Two years was enough. Music was his life's purpose, his destiny, as the revered poet Jean Paul would have written the storyline. One day, Herr Wieck asked Robert if he would like to study piano with him. *Natürlich!* Certainly he would. That October, when he was twenty, Schumann moved into the Wieck's house as a boarding pupil. Robert's mother gave her blessings to the arrangement, only convinced by a letter from Wieck that "pledged within three years, by means of his talent and imagination, to make your son Robert into one of the greatest pianists now living." As proof that he could do it he said simply, "I present you with my eleven-year-old daughter."[11]

Schumann's nascent career was launched. Meanwhile, the young man had not been idle, in either a music or social sense. He'd met another young woman during a music fest in Mannheim. She was one of many delicious diversions for Robert Alexander Schumann. This one was the Countess Pauline Meta Abegg. Schumann returned to the Wieck household with the draft of a composition, "*Theme and Variations on the Name Abegg*" – a short piece for piano. It was another breakthrough work for the eager young composer. Robert Schumann completed the work, translating the letters of her name into the musical notes: A, B, E, G, G – then devising an impromptu, original theme. Not surprisingly, he dedicated the work to Countess Pauline. After all, Clara was entirely too young for him to be fawning over, musically or otherwise.

For her part, Clara was captivated by Schumann's looks, by his demeanor, and by his boyish charm. They read poems and played piano together. Undoubtedly they fascinated one another. Though still a girl, Clara was an accomplished pianist – better than Robert. This young woman, her big, bright blue eyes and penetrating gaze, now captured his dreams and fantasies. Although she had many casual competitors, gradually, Clara Wieck was becoming the most significant person in Robert's life. For now, while it was hands off Clara, Robert had other girlfriends with whom he was intimate. He made the results of these encounters quite clear in his diary with the use of a standard letter of the alphabet for his deed.

Undaunted, and though much younger, Clara may have suspected she had the upper hand. Perhaps she had an insight into the difficulties of holding a romance together – her parents had divorced when she was not quite six-years old. Her mother had gone off to live in Berlin. Likely, for Robert Schumann, the attraction had as much to do with her musical genius as with her pretty face and winning personality.

Clara taught Robert something else about himself, about what he wanted to do with his gifts. He admired her skill and energy, particularly since she was already composing. He wanted to write music, not just to play it. Clara's *Four Polonaise* was published when she was eleven years old, in 1830. Schumann took notice. He was proud of his Abegg composition; and he had already written parts of his *Twelve Pieces for Piano,* including *Papillions*, or Butterflies. The work remained incomplete until 1831. *Papillions* is said to be a musical interpretation on Jean Paul's *Flegeljahre,* the story that so captivated the young Schumann. He would do something similar, designing a much more ambitious project, with four letters again in his *Carnaval.* That story is yet a year or so away. Pleased as he was with his work, he was drawn to the girl he knew had at least as much talent.

Beyond Bach, Mozart and Beethoven, other composers now began to draw his interest. While he was deeply interested in Schubert's music, about this time Robert became fascinated as well by Paganini as a performer. Robert traveled to Frankfurt to see the violin virtuoso. The possibilities of music seemed endless.

Schumann also met Felix Mendelssohn at about this time, and they remained close for another seventeen years, until this other great, young figure of the Romantic era of music died at the age of thirty-eight. Over the next couple of years, Schumann worked on *Six Concert Studies on Caprices by Paganini.* Then something happened that made extended piano play a near impossibility. He injured his right hand in an attempt to strengthen the fingers of his right hand – perhaps as an attempt to overcome a kind of tendonitis. He truly wanted to be a virtuoso pianist, but he knew he was not as good as the girl he was coming to love. At the age of twenty-three, with his right hand degraded, Robert decided to concentrate on composition. He did not quit playing, entirely, but he put significantly more time and effort into his creative work than performance. He also paid attention to what this one young lady was up to. Robert was infatuated.

Clara Wieck was the featured artist at a gala concert in Zwickau, in November of 1832. Robert's play of the first movement of his first *Symphony,* the *G minor,* did not go over well, even as Clara's "own recently composed *Scherzo for Orchestra* was enthusiastically applauded. She dominated the performance with no less than four solo performances."[12] Robert's mother was so impressed with the thirteen-year-old Clara's performance that she told the young teen she must one day marry Robert. This was a remarkable thing to say, but it did prove prophetic. Her son was more concerned with the present state of affairs, however, and knew that his talent had not shown as brightly. Hurt and depressed, he elected not to return with the Wiecks but to stay in Zwickau in his mother's house. His spirits could not have been lower.

Worse than his concert disappointment his baby nephew, also called Robert, had died only days before. The loss of a close relative, and eerily another Robert Schumann, shook him.

The composer fell into a deep funk, remaining away from Leipzig for four months, away from his work and whatever his future might hold. He had little energy, updating sporadically his symphony, but his heart was not in the work. This was arguably the beginning of Schumann's life long struggle for mental health.

Acting on a fear that was beginning to haunt him, that he might be mentally unstable, as had been his sister, Robert decided to take electroshock therapy. One less costly diversion proved palliative. He needed something creative to occupy him. Robert and a few friends, along with his two imaginary ones, Florestan and Eusebius, began a literary magazine to "again bring the poetry of art among man."[13] The purpose was to serve as an alternative source of reviews of serious music. The *Neue Zeitschrift für Musik* appeared in April of 1834. Robert had read Chopin's *Variations for Piano and Orchestra in B-flat major*, although he had not actually heard the work, and declared "Hats off, gentlemen – a genius."[14]

The review was written as a conversation among Schumann, the droll Florestan, and the diffident Eusebius. Robert Schumann was now a critic and an editor. He had made an important breakthrough in consciousness, but he was not yet ready to resume his relationship with either of the Wiecks. Schumann needed time to think.

When Robert returned to Leipzig, in March of 1833, he took an apartment with a fellow who had been his law-school friend. He also decided he probably needed more psychological counseling. "It was in this socially isolated condition, and while still smarting from the artistic defeats of the preceding year, that Schumann began to feel in some magical way drawn to Clara – 'a chain of sparks,' he wrote, 'now attracts us or reminds us of one another.'"[15] But providence and Herr Wieck saw matters differently.

In the summer of 1833 Robert was ill with malaria. His brother Julius was dying. Surely every woe, every doubt, every negative idea came racing to Schumann's mind. Predictably, he had a nervous breakdown. The culminating event in Robert's decline may have been the death of his brother Carl's wife, in nearby Schneeberg. As he wrote in his diary, "[W]e were the same age; she was more than just a sister-in-law to me," and her death seemed to leave him defenseless.[16] Here was one loss too many – his sister Emilie had killed herself when Robert was fifteen. To make matters even more complex and bizarre, the infant Robert Schumann, the composer's nephew who had only so recently died, was in fact the child of the now deceased Rosalie.

Robert's family was crumbling. His own musical capabilities were in doubt. There was one further complication, the man's sexuality. "Schumann's propensity for loving unattainable or forbidden women was associated with a desire for intimacy with men, a yearning that we can conjecture had been effectively reduced through the imaginary companionship of Florestan and Eusebius. Recently, however, a group of attractive young men had begun to cluster around Schumann in connection with his newspaper work. Considerable revelry as well as rivalry prevailed in that circle, so that homosexual or bi-sexual interests may have contributed to his confusion and sense of self." Panicked, Robert could no longer control his thoughts and was incessantly preoccupied with suicide.[17]

Meanwhile, he had reportedly been intimate with his Leipzig roommate Carl Günther. What affect this outré relationship had on his feelings about Clara is anyone's guess. It took Schumann the best part of six months to recover, during which time he wrote to his mother about his roommate and friend, "he stimulates and warms me." If anything, perhaps Günther helped Robert to find some inner balance. His next roommate, Ludwig Schunke, a brilliant pianist, also seems to have helped Schumann to get back to what passed for stability. Schumann's doctor told him in no uncertain terms that if he wanted to truly get well he must "go find himself a woman." Robert hesitated. He was not sure he was ready to return to Clara, but the idea worked on his mind. He figured he probably needed her support. Would she still want him? Did he really love her?

Their reunion would require more time. For one thing, Clara's father was dead set against it. Robert's mental collapse must have weighed heavily on his mind. While working with Robert at the keyboard, shortly after the young man's return, Herr Wieck lamented the young man's so-called temperamental instability. Soon they became openly hostile. Schumann needed distance. The older man was suddenly too rigid in his teaching style. Robert talked of finding another mentor. Then, "in 1834 Wieck noticed that Clara, now fifteen, was showing signs of calf love for their lodger. He immediately sent her to Dresden on the pretext of her having lessons in musical theory."[18]

There may have been more to the story. Clara's feelings were hurt, as well. Clara was, in Robert's estimation, too young to become physically involved with him. But his yearnings were strong; Robert needed someone to love him. He'd always craved affection, which probably contributed to his bi-sexual disposition. Nature was listening. Sometimes the straight line is not the shortest way home.

Suddenly, Schumann fell in love with seventeen-year-old Ernestine von Fricken, the illegitimate daughter of a wealthy Baron from the Bohemian town of Asch. She, too, had come to Leipzig to live with and to study with Clara's father. The teen-aged Clara backed away and let them have their time together, telling Robert later that it was because of Ernestine that her father had sent her to Dresden. Robert, apparently unphased by Clara's departure, wrote of Ernestine to his mother: "[She was] a wonderfully pure, child-like character, delicate and thoughtful. She is truly devoted to me, and loves anything artistic. She's extraordinarily musical. [She's e]verything, in short, that I would want in a wife."[19] Robert Schumann could be so injudicious.

This testament certainly represents quite a reversal of fortune for all concerned. The couple became secretly engaged in the summer of 1835, but the Baron, upon hearing of this alarming development, returned to Leipzig and took his daughter back to Asch. Schumann evidently made the best of this reversal of love's fortune.

"In any event, the affair had a catalytic effect on Robert's music. He had the idea of writing a series of [twenty-one] piano pieces based on the letters ASCH; these he turned into *Carnaval*."[20] What was in the composer's mind as he constructed this music? "Schumann's interest in cipher, number symbolism, and musical/word puzzles is frequently encountered in his writing… Evidence of his interest in the playfulness and symbolism of number can be found in his diary, and, from later in life, a sketch of a letter to Brahms… an arrangement of numerical patterns, though of unknown meaning." We learn, "It is not surprising then that Schumann took pleasure in creating compositions based on words such as ABEGG and ASCH. Such an approach permitted him to add both mystery and an extra-musical significance to his work."[21] Ernestine was not the only force behind these tightly designed compositions. *Carnaval* also includes the *Chariana*, his miniature No 11. The name is the Italian equivalent of *Clärchen*.[22] Evidently, Clara Wieck was never far from his mind.

Not giving up on the fair Ernestine, Robert convinced papa von Fricken that his intentions were honest – which is doubtful – and he was permitted to visit Ernestine at Asch during the last days of October, returning again to see her in early December.[23] Robert wrote again that he was tormented. This must have been the understatement of the decade, as we know how sexually motivated the twenty-five year old composer was at the time. By the first of the year they decided to suspend whatever their arrangement had come to be. Making the best of the outcome, Schumann composed some piano variations on a theme, taken from the whole, bizarre von Fricken epoch. Schumann later wrote and dedicated a book of songs to Ernestine.[24] His music for her was the *Three Songs by Chamisso*, op 31. Short-lived though she was as a Muse, the young would be Countess certainly proved to be inspirational for Robert Schumann. That chapter closed, he had someone else to worry and dither over.

By this time the composer had returned to the Wiecks, wiser, perhaps, and somewhat more mature. Clara, back home, was now sixteen-years-old, still fascinated by the strange and wistful Robert. But the young man, ever something of a dilettante, was slow to commit. As a musician, he was drawn to the Wiecks in no small part because Chopin and Ignatz Moscheles were frequent visitors to their home; Robert loved their music. But what to do about Clara? Robert discussed his feelings for her with his friend Mendelssohn. He envied her talent, her success, and he supposed that he loved her. Finally he admitted to himself that Clara was the young woman he most needed.

Friedrich Wieck saw what was happening and sent his daughter off again – back to Dresden, likely thinking he was sparing her from Robert's hurtful, whimsical ways. Both parties were unhappy for the forced separation. It would not hold.

Unexpectedly, adding immensely to the drama of the day, Schumann's mother died. Her passing was a monumental event in his maturation. Robert had counted on her for emotional and financial support. So much of what he had done, he did to please his mother. After all, his father had been gone a long time. To whom would he turn for succor, for love? Whom would he now offer to please? Clara, who had been motherless since she was five-years-old, gave Robert the comfort he needed to get past the ordeal of her funeral. This was the quintessential romantic catalyst. Now Schumann knew he wanted Clara to be his wife.

Her biographer, Bertold Litzmann, says only that "both lovers renewed the oath of loyalty never to separate from each other again."[25] How would they convince Friedrich Wieck to give his consent? Her father, when learning that the two had been meeting behind his back, was outraged. Clara represented, in at least a rather utilitarian sense, the man's life's work. Now she would sacrifice all for this aimless, demonstrably unstable and fickle young man? Besides, she was still only sixteen.

Robert had a problem. For the composer there could be no turning back. Clara was his all. His compositions now were to her and about her. Soon he finished his first piano sonata, in *F-sharp minor*, Op 11, dedicating it to Clara from Florestan and Eusebius. The later two, of course, were equal parts of his tumbling psyche. "Schumann later told Clara that the music was a 'solitary outcry to you from my heart… in which your theme appears in every possible shape.'"[26] The *F-sharp minor* was one of four solo piano works that he wrote with Clara in mind. She obsessed him. She also encouraged a great deal more work from him, but that's getting ahead of the story.

Meanwhile, Friedrich Wieck was still saying no to their union. He wanted Clara to remain with him – his alter ego. Again, Friedrich flatly forbade his daughter from seeing Schumann. Wieck actually threatened to shoot Robert on sight. Non plussed, the young man did the only two things he could to compensate: he took to drinking heavily, he also returned to his compositional efforts.

There was a good deal more of the former than the latter. Schumann began work on a *Fantasy in C Major for Piano*, in three movements, but he did not finish it for two more years. Schumann told Clara "the first movement is probably the most passionate thing I have ever written – a deep lament for you."[27] He had faced difficult barriers, but this one seemed unfair.

For his part, Herr Wieck was still vigilant in his desire to keep his daughter and Robert from marrying. He spread rumors that the composer was a slovenly drunk and a great womanizer. He also encouraged Clara to see her singing teacher, Carl Banck. She did not warm to the idea. Things would be different, she knew, when she turned eighteen, and on 13 September 1837, Clara knew that her father's hold on her was tenuous.

Robert had kept up the good fight; he wrote to Herr Wieck explaining that he loved Clara; his prospects as a professional musician were bright. He again asked for her hand. The old man again said no. Wieck was standing firmly against the marriage. To complicate matters, Clara began a concert tour of major European cities.Now, Robert began to doubt himself. Was he good enough, talented enough for her? Clara Wieck needed little persuasion, his letters had won her over; she told her father in no uncertain terms that she would marry Robert. Again Wieck objected; outraged, he threatened to send Clara to live with her mother in Berlin, and then pouted that if she married Robert he would disinherit her. Recall that this is the same stunt Leopold Mozart pulled on his prize child when Wolfgang insisted on marrying Constanze Weber.

Finally, the nastiness went to court. Robert asked a judge to overturn the paternal ban, also gaining the support of Wieck's divorced wife, Clara's mother. The judge ruled for the young couple. It had taken three years to settle the row, the legal and personal battles, though it never was harmoniously resolved. Clara and Robert were married in tiny Schönefeld, near Leipzig, on 12 September 1840. It had taken three years to beat down the obstructionist father. Schumann had been planning for the big day.

The composer wrote and now presented to his bride a celebratory song cycle, *Dichterliebe*, meaning Poet's Love. He was a poet again as well as a romantic composer; and for now all seemed right with the world. Poetry and music would sustain them. Wouldn't it?

By and large, Robert and Clara enjoyed a largely contented and productive few years, although Schumann went into a devastating funk in 1842. His creative energy was, even so, usually high. Schumann initiated a wealth of love songs, including his *Frauenlieder*. He began, with Clara's support, what would be his first full symphony. This was *The Spring*, in B flat Minor, completed in 1841. Their first child, Marie, was born that year, followed by another daughter in April of '43. Robert was delighted he was able to move into another compositional genre when he completed the secular oratorio *Das Paradies und die Peri*, in June, "thus bringing to a close a project that had occupied him at various points for over two years."[28] The work allowed him to combine virtually every musical resource: solo singing, choral writing, and broad, symphonic construction. It's fascinating that Peri is an androgynous fairy kicked out of paradise, now wanting back in. The protagonist must make a special penance. Was the work a cipher for something Robert was working through? Was it in any way autobiographical?

Clara became concerned about the time he spent on the work. "The ambisexual Peri seeking redemption is a lovely symbol of Schumann's guilty innocence, the passive aggressiveness displayed so often in his social behavior."[29] Did the thirty-three year old Schumann figure he had some personal history to atone for? He was also interested in composing in other musical forms. *Peri* offers many tempting ideas for musicologists.

From a practical sense, we should be aware that oratorios were highly popular at the time, in no small sense because of his friend Mendelssohn's work. Schumann said his own oratorio was the largest work he had yet undertaken. *Peri*, first heard at the Leipzig Gewandhaus, was well received and reviewed. It was a watershed event in his early career, but a second symphony was less than a year away and soon thereafter an opera. Toward the end of his career he devoted much of his creative energy to choral music.[30]

Robert now had about ten years to go before he would begin to give up on life and on his work. Clara was urging him to try more orchestral music, which was good advice, for he wrote his *Rhenish symphony* in 1850, well after his deterioration had begun. Except for one cello concerto, that was all he managed that year. Until the very end of his life Clara helped her husband to keep his fragile world together.

The couple wrote one piece together, *Liebesfrühling*, or Springtime of Love. They often they inspired each other in their work, as Clara was now growing more interested in her husband's music, wanting to help him focus.[31] In fact, it was Clara that helped Robert to make some of his music derivative of Bach more accessible to the public. As Schumann tended to be abstruse, "[s]he advised him to compose something 'brilliant, easy to understand,' without a program and titles – 'not too long or too short …perhaps some variations on a rondo.' It was well intentioned advice, and in his way Schumann complied with the *Arabesque*, op 18 and the *Blumenstuck* op. 19."[32]

Toward the Christmas holiday, in 1843, the couple even reconciled with papa Friedrich, but Robert was not happy about the significant travel Clara was committing herself to. She, for her part, wanted to earn some money for the growing family; her tours paid her well. Clara was much in demand.

Robert hated to travel, and he certainly did not want to be perceived as Clara's travel partner. Soon his music began to wane; as his compositional interests declined, he began to suspect that he was ill. In fact, he wrote no significant music in 1844, the year in which the couple moved to Dresden. Then, from precious little harmony in their first few years came discord. Robert wrote almost nothing for the next two years, only completing his single opera, *Genoveva*, in 1847, a work never seen as particularly strong. Schumann tried his hand at teaching – at the Leipzig Music Academy – and then at conducting, but came to consider himself a failure at both. His state of mind was not improved by Clara's travel, which oft times made him feel superfluous.

Their trip to Russia in 1844 seems to have tipped him over. The catalyst was nothing other than rank jealousy. Robert was unhappy with the adulation Clara received, while he could barely make small talk in the presence of many flattering strangers. He began to write tragic poems, filled with images of death – a hangman and corpses. "But by proving once and for all that he could do no work as long as Clara was actively pursing her own career, this trip had damaged their marriage. Schumann's complaining, physical and mental symptoms, depressiveness, and unsociable behavior became a terrible burden for them both. Clara's future as a performing artist was in jeopardy.[33] Now, Clara too was hurting.

In the next years, Robert Schumann suffered a series of staggering depressions. Until his final illness, these were the lowest days of his life. What to do? With his doctor's encouragement the couple thought Dresden could be the new start they needed. The relocation did not go well. Clara would often find him in tears. Robert was drained; he said he was discouraged. He thought of giving up his duties as a critic, which had always been a source of satisfaction and renewal for him. Then he did just that – selling the beloved *Zeitschrift*. As a critic Robert Schumann had always been fair and usually kind, promoting any musician who seemed to show promise. Sadly, his own music was less understood and therefore less supported. Now nothing seemed to go well.

Robert had to fight his way through this stage of anxiety and misery as he had the similar bout with depression a decade before. Clara stood by her husband, listened to him, perhaps cajoled him to get back to work. Gradually, his condition seemed to improve. He was inspired to write one more oratorio; this would be his *Faust*, but he soon found it intractable. By Christmas time, in 1844, he was indeed working, just a little, now and again, with the help of what then passed as hypnotherapy. Today, only the overture and "scenes" remain from the aborted *Faust*. In 1851 he again tried an oratorio. This was *Luther*, spurred by Handel's magnificent *Israel in Egypt*. But it, too, collapsed from too much promise and too little concentration.

Biographers agree that from this point Schumann was never truly well again. Moreover, one condition that seems to have brought all of Robert's demons to the surface was not going to change. Clara simply had to travel; this was her work. Robert felt abused by travel. In August of 1845 they left for the Beethoven Festival in Bonn. The weakened Schumann complained of anxiety and dizziness. He fought through it, and soon reported that he felt better. Returning, he set to work on what we know as *Six Bach Fugues*. Except for revisions to the *Second Symphony*, this was Schumann's only real output for the year. In 1846, as he had struggled in 1844, he wrote nothing.

Recall his disappointment with the opera *Genoveva*, which he had worked on, here and there, for two years. The impetus for St Genevieve came from Clara, who told her husband that she liked the story. This is the parable of "an adventure-seeking husband leaving his castle while his demure wife remains obediently at home – [It] is almost an exact reversal of Schumann's marriage."[34] Was he attempting to honor Clara? Robert imitated a series of "sea baths," expected to clear his head – to somehow settle his anxieties. The couple spent time in the Frisian Islands for just this purpose. His affection for and apparent trust in such immersions would prove to be dramatically significant in the near-immediate future.

Whatever we choose to make of the rejuvenating baths, something happened after they returned that helped Robert to get turned around enough, albeit briefly, to resume his concentration and rediscover his vigor. Perhaps it was perceived genius in another musician. After all, he so loved to sponsor new talent. Or could it be a perceived rival?

"By coincidence another volatile musician was at work in Dresden at the same time. [This was] Richard Wagner, Kapellmeister at the court theatre."[35] While Schumann did not think much of Wagner's sense of orchestration, upon hearing a performance of *Tannhäuser* he soon recognized the stupendous power of Wagner's dramatic skill. For his part, Richard Wagner thought the man three years his senior to be too conservative. Complicating the men's poor chemistry, Clara was not a fan. Wagner had tried to kiss her once while she was on tour. She thought him presumptuous, which of course he was. It was a conscious, studied part of Richard Wagner's flair.

There were other people to both prod and support Schumann. Felix Mendelssohn was particularly important at this time, and his friendship helped Robert to return to something approaching normalcy, at least for a little while. Meanwhile, Clara was pregnant again. She recorded in their Household Account Book, which they kept together, that this would be their third child – actually they had already lost a couple. Robert wrote of her pregnancy, "children are a blessing." He was looking hard for blessings. More to the point, he was focusing again.

Schumann wrote two highly regarded piano trios in 1847. Then, that November, Mendelssohn was gone; dead at the age of thirty-eight, and things quickly began to look bleak for

Schumann. Mendelssohn had probably been his best friend, besides Clara, in the music world. Robert was never emotionally resilient. One professional breakthrough, totally unexpected, seems to have kept him upright.

Two days after Mendelssohn's funeral, Schumann was appointed to succeed Ferdinand Hiller as Director at the Dresden men's choir. It was not a prepossessing assignment, but it brought Robert back to song, where he had always been comfortable. Soon forming a mixed choir, he quickly pronounced the work a "great joy." He returned to his own composition, the next year completing his dramatic tone poem *Manfred,* from Lord Byron's verse. Schumann had reached the age of thirty-nine. He had not been at all sure, for some time before, that he would do so. Forty would be another matter.

This was a busy and productive time, a period of flow. Florestan would have been happy for his friend. But ebb quickly followed, as it must, and as *Faust* did not come together; *Genoveva* faltered; Schumann began to wonder what he was doing in Dresden, after all. When his friend Hiller, who had vacated the Dresden choir position, suggested he take over for him as Director of the Düsseldorf Music Academy, Robert was tempted. One thing that bothered him was that the city was known for its madhouse. Robert said its very presence bothered him, haunted him. Clara, however, who found Dresden too provincial, too narrow-minded, was all in favor of the relocation; maybe Düsseldorf held a better future, more promise. They decided to go live in what would become, unknown to either, their final home together.

The Schumanns could not have anticipated a warmer welcome to the Rhineland city. Robert's confidence grew as he became convinced that he had inherited a fine musical program, one honed by Hiller and his great friend Mendelssohn. Here he would have time and motivation to compose, as he kept up with his positional duties at the music school. As we know, with Clara's encouragement, Robert set to work on his third *Symphony* in *E flat Major,* the *Rhenish.* Schumann's gift, however, was for the smaller, less complex forms, and soon he wrote his only cello concerto. This was also the year he returned to sacred music. Perhaps his return to the Catholic Rhineland provided the impetus for his irresistible wish to compose music that would be "suitable for church as well as concert hall."[36] He was disappointed; his *Luther* oratorio was stillborn.

Nevertheless, Robert was feeling stronger than he had in years, he and Clara resumed limited travel, including a short trip to Switzerland. The next year they enjoyed the visit from Franz Liszt and his paramour, the Princess Carolyn Sayn-Wittgenstein. But, as had so often happened when he was feeling fit, Robert soon began to lose focus on his responsibilities. His musicians, and especially his singers, found him too distracted. Some called for his resignation. All this lead to Robert's final tumble. Another complication, his long-time fascination with the occult grew stronger. At one point Robert thought the table on which he composed music was dictating a cadence, a rhythm for him to follow. Clara was despondent.

In April of 1852 "he suffered a form of paralytic attack, which was accompanied by sleeplessness and depression. By June he was worse still…Many of his old symptoms returned, together with an alarming new speech impediment."[37] His condition worsened as he tried new and stranger cures, including bathing in the Rhein at Bad Godesberg. This last bit of jiggery-pokery would be the one that may have led to more harm than any other. His work fell off and his confused charges found others to lead and direct them.

Schumann suffered a stroke during a visit to Bonn the next year. Then, incredibly enough, as had happened so many times before, he rallied. Schumann began again to compose. The year 1853, nearing the end of his productive life as a musician, he composed the *Concerto in D Minor for Violin*, *Four Pieces for violin, piano, and viola*, the *Introduction and Allegro for Piano*, and his *Fantasy for Violin and Orchestra*. It was a very full year for a man now running on manic fumes.

That September the couple celebrated their fourteenth wedding anniversary. Robert presented Clara with a score he'd been working on for a number of years and had now finished. This was the *Concert Allegro for Piano and Orchestra* (op 131). Naturally enough, he dedicated it to her, his caring, tireless, loving Muse. There remained one more sea-change ahead for the man.

Toward the end of the month a twenty-year old fellow came to visit. Like none other, this young man would impact Robert's remaining few years and more so those of Clara Schumann. Their daughter Marie tells the story: "A very young man, beautiful as the day, with long, fair hair, stood in front of me. He asked for my father… He had brought his compositions and my father said that, as he was there, the best thing was for him to play them himself." Marie further notes that his play was so fine that Robert raced off to bring Clara to hear, as well. They were enchanted, and later "could not stop talking about the genius who had visited them that morning, Johannes Brahms."[38]

Brahms continued to visit, continued to honor the Schumanns – for their work, their tutelage, and their friendship. The threesome became close. To Robert, this Brahms lad must have seemed a gift from the heavens, maybe more so to Clara. "And from this date till November 2, the diaries of both husband and wife are full of nothing else."[39]

Another young talent, the violinist Joseph Joachim, was invited to join them; together the four, along with the Schumann's four children, celebrated what proved to be the final sensate months of Robert's life.

Schumann briefly returned to the role of music critic, writing a piece for Franz Brendel, who had taken over as publisher of the *Neue Zeitschrift für Musik*. His article, *Neue Bahnen*, which means New Paths, described the "flight of the eagle," the coming of one who soars alone – the musician so heralded, this Messiah, was Johannes Brahms. The very presence of the young man from Hamburg seemed to help Robert to regain a bit of confidence and optimism.

Things were not going as well in Robert's capacity as Düsseldorf's municipal music director. Abruptly, he offered his resignation, effective 1 October 1854. The city fathers demurred. True, he was not doing the job they expected, but perhaps things could be worked out. Clara knew that Robert did not really want to resign, and she encouraged her husband to stay at the podium. After all, Julius Tausch, Schumann's able deputy, could handle some of the concert series. For her part, Clara also wanted some time away from Düsseldorf for her own performance options, or just to get away from domestic duties.

With more time away from program rehearsals, Robert could work on new music, including the sacred pieces he was now so fascinated with. He was again working on a Mass. "A formidable work for organ, orchestra, chorus, and solo voices, this *Mass in C minor* (op. 147) was designed to meet the spiritual needs of his new community in the Rhineland."[40] Schumann was pushing himself in other creative directions as well; he was working on a book about music he called his *Poet's Garden*. Writing was therapeutic, for a while. Schumann had always taken immense satisfaction in writing poetry.

The year before, Julius Tausch had brilliantly led the summer concert series and would soon take over the winter program as well, seriously impacting Schumann's income. The couple did not have any room for financial setbacks. Robert's medical bills were already significant, and Clara found herself with fewer performance options. The young Herr Brahms helped them financially. Something had to change.

He needed to work, but Schumann did not seem overly worried about the failing directorship; likely he had already, mentally, backed out. Robert's fascination for young Brahms, however, was something that caused his contemporaries, such as Franz Liszt, to question Robert's sense of proportion. Brahms may have inadvertently created something of a rift in the Schumann marriage, and not by anything he actually did; whether or not, as some biographers think, there was then anything overtly romantic going on between Clara and Johannes. Robert was truly, deeply, fond of the young man. Likely there was little second-guessing as to whose star was ascendant.

While his motivation for doing so cannot be known, at the end of his tenure as city music director Robert dismissed his wife from her position as his associate choirmaster. Why? He told Tausch that it was no job for a woman. Away from any outside responsibilities, he wrote some tentative musical sketches, most of which came to him unbidden – voices in his head – as he worked on his *Poet's Garden* manuscript.

On January 18th the Schumanns left town for Hanover, intending to see Brahms and his good friend Joseph Joachim and to give a few more concerts.

Robert had difficulty keeping his mind on much of anything. There were too many distractions. Then he surprised everyone close to him. Out of the deep blue, Robert asked to be relocated to an insane asylum. He could not keep the noises he heard from becoming the most intractable music. By January, 1854, Schumann had apparently lost control of his mind. He had been delusional, off and on, for months – angels and demons talking to him, in turn. He told Clara they must move the family to Vienna, although he had no prospects there. Why to Vienna? Clara, again pregnant, was not happy about making a reactive move. She had already been treated rudely in the business of the choir.

By February the noises became insufferable. Schumann slept little. Then the great annual German *Fasching* celebration began, the carnival that immediately precedes Lent. Revelers must have put Robert's precarious sense of reality to the test. At noon on the 27th Clara set out to find her husband's doctor, asking her daughter to watch her father, but Robert had left the house by an unwatched door. Wearing only his dressing gown and slippers, on this wintry day, Robert walked the few blocks to the Rhine and threw himself in. He was rescued by fishermen who saw what he had done. Was it an attempt to heal himself by sea bath? A cry for help? Was it a genuine suicide attempt?

The men brought him back to the house, but this was the end of the line, as far as his mental health was concerned. The psychiatrist who had recently been treating Schumann told Clara that her husband must be committed. He knew of a small, private hospital in Endenich, near Bonn. The next week, on March 4th, Robert entered the institution from which he would never return.

Although Schumann periodically showed signs of regaining mental equilibrium, even writing a few lucid letters and receiving a few guests, including his young friend Brahms, the moments of apparent clarity were short. Robert's doctor told Clara that her husband's symptoms were getting progressively worse. Some biographers suggest that Robert was also showing symptoms of the syphilis he had contracted many years before. But this diagnosis is speculative. Whatever the cause, Robert faded quickly that summer. On July 23rd Clara received a telegram that she should come at once if she ever wanted to see her husband again; Robert was dying.

Accompanied by Brahms, she visited with him for two days – it was the first time Clara had seen Robert since he had been removed to the asylum at Endenich. In his last year Schumann actually wanted out of Endenich, he tried to talk Brahms into helping him relocate to another institution. Could not Clara, with her superb connections, arrange something? Nothing came of the request.[41] Maybe by now, Clara had come to realize some degree of respite.

Schumann died on the 27th and was buried in Bonn two days later. His young friend Brahms was asked to walk in front of the casket. Clara wrote: "His dearest friends walked in front, and I came unnoticed behind. It was best this way. He would have liked it so. With his departure, my happiness is ended. A new life is beginning."[42] A review of the couple's Household Account Book reveals that on the day Robert went into the river, on the 27th of February, two and a half years before his passing, the handwriting "changed from Schumann's to Brahms's, as the younger man touchingly took on the daily chores for Clara. 'Housekeeping, Postage … Letter to Dublin … half-bottle Moselle wine.'"[43] The old order had changed.

Clara Schumann resumed her travel as a great pianist and was finally recognized for some of her own compositions. She outlived her husband by forty years, passing away in Frankfurt on 20 May 1896. The vaunted third member of this storied relationship, Johannes Brahms, died just eleven months after Clara, having never married. Sometimes such stars cannot align. Robert, then Clara, and finally Johannes passed away; all were gone three years before the dawn of the twentieth-century, a trio of talent and mutual affection such as would likely never come again.

CHAPTER SIXTEEN

STRAUSS, Richard (1864 - 1949); German

"Richard, go compose!" (attributed to Frau Pauline Strauss)

Not every musical muse is necessarily socially gifted, or even particularly accommodating, as Richard Strauss discovered when he married Pauline de Ahna in the resort town of Marquarstein, south of Munich, in the fall of 1894. Just such an intemperate, boorish woman as she, however, nevertheless proved a great source of inspiration for the artist, especially since Richard needed a periodic boost. In short, Pauline made her husband work when he would rather be playing cards or walking about the Bavarian countryside. Arguably, a couple of Strauss's best known compositions would not have been possible without the outrageous conduct of the woman to whom he was so inexplicably devoted. Strauss had few other "girl friends," in the romantic sense, but his life with Pauline seems to prove that inspiration does not always need sweetness and light to flourish.

This is a story that begins in Munich, the 11th of March, in the year 1864. It was also the year in which Toulouse-Lautrec was born, when the popular opera composer Meyerbeer died in Paris, when Abraham Lincoln was reelected President of the United States, and when Tolstoy wrote *War and Peace*. Like all these men, Richard Strauss would be a man of vision, of innovation, and perseverance. Unrelated to the celebrated Johann Strauss family, this turn of the century composer was also marked for greatness. Coming into his own as he did at the end of the Late Romantic era Strauss had a great deal of work before him. In fact, this fellow would change the face of "classical music" in Germany as much or more than even Wagner, fifty years before, is said to have done. Richard Strauss was a marvelous innovator.

Composition of his symphonic poems, which he subsequently called "tone poems," perhaps especially *Don Juan*, led him to redefine the size and scope of orchestral music. Richard's grand operas which followed dominated the beginning of the twentieth century, the great transitional period in classical music. Few composers were as bold and pioneering as this German harmonic master.

Strauss, though not a singularity in his range of musical gifts, was blessed with the skills to compose, to conduct, and certainly to play. The blood lines were strong; his father Franz was for many years the principal horn player in Wagner's Munich Court Orchestra. Franz was also a highly respected professor at the Royal School of Music, in Munich. Son Richard showed early signs of genius, comparable to that of Mozart's. He played – no, he studied – piano at the age of four, violin the next year, and was composing at six. Strauss's first piece was the *Schneiderpolka* for pianoforte.[1] The first work he gave an opus number to was his *Festmarsch, in E flat major*, which dates to the year 1876. Strauss's principal biographer, Norman Del Mar, writes that the work was remarkable. The boy had tenacity as well as the skill, "to complete the full orchestral score." What the piece lacked in sophistication it made up for in precision and detail.[2] Richard began his studies at the university in Munich at the age of seventeen, studying philosophy and the history of art – somehow he avoided law school – but he dropped out to concentrate on his music study.

He was a precocious teenager, keeping up a heady correspondence on music criticism with his good friend Ludwig Thuille, some three years older, and a fellow who apparently was an adjunct member of the family. When Richard was fourteen he wrote to Thuille: "I am now playing Mozart piano concertos diligently from our Mozart edition, and I tell you it is splendid, for me it is the greatest enjoyment. This wealth of ideas, this richness of harmonies and yet moderation in everything... But to play anything like this is not possible anymore! Now nothing but smarminess will do –harsh booming and thundering... what I have sworn is that when some day I perform in a larger concert, and can be accompanied well ... then I will play a Mozart concerto."[3]

It is interesting to see that the young man who cherished Mozart, as the "greatest enjoyment," suspicious of bold innovation, led the vanguard into early modernism, with its attendant rustling, thunder, and boomings. Perhaps because he chose to be open to new forms, Richard quickly matured as a composer. Some of his best known and most popular works date to his early twenties, but he was active for all of his eighty-five years.

Richard's father arranged for the boy to study with his harpist colleague, August Trombo, and from this work Richard came to know the Wagner operas, as well as the work of the old masters that had so captivated him in his teens. "His childhood was musically blessed by talking place within the Munich Opera. But his first experiences of Wagner on the stage left him puzzled."[4] Richard had no guideline to help him find his way from Brahms to the often startling work of Liszt and Wagner. Left to his own devices, he surveyed all that had gone before and forged a way ahead. It's not that he didn't have some well-timed help; help from the ladies, however, was less propitious.

Strauss's young career took an exciting and challenging turn in 1885 when, now twenty-one, he was offered his first job as conductor. The position was in Meiningen, and his would-be sponsor for the job was the brilliant, iconoclastic Hans von Bülow. The conductor had recently had a falling out with Johannes Brahms and decided to move on from his post at the same city. Maestro von Bülow's departure opened a significant door for Strauss who, after limited training, became his successor on the 1st of November.[5]

By mid-December Strauss was not sure he had made the right move. Richard seldom found himself settled and was constantly on the look for the next great offer. Munich made him one. Richard asked Bülow his thoughts, stating that he found himself "unlikely to find anything better." He also admitted that the present outlook for this orchestra is not bright.[6] Actually, von Bülow advised him to stay put, and he did for six months, finessing the question by taking a holiday in Italy, in May and June. Strauss loved Rome, found Naples too smelly, and agreed with Bülow that he had probably spent too little time in Florence. He reported that he loved the countryside, mistrusted the people whom he said had cheated and stolen from him, and he came back full of ideas.

By the end of June, Richard was back in Munich, explaining to Bülow that he was now at work in his new position as Music Director – actually as the company's third string conductor. More importantly, however, for the development of his compositional career; what he had brought back from Italy was a sheaf of notes and a wealth of inspiration that lead directly to his symphonic fantasy, *Aus Italien*.

We have seen in this book that many composers from central Europe found Italy to be a catalyst for their work. Apparently, Richard Strauss acted on advice from Brahms to go to Italy while his generous father footed the bill. The result, *Aus Italien*, was everything he or his loving sponsors could hope for: "[T]he Fantasy has the outward semblance of a traditional four-movement symphony; yet it became, as Strauss once said, 'the connecting link between the old and the new methods.'"[7] Strauss believed in the transformational. He was now, and for long would remain, fascinated with the prospects of "new methods."

The young Richard had made astonishing progress in the world of professional music. The correspondence between the old master and Strauss helps us to understand not only the trust the two placed in each other, but how dependent Strauss was on von Bülow for guidance, surpassing that which he sought from his father. Franz Strauss, of course, did not have the range of musical knowledge that the conductor did. As time passed, Richard must have begun to second guess his father, no fan of Wagner's music, even as the younger Strauss came more under its spell. The vibrant city of Meiningen offered more.

There was one further result from Strauss's decision to follow von Bülow, and this bit of Kismet would reshape the musician's interests and passions as a composer. His boss, the Duke of Sachsen-Meiningen, was a great supporter of theater. The players in the local theater were strong, Strauss found, and their productions first rate. "Strauss attended as many performances as he could; his profound sense of theater was developed there."[8] He would not have known then where such interests would take him in composition, for he had also picked up an interest in what he called *Zukunftsmusik* – the music of the future.

Recalling his <u>Youth and Years of Apprenticeship</u> he wrote: "New ideas must search for new forms – this basic principle of Liszt's symphonic works, in which the poetic idea was really the formative element, became henceforward the guiding principle for my own symphonic work."[9] Liszt, fifty-three years older, also became something of an alternate father, or grandfather figure for Richard. Now the young man needed something or someone in his life to inspire, not only to instruct.

During such a pivotal time in Strauss's life, and with his career developing most successfully, Richard found time to fall in love. In 1883 he met Mrs. Dora Wihan, wife of the Czech-born cellist, Hans Wihan. Evidently, the couple's marriage had long been rocky and Richard may have inadvertently helped to force its termination, as he and Dora clearly had a romantic interest in each other. The woman was four years older than Richard and considerably younger than her curmudgeonly husband, who examined his limited options and headed to Prague the next year.

Dora and Richard's sister Johanna, who described the young woman as "rather coquettish," also became good friends. In fact, Johanna apparently acted as something of a match-maker when it looked like the relationship could lead to something. Richard wrote for his Dora the 1882 -1884 *Intermezzo, for piano*, Op. 9/3. Much later in life he wrote another piece for her, something grander than anything he might be able to offer her now.

Richard and Dora wrote each other countless letters over a period of years, but somehow their attraction for each other was not enough to sustain any permanent relationship. In fact, both agreed to destroy their correspondence, perhaps thinking the contents would be too revelatory and potentially embarrassing. "Dora went to America then took a position in Greece. At one point they made plans to meet in Italy, but appear not to have done so."[10] Apparently this would-be liaison remains a mystery. They were good at covering the details of their physical relationship, so their *belle epoch* was evidently one rendezvous that stayed private. Gradually, both realized the magic had faded.

Another woman entered Richard's life in 1887. Complicating the now tenuous affair of Dora was the larger than life presence of one Pauline de Ahna, whom Strauss was immediately attracted to and was soon, for complex reasons, more interested in seriously pursuing. Richard's uncle introduced them at a resort in nearby Feldafing. We'll have more to muse upon the guiles of Pauline, shortly.

Fortunately, for anyone interested in the long lines of the Richard Strauss – Dora Wihan relationship, one of Richard's letters to her survives. He wrote to her in 1889, fresh from composing the *Don Juan* symphonic poem, his opus 20, which takes its inspiration from his uncertain Muse, Miss Wihan. "The fact is," he told her, "your letter, putting off the prospects of seeing you again, my sweet Dora, for the foreseeable future, has upset and distressed me deeply. God what wooden expressions those are for what I really feel… Strauss the artist is doing very well! But may no happiness be complete?"[11] His being or not being "complete" is obscure. Was he pining for his Dora?

Let's return to the inspiration of *Don Juan*. Michael Kennedy, arguably the best known of Strauss's biographers, credits Dora with the work's fire and purpose. Strauss, "inspired by his love for Dora," began the "tone-poem dealing with the perennially fascinating figure of Don Juan."[12] At least one alternative explanation was that he was already thinking of Pauline, whom he found inspirational, even as the Dora affair became less and less certain. Either way, the theme, taken from the verse-play by Nikolaus Lenau, intrigues the listener today. Don Juan deals with a man's quest for the perfect woman. Was not Strauss pursuing his own such quest? It would take Richard six more years to be sure Pauline was right for him. Or wrong. There were unexpected complications, as well.

Paternal instincts run deep. We learn that Franz Strauss had long been weary of his son's love affairs. "His father wrote to him after he went to Meiningen that, nice as it was for him to enjoy himself with good, cheerful women …he should be careful not to smear his good name and damage his career."[13] The selection of the Don Juan theme, then, seems particularly significant. It is a vehicle for the expression of sexual desire. "[Richard] chose the greatest erotic subject of all time… trac[ing] the main outlines of Don Juan's career from the scene where his father vainly sends Juan's brother, Don Diego, to fetch him home."[14] Don Juan's exploits take him to the depths of five passionate and pointless affairs. Rejecting any family counsel, the man lives his life in pursuit of perfection, but despondent and unable to find it, he allows himself to be killed in a duel, having turned from an outcome that would have assured him victory.

Strauss's *Don Juan* is "on the one hand a symphonic movement, fully worked out according to the requirements of the thematic material, while on the other hand it portrays the development of a human personality…"[15] To what extent Strauss placed something of his own aspirations into the tale we can only surmise.

We should return to Strauss's other closely related compositional work. After all, *Don Juan* was not the first of its kind. That is to say, the music was not Richard's first major "programmatic work." Strauss took up this cause, as he called it, for music written around a poetic theme – the term "symphonic poem" came from Franz Liszt, whom Strauss revered – and "devised his own name for it – tone-poem – and imparted to it new life and urgency.

Liszt had died in Bayreuth in 1886, the year of the much heralded *Aus Italien*. Strauss knew that Smetana, Saint-Säens, Dvorak, and César Frank had all experimented with the idea. Richard was particularly fascinated with where he could take music, with what he called "the creation of new forms [of music]."[16]

Strauss and von Bülow, who had begun a lengthy correspondence some years earlier, now exchanged ideas about the limitations of the sonata form, brought to its highest point by Beethoven. Strauss wrote to his mentor von Bülow, on 24 August, 1888, "If you want to create a work of art that is unified in its mood…and if it is to give the listener a clear and definite impression … this is only possible through the inspiration of a poetical idea… I consider it a legitimate artistic method to create a correspondingly new form."[17] That is precisely what Richard Strauss did.

His break through work was *Macbeth*, also completed in 1886. *Macbeth* was heralded by his friend and champion as 'the most independent and purposeful work the young man had ever composed. Richard wrote to Dora the next year telling her that he had joined the ranks of the Lisztians. "I feel wonderful," he said, "a new clarity has come over me."[18] What higher aspiration than to join Liszt could the young man have for his ambition as a serious, progressive composer?

Dora was the inspiration the man needed, but his family intended to see to that such inspiration would never be built on anything tangible. They could not control his pining and dreaming, but they could say no to anything legal. Richard wrote one other major piece of music for his lost love, his Dora. He began the work when he was seventy-three, in 1937, and worked on it off and on for four years. The result was the opera *Die Liebe der Danae*, op 83, which is has been called especially autobiographical. Danae is Dora. Strauss takes as the opera's central theme Donizetti's aria *L'elisir d'amore*.[19] By most standards now an old man, Strauss told his librettist to use the Donizetti work because he loved it and it had special meaning for him. We'll soon learn why.

The theme, so dear to Strauss's heart, was that money does not begin to compensate for love. Surely he was still in love with his passionate, youthful Dora. "This moment of idealistic love, opposed by his parents, lingered on well into the years in which his marriage with the decidedly unpleasant Pauline had settled into a comfortable domestic routine… Dora was the inspiration for the work, which poses the question as to how happy a man will be in his mundane respectability when his passionate, rebellious ideals of youth are forfeit."[20] Let's return to the young, energetic, and less-settled musician, a man who would never again find that level of infatuation. Whether or not it is accurate to declare de Ahna "unpleasant" will have to wait a few pages.

While the Strauss family would not accept Dora as more than a passing affair, there was a bit of intervention on behalf of the "other woman." Here's how it all came about: Richard was encouraged by his maternal uncle, George Pschorr, heir to the famous Bavarian brewery, to visit him in the resort town of Feldafing, south of Munich. One prominent family in the village was that of Bavarian army Major General Adolf de Ahna. He was an amateur musician who, with his talented daughters, gave local recitals. The older girl, Pauline, trained as a soprano at the Munich Conservatoire, took a quick liking to Richard, whose early fame preceded him. Recall that Dora Wihan had been physically out of his life for years. Pauline de Ahna had another advantage – proximity.

For his part, "Strauss was entirely captivated by the girl and, like many other musicians, made use of his art to further his courtship by undertaking the instruction of his beloved."[21] In all likelihood, the Strauss and Pschorr families had been doing everything feasible to wean Richard from Dora, and what they thought to be an ill-conceived relationship. Her divorce may have had something to do with their feelings, or the fact that she was older than Richard. Their match making with Richard and the young de Ahna would prove to be far more successful than they could have imagined. The de Ahnas didn't much care for it either, thinking she would be marrying below her station.

After all, papa was the very model or a modern major general, and the daughters of same marry only into the gentry.

Meanwhile, with his tenure in Munich becoming uncomfortable, owing to what he perceived to be left-over assignments, Richard found himself eager to move on, to find better conducting opportunities, and to find his future a good bit further from home. He wrote to Dora once again. He told her of his acquaintance with the Wagners; that he was leaving Munich – too provincial; that he still wanted to follow the footsteps of Liszt in Weimar. Richard was sketching out his first opera, *Guntram*, in 1892. He wrote, "[i]n addition I have sketched out a new tone-poem, to be called *Tod und Verklärung*."[22] Dora had been his first serious girl, his first important Muse, and he wanted to share his dreams with her. That he would write another major work based on Dora long after he was married does not belie his feelings for the dauntless Pauline, but speaks convincingly about the power of reverie.

Richard spent the high summer in Bayreuth, coming even more under the spell of Cosima Wagner, widow of the lion of German opera, who had died in February of 1883. Frau Wagner entertained Richard and his lady friend Pauline, traveling as his pupil, convincing Strauss that his future might well rest every bit as much in conducting as it would in composition. Strauss, well aware of his dual callings, did not actually need anyone to tell him to push his opportunities to conduct. Cosima, of course, enjoyed mixing in the business of wielding influence and favor. She had done it before. It's interesting now to speculate now to what extent Cosima may also have been jealous of Strauss's affection for Hans von Bülow, to whom she was married for many years before running off with Wagner. Supposedly, Cosima left Bülow because she determined that he would never make a first-class composer.[23] The lady may have been right on that count.

Cosima was also quick to cast doubt on those she did not favor. She had a special animosity toward Jews, which she shared first with her husband, a world-class anti-Semite, and then with anyone else who would pay attention to her ugly rants. Thus, she shared such bilious feelings without hesitation with the impressionable Richard Strauss. It is not surprising that, with her peculiar pedigree, the illegitimate daughter of Franz Liszt and his paramour, the countess Marie d'Agoult, Cosima did have an ear for *ad hominem* intrigue.

Meanwhile, Pauline de Ahna was growing in Richard's favor. The two were friendly for six years before they actually became engaged. She was his student and he thought her gifted, if not brilliant, solid and well trained. Perhaps romance would come of its own volition. Strauss made the most of his opportunities to make Weimar "the center of musical life in Germany," as his star soprano, Marie Gutheil-Schoder announced. "He conducted operas by Mozart and Wagner … [then] Pauline joined the company, and under his tutelage, was good enough to sing the roles of Pamina in *Zauberflöte*, Elvira, in [Mozart's] *Don Giovanni*, Elsa in *Lohengrin*, and Elisabeth in [Richard Wagner's] Tannhäuser."[24] Who stood the most to gain by the

Pauline's breakthrough assignments? "Strauss's extraordinary understanding of the voice, particularly the female voice, was instinctive; no doubt he was helped and advised by Pauline, but there is also no doubt that he made her career."[25] Intrigue sharpens romance.

Cosima must have been aware that she could also get Richard to do her bidding without much struggle. In fact, "[i]n his staging of Wagner at Weimar, Strauss worked directly under the influence of Cosima. This alarmed Hans von Bronsart, the Intendant, [principal administrator] who did not fancy his opera house becoming a subsidiary of Bayreuth." Bronsart told "his young conductor" that "other musicians had 'a better and more reliable knowledge 'of Wagner's works than 'the Meister's unmusical widow.'"[26] To what extent Richard followed the senior man's guidance is unclear.

Strauss spent Christmas of 1891 with Cosima, planning for his first, much anticipated performance of Wagner's *Tristan und Isolde.* Following a highly successful presentation, on 17 January 1892, he told Wagner's energetic widow who was now so much a part of his creative world that it was the "most joyful day in his life." Whatever impact or influence Cosima had on him, following Strauss's triple success with the tone poems *Macbeth*, *Don Juan*, and *Tod und Verklärung*, and his conducting of the pinnacle works of Wagner, still following the master, he returned to composition with sketches for his first opera.

Guntram premiered two years later. Richard now became a champion of Wagnerian Music Drama. "Strauss determined to draft his own libretto in the Wagnerian manner, basing it upon the Teutonic legend or medieval history."[27] Meanwhile, Pauline was not out of his thoughts. Richard subsequently found another part for her as *Isolde*. Interestingly, as early as 1892 he began to refer to Pauline in letters as "my fiancée" although they were not truly engaged. Was he staking some kind of claim? When they did become engaged, in January of 1893, it was in the most dramatic fashion, for Pauline had stormed off the stage in rehearsals for Humperdink's *Hänsel und Gretel,* much of the cast refusing to work with her because of her temper and bizarre antics. In his surprise announcement, Strauss not only saved their on-again off-again relationship but, a master of good timing, he apparently solidified the opera company behind him. Pauline and Richard were not yet ready to marry, not for a good while. They were thinking about it… She even wrote to him asking if he was sure he knew what he was getting in to. Good question.

Richard may have had something more than matrimony on his mind. He was contemplating a return to Munich as associate conductor. In fact, he did return for four more years. Pauline told him that she wanted him to do so – more money and more prestige. About that time Richard took ill; he used his recuperation time to travel to Egypt and Italy, to heal, to read, to find his center. Strauss wrote most of the score to *Guntram* while feasting on the euphoria of these enticing new places. He even managed to write in a role for Pauline. She would be his *Freiheld,* something of a bringer of spiritual truth. Not surprisingly, and not for the first time, rehearsals were difficult with Pauline de Ahna in the mix.

When the opera opened in Weimar, audiences found his *Guntram* by no means a great draw. This was largely due, at least in part, to its disestablishmentarian theme, specifically it's theme against organized religion. *Guntram* was difficult for some patrons to accept. We learn that Richard's publicist lost a good bit of money on the work, to which even Cosima objected. The opera played only a single night in Munich. But Strauss, steeped in high Wagnerian drama, was writing with a message, and he would remain true to his need to innovate. There would be other themes, other opportunities. Something was missing…

Strauss decided that he would take a wife, and in so doing take what he hoped would be a step up in his career. Richard and Pauline married that September, he assenting to her request for a Roman Catholic wedding, although he had no ties to the faith. Strauss, for all his fascination with new forms and for pushing the boundaries of creativity, was also a world-class accommodator. Maybe he was maturing. Certainly he was wiser. In a manner he had not yet fully understood, his family life and career were now as one. The woman who would act as a prime mover in her husband's work, in so many ways assure his daily bread, was now in the house.

The next year Richard wrote the whimsical symphonic poem *Till Eulenspiegel's Merry Pranks,* followed closely by *Don Quixote*, and then *Ein Heldenleben*, or A Hero's Life. In the latter Richard shows the listener his autobiographical side, making himself the unabashed hero, as well as offering what was said to be "a musical portrait of his wife." In the first performances of *Heldenleben*, Strauss also gave Pauline the honor of singing the principal soprano parts. During his initial scoring of *Eulenspiegel* an audacious Pauline annotated her husband's score with such comments as "dreadful," "mad," and "lousy composition." From the beginning, Pauline was nothing if not vexing and compelling, outrageous and endearing, in nearly equal parts.

"She had enough temperament for three." We learn "[i]t was her habit to say what she thought, uninhibitedly, and with disarming directness."[28] But Strauss was enchanted. He wrote his opus 27, *Four Songs*, as a wedding gift for Pauline. Actually, he wrote many more songs for her, but as her voice began to change, to fail, touchingly he wrote fewer. In 1904 Strauss wrote the tone poem *Sinfonia Domestica*, a complement to *Ein Heldenleben*, which treats the quiet satisfaction of an untroubled marriage, even to include "merry arguments."[29] In 1922, when Strauss was fifty-eight years old, he wrote the opera *Intermezzo* with his wife firmly in mind, and his tongue firmly in his cheek.

Here, the churlish woman, mistakenly thinking her husband has been cheating on her with a bar girl – the event actually happened – initiates a terrible row with the hapless hubby. The opera ends with their complete reconciliation. Richard got a great deal of inspiration for his work from his life with his Pauline.[30] The stage sets were even copied from the walls of the Strauss family home in Garmisch. Call these two compositions *Tales of Pauline*.

"Her temperament was as necessary to him as the air he breathed,"[31] and no one ever said he did not love her. There was never a hint of scandal, no vacation from their vows. Even if an aging Richard held tenuously and fondly to the traces of his early love for Dora Wihan, he was always true to his wife, the outlandish Pauline.

Of course this brief treatment of Strauss's work, especially that as composer, has been select and may seem to some Strauss lovers as somewhat arbitrary. As with twenty-eight or so other composers, however, their vast production is treated here only in the light of some demonstrated Muse-ical inspiration. That said, Strauss, as much and maybe more than most of the men in this volume, owed his accomplishments to one particular woman. "The man who had no equal in the composition of music for and about women…who loved the company of women – that man was irreproachably faithful. He knew only one all-embracing love, enjoyed complete trust, complete harmony with the woman who was his other self: Pauline."[32]

His other great love, as we know, was conducting, especially so where travel was involved. Richard loved to travel as much as Schumann, fifty years before him, had not. The couple had gone to live their final years in Garmisch, after highly successful years in Berlin, and then as director of the State Opera in Vienna. Strauss had been injured by the vagaries of the coming war and nasty Nazi politics, but his last years were peaceful.

After celebrating his 85th birthday, in June of 1949, Strauss traveled the next month to the city of his birth, to Munich; here he conducted the Moonlight Music from his 1940 opera *Capriccio*. It was his last performance. Richard had a series of heart attacks and his health failed quickly. His friend and Munich producer went to see him in hospital late in July and Strauss told him that he was dying; he asked him, almost as a favor, *"Grüss mir die Welt!"* Greet the world for me.

Richard Strauss had written music for all the world, and in the last fifty-five years he often wrote specifically for Pauline. He died in his bed on 8 September 1949, but not before he completed one particularly significant composition. Recall that he wrote *Four Songs* for Pauline as a wedding gift in 1894. They would prove a worthy theme once more. In tranquility, Richard returned in 1948 to those four final songs. They were, more accurately, his *Vier Letzte Lieder* – Four Last Songs, performed only posthumously.

Herein his music complements the poetry he had selected of Herman Hesse, to whom he had often turned for an appropriate back story. Hesse, too, was a man transfixed by the rise and fall of his fellow man's spirit. While we learn that Strauss dedicated the four songs specifically to many of his closest friends and contemporaries, suggesting a mood of reconciliation to one's death and transfiguration, "it cannot be doubted that it is Pauline who haunts every bar of each song."[33]

Mrs. Pauline de Ahna Strauss, the ideal complement to Richard's magnificent spirit, died the next year in their home in Garmisch, nine days before the world premiere of those songs in London.

Arthur McMaster

CHAPTER SEVENTEEN

STRAVINSKY, Igor (1882 - 1971); Russian, American

"Minor composers may achieve great popularity in their day, but they never influence the course of music. Stravinsky did. He always was at the end of the rope, pulling everybody along with him. [1]

This chap was destined to become no minor composer. Named for St. Igor, on whose feast day he arrived, this fellow grew up in a home where music mattered. Stravinsky's parents were well-to-do and highly educated people. Music in the Stravinsky home was as constant and the sharply defined seasons of his native land.

"At the age of nine he was given a piano mistress and quickly learned to read music – particularly the opera scores he found in the family library, for his father Feodor [more often written as Fyodor] was one of the most celebrated bass-baritones of his day."[2] Papa began his singing career with the Kiev Opera, then sang with the Imperial Opera in St. Petersburg. Among his standards were several of the works of Mikhail Glinka and Modeste Mussorgsky. Whether he meant to do so or not, Fyodor gave his son a taste for opera as grand construction. Only later did the boy actually get to hear the music, to see the performers. Stravinsky himself suggests that he inherited his ability to read musical scores from his mother, an accomplished pianist, and who was particularly gifted at this kind of work.[3]

Other family members demonstrated interests in wider musical forms, as well as in broad social issues – in social problems, politics, and art.[4] Young Igor Fyodorovich, then, was surrounded by radicals and "free thinkers," especially among his mother's family. There is little wonder that the boy grew up curious and precocious.

His piano teacher, one Mlle. Leokadiya Kashperova – Igor called her a talented blockhead – was a student of the esteemed Anton Rubenstein. Strict in her pedagogical approach to form, she nevertheless encouraged Igor's broader interests in music. Kashperova helped Igor to master, at the age of ten-years, Mendelssohn's *G minor concerto* "and many sonatas by Clementi and Mozart, as well as sonatas and other pieces by Haydn, Beethoven, Schubert, and Schumann."[5] The boy's background was solid in the classical and Romantic forms. He also "knew all the Wagner works from the piano scores."[6] He soon realized that none of these would do. The little Russian was about to become another revolutionary. He had some preparatory work to do first.

If not necessarily a scholar, master Stravinsky was a voracious reader, enjoying Horace and Flaubert. Later, he read Dickens; and his hero during his university years was Dostoyevsky – socio-political commentary at its finest. His early exposure to such timeless themes of hero and anti-hero, peasant and privileged, would factor in to his music in a demonstrable way. Moreover, such broad exposure to the arts and intellectual discourse foreshadowed his highly eclectic tastes throughout his long life, even to include an infatuation with American jazz, which Igor Fyodorovich managed to incorporate into his breakout material between the wars in Europe. While his actual music training was certainly solid, the young man showed little interest or affinity for harmony, focusing rather on counterpoint, which led him to a fascination with composition. Igor was not interested in writing more sonatas. His road would be less traveled by. Equally significant was the young Stravinsky's interest in variations on themes. Self-imposed exercises "opened up a wider vista in the domain of musical composition and did more than anything else at this period of his life to stimulate his imagination and desire to compose, and to lay the ground work of his future technique."[7]

Stravinsky wrote about the significance of such broad experience in his 1936 autobiography; he wrote about how much he admired Mikhail Glinka, a premier Russian nationalist composer. He offered that such improvisation sowed the seeds of musical ideas.[8] He later studied under Rimsky-Korsakov and excelled as a pianist under his tutelage. Rimsky was professor of composition and instrumentation at the prestigious St. Petersburg Conservatory, sharing his lodgings with Mussorgsky. Igor Stravinsky did not want for exposure to the best and the brightest.

But his musical career was anything but pre-scripted. His father demanded that Igor study law, which he dutifully did for years. His father wanted Igor to take this study into a career. That part of the agreement he steadfastly refused.

Fyodor had also expected to become a lawyer, and was determined that his son would do so if he could not. In fact, two of Igor's brothers were also expected to pursue such studies. Music, said father, was too unpredictable. This business of law was an obstacle to Igor, but he got over it, as did, presumably, the young man's father. Maybe he rejected the law because he was drawn to music as an alternative career, or maybe because he never had a loving relationship with his father, whom he described as "cold and cruel."

The only member of his family Igor was close to was his younger brother Goury, also expected to study law, as was an older brother, Roman, who died of illness at age twenty-one. The composer says Goury, two years younger, "had inherited my father's voice and musical ear… and he was determined to be a singer."[9]

The Stravinsky family was large and made larger by the inveigling of his mother's people into the circle. As a young boy, Igor would accompany his elders, sometimes with or without brothers, to his mother's aunt's estate at Pechisky, in the heart of the Ukraine. Little Igor disliked most of the people there, certainly to include Aunt Yekaterina. One young member of the entourage, however, would change his life.

Before meeting her we should consider how early images and experiences of the region where they met came to play a significant role in Stravinsky's later work. For example, it was in this countryside that he conceived ideas for his beloved *Petrushka*. "One pictures [the town], from the description in [Stravinsky's autobiographical] *Expositions and Developments*, amid a sea of wheat, vibrating with peasant dancing, the heel dance (*presyatka*) and the Cossack kicking dance (the *kazachok*), and the wonderful costumes in the primary reds, blues, and yellows – the whole setting for a kind of rural *Petrushka*."[10]

Fair Pechisky offered much more. This is where he came to know and to grow close to his cousin Yekaterina Nosenko – called Katya, no doubt to distinguish her from her mother. Katya, often anglicized to Catherine, would become Stravinsky's first wife. Immediately she would begin to shape the first decades of the man's creative future. They became fast friends, kindred spirits, while still young and much in love. "'From our first hour together, Stravinsky wrote seventy years later, "we both seemed to realize that we would one day marry – or so we told each other later… Catherine, who was my first cousin, came into my life as a kind of long-awaited sister in my tenth year. We were from then until her death extremely close, and closer than lovers are sometimes, for mere lovers may be strangers though they live and love together all their lives."[11]

Their cousinly love grew over the next few years, Igor writing to her and asking for letters in return, telling his mother how "wonderful" he thought Katya was. One year older, Katya played her part equally well. This bright and attractive girl, who had gone to Paris to study music, to become a singer, made it clear she was captivated by Stravinsky. A reader of Pushkin, Catherine was a serious-minded girl whose love of music and painting mirrored his own. She found in him something exceptional and astonishing.[12] Given the awkwardness with his father, Igor needed just such validation.

Stravinsky fed on Katya's support and reassurance. In fact, her dedication was vital. Igor's parents, though musicians themselves, did not give him the kind of encouragement the boy expected and needed. The elder Stravinskys made it clear to Igor that his music was somewhat "amateurish." Forget music; be a lawyer, they said. He never forgave them for their lack of support. But the man had plenty of determination. He never doubted his talent. For Igor Fyodorovich it was only a matter of where to focus his boundless energy.

At nineteen, Stravinsky was still looking for his own creative center, still sorting out in his own mind what kind of music he would compose. He took a deeper interest in Chabrier and Bizet. With these composers, aided by his study with Pokrovksy, Igor found "a different type of musical writing, different harmonic methods ... a freer and fresher use of form."[13] Soon he was experimenting with his first compositions, and at least one, the romance *Storm Cloud*, for voice and piano, evidently took its inspiration from some romance of his own. *Storm Cloud*, taken from a Pushkin poem, is the earliest vocal work of the composer to survive. Was it music composed for his new love?

The year 1905 was important in Russian history for a number of reasons, not least for the first major uprising against the Tsarist system, that October. It was also the year Igor finished his course of study, largely at law, at the university in St. Petersburg. Stravinsky decided to complete his coming of age by asking for the hand of the young woman he loved.

Igor and Katya became engaged to be married that August. They were twenty-one and twenty-two years old. They were married five months later in the village of Novaya Derevnya, near St. Petersburg, "with not one member of their families present. The only attendants were Andrei and Vladimir Rimsky-Korsakov, sons of the composer."[14]

Stravinsky's best man was the one he called "master," Nikolai Rimsky-Korsakov. The break with family could not have been clearer. Igor had chosen his own path, unable to forget the hurtful memories he associated with his parents' rejection of his chosen career in music.

His formal education now behind him, Stravinsky spent time developing his musical talents, especially in composition. He grew particularly close to Rimsky-Korsakov, arguably the center member of "the five," Russia's preeminent group of nationalist composers. The music of these men dates from about 1860 -70, and includes Rimsky-Korsakov, Cui, Balakirev, Borodin, and Modest Mussorgsky. Their purpose was to express a Russian spirit in music. Rimsky was also the only one of the five whom Igor considered especially influential. Stravinsky became close to Rimsky's esteemed friend Alexander Scriabin, and the brilliant, youthful Sergei Prokofiev. Igor Fyodorovich knew, however, that he had learned from them all he needed in order to move in a different direction. Stravinsky, with Katya steeling his often tenuous resolve, had a head start in making a new kind of music.

The next year he was working determinedly on a number of new pieces. Katya, trained in voice, had also studied music calligraphy. She regularly helped her husband with copying out scores. She did a great deal more. The honeymooners had settled in Ustilug, a city they knew well from frequent visits with family members, before the schism that followed Igor's graduation from university. "They had with them the score from Rimsky's *Kitezh*, which the composer had given to Igor before the wedding."[15] Igor was putting together the basic construction of something compelling and exciting. He wrote that spring to Volodya Rimsky-Korsakov, "the music of the *Faune et bergère* was growing in my head." Again, the young Rimsky-Korsakov was a member of Igor and Katya's wedding party. Stravinsky soon began the *Faun and Shepherdess*, a symphonic suite for soprano and orchestra. He launched the project while on his honeymoon, dedicating the highly unusual work to his young wife.

Perhaps it was also meant to be a wedding gift, although by any standards the theme of a teen-aged girl being ravished by a randy forest creature seems a bit overly erotic to serve as a proper present. Responding to the common wisdom that their relationship was romantically somewhat subdued, we find "[i]f Igor chose them [Pushkin poems, upon which the suite is based] as a suitable offering for his cousinly bride, then we may well need to adjust the usual view – encouraged in later years by the composer himself – of the couple's early relationship."[16] In later years, and certainly after Stravinsky began his active affair with another woman, he referred to Katya in ways that would suggest their marriage was missing something. Igor, for his part, was never slow to look ahead.

Whatever the pitch and timbre of his personal life then there was something changing in his appreciation for music. He became more curious about music from abroad. Specifically, he was becoming attentive to a few non-Russian composers whose work he enjoyed and, to some degree, he'd begun to emulate. None was more influential than Claude Debussy, whose *Images*, for piano, composed between 1905 and 1907, were so distinctive. Actually, Rimsky-Korsakov had encouraged Stravinsky to experiment with orchestration. RK was not fully comfortable with the direction in which musical forms were leading. Stravinsky writes: "When I asked to go to a concert to hear Debussy's music he [Rimsky] said, 'I have already heard it. I had better not go: I will start to get accustomed to it and finally like it.'"[17]

Besides the fact that Stravinsky thought Rimsky to be overly provincial in his literary tastes, the only apparent source of disagreement between the two was over the relative worth of Tchaikovsky as a major Russian composer. This was no small disagreement. Stravinsky, writing in his *Memories and Commentaries* with his friend, the conductor Robert Craft, says Rimsky Korsakov was jealous of the larger recognition Tchaikovsky was getting in the rest of Europe, especially in Germany. Ironically, Pyotr Tchaikovsky, in most ways more balanced in his dealings with "rivals," was always a great admirer of the man four years his junior.[18]

Nicolai Rimsky-Korsakov died of heart failure in 1908, at the age of sixty-four. Stravinsky was saddened but not surprised. He'd become particularly close with Volodya, himself a fine musician. They were both witness to the old man's two year decline. As close as he was to both men, it is likely that Stravinsky had steeled himself against the day he would lose Nicolai, in a real sense his substitute father. He also knew that Rimsky likely had taught him all he could, or might.

Another figure, this one also larger than life, was about to become an influential force in the life of the young composer. Stravinsky was twenty-eight years old when Sergei Diaghilev heard Igor's orchestral suite, *Scherzo Fantastique*. The impresario, a man of wealth and influence, was impressed. Maybe Igor was in the right place at the right time.

"As artistic director of the Russian Ballet (*Ballets Russe*) he was entirely responsible for the conception and production of its entire repertoire… [he] liked Stravinsky's compositions, he liked the fresh rhythms and especially the glittering cascades of sound he heard in *Fireworks*." We learn, "It was a highly inventive and compelling new work, in which one could hear the arresting rhythms that would change musical history."[19] Stravinsky was about to enter into the next phase, so far the most important phase, of his career as composer.

Some biographers speculate that with Rimsky dead, Igor Stravinsky actively sought a new patron, a new protector.[20] It seems likely that the young man needed someone to open the right doors, to sponsor his outrageous genius. There is also the fact that Russia was now unsettled. Politically, she was a tinderbox of conflicting radical and revanchist ideas. Worse for Stravinsky, a composer who insisted on "making it new," to echo Ezra Pound, an almost exact contemporary of the composer; few seemed to want to hear the music he wanted most to make. It was time to move on. Paris was calling, and it was calling for *avant-garde* Russians. With the arrival of Diaghilev, Stravinsky, and the Nijinsky siblings, French theater goers would get much of the best in Russian ex-patriots.

Diaghilev was looking for a way to reinvigorate one particular ballet, in its many components, when his *Firebird* stalled in the summer of 1909. The impresario thought he wanted Maurice Ravel. No; Ravel was already committed to *Daphnis and Chloe*, which, as it turns out, did not materialize until 1912. Diaghilev's in-house composers would not work out either. Could Stravinsky possibly accept the assignment? If so, there would be a clear deadline. Stravinsky was excited: "the legendary figure of the Firebird was already a kind of insignia for the modern style in Russia."[21] Diaghilev made a firm offer to Stravinsky that December, and Igor Fyodorovich immediately began working on the libretto. "Not only did he manage to compose three-quarters of an hour of sumptuously orchestrated music in less than six months … but he accepted a collaborative element in the writing which would have been dust and ashes for him later on."[22]

The collaboration, of course, refers to work with Mikhail Fokine, the original choreographer, whom Stravinsky thought bright but a bit ham-handed. Such complex collaboration is hard to get right, especially when the principals have not worked together before. For his own part, and where his work truly succeeded, Stravinsky was able to call upon his training in orchestration that he learned from his friend Rimsky-Korsakov.

The Firebird was an enormous success. The composer had worked from his place in St. Petersburg on this, his first ballet. It was also his first cooperative foray into ballet. The Stravinskys arrived in Paris early the next spring for rehearsals. *L'Oiseau de Feu*, to use it proper French title, premiered on 25 June 1910, at the Paris Opéra. *Firebird* was only the first of many collaborations. A few years later he worked with Pablo Picasso in *Pulcinella* (1920) and then Jean Cocteau for *Oedipus Rex*, in 1927, and finally George Balanchine *(Apollon Musagete)* in 1928. In any event, this was the one that led to his greatest fame. *Petrushka* and *The Right of Spring*, followed over the next few years.

One night during rehearsals for *Firebird*, Diaghilev told the dancer Tamara Karsavina, "Mark him well. He is a man on the eve of celebrity."[23] We are reminded of the prophetic words of Mozart upon meeting the nineteen-year old Beethoven, almost two hundred years before, in Vienna. Claude Debussy, present on opening night, came back stage to congratulate

Stravinsky on his score. Igor could not have been more pleased; Debussy was one of the "new composers" he most respected.

This was no Romantic ballet; it was a music none had heard nor expected. Some patrons were scandalized. What was at least as significant in all this is that Stravinsky had demonstrated the strength of using a new score for ballet, something written on demand for ballet, when it was standard practice to find something only "suitable." Stravinsky's reputation was made that night.

The composer, then twenty-eight, would collaborate with Diaghilev for another twenty years, composing seven more ballets. Yes, there were speed bumps. Stravinsky and Diaghilev had a big falling a few years later, but to be fair Stravinsky eventually had a big falling out with almost everyone he worked with, at some point. The more celebrated the individual the more likely there would be some artistic tension, a perceived slight, the awkward contractual dispute.

Igor Fyodorovich found that over the next few years he was required to spend much of his time in Paris. He also had a conundrum – his wife. Stravinsky found that he very much enjoyed the work in this most engaging city, but where did that leave his Katya? They usually made camp away from the busy city, yet Igor was drawn like a Luna moth to the light. When not in France they were often in Switzerland, thought to be good for Katya's fragile lungs. Wherever they were, Igor was working incessantly. Katya supported as she could.

Here, Stravinsky thinks back to the time he struck upon the theme for his next major work: "I came up with the idea for piano and orchestra – a kind of *Burlesque* or *Scherzo* … in which the piano would represent a puppet, suddenly endowed with life, exasperating the orchestra with diabolical cascades of *arpeggi*, and the orchestra replying with menacing fanfares."[24] Stravinsky brought the idea to Diaghilev who, along with another librettist, developed the idea for what became *Petrushka*, the love-struck puppet who finds both life and sudden death at the St. Petersburg Carnival. Stravinsky called upon Russian folk songs and some previous musical sketches to complete the zesty, garish, morality play that so captivated the Paris theatre crowd when it opened the next year, in 1911.

Even before *Petrushka* had taken its final form Stravinsky was putting together the ideas for *The Rite of Spring*, his third great collaboration with Diaghilev and the *Ballets Russe*. Also set in Russia, more importantly so set in pagan times, *Le Sacre du Printemps* is another expression of man's inability to survive the elemental forces of nature. This ballet, opening two years later, would mark Stravinsky as one of the great geniuses of early twentieth-century composition. As mentioned, not everyone was convinced it was genius at all, at least as many people could not understand the music, trying to find some reason and interpretation in known entities. Not even Igor's mother, living with her son and family at the time, was particularly supportive, telling a friend that it was not her kind of music.[25] All this apparently struck Stravinsky as quite right, affirming his believe that most music patrons were bourgeois idiots. He was more than content riding Occam's razor.

As Stravinsky's star rose he began to look for personal and, for lack of a better word, intellectual stimulation in the other arts, thinking he would find ideas good for composition there. The composer had already been intrigued by such breakaway groups as "the futurists," and *Les Fauves* (the Wild Beasts), and he new that what was bold was becoming all the more acceptable. Igor was looking to do something besides the ballet music, which was quickly becoming a burden. He did not want to be identified as just a Russian ballet composer. Igor wanted to work outside the ropes. In doing so, other musicians became important to him – men besides Debussy, men whose music he respected as they did his *avant garde* work. Central to this movement was Erik Satie, who later wrote of the Russian composer: "I love and admire Stravinsky because I perceive also that he is a liberator. More than anyone else he has freed the musical thought of today, which was sadly in need of development."[26]

But Paris life was wearing him out. He needed to get away; he needed quiet to work. Igor and Katya, now with two children, found respite away from the city. They began spending time in Switzerland, away from the cacophony of Paris. No doubt this time away permitted him to work. Igor Fyodorovich returned to some orchestrations he had set aside. In 1910 he set to music, for voice and piano, *Two Poems by Verlaine*. The work came between his ever-so popular ballet scores. The next year he wrote, again for voice and piano, *Two Poems of Balmont*. Something was missing; for at the same time he needed the energy of the city, and he knew that Katya never felt at home in Paris. The contradictions wore on him, wore on this man whose home life and career would always be complicated. Not surprisingly, it was another woman who would make things more difficult, more confused. Katya was still in the picture, but another Stravinsky Muse was heading his way.

When in 1921 Diaghilev introduced Stravinsky to Vera Sudeikina, wife of the impresario's costume designer at the Opéra, the young composer quickly fell in love with her. It is not that Katya was unloved, far from it; but Vera was somehow the breath of fresh air Stravinsky told himself he needed, as the physical marriage with Katya atrophied. Theirs was not a casual or even a discreet affair. "Catherine accepted her husband's infidelity, bearing it with a mixture of magnanimity, bitterness, and compassion. Given the nature of her marital relationship, Catherine's passive acceptance of her husband's indiscretion is not surprising. She had always been submissive, viewing herself as the wife of a great man destined to transform the musical world."[27] Yet, even the youngest of the Stravinsky's four children, Maria Milena, born in 1914, told one biographer "that her mother was the person her father loved most in his life. She recalled that in his final years he [Igor] said of her mother 'The minute I met her, I loved her and I still love her.'"[28] While a daughter may pad a memory to flatter her mother, she could well have it exactly right.

Others would say that it was Vera Sudeikina who was ultimately the love of Stravinsky's life, but it is hard to argue with the daughter's testimony, or with the fact that Katya saw her husband through his most trying period – the beginning of his compositional career. For nearly eighteen years, and until Katya's death in 1939, Stravinsky simultaneously led two lives, one with each woman. He was hardly the first major composer to do so. On top of such complications, he had time to have affairs with two other women, at least one of which inspired some original music. More on the fellow's peccadillo's in a moment.

Whether or not we choose to see Katya as saint, martyr, or dupe we have to recognize that, by staying with her husband, she showed amazing will power. We may believe the couple's youngest daughter her father always loved his first wife, but we also know that he needed a source of elemental energy from somewhere else for his work. In this sense he favored Puccini. Stravinsky needed a Muse on familiar terms with the Eros, or certainly with Erato.

Could he not have simply gone back to Russia to work, possibly making a move that could have helped to keep Igor and Katya closer? We don't know if Stravinsky ever considered it in that light, but he expected he would be financially better off in his homeland.

It was not to be. The Russian revolution and the First World War effectively blocked his return. Like Diaghilev, "and many Russians then living in Western Europe, he had felt exhilarated by the 1917 revolution …[but] found himself cut off from his private resources in Russia; and for the first time the possibility must have occurred to him that he might never return to his native country."[29] Igor Stravinsky was suddenly out of funds and, in essence, forced to become an exile.

The ex-patriot composer got by financially, but he found himself forced to write music just to pay the basic family expenses. The family spent time both in France and in Switzerland for the next few years. Actually, this quiet time proved something of a boon for Katya and the children – a period of domestic tranquility for the Stravinskys. During these lean years Igor found the time to write several children's songs and two more sets of piano works that have aged well. Igor composed *Three Easy Pieces* (March, Waltz and Polka) for piano duet, keeping the left hand simple and accessible for novice pianists. Did he write them for his children? The composer and Katya's third child, Soulima, says they were written specifically for him.[30] In 1916-17 Igor wrote *Five Easy Pieces* for piano duet, and here he moved the simpler construction to the right side. At the age of thirty-five, in late 1917, he wrote a *Berceuse for Voice and Piano*. Over the next few years, still with Katya and the kids, Igor wrote *Four Russian Songs* for voice and piano. Remember that Katya was an accomplished singer. She had studied in Paris as an eighteen year old. True, we have no proof that all or any of these works were done expressly for Catherine and the children. They do offer, however, a cogent explanation for the composer's motivation. His wife's health was not good; her lungs were getting weaker. Perhaps he was being considerate, affectionate. It was not a common trait in this man who eschewed emotion in music. Of course there was "the other woman" and with her arrival there would be a profusion of emotional feelings.

Sergei Diaghilev was well connected to the larger arts scene, to "a whirlpool of artistic enthusiasm."[31] He had made it a point to introduce his friends, colleagues, and his prized talent to all the literati, to all the artistic elite, and especially so in Paris which demanded such celebration. Stravinsky met Pablo Picasso through Sergei. In every sense of the word, Diaghilev was an inveterate glad-hander and matchmaker. In May of 1920 Stravinsky's neo-classical ballet *Pulcinella* opened to packed houses. The highly respected Ernest Ansermet was the conductor. Picasso did the sets, having suffered through a wild disagreement with Diaghilev as to what they should look like. But on opening night the public knew they had been witness to a most fabulously chic bit of musical theater. Diaghilev was not shy about taking credit. "Pulcinella had brought together two such geniuses [alluding to Picasso]; in another of those dazzlingly integrated shows which proved that the World of Art spirit was still in command at the *Ballets Russe*."[32]

Sergei Diaghilev's extra-curricular work in human dynamics was not finished. He introduced Igor to the wealthy and scampy fashion designer Gabrielle "Coco" Chanel during rehearsals of *Pulcinella*. Speculation abounds as to whether or not the composer and the well-to-do lady had a fling. She says they did,[33] but she would not count as a true Muse unless she inspired some of Stravinsky's music. What she did do, and which could give her certain minor credits in that department, was to provide the composer money to continue work when his accounts were running unexpectedly low. With his limited assets frozen in Russia, "Chanel, one of the great French couturieres of the time, came to his assistance, not only lending him financial aid but going so far as to have all the new costumes executed in her dressmaking shops.[34]

The one biographer who became the composer's friend and the ghost writer for some of Stravinsky's late autobiographical work, Robert Craft, holds the opinion that Igor and Coco were intimate. Perhaps more significantly, however, Mlle Chanel also provided additional logistic support Igor Stravinsky needed while staying in Paris. She had a villa outside the city, called Bel Respiro, which seemed to suit Igor well. Katya lived there too, for a while, until the family had to relocate to a sunnier clime for her deteriorating health. It was the unfortunate Katya's shaky constitution as much as any other consideration that brought the Stravinsky family to live in Biarritz.

We know that Igor couldn't stay away from Paris. Performances of his work, now international, nearly always premiered in Paris. Igor Fyodorich reveled in their success. Whatever else was happening at Ms. Chanel's villa, it was here that "Stravinsky at last finished his string quartet piece for [violinist Alfred] Pochon, a four-minute, single-movement work which he called *Concertino*, and he was now mainly at work on the full score of the *Symphonies of Wind Instruments*."[35] The coastal town near the Basque region of Spain boasted a large Russian émigré presence and even its own Russian Orthodox Church. For Katya, slowly fading from her tuberculosis, Biarritz was as close to Russia as she would ever be again.

Vera Sudeikina, who along with her husband was much a part of the Diaghilev retinue, was a presence if not yet a major factor. She was never far from the busy artistic center, however, and Igor Fyodorovich was likely interested. Theirs was no fast passion. This is not to say that, whatever was going on or not going on at Bel Respiro, Stravinsky wasn't about to lose his head. Perhaps he was simply in the mood for something outré. The usual suspects were having a late dinner following a performance of a production at the *Theâtre Femina*, in May of 1921. We know Stravinsky was feeling a bit low, so Diaghilev, ever the fixer, asked Vera to intercede. She'd help by trying one of her parlor tricks. Might she read his fortune? He agreed. Vera proclaimed him, this awkward and uncertain Mr. Stravinsky, "'the wittiest, most amusing man I had ever met.' The cards, if she read them correctly, will have warned her of more than an emotional attachment."[36] Whatever she saw, it was not likely to have been the impetuous composer's reaction to another woman.

This one was a spirited dancer, Zhenya Nikitna, performing at a theater pandering to Russians in the city. She strutted and cavorted in the role of Katinka, another Russian doll come to life. Hers was fine timing. Apparently, at least for the moment, she brought Igor Fyodorovich to life, as well.

Artur Rubenstein, a late comer to the ex-patriot pack, recorded that the composer "fell head over heels in love with the voluptuous Zhenya. Whether or not we believe Rubenstein's highly colored account of the composer coming to him in despair at his supposed impotence in the ultimate presence of this mock-exotic creature, it seems certain that there was an affair." We learn that Zhenya asked the composer to write something for her, and the result was the orchestration of a four-hand piano polka, "originally a portrait of Diaghilev as a circus master, but now transformed into a Chauve-Souris [theater] dance, completed with Katinka's own theme added by way of a brief coda on flute and trombone."[37]

Theirs was also a meteoric relationship, based on elemental lust and celebrity; but we do have some fresh Stravinsky music as a bumper crop. The interlude passed quickly enough; and with Coco and Zhenya now consigned to the man's memory, Vera was primed to find her way to the forefront of Igor's passions and musical soul. Not to put too fine a point on it; Igor Stravinsky needed the physical side of marriage, and his life – not to say his love – with and for Katya was essentially doomed when she became too ill to share his bed. His next Muse was getting impatient.

Vera de Bosset Sudeikina was born on Christmas Day, in 1888, in St. Petersburg, to French and Swedish parents. Her father was a well-to-do French businessman with factory in Russia. The young Vera was largely educated by her governess, in Gorky. She was an accomplished pianist, playing a Scriabin etude in her graduation recital.[38] Vera also loved theater and became an actress, appearing in the film, "War and Peace," in Moscow, in 1915. Months earlier she had married an Englishman who fancied gambling more than providing a secure home. Unable to deal with such a topsy-turvy situation, and being raised to expect comfort and style, Mrs. Vera Shilling eloped the next year to marry the more artistic-minded Sergei (Serge) Sudeikin, Diaghilev's friend and sometime set designer. We can assume there was a comfort in staying close to what passed for her "Russian roots." We'll return soon to the idea of her ethnicity.

More importantly, Vera was drawn to the theater world and to those that populated it, drawn as much as she was to Sergei Sudeikin, himself. Vera and Serge actually married without the convenience or benefit of having obtained divorces from their legal spouses, an engaging oversight perhaps attributable to the chaos of the Revolution.[39]

To say that Mlle. de Bosset was Russian is only to make a statement about where she once lived. When the revolution barred the Sudeikin couple's return she easily accommodated to a life in the west, no doubt more so than did any of the true ex-patriots making up her social circle. A confident actress, Vera had no trouble staging a romance in the heart of the little Russian composer. It would not be unkind to say that she was also a master of timing, having watched a few women enter and leave Igor's fancifully romantic world. Biding her time, Vera emerged as Stravinsky's true inamorata. She must have been kind-hearted as well. If we take their letters to each other at face value, Vera and the ever failing Katya seemed to get on swimmingly.

Back to the hearth and home, everyone in Igor's circle knew that Katya was gradually losing her battle with tuberculosis. She succumbed in 1939, just after the Stravinskys had lost their daughter Lyudmilla, affectionately called Mika, to the same disease. Igor and Vera married the year after Katya's passing, but they had been lovers for eighteen years. For his part, Stravinsky had managed to find a way to lead two nearly parallel lives, spending "some of his time with his first family and the rest with Vera. Katerina [accepted] ... the relationship as inevitable and permanent."[40] Igor evidently took her generous understanding in stride.

The couple was married in New York, where they had gone from France to escape the onset of yet another European war, in 1940. Stravinsky had not been idle in these many years he shared with both women.

The first instance in which Stravinsky clearly celebrated his paramour Vera as Muse dates to the completion of his *Octet for Wind Instruments*, in 1923. This was two years after they had met and followed quickly his rather poorly received opera bouffe *Mavra*, with its clear tribute to Glinka. Few besides Vera gave Stravinsky any support on the latter, though the composer says that it marked a clear change in his development as a composer.

Indeed it did; Igor Fyodorovich called it "a turning point in the evolution of my musical thought."[41] At least as important, *Mavra* was a private success which he could, and did, share with Vera. As for the *Octet* itself, Stravinsky says he received his inspiration for the music in a dream. He supposedly found himself in a room listening to musicians playing something particularly delightful. Next morning he wrote down what had come to him in the night. "Perhaps I had Bach's *Two Part Inventions* in mind while composing this movement. The *Octet* is dedicated to Vera de Bosset."[42]

We should not assume that Stravinsky had stopped writing music for his Katya, or that she was no longer a part of his compositional efforts. Igor Fyodorovich was a slow and careful composer, and we know he was careful to include his first wife in the preliminary reviews of many of his works. His jump from the so-called Primitive, or Russian Impressionistic period to these mid-career, neo-classical compositions was not easy. The one piece we know that he wrote for Katya, even though he was now more Vera's lover than Catherine's husband, was inscribed "a ma femme," in the summer of 1925. This is his *Serenade in La*, for piano.[43] It's interesting that what he was dedicating to her was another break-through piece of music.

Peter Serkin writes that the composition was written specifically to be recorded on "plastic"– that Stravinsky was in negotiations with Columbia, who would not actually bring out the music until 1934. Stravinsky explained that the concept of "en la" meant "all the music [must] revolve around an axis of sound which happened to be *la*."[44] It was one of the composer's first important foray's into polyphony. Why he decided to give this piece to Katya is unclear, as Vera was more active in supporting his metamorphosis as a modern composer. Maybe Katya represented a singleness of purpose that Vera did not.

Stravinsky no doubt knew he would have plenty of time to write for or about Vera, who would share his life for fifty years. The longer they were together the closer they grew. Both took French citizenship in 1934, and then, in 1945, American. We know Vera was the inspiration for 1931 *Violin Concerto*. The background to this loving assignment comes from someone close to the source. Lindsay Fischer, George Balanchine's principal dancer, recounted: "I'm going to commit a ballet indiscretion by kissing and telling the meaning behind [the] *Violin Concerto*… It was [Fischer said] the "music maker's infidelity – not his high fidelity."[45] We can forgive Mr. Fischer his purple prose, as he seems only interested in telling the news Balanchine knew to be true about his friend and collaborating musical genius. Whatever we may think about the descriptive rhetoric, Vera was entitled to her due as Muse.

Two years later Stravinsky's highly introspective melodrama for symphony, chorus, and dancers, *Perséphone*, taken from André Gide's traditional libretto, was performed at the Paris Opera House. The storyline is classic: After a nasty turn in the underworld the heroine Persephone is reborn and returned to earth as queen of the spring. It is all very romantic, recalling "the serenity of Gluck's Elysian music in *Orpheus*."[46] Stravinsky had romantic themes in mind when he wrote it, even though this was a style and form no longer thought to be of much interest to the middle-aged composer. Actually, his interest was great, his sense of gratitude even deeper.

Igor Fyodorovich traveled to London to conduct the British premier of the work in November of the same year. Why did he write the music for something so far from what we take to be his core? Stravinsky explained to his friend Robert Craft, the conversation reprinted in *Perspectives of New Music*, in 1962, that there was a sense of romantic love which the composer had to manifest. He describes what effect he wanted from certain passages. "I love, above all, the lullaby *Sur ce lit elle repose* [roughly, "she lies on the bed."] I composed this *berceuse* for Vera de Bosset [they were mot married yet] in Paris during a heat wave, and I wrote it for her in my own, Russian, words originally. But the whole of *Perséphone* was inspired by Vera, and whatever tenderness or beauty may be found in the music is my poor response to those qualities in her."[47] Perhaps the composition has more to do with what Igor thought to be the taste and preferences of the woman he so loved, and for whom he had written this work.

In the late 1940s and entering the fifties Stravinsky was spending a great deal of time in the United States. He brought most of his earlier music with him, which is to say he conducted frequently – so much so that he had little time to write. Igor Stravinsky had learned long ago that he could make more money as a "performer" than a composer. With the help of his friends, notably Robert Craft, he began to write autobiographically. The New York theater-going crowd knew and loved *The Fairy's Kiss* and more so *Apollo*, in 1935, another Balanchine choreography that helped to set up another in a long list of highly successful collaborations.

From the success of another ballet he was tendered and accepted a commission to write the *Concerto in E flat*, for chamber orchestra, which came to be known as the *Dumbarton Oaks*. Ever alert to the possibilities of maintaining favorable influence, Igor quickly followed that bit of Americana with his own orchestration, performed once in

Boston, of *The Star Spangled Banner*. The American public, and importantly the critics, had applauded and praised his foray into opera – *The Rake's Progress*. Again, the value of collaboration with proven genius, W.H. Auden, had worked in his favor. Igor was not slowing down. Stravinsky had Vera settled quickly into the Los Angeles suburb of Hollywood Hills. There was always another project to attract him.

Stravinsky found time to begin a lecture course at Harvard, but the war put cancelled to that plan. Here in the United States, which had shown him so much admiration and respect, not to mention had fostered his affinity for jazz, he would not be politically or socially isolated. Then, in 1945, wanting to come ever-closer to the nation and its people, he and Vera, now his wife for nearly five years, became American citizens. Still, something was missing – something visceral. Simply; it was Russia.

Igor returned to his homeland once more. He had long said he was ambivalent about doing that. In fact, he flew at the invitation of First Secretary Khrushchev's government in 1962, marking the composer's 80th birthday. Stravinsky had traveled the world, giving concerts in most major cities, and many smaller ones as well. In 1960 alone he conducted in New York, Los Angeles, Toronto, Mexico City, Bogotá, Buenos Aires, Rome, Venice, Genoa, Paris, and back to New York. In the next eighteen months he would perform, in the truest sense of the word, in Caracas, in Israel, and even in Johannesburg. Still, going to Moscow was something he had difficulty preparing for.

Emotions were high, expectations even higher. His colleague, friend, and business manager, cum-biographer, Robert Craft, recalls the moment they walked in to the Moscow arrivals terminal. Craft tells us that Vera, whom he calls V., was choked with emotion. He writes "… [for some] it fulfills a lifelong dream. Which is the reason why the atmosphere is like a child's birthday party, and the reason why everyone, not least among them I.S. himself, is bursting with relief."[48] Moreover, the composer felt some obligation to tell the Soviet sponsors that he was returning not for nostalgia but "for the younger generation of Russian musicians." He had evidently decided to leave behind his difficult and generally less appreciated serial music, his twelve-tone works.

Instead Igor chose for his first concert in his native land the proto-Russian ballet score *The Rite of Spring*, along with his *Orpheus*, and the *Ode* he had written in honor of his friend Serge Koussevitzky's wife. Craft shared the conducting chores.[49] Helping to make the night even more of a homecoming, Soviet music luminaries Dmitri Shostakovich and Aram Khachaturian were on hand to welcome and toast the Russo-American conductor. Stravinsky likely saw both of them more as representatives of the state than as kindred spirits. But he could not long maintain any sense of indifference to the land as he told the people gathered at his official reception "a man can have but one birthplace – one fatherland, one country … and the place of his birth is the most important factor in his life."[50]

Igor Fyodorovich and his wife Vera took a drive to look carefully at the land they had left, nearly fifty years earlier. It was a time filled with emotion for the man who often said he had no truck with sentiment. The Stravinskys were hardly able to comprehend all that had happened, all that had changed, in the time away as they now attempted to find their way back.

In his final years, as his pace slowed, the feisty old composer who had changed the nature of classical music, who had been a citizen of three nations – never certain that he belonged to any one – became more circumspect. Vera wrote that Igor developed what she called "a new gentleness." Her husband even found an appreciation for Beethoven, a composer he once said was too romantic. Stravinsky had long professed that he loved "the system" over the emotion. But if all things attempt to find their center at their natural close, this gentleness and acceptance of the romantic heart fit him well at the close of his most remarkable life.

In the last months of their life together, Vera purchased an apartment in New York City. Igor said he wanted to see the park. They lived in their new home together only a week before he died, at the age of eighty-eight, on 6 April 1971. The woman whom he called "my dearest Persephone" would live another twelve years. Following Stravinsky's funeral, Vera was remembered by the editor of *Gramophone* with these words: "She was his necessity, his reason for living… and with her he was utterly romantic."[51]

CHAPTER EIGHTEEN

TCHAIKOVSKY, Pyotr Ilyich; (1840 - 1893); Russian

"… I am passionately fond of the national element in all its varied expressions. In a word, I am Russian in the fullest sense…"(letter to Nadezhda,1878)

Few composers can measure up to this man either for innovative genius or for popular appeal. Few composers ever felt less comfortable in society, or more painfully shy among his peers, many of whom he clearly outshined. Such anxiety was the engine of what Harold Schonberg called his surcharged emotionalism.[1]

Tchaikovsky was gay – more decidedly so than such sexually curious or bi-sexual men as Handel, Schubert, or Schumann. Therefore, the role of the Muse in his career is tenuous, but only if we insist on gendering the muse. It is not that he didn't try the so-called straight and narrow. Nor does his sexual preference mean that Tchaikovsky did not have a woman in his life that influenced his music, but to say that he did requires some explanation. We'll find the sources of inspiration, in all shapes and dispositions, as we make our way through the musical development of one of the most important musicians and composers of the late nineteenth century.

Pyotr Ilych was descended on the paternal side from "government-men" – his grandfather was a Cossack officer, his father a police captain, then a senior civil servant. His mother came from a well-to-do French family where music was foundational to their lives and often to their livelihoods. This combination suggests a kind of privilege that influenced the boy's expectations for success in the mid-to-late nineteenth-century Russian arts community. It also came with enormous pressure, something this most sensitive of boys found difficult to deal with.

His mother, Alexandra (neé d'Assier) called him Pierre. She spoke enough French at home to facilitate the boy's mastery of the language. Pyotr was writing poems in French at eight, and then quickly learned German when he was nine. This was about the time the family moved from Votkinsk, where he was born in 1840, through Moscow, and on to St. Petersburg, where he spent most of his life. The family also hired a French governess for the children, and this woman gave young Tchaikovsky his first head start in music. When he was bored with his lessons he took to improvising on the family piano. His nanny taught him to read music.

What composers did he particularly like? Mozart was clearly his first choice, but within a year he was playing Chopin etudes. Tchaikovsky soon became so good that he surpassed his first teacher, presenting a problem for the boy's parents who wanted him to concentrate on his other studies. A close family friend brought Pyotr to see Mozart's *Don Giovanni* in 1850, and the boy was overwhelmed with joy and inspiration, marking that evening as the day he decided to devote his life to music.[2]

Pyotr's first notable composition – *Symphony No 1, in G minor* – did not come along until the young man was twenty-six years old, following a late graduation of the conservatoire. His tardy arrival is easily explained; Pyotr had initially followed an academic track at the university and briefly tried a career similar to that of his father. Listening to his heart, he decided at the age of twenty-one to dedicate his life to music. It took only a few years for things to come together.

Tchaikovsky at twenty-one is a good place to focus for a moment. He studied the masters that were most appealing to him: Mozart, Haydn, and the late classical period. We have already found that he was drawn to the profound and elegant Chopin piano music. His so-called orthodox classical study, however, did not leave him helpless in developing his own style, for Pyotr successfully melded the earlier style with his affinity for Russian folk music and harmony. One musicologist suggests that Tchaikovsky was able to offer was largely what "the Five" did not: "a sweet, inexhaustible, super-sensuous fund of melody."[3]

It was his melody that would make him famous. To go further, it was his surcharged emotionalism, melodic and sensuous, that made the composer at once so popular with many and so anathema to quite a few others. Some critics felt some emotion can be too cloying or hysterical. Think pathos plus! Few composers could or would transcribe their feelings as fluidly as did Mr. Tchaikovsky. He got a lot of help from both sexes.

In the year before the *G minor symphony* Pyotr wrote one piece of music he liked well enough to give his first opus number to. This was his *Scherzo a la Russe for piano*, Opus 1, no 1. He was still trying to find his strong suit as a composer the next year when, in 1867-68, he wrote his first of eleven operas, the best known of which is perhaps *Eugene Onegin*, ten years later.

Tchaikovsky may have gotten a late start but he had some talented and influential friends in music to help him. The young composer had met and became fast friends with Anton Rubenstein, who became his true mentor.

He also met in Moscow Nikolay Kashkin, a music critic and fellow hard drinker. Soon the young man made the acquaintance of some highly regarded literary scions, one of which led Pyotr to his first romantic entanglement with a young lady. Fortunately, or unfortunately, the tale of his sexuality not yet told, young "Mufka" married an army officer and was soon out of Pyotr's life. After a couple of difficult years, health-wise and in terms of income, he found a new lease on life when his opera *The Voyevoda* was warmly received in Moscow, and one young mezzo-soprano temporarily won his heart. One of Tchaikovsky's better known biographers tells of a talented young Frenchwoman, Désirée Artôt, "on meeting her he discovered a 'nice, good, sensible woman,' and by the end of the year the friendship had progressed to the point where marriage was being considered."[4] This would not have been a strong move in any event, but Tchaikovsky had some serious work yet to do on his psyche.

Tchaikovsky's closest friends, not a few of who doubted the viability of the chemistry of the whole affair, tried to talk him out of it. Undaunted, he wrote a number of choruses and recitatives taken from Auber's *Le Domino Noir*, as well as other original vocal music, for the woman. He then wrote a *Romance in F minor* for her. We have no word of just how she received these honorifics to her Musedom. Pyotr was devastated to learn from his friend Nikolay Rubenstein during rehearsal of his opera that Désirée had run off with another man – none other than a Spanish baritone she had met in Warsaw. Désirée perhaps saw that the match would not be uncomplicated.

Like Berlioz wife Harriet Smithson, the young Russian saw the stage presence before he saw the real woman. Perhaps Pyotr was not seeing clearly until the woman ran off, "but in his case, the impossibility of achieving any real emotional contacts with a woman condemned him to situations in which a strong element of fiction was an essential ingredient. The reality of Désirée Artôt would probably have proved almost as disastrous as his later marriage did."[5]

When not writing music, and before enjoying his evenings out with friends, Tchaikovsky was employed by the St. Petersburg Music Conservatoire as a teacher of music theory and composition. He was, however, first and foremost a composer. He was frequently in a funk about how well he was doing, or not doing. His next two operas were not especially well-reviewed, though he had hopes for *The Oprichnik*, following some revisions. While the premiere was warmly received the ambiance did not last and key critics tore it up. Worse, the composer could not even bring himself to consider that the work was worthy of him. Pyotr lapsed into one of his periodic fits of gloom and doubt, traveled briefly to Italy to refresh himself on more opera, then got back to work on his stalled compositions.

Into the early to mid-1870s the fellow was prolific; his brooding D *major Third Symphony*, in gestation since 1874, may have cleared the way for his much more spirited ballet *Swan Lake*, in 1875, or his *Slavonic March*, the next year. Biographers also suggest that he was depressed about his ever-more certain feelings about his urges. For a while at least, his homosexuality may have served him well in one unexpected manner. The year 1877 was a crisis year, but it began under the most advantageous circumstances. It seems the brilliant and quixotic widow Nadezhda von Meck decided she loved Pyotr's music and wanted to show him just how much. She set out to become Tchaikovsky's friend, financier, and platonic lover. Theirs was a relationship probably never since duplicated in the world of serious music, one in which they became both devoted to and dependent upon each other, yet they had vowed to remain ever apart, to have no physical contact, not even to meet.

The couple exchanged what has been estimated as 1100 letters, but there was no physical relationship – not so much as an embrace. Why? She had had enough of the physical side of relationships; after all she had given birth twelve times, complements of her German husband, a well-to-do engineer. More to the point, they both knew that it would not be a good idea to put Pyotr to the test. She requested certain compositions, he complied. Her support when times were difficult kept him not only solvent but actively composing when he might have decided to abandon writing music in order to teach more and be able to pay the bills. Was she a Muse?

In broadest sense of the word she answers the calling; in fact, Tchaikovsky told his publisher, Nikolay Jügenson, that "for her he would write only the best music."[6] Perhaps the success of this unlikely relationship prepared him emotionally for one that was more mainstream. Finishing his *Fourth Symphony,* complements of a loan from Mme. von Meck, and fully under the spell of Pushkin's poetry that launched his spectacular *Eugene Onegin,* Tchaikovsky got a letter from another admirer. She confessed, out of the blue, that she was in love with him. The next part of the story does not end well for anyone concerned.

Her name was Antonina Ivanovna Milyukova, one of his students at the Conservatoire. Pyotr realized that he should have discouraged her affections, but he was too much in love with the fiction of his potential marriage. He longed for a conventional family life, but "with no experience whatever of a relationship with a woman, he could only interpret the situation in terms of fiction; and the fiction closest at hand was Pushkin's."[7]

She was at least as ignorant as he of what lay ahead. She was twenty-eight, not particularly bright or artistically gifted, yet thought herself to be highly desirable. The woman offered Tchaikovsky her undying passion and loyalty. A nuttier, unrealistic relationship cannot be conceived. Incredibly, he proposed marriage that June; Antonina promptly accepted. Three days before the wedding he wrote to his friend and confidant Nadezhda that he feared he was making a mistake but was unable, or insufficiently callous, to break it off now.

They married on 18 July 1877, in Moscow. He wrote he hoped she would leave him alone and let him write. It would not be. Within two weeks Pyotr was in a panic and near despair for what he had brought upon them both. Nadezhda tried to be supportive, sending him money and her best wishes. A veteran of love and a true philanthropist, she may have felt some sense of *noblesse oblige*.

Now fully realizing what problems he had keeping his wife as well as himself solvent – he did not need another dependent – he told von Meck that he had awakened to the reality that he did not have even a feeling of friendship for the woman, his bride. Tchaikovsky feared his musical talent would be adversely affected. He said what was left was simply "to pretend." Two weeks later he walked into the closest river, as had Schumann twenty-three years before, expecting never to return. Pyotr wrote to his friend Nikolay Kashkin that he had fallen in to the water, but most of his close associates suspected something more dire.[8] Defeated even in his half-baked attempt to kill himself, he went back to work the next day, lapsing into a coma some eight days later – totally exhausted.

Needless to say, the new Mrs. Tchaikovsky did not inspire any music in the man. In fact, she likely retarded it. Pyotr was miserable. Shortly, they broached the subject of divorce, but on what grounds? It would be ludicrous to claim adultery – or would it? Pyotr's friend Jürgenson did some spade work and found that she had taken a lover and had given birth to his child. What a boon! Now the marriage could be legally ended. Tchaikovsky fled to Switzerland to sort things out. The marriage was kaput.

Antonina went on having children with casual lovers for years, leaving the hapless foundlings at orphanages. By 1896 she was committed to an insane asylum, still delusional about Tchaikovsky's passion for her. The crisis was over long before, but the recriminations dragged on for years. Antonina actually stalked her ex-husband, prior to her commitment to the asylum. She died in the same institution, twenty years later.

In late '78, the acute part of the crisis past, Pyotr Ilych Tchaikovsky got back to his life. Over the next three or four years he wrote some of his best known and most highly regarded music, including the orchestral *Capriccio Italien*, and his *Fourth Symphony*, which he dedicated to von Meck. He wrote to her: "I am now busy with the symphony I started this winter which I very much want to dedicate to you, because I think you will find in it an echo of your innermost feelings and thoughts. I shall write on the symphony 'Dedicated to My Friend,'"[9] Mme. von Meck was present for the premiere that night in Moscow, February 22, 1878. She was the only one besides the composer to know the identity of that "friend."

Of course there were other friends. The one he was closest to before his doomed marriage was Vladimir Shilovsky, son of Maria Shilovskaya, with whom Mussorgsky had had a brief affair. Vladimir was a student at the Conservatoire, and Pyotr took a strong liking to the boy, frequently traveling abroad with him. They spent much of January of 1874 together in Nice, then in Genoa. Tchaikovsky wrote while they dallied, and upon their return he dedicated a couple of piano pieces to the lad, including an *F major Nocture* and a "the sprightly *G major Humoresque.*"[10]

This youth was not the biggest love of Pyotr's life, however. That distinction would fall to his nephew. Finally, for this composer who in his younger days was so uncomfortable with his sexuality, he'd found a life-partner. Theirs was a love that came to pass late in Pyotr Tchaikovsky's life. The lad was Vladimir Davydov, nick-named Bob, or Bobyk. By 1890, most of Pyotr's best work done, the composer confided in Bob that year that he felt his powers were declining, noting that the *Nutcracker*, surely his best known and performed ballet, was weaker than *Sleeping Beauty*, which he had completed two years before. This was also the year his subsidies from von Meck ceased. She claimed she was going broke; she was not. Still, that pipeline was closed.

For better or for worse, and this would seem ironic to Tchaikovsky, he has come to be identified with his ballets; although his more classical violin and piano concerti are often extraordinary. He also wrote four wonderful orchestral suites. In fact, Tchaikovsky actually wrote more operas than any other form, but few people consider him an opera composer. One could say, perhaps, that Tchaikovsky had difficulty finding his métier. He seemed ever in search of the answers posed by Fate – he even wrote a symphonic poem with *Fate* as the title, in 1868. Clearly, Fate gave Tchaikovsky enormous talent, gave him many blessings, and presented him with even more vexatious problems. Pyotr Ilych died much too young, at fifty-three, of cholera – probably from drinking unclean tap water. He was never happier than in his final ten years with Bobyk.

One other work remains to be considered. It was the last major piece he wrote and many think it was his finest work. He finished his *Sixth Symphony, in B minor*, in 1893, shortly before his death. He wrote it for and he dedicated it to his beloved Vladimir. Tchaikovsky told his brother Modest that he had "put his soul into the work." He had considered titling the symphony, which premiered two weeks before his death, the *Tragique*. We know the piece by its original title, the *Pathétique*.

As we conclude our examination of Tchaikovsky's musical genius, and the complicated nature of his Muses, it must be said that in his last decade he came to know his mind, not to mention his oh-so romantic heart. At least as importantly, whatever fear of anxiety Pyotr Ilych Tchaikovsky had about Fate, arguably his quintessential Muse, the man's music was all the more splendid for her frequent intervention in his short but magnificent life.

CHAPTER NINETEEN

VERDI, Giuseppe (1813-1901); Italian

"You can write anytime people will leave you alone, but…the best writing is when you are in love."[1]

He was born to poor, illiterate parents in the unprepossessing village of Le Roncole, in the Duchy of Parma, the night of 10 October 1813. His parents, Carlo and Luigia, had no known musical talents or experience, and they certainly did not have what is often called opportunity. They did recognize that perhaps their son might do more with his life. Luigia's parents had kept a tavern, of sorts. Giuseppe Verdi's story as a bright but financially strapped youth is uncommon only in this book, where privilege, or at least pedigree, is often a given.

Dvořak and Wagner were a few who would have experienced similar straights. His first good fortune was that his parents recognized an extraordinary potential in their child. Against all odds, Verdi became the most celebrated opera composer of his generation, unless one wants to give that distinction to Richard Wagner, born five months earlier in Leipzig. In Italy, only with the arrival of Puccini forty-five years later would there be a force so strong in musical theater.

Because little Roncole had no music school, and little else to satisfy a growing curiosity of the world, the Verdis sent their only son to the town of Busseto, so that Giuseppe could continue his formal studies beyond elementary education. The young man's musical interests were encouraged by one Antonio Barezzi, the founder and president of the local Philharmonic Society. Barezzi played the flute and clarinet, but he was an even better champion of talent. It seems that Barezzi was to become, in all practical ways, Verdi's father.[2]

When Giuseppe was twelve years old a village priest suggested that the lad might enroll in Ferdinando Provesi's music school in Busetto. Provesi, a composer of operas, masses, songs, and symphonies was something of an infamous character, having been imprisoned on what were likely trumped up charges in Parma. His attention to the needs of the budding young genius from Roncole proved transformational. Young Verdi traveled to Roncole to handle his weekend church organ duties; he did so for nine years more. Arguably, under Provesi the boy became a true musician.

Verdi studied harmony and composition, and taught himself piano from self-help manuals.[3] At least as propitious for Giuseppe was his master's knowledge of, and love for, drama which, with his "classical" music study, formed the necessary background of Verdi's coming career in opera composition. Absent the "felon of Parma," what might have become of the man musicologist Harold Schonberg named the Colossus of Italy? At the age of fifteen Verdi was playing the piano so skillfully that he landed a position with the Busetto Philharmonic Society. He began to teach locally, spelling Provesi when the old man was indisposed.[4] Verdi graduated with honors in 1827, prepared to pursue his dreams of becoming a respectable, responsible musician.

Before Giuseppe Verdi found his first Muse there were some extraordinary early compositions. His first work was an added "overture" to Rossini's *Il Barbiere de Siviglia*, evidently thinking that the opera needed a proper overture of its own. After all, Rossini had used it before. The teenaged Verdi's music was well received and "within a short time he had composed several other overtures, arias, duets, concertos, and variations on themes of other composers." The high point of Verdi's first work was said to be *I deliri di Saul* (The Madness of Saul), a cantata in eight movements for baritone and orchestra.[5]

Still acting as his musical patron, Barezzi, also one of Busetto's wealthiest merchants, advised Carlo Verdi to apply for a scholarship on behalf of his son, now seventeen, so that the lad could study in Milan. In the meantime, Giuseppe needed some income, and with his formal schooling complete he needed room and board. Barezzi invited young Verdi to come live with him and his family. For his part of the deal, Giuseppe would give piano lessons to the merchant's five children. The eldest, Margherita, herself only a few months younger than Verdi, may have been his prize student, and in more ways than one. Although they were only together about six months before the young man left for Milan, "[a]n affectionate friendship had already begun between the young teacher and his pupil. During the months in which Giuseppe lived with the family, this friendship ripened into love."[6] We'll find Margherita again shortly.

Verdi went to Milan fully expecting to be accepted into the Conservatorio. There he found that the school was already overcrowded. His age also worked against him; he was two years too senior. Verdi was crushed. Whatever the examining faculty might have thought of his preparation, Giuseppe would not be admitted. He was advised by the director to stay in the city and study with one or two teachers who enjoyed a reputation for excellence. Verdi selected Vincenzo Lavigna, a composer of mostly fugues and canons, and a sometime conductor at La Scala.

While the work was narrowly focused, too much so for Giuseppe's taste, he learned a great deal, especially about counterpoint. His progress sufficiently pleased his benefactor Barezzi, who rewarded him with something that would be both enjoyable and would further his instruction. He bought young Verdi a subscription ticket to La Scala so he could follow the best work being performed in the city.

His next major breakthrough came shortly after the death of his first music teacher, Provesi. Though Verdi may have considered trying to make his musical career in Milan, there were too many reasons to return home "where his obligations were: Carlo and Luigia Verdi, [were] now alone in Roncole, with their daughter dead [his sister had died the year before] and their son living in the city." They needed him. Moreover, there was "Margherita, Barezzi's high-spirited, red-headed daughter, whose love for him [Verdi] had been known for years."[7] Did she need him too? Suddenly, returning home had a powerful appeal.

Provesi's passing created a major drama, for in 1834 a battle began in Busetto that would drag on for two years. The problems lay in selecting Provesi's successor. Young Verdi was vocally opposed by members of a conservative faction, some of whom were clearly enemies of Barezzi, and who stood against Verdi because he was considered to be "a theater-oriented musician."[8] He initially lost the job as organist to a man far less qualified, but the war was far from over. The intrigue lasted for two more years, and though he lost the church job, Verdi eventually secured, by direct examination and competition, the more highly prized position as *maestro di musica* and director of Busetto's Philharmonic Society. Giuseppe actually did better financially and wound up in a situation that would better lend itself to his development as a so-called theater-oriented musician, which is where his heart wanted to go anyway. "His position assured, Verdi became officially engaged to Margherita Barezzi on 16th April [1836] and on 4th May they were married."[9] The young lovers were each twenty-two years old. Giuseppe Verdi remained as Busseto's premier musician for three years. It was a time given at least as much to his young family as to the town's music patrons who had supported him.

The marriage was initially blissful. Their lives were suddenly saddened, however, by the loss of the couple's first born, a girl named Virginia. Instead of giving up his energy for composition seemed to boom. Now he had a wife to take care of. Verdi wrote: "Back in my home town, I began to write marches, *sinfonie*, vocal pieces, etc., a complete mass, a complete set of vespers, three or four settings of *Tantrum ergo* and other church music... Among the vocal pieces there were choruses from the tragedies of Manzoni for three voices, and *Il cinque Maggio* for solo voice."[10] Verdi had also worked on an opera, *Rocester*, but the early scores are lost. Apparently, he used at least some of the music in his *Oberto*, which the next year would be his first produced opera. Then more tragedy struck, as their second child, a boy, died at seventeen months.

Verdi and his wife were despondent. Now the couple was determined to get out of Busetto, which they were convinced was against them. Verdi wrote to his father-in-law, telling him that he and "Ghita," as he called his wife, were short of the funds needed to get a fresh start in

Milan. He asked Barezzi for a small loan. After all, Milan offered opportunity; there the young composer's work was known and respected. Meanwhile, he had the problem of his contract with the Busetto town council. Giuseppe regretted his hasty decision to enter into the contract and insisted on cutting lose; he pleaded his case. With all that had befallen, the personal tragedies, Verdi had to clear his head, had to work on his opera exclusively, which would mean forgoing any other source of income.

Margherita was supportive of his decision. They would make a new life, have more babies; Giuseppe would write more. The old man came through. The Verdis left Busetto a few days later, entering Milan on the 8th of September, 1838, full of hope and promise. In point of fact, Verdi was still officially under contract to the city of Busetto, but they agreed to let him go after satisfying his six-month termination clause. Verdi's decision was remarkable, because in Busetto he had an assured income, something as yet undetermined in the large, northern city. Their choice to start again took both courage and high hopes, not to mention trust in his talent. The couple was so strapped for funds when they arrived in Milan that Margherita had to pawn her jewels to help pay for rent. Soon the Verdis began to meet the right people. It was just a matter of timing, luck, and perseverance. Wasn't it?

By early the next year Verdi's music was being widely published and was well received. His hopes for an opera at La Scala were high. Verdi got the break he was angling for when, "in the late spring, the composer got a firm offer from La Scala... His opera [*Oberto*] as he had expected was to be put on, as a benefit, by the Pio Instituo Filarmonico."[11] He had to share his joy with Ghita. In the interval between the two acts of *Oberto*, "on the great night of the first performance, Verdi ran home to tell her that everything was going, or seemed to be going, as they had hoped."[12] Margherita, still lamenting the death of her two children, did what she could to support her husband, celebrating his important first triumph in the city.

Finally, Verdi had gotten what he most wanted. The success was made sweeter with the expectation that there would be a good number of performances, as this production would also be for a charitable cause. Charity meant repetition. Repetition meant celebrity. The young man was delighted to find that two of the biggest and brightest names in the business would sing the most important parts of his work. The third would go to a highly regarded young soprano by the name of Giuseppina Strepponi. He could never have known what this assignment would lead to.

The young lady had experienced her own personal traumas and dramas, having to give up her second child to adoption because she was not married and paternity was uncertain. The baby had been born only six hours after her mother finished singing *Il giuramento* at the Teatro Alfieri,[13] at another Milanese opera house. Her own mother was near destitute, and Giuseppina took on extra work – likely too much, to help with her support. Even as a young woman, Ms. Strepponi, not unlike Ghita Verdi, seemed to embrace the satisfaction of dutiful love.

Handed the music for Verdi's *Oberto*, Giuseppina could not foresee, nor could the delighted composer, what future they would come to share. As for the immediate opera production, "[b]ecause of its stars' reputations, expectations ran high for that season at La Scala, where it seemed that Verdi's promise was about to be fulfilled."[14] *Oberto* was a clear success, and soon Verdi had the offer to write three more, at eight month intervals. Just when his career and his personal life seemed to be moving ahead, tragedy struck again.

Margherita became suddenly ill, diagnosed with what was later determined to be encephalitis. She died on the 18th of June. His beloved wife was gone just one year after the death of their second child. Verdi was shocked, despondent; he swore he would never work again. He'd taken so much energy from his love for this woman. Adding to his grief was the realization that his new *opera buffa* work, called *Un giorno di regno* (King for a Day), which was in production when Ghita died, was a complete failure. Verdi's spirits had never been lower. He seems to have envisaged this section of his own life, in recollection, "as if it were a page from one of the violent romantic melodramas which occupied his imagination."[15] Verdi wrote to his friend and publisher, Giulio Ricordi, "with a mind tortured by my domestic disaster, embittered by the failure of my work, I persuaded myself that I had nothing more to find in music and I decided never to compose again."[16] Fortunately, Giuseppe reconsidered.

The single, propitious event that turned Verdi's thinking was a chance meeting with La Scala's impresario, or opera manager, Bartolomeo Merelli. As the story goes, one evening in the autumn of 1841, Merelli accompanied the composer to the theater. He handed Verdi a libretto and asked him to read it, to give Merelli his opinion. Verdi took it home – did not really want to read it, but when he dismissively tossed the manuscript aside he saw that it had opened to a page containing a particularly compelling phrase, a reference to the Jews fleeing persecution. This was a bible story Giuseppe knew; he was transfixed by the hopeful message. Reading the rest of the libretto he quickly decided to commit to the work. The twenty-seven year old had figured out how to move ahead. He was bigger than the hurt of any one failure. Giuseppe Verdi had strength and passion.

Identifying with the theme and the possibilities, Verdi began work on the opera that would make him famous. Rehearsals began in February, with Signore Strepponi agreeing to take the lead soprano role. This, then, was the genesis of *Nabucco*, which premiered on 9 March 1842. The coda of the work, *Va, pensiero,* became popular for nationalistic reasons. Recall that Italian nation had not yet come to pass, and the duchy of Parma was under Austrian occupation until 1882. Verdi became closely associated with the *Risorgimento*, the movement for a free Italy. In fact, the work became popular even with men and women who had never seen the opera, but recognized the music. His friendship with Merelli had proven invaluable, and now Verdi's confidence was restored. Two years after his wife's passing, Verdi had his second successful opera.

A liaison, at least as strong, was now being forged. While *Nabucco* far surpassed the less sophisticated collage that was *Oberto*, Verdi needed additional validation, both personal and professional. His loving wife was gone, but he had met the woman with whom he would next fall in love, the one who would inspire and sustain him in his work for the rest of his life. We return to the beautiful and talented soprano, Giuseppina Strepponi.

Recall that Verdi met her during rehearsals for *Oberto*. She reportedly took more than a passing interest in his music, and shortly thereafter she was clearly interested in the composer himself. Their relationship was platonic, at first – built on mutual admiration and respect. No doubt Verdi had left a favorable impression with her when they worked together on *Oberto* two years before. An interesting account of the part Giuseppina Strepponi played in the opera's success states that one influential patron agreed to put up the necessary financing only when the famous soprano decided to participate. Verdi and his benefactor "went at the hour set by Strepponi; she went over her part with Verdi at the piano and then said to him: 'I like this music very much and want to do it for my debut opera' [of the season]."[17] They saw something in their mutual love for opera that would tie Giuseppe Verdi and Giuseppina Strepponi more closely.

Each been through a great trial and tribulation. She was twenty-four when they met; she'd been singing professionally for five years. Giuseppina sang the part of Abigaille, and with her voice talent to match the composer's Verdi's *Nabucco* enjoyed fifty-seven performances at La Scala. No other opera had ever had such a success at that theater. The composer and the soprano formed a winning team.

Giuseppina's own story deserves some review. Her parents were both musicians; in fact both were accomplished singers. Their daughter, whose talent exceeded that of her parents, studied at the Milan Conservatorio, gaining in 1830 an exception to the age limit that had kept Verdi out of its vaunted program. "She was a good pianist and showed exceptional promise as a singer." When tuition money ran out, "Giuseppina was then granted a free scholarship, which enabled her to complete her training, and in the autumn of 1834 she carried off the first prize for her *bel canto*."[18] She made her reputation singing principal works of Bellini and Donizetti, but "her success in Rossini's *Matilde di Shabran* at the Teatro Grande, in Trieste, during the Carnival season of 1835, established her as a rising star."[19]

Following the success of *Nabucco*, Giuseppe and Giuseppina's relationship grew. Her career was strong, but she was advised she was wearing herself out with the pace she had been keeping. Her doctors advised her to cut back lest she become seriously ill. Nevertheless, "she sang in the eight scheduled performances of the season; she needed the money. After the triumphal premier, [impresario] Merelli offered Verdi a new contract; leaving it to the young composer to state how much money he wanted. During the second performance Verdi went to see Strepponi in her dressing-room, asking her advice. She told him he should not ask more than Bellini [1801-1835] had been paid for *Norma*."[20] Giuseppina's role in their relationship was perhaps based primarily on respect and friendship, less so on romance. They already shared a love for theater and music. The full blown romance would take its time in arriving. For now, the woman was proud of her part in supporting, counseling, advancing Verdi in his career.

Strepponi no doubt also sensed she had reached the pinnacle of her career just as Verdi's was beginning to take off. After *Nabucco* she took some time away from the stage to regain her strength, and for a few years Giuseppina accepted only the occasional assignment. Her final appearance was in January, 1846, when she reprised her role in *Nabucco*. By the age of thirty-one, her voice having been overly stressed for too long, she was through as a performer.

Strepponi moved to Paris, which now challenged Vienna as Europe's musical center. She made her living giving voice lessons. Verdi came to visit and at least one biographer says that it was here, in 1847, in the city of lights, that Giuseppe and Giuseppina became lovers.[21]

The immediate source of their mutual affection was, quite simply, their shared triumphant *Nabucco*. "Verdi and Strepponi may have worked together late that summer or autumn… One of the most successful pieces in *Nabucco* was the aria of Abigaille, La Strepponi, in the second part [of the opera], especially the adagio recently written expressly for her by the composer,"[22] There is no doubt that they were drawn to each other to a large degree in appreciation for mutual genius. Verdi was not necessarily ready for a major romance. He was still working on his reputation as a major composer. His next stop was Venice, where he committed to another series of operas. He may also have thought that he was too young to get tied down to one woman so soon after the loss of his Ghita.

In 1843, Verdi was at work on his next opera. This was *I Lombardi*. History has a way of repeating itself and this opera also failed. Even Verdi pronounced it a fiasco. Must it be only every other opera that would succeed? He was adept at getting into a funk and staying there. Later in life he had long periods of depression. Now his *Ernani* was looking like something of a disappointment. Verdi blamed the singers; the stage was ill-prepared. Costumes had not been delivered. Still, he persevered, and by the time the opera entered its full production run all these problems had been addressed.

The reviews were mixed, but Verdi knew he had a hit. Although he was eager to leave the city when *I Lombardi* failed, a little success proved to be highly restorative to his psyche. "Verdi gradually came to like Venice, which, he said, he would regret leaving. While there he also became involved with a woman friend in whom he was interested for at least seven years."[23]

Curiously, biographers are unable to identify the woman from a half-dozen or so who were on Verdi's mind, who gave him the energy to press on that year, 1844, and write the opera *I due Foscari*. Certainly the Muse was a presence. Verdi referred to her in letters to his friend Francesco Piave, the librettist of *Ernani*, as "that angel." "She may have been a singer such as Geltrude Bortolitti, whom Verdi liked a great deal and often mentioned in letters." Apparently "the woman Verdi loved was the daughter of one of the city's old families, the Soranzos, the Papadopolis [a Greek], or the Venturis."[24] Whatever happened to break them up a few years later was so stark that he never mentioned "that angel" again. Giuseppe decided it was time to leave Venice. He'd always loved to travel, to be on the road. Travel was essential to the man, as it would be to Stravinsky some two generations later. For Verdi travel was restorative.

He journeyed in 1847 to Paris. Did he go expressly to reconnect with Giuseppina?

Probably; he knew that she was there. Fresh from the success of *Macbeth*, perhaps his best known mid-career opera, Verdi became interested in producing his work abroad. His London experience was particularly satisfying. The opera *I Masnadieri* was the first Italian opera performed in the city in a long time. Even Rossini had not brought an opera to London. And now the French capital called. Verdi felt alive again; he had serious work to do in Paris. And Giuseppina was in the city.

The Paris Opéra had requested a new libretto to his *I Lombardi*, but this time in French. Verdi worked with the French translators for four months. The result would be the adaptation called *Jerusalem*. Biblical themes intrigued the composer, but he also wanted to see what kind of welcome France would give him. Then there was the matter of Ms. Strepponi. Perhaps after his failed "my angel" romance, an attraction that lasted some years, he was ready to reconnect with the woman with whom he'd shared an abiding love for music – and a shared music history, at that. This time the chemistry worked.

Giuseppina had left her children in Italy as she made a life for herself in Paris. "Autumn, not spring, in the loveliest season in Paris, and the autumn of 1847 must have been very special for Verdi and Giuseppina. What happened no one knows, but by the end of the year they were openly living together… They had known each other for eight years, since the spring of 1839, when Verdi, carrying the score of *Oberto,* had called on the prima donna in Milan. Since then, both had gone through their private agonies. It was perhaps suffering and compassion, as much as love and passion, that brought them together,"[25]

Now they might come together in a way they had never attempted. They worked on a collaborative composition. "[I]n one scene of the manuscript *Jerusalem*, the dialogue was written, alternately, by both of them. The following exchange can be read:

In Strepponi's Hand:	Alas! Hope is banished. My glory has faded! Family, fatherland, all I have lost!
In Verdi's Hand:	No, I am still left to you! And it will be for life!
Strepponi	Angel from heaven! May I die in the arms of a husband!
Verdi	Let me die with you! My death will be –
Strepponi	sweet."[26]

The sentiment is almost too cloying to bear, but the text seems to underscore the degree to which their romance was rekindled. Giuseppe had his Muse back.

The change in setting from the eleventh century, populated by Lombardy Crusaders, was not inconsequential. *Jerusalem* also required a new orchestral introduction. Attuned to the Parisian expectations, Verdi also found he had to write a ballet scene for the remodeled work. The

French crowds and critics agreed; *Jerusalem* was a major success. Actually, Verdi's revisions were considered significant enough that he convinced his friend and publicist, Giulio Ricordi, to support a transcription of the libretto back to the Italian. As a result, *Gerusalleme* opened at La Scala that December. While living with Giuseppina he also wrote the song *Il Poveretto*, based on a poem they enjoyed. His next major work was also demanding significant attention.

Verdi had contracted to write *Il Corsaro*, based obviously enough on George Lord Byron's The Corsair. The work seemed to interest him little; he was simply fulfilling a business deal. Meanwhile, as war broke out in 1848 across much of Europe, and Austrian troops were actively engaged in Milan, Verdi was enjoying Paris. Giuseppina and Giuseppe took a house in the Parisian neighborhood of Passy. Here, at least all was right with the world.

This does not mean to suggest that Verdi was unsympathetic to the cause of nationalism among Italian states, opposing Austria. He was anything but. In fact, he wrote a few patriotic songs, then turned to *La battaglia di Legnano*, after a French resistance play of a similar name. "The opera was short, simple to understand, and full of stirring music. For the first time Verdi had deliberately set out to appeal to his audience's patriotic feelings." The play made him a national hero on a second plane. Italy saw the composer as a patriot. "Parts of Verdi's earlier operas had frequently been taken up by the fighters for a united Italy, but this time the composer had given the movement its own opera. It was his contribution to Italy's future... [and] a valid work of art."[27]

In the next few years, between 1851 and 1855, Verdi wrote what are generally recognized as three of his greatest operas:" *Rigoletto, La Traviata*, and *Il Travatore*. Actually, *Aida* may be his best known and most often performed work. These three, however, were created at a time when Verdi seemed to be at his creative best. They married the next year. Their union was kismet in its clearest manifestation. "From the very beginning of his operatic career, Verdi's life had been strangely linked with that of Giuseppina Strepponi. In a sense, Giuseppina discovered Verdi... Giuseppina was the first person *inside* the magic circle to sense his greatness, to recognize the right of entry that belonged to this pale, black-bearded young man knocking at the door."[28] Perhaps she "discovered" him because Strepponi had played an influential part in launching both *Oberto* and *Nabucco*. Both were successful and proved influential in Verdi getting the attention and the contracts he subsequently received.

It seems of especial interest that Verdi's former father-in-law, Antonio Barezzi, was particularly charmed by his visit to Paris in January of 1848 to stay with Verdi and Signora Peppina, as the old man called her.[29] Giuseppe was charmed, as well. The lovers had known each other for nearly twenty years when they got married in 1859. They had been living together, much to the chagrin of the people of Busetto, for nearly eleven years. Barezzi, predictably, was upset with their living conditions, early on becoming angry with Verdi for the couple's unmarried, life-style – simply put; Verdi was not a big believer in social convention. They were together. That's what mattered.

The vocal score to *Gerusalemme* is dedicated to Giuseppina, not because it is one of Verdi's strongest works but more likely because they shared the same emotional connection to the uprising, the *Risorgimento*. They were kindred spirits. They left Paris together to return to Italy, specifically to live together in Busetto.

After the successful 1851 production of *Rigoletto* the couple bought a farmhouse in nearby Sant'Agata. They had both been wounded by some ill-feelings on the part of Verdi's parents. There was a big family falling-out, by and large placing Busetto off limits. Perhaps their living together, unmarried, was too difficult for Verdi's parents. They knew they would face the same question from friend Antonio Barezzi.

"While Verdi and Giuseppina were alive it was never explained why they did not marry until 1859, when they had known each other for more than seventeen years. The only one who asked that question was Barezzi. Verdi wrote to him, early in 1852: 'Dear Father-in-Law," he wrote …"You live in a town that has a bad habit of meddling in the affairs of others... the gossip, the whispers, the disapproval… I have nothing to hide… In my house there lives a lady, free and independent, who like me prefers a solitary life… What rights do I have over her, or she over me? Who knows whether or not she is my wife?'"[30] Verdi explains that their situation is no one's business, and that, in spite of this awkwardness, he still considers Barezzi in the warmest sense his benefactor and friend. He had less sympathy toward the townspeople. Some force of convention eventually did move them.

The couple married in a little village just outside of Geneva, Switzerland, about 160 miles away, on 29 August 1859. They could have married at any time in the many years they lived together before nuptials; why they did not has never been satisfactorily addressed. Was it some pact or promise? Some sense of obligation? In any event, this family dispute did not adversely affect his work. *Traviata* and *Travatore* followed, splendid works, both. Something was working well at Sant'Agata.

The composer, long interested in the course of Italian politics, was elected to the Assembly of the Parma Provinces a few weeks after his marriage. He was probably more popular in the many provinces seeking a national identity than he was in Busetto, and he remained active in politics for nearly five years.

Now "legal," Giuseppe and Giuseppina remained at Sant'Agata, usually involved in some addition or remodeling effort to the old farm house, for nearly fifty years. The sanctity of their union was damaged only by Verdi's inexplicable love affair that began in 1869, ten years after their marriage, and lasted for seven years. The object of his affection, and of Giuseppina consternation, was the soprano Teresa Stolz. Seldom has there been a more definitive Muse.

Verdi found the woman at mid-career. She must have seemed a gift of the gods. Teresa became the preeminent soprano of her day, fifteen years after Strepponi held the same distinction. The composer first heard of her and her early successes in August 1865, through his friend, conductor, and concert master Angelo Mariani. It seems that the Bohemian-born Teresa had performed exceptionally well in Rossini's *Guglielmo Tell*, Mariani conducting.[31] Stolz, in fact, was more than Mariani's prima donna; she was briefly his fiancé. A few years later, when

Mariani was struggling, Giuseppe Strepponi who knew Mariani well and thought him a friend, warned him about the women he was involved with.[32]

Little did Giuseppina know what Teresa-trouble was heading her way. Verdi first heard her sing in a performance of his *Don Carlo*, in January, 1869. She would later be his *Aida*, and along the way she successfully ingratiated herself into the lives of both Verdis – once she even discussed buying a home near them by Sant'Agata. Teresa began writing letters to Verdi – many letters – some were silly; all suggested a strong bond with the composer. Meanwhile, Verdi was traveling a great deal. He liked to keep his work in front of as many people, in as many cities, in as many opera houses, as feasible. This is not to say that he was uncomfortable at home, though there had been a few spills for the Verdis.

Actually, there was a strain in their relationship in the early months of 1869. Giuseppina felt Verdi had been unkind and inconsiderate of her. Had she gotten word of Teresa? She rejected his offer to come to Milan and join him for rehearsals of the much revised *La forza del destino*. He'd been working on it, especially the ending, since it opened in 1862. Verdi wrote to his wife, who was determined to remain at home, that "La Stolz and Tibernini [the tenor] were superb,"[33] *Destino* was now complete. Perhaps three people's destinies were at risk.

We cannot tell what Strepponi made of this review, but it is unlikely that she saw it as anything but news from the front. Only when Giuseppe and Teresa began to work together on the next opera, *Aida*, did strong rumors of romance begin. It seems ironic to consider that "the force of destiny," a romantic farce, would also come to suggest infidelity.

By March, Verdi was again in Paris, then on to Genoa, and finally back to Marseilles, where he was first tempted by an old friend to consider writing an opera that would take Egypt as its theme. Verdi had collaborated with Camille du Locle, the co-director of the Paris Opéra-Comique, on *Don Carlos*. Verdi was unsure he wanted the assignment, but he returned home that summer to read the libretto, based on the story by Auguste Mariette, "*La Fiancée du Nil.*" Yes, this one would work! The Cairo premier of *Aida* was Christmas Eve, 1871 – having been delayed nearly a year because of war. The Italian premiere would quickly follow, and this time Verdi, who had no interest in going to Egypt, would take a hand. The principal cast came to Sant'Agata to rehearse. Teresa Stolz was cast in the title role to no one's surprise.

Their romance, or infatuation, or whatever emotional energy one will call it, began in earnest during *Destino*. Verdi was struck by her style, her brooding good looks her copious talent. Giuseppe praised Stolz's performance to an acquaintance, who was one of Angelo Mariani's closest friends, suggesting that Teresa's work was "sublime." It is an artful word, and one that seems loaded with extra meaning. Surely such unfettered adulation would get back to both Mariani and Strepponi, who had her own sources. As if she had some second sense, and while her husband was joyous about the immediate details of his career, Giuseppina Strepponi became morose, said she "regretted having been loved by so few people in her life," but she thanked God for Verdi, anticipating finding him in eternity."[34]

Recall that Mariani and Stolz had been engaged. Did Miss Stolz simply lose interest or was she drawn away? The ensuing breach between the two men was painful, especially so for the conductor, who seemed genuinely hurt at the sudden loss of friendship. Supposedly their relationship had declined with Verdi's disapproval of the way in which Mariani handled, or did not handle, arrangements for a proposed Requiem for Rossini – dead in Paris in 1868. Verdi was not happy his pet project was ignored.

There had been other grievances. Before the Requiem misunderstanding Mariani had conducted Wagner's *Lohengrin* when Verdi thought he should have been working on his scores. Was Mariani trying to keep Teresa away from Verdi? Maybe… There's more to the story.

Truth be told, there was a kind of artist-to-artist connection which Mariani could easily chart. Verdi's and Teresa's careers were on a common track. After all, she had been Verdi's prima donna in the Turin production of *Don Carlo*. For her part, Teresa Stolz did all she could to promote their friendship, also trying to ingratiate herself with Strepponi. "Because the soprano was free from the end of the Turin season until the beginning of July [1871], she had a chance to be with Verdi, Strepponi, and [impresario] Corticelli on a regular social basis, as they dined together in Verdi's apartment and celebrated his and Strepponi's name-days." The Verdi couple had the same root Christian name. Stolz was angling for access, and Mariani saw something much more in the friendship. Surely Carlo Gotti, Verdi's first serious biographer, thought so too.[35] What of Mrs. Verdi?

We sense that Strepponi was liberal-minded about the affair and chose to accept it for what it was, a rite of passage not uncommon "in the operatic world….[and] not regarded in quite the same way in ordinary society"[36] Another insight into the source of Giuseppina's remarkable acceptance is explained this way: "she and Verdi had not had an active love life since about 1860, when she was 45 [he was 48] … he may have been pleased to find a young, responsive partner. At the same time, Stolz could give the composer what he needed on the stage to guarantee his operas' success: a powerful, luminous voice and an imposing dramatic presence."[37] Verdi saw Teresa as his lifeline to the theatre. For her part, Teresa got recognition as Verdi's chosen. Some Muses get as much as they give.

The affair was stranger yet for its duration and the fact that Strepponi, though vexed by her husband's openness about the liaison, seemed to remain cordial to Stolz. They exchanged letters when the younger woman was not actually staying with them, which she did, off and on, for seven years. There must have been periodic strains.

In the summer of '75, Teresa suggested by letter to Giuseppina that she was feeling guilty. She said she sensed that she was no longer welcome at Sant'Agata. Mrs. Verdi thought about it, then responded from Florence, a city she enjoyed visiting when she could: "That you love us, I know, or rather we know. We believe it and we are confident that, over you, we shall never suffer disillusionment… For you, we shall be the same as long as we live… And with that and a kiss I close the paragraph."[38]

Teresa was a most uncommon visitor. We can only surmise the genesis of Strepponi's refusal to deal with the larger implications of friendship and fidelity. Finally, by 1876, any active relationship between Giuseppe and Teresa was likely past. In any event, having returned again briefly, Teresa abruptly left the villa at Sant'Agata and that year went off to St. Petersburg, reportedly in an attempt to extend her career. Strepponi, ever the conciliator, had advised Teresa to retire while people still loved her.

Stolz considered a return. Was it to set up a house for the three of them again? No. By now Strepponi had had enough. We have this fragment of another letter to Teresa from Giuseppina: "I hope you will never have to struggle with the sorrows of life, especially the delusions and sorrows of the heart… Yes, my dear Teresa, in joy and in misfortune, may God save you from it, say a Sunday prayer and, while saying it, think of me sometimes and beg for me the mercy of God, that God that the beautiful souls refuse to believe in, because they do not want to look at their own consciences."[39] Strepponi was referring, of course, to her husband who, while he seemed to be spiritual in his own way, did not attend church. Further, Giuseppina was perhaps chiding Teresa for keeping Verdi from "the mercy of God." After that the letters, which had been coming like the snows of Alpine winters, began to slow. By 1880 the letters, many of them exculpatory, had virtually stopped, except for the episodic chatty news the women sent to each other. Maybe they'd reached a tacit understanding.

Time would do what it always does to heal wounds. The women became friendlier again, "developed a sisterly relationship as they sent [notes about] lace, furniture, and [other] advice back and forth, traded coats and furs, paid each other's small bills… Whatever had happened, Strepponi had put an end to what she called Verdi's exclusive attention to the soprano. The semblance of propriety was restored."[40] The next year, in June of 1878, Teresa wrote once more to Verdi, addressing him as Maestro, and telling him that she had not written "because she was afraid of causing problems for him."[41] Perhaps the two women had, by now, completed all essential work as Verdi's sources of inspiration. As Muses they had earned a rest.

Teresa Stolz retired from the stage in 1879, but she had had quite a career, having been chosen by the composer as his first singer of *Aida* in Italy, and for the world premières of *Don Carlo*, in Paris, and Verdi's *Requiem*, in Vienna. The man who struggled with his faith, who was so ambivalent toward the church, had now returned to sacred music. There would be a more, and some of it, perhaps, could be called sublime.

It's interesting to speculate on what was going on, or not going on, in Verdi's life between the production of his *Requiem Mass*, in 1874, when he was sixty-one years old, and 1887 when his next major work was complete. He had great periods of depression. He traveled. Finally, his next work came together, the opera *Otello*, which, along with his final opera in 1893, *Falstaff*, were considered his operatic masterpieces. Learning much from his venture with *Macbeth*, "he had learnt to turn Shakespeare into music, Italian music."[42]

Verdi knew that he owed a debt of gratitude for *Otello*'s success to his librettist, Arrigo Boito. They would work together again on *Falstaff*, as Verdi became, in his enormous success and veneration, the embodiment of Italian opera. Such popularity has a way of alienating some people, and now there were heated discussions in the newspapers and journals about the feud over Italian and German opera, meaning Verdi and Wagner, the personification of each "school." They personally did little to advance the struggle, and little to defuse it. Each had devoted soldiers who advanced it anyway. For his part, Verdi "apparently had a strong distaste for Nordic myth, and for the entire paraphernalia of Wagner's *Ring*."[43]

It is interesting to find that one result of the feud was that Hans von Bülow, obviously steeped in Wagnerian prejudice, wrote to Verdi, apologizing for his blind fanaticism. Verdi accepted the surprising flag of truce with good spirits and told a colleague he thought Bülow was going mad.[44] Certainly, their music need not be seen as in any way in competition. Wagner worked from the illusion of the stage to the reality of music. Verdi always began with human beings singing, singing on the stage. In fact, one biographer offers: "Even today [1974] there are Wagnerians who have no use for Verdi and, more regrettably, Verdians, a more mature, more civilized group, who take a dim view of Wagner's work."[45] Here is a critic in search of the last word.

The young Richard Strauss, fifty years Verdi's junior, also made a point of befriending the old master, evidently recognizing as well that there might well be two titans of opera. After all, he would become the recognized master of the tone poem, while retaining close ties with composers he was leaving behind.

Recall that Verdi returned to sacred music in his mature years. That is where he began, as a church organist in Busetto. He followed his *Requiem* with a *Pater Noster* for unaccompanied five-part chorus, in 1880. Requiems are wonderful good-byes.

His beloved Giuseppina died in November of 1897, and the next year he finished his *Four Sacred Songs*. Verdi had been working on the *Stabat Mater* when she died. He'd written the *Ave Maria*, the first of the four songs, some years before, actually between *Otello* and *Falstaff*. Ever devoted, Strepponi was helping him with even these last pieces as she was beginning to fail.

Come to that, Giuseppina may have led her husband back to scared music. She told him that all of his friends were dying, leaving him, going on to whatever might be their reward.[46] We do not know if he found this news particularly motivational. The musical results, however, are undeniable.

The arrangement of these four scared songs was his final work, and all four were presented at La Scala, in Milan in 1899. His work as a composer was over. Verdi had written thirty-two operas. His sacred music, the form with which he began and concluded his career, is now considered some of his best work. At the end, the composer looked outward, became more magnanimous.

In his last three years Verdi turned his attention to those without means. He'd once been poor, and save for Barezzi's care he might have missed his chance to excel in music. Verdi had already set up three scholarships for deserving, needy music students in Busetto. Next he ordered built three work farms to keep people without employment busy and productive. He subsidized the operation when it needed a little help to remain solvent. Then Verdi hit upon the grandest plan of all. He would build an old people's home, and specifically for musicians whom time had passed ungenerously.

There was an order of merit, though somewhat tendentious. Composers would be admitted first; then singers, conductors, chorus masters, and orchestral players might enter.[47] Casa Verdi operates today much as it did in 1900 when it was complete, accommodating 100 guests. Today it is a "co-ed facility." Verdi did not live to see the home actually open. He died of a stroke on 27 January 1901, at Sant'Agata, in the home he and his long supportive wife Giuseppina had built and loved.

"'Not everyone can write *Aida*, Giuseppina once said, 'but somebody has to pack and unpack the trunks.' Giuseppina understated her lifelong role as the woman behind Verdi. She was in every sense his source of strength, "his most influential critic."[48] Verdi had lain in a coma for a few days before he died. Hearing of his condition, friends and loved ones could come to pay their respects. At his side on his last day was the priest he had asked for, along with the sixty-seven year old Teresa Stolz.

Also beside him were Giulio Ricordi and his friend Arrigo Boito. It was Boito, the librettist and poet, who had helped Verdi to reach his greatest acclaim. It was Boito who recorded in his own diary the final wish of the grand old man. Italy's greatest opera composer, a man comfortable on nearly every European musical stage, had asked for only this when he would be laid to rest: "one priest, one candle, and one cross."[49] Someone had found his way home.

CHAPTER TWENTY

WAGNER, Wilhelm Richard (1813 - 1883); German

"... Mine is a highly susceptible, intense, voracious yet uncommonly sensitive and fastidious sensuality, which must somehow or other be flattered if my mind is to accomplish the agonizing labour of calling a non-existent world into being." [1]
(Wagner to Liszt, January 1854)

The word "Muse" gets stretched a bit, now and again, when meant to show a woman's influence on an artist. Some worked tirelessly to inspire their romantic others to achieve greatness, or at least to laudatory efforts. In the case of Wagner's women, the properties of the word "Muse" become pretty elastic. That's because Wagner inspired himself though self-promotion and selfishness almost as much as any woman awakened or sustained his creative spirit. Nevertheless, of the seven principal women in his adult life some were particularly inspirational; two of them proved to be catalysts in compositions that made Wagner "great" – whatever one may think of his outrageous mendacity, selfishness, and pomposity.

We begin, as by now we are accustomed, with the arrival of the scamp himself. Richard was born 22 May 1813, in Leipzig – born healthy, if perhaps not truly legitimate. His biographers have trouble deciding whether or not the paternal impetus came from Carl Friedrich Wilhelm Wagner, married to Johanna Rosine Wagner, with whom he had already had eight children, or from another gentleman. Even the composer's highly charged autobiographies – he had many of them – suggest that the real dad may have been family friend Ludwig Geyer, a painter and sometime-actor who had come to live with the Wagners in the year before Richard was born. When the nominal father, Carl Friedrich, died from typhus six months after the boy's birth, Johanna promptly married Ludwig. That tidied up a few loose ends and may help explain why she traveled nearly 150 miles just weeks after Richard was born to visit her friend Geyer, who'd decamped to the Bohemian spa town of Teplizt.[2] Such travel might seem unwise or unwarranted for brand new moms. Maybe it was an obligatory report.

Add to the plot the fact that Europe was still much in distress and Napoleon's campaign was at another impasse. Johanna's elective journey would have been perilous for her and her child. The mother's husband was clear in his sentiment. "Evidently Carl Friedrich wanted no part of the new child," his wife Johanna making the trip, essentially, alone.[3] While the truth of Wagner's paternity has never been satisfactorily settled, there is no doubt that it was Geyer with child's mother who exercised a significant influence on the musician's future.

Carl died three months later, setting Johanna was free to join Geyer, with whom she was certainly involved. Six months after their marriage – it was her second – the newlyweds celebrated the birth of their first child, or was it their second? There were now ten little and not so little mouths to feed in the Geyer demesne. Richard's spanking new little sister, Cäcilie, became his first childhood companion and playmate.

It is difficult to determine whether Richard had any great animosity toward or sense of ambivalence about his real father's identity. The fact that Wagner thought Geyer might have been a Jew certainly vexed him, as Richard spent much of his youth and maturity insulting and tormenting Jews. He even wrote an absurd tract many years later against their influence in classical music called *Das Judenthum in der Musik*. We must return to this important though disagreeable sub-text later in our examination of the man whom who has been called The Colossus of Germany. In any event, Wagner had to overcome a confused early identity.

The vagaries of war in Europe and the lack of any substantial income in the home of Wagner, like Verdi, only made their triumphal stories the more compelling. Both were in their late twenties before much of anything noteworthy came of their compositional efforts, yet both became enormously influential and successful, in part because of willpower and determination, and because of vital romantic links and liaisons.

Wagner's early theater training was strongly influenced by Geyer, the only father he ever knew. Geyer playwright, too. "His oeuvre included a number of small, domestic dramas written to celebrate anniversaries in the household, anticipating [son] Wagner's predilection for similar pantomimes at Tribschen and Wahnfried years later."[4] What about the boy's primary education and his formal musical training?

Richard developed not only a taste for theatrical production but an ear for dramatic music. Apparently, he could also recall and duplicate music he'd briefly heard. Beethoven fascinated him. One event stands out as particularly prophetic and revelatory. On a day when the boy was home from school Johanna asked her son to play in the next room – to go in and entertain yourself on the piano, she said, so as not to disturb your father, who was then deathly ill. "The eight-year old boy strummed [sic] a folk-tune and an air from [Weber's opera] *Der Freischutz,* and Geyer turned to Johanna and asked, 'Is it possible that he has a talent for music?'"[5] He did.

This proud observation may have been the paradigmatic breakthrough each of them needed. If not an artist or actor, could young Richard be a musician? Perhaps it was the culminating moment for the fast failing Ludwig; the next day he was dead. Johanna now had a number of unexpected challenges. The family found itself nearly penniless, a condition Wagner would take years to remedy for himself.

Frau Geyer encouraged her son's formal instruction, though at age eleven he was determined to be a poet. In fact, his assigned poem on the death of a school friend won high praise from his teacher,[6] but Richard had inherited some musical abilities as well. His father, that is; Ludwig Geyer, was a decent singer. In fact, "Geyer's tenor voice was serviceable enough for the Dresden conductor Carl Marie von Weber to draft him for duty in various Singspiele and operettas. He appeared in Méhul's *Joseph*, Weber's first operatic production in Dresden."[7]

It makes sense that this is where Richard encountered *Der Freischutz* – he had heard his father in the production. Meanwhile, there were other Wagners in music. Older brother Albert had left his medical studies for a career in opera. Other siblings were actors or singers. Johanna passed on some worthy genes.

Richard's call to music ran deep; and nothing fascinated him as much as composition. He copied two of Beethoven's symphonies to get a sense of scoring and he attempted to teach himself something about string instruments, although this kind of "blind groping," can not have been very satisfying to the teen wanting to become a great figure in the world of music. He had another epiphany at the age of sixteen when he heard Wilhelmina Schröder-Devrient sing Beethoven's *Fidelio*, at the Leipzig Opera. The soprano likely only added to the sense of ache and awe felt by the young Wagner for one Jenny Pachta. Richard had fallen in love with the aristocratic Miss Pachta while accompanying his mother and older siblings to Prague, in 1827. Jenny tormented Richard, indirectly at least, for a number of years.

We might credit Jenny, as does Derek Watson, with an "enduring influence" on Wagner's sense of the romance in music.[8] Wagner returned to the Pachta estate five years later, unable to quite get little Jenny out of his mind. He realized that the "social gulf" between them was great, but he was willing. Arguably, any number of Wagner's tangled love themes – love thwarted by outrageous circumstances – may have a connection to his impossible love for the daughter of Count Pachta. Wagner was always banking ideas.

Jenny was only to be the first of the composer's notable infatuations. Then there was Schröder-Devrient. Richard seemed to worship her from his first experience of seeing her on the stage, in Leipzig. He immediately wrote to Wilhelmina and confessed that she alone gave his life meaning. Thus inspired, Richard told the beautiful soprano that he vowed to make a name for himself in the artistic world. Wagner had found his Muse; he never forgot his oath.[9]

The next year, for whatever reason, or from whatever impetus, Richard Wagner began to study music somewhat more seriously, concentrating on harmony and counterpoint under the tutelage of the Dresden church cantor Christian Theodor Weinlig. He entered the University of Leipzig, but study and discipline were neither his long nor his strong suits.

Richard did enjoy gambling and getting involved in social and political causes and "[w]hat he composed in those [early] years – a piano sonata [in B flat major], several overtures, a symphony – gives evidence of sound training, nothing else."[10] Richard's *Symphony in C*, alluded to in the quote above, owes much to Beethoven. After all, Wagner was largely self-taught, so he was drawn to the masters. Christian Weinlig, who was not a full time music tutor, helped the young man to focus his uneven and undisciplined talent. In this manner alone Weinlig was a gifted teacher.

Wagner seems to have found his métier, in opera, at age twenty. His work *Die Feen* (the Fairies), taking a libretto based on German folklore, was not a big hit, but it proved to be a solid start. One year before, Richard had tried the opera "The Wedding" *(Die Hochzeit)*, likely inspired by his affection for and loss of Jenny Pachta. Maybe both operas were so inspired, but he abandoned *Hochzeit* much as he must have thought love had abandoned him. The heroine in *Hochzeit* is a half-fairy whose identify must not be revealed. Wagner would torment himself for the rest of his life, regularly second guessing not only his paternity, but his own purpose.

In any event, shortly after the initial run of *The Fairies*, in 1833, Wagner gave up his five-year struggle with Jenny's rejected affection. Such disappointment is the theme of *Hochzeit*. Richard had had enough of unrequited love. He did not have long to wait to find another contender, and this one would become his first wife.

This story has everything to do with Wagner's attempt to leave Leipzig, where his finances and future seemed ever in doubt. An appointment as conductor in Magdeburg looked pretty good. It looked even better when he met Christine Wilhelmina Planer at the hotel he had chosen to stay at. Minna Planer was everything Richard told himself he wanted and needed – beautiful, talented, and perhaps interested in him? At the tender age of fifteen, Minna had been "involved" with a military man and she now had a daughter to show for her troubles. Since the two women were so close in age, Minna passed off the child as her little sister, a charade Richard accepted and abetted. Minna and Richard's life together would become much more complicated than the problem of protecting little Natalie's embarrassing identity.

Wagner's choice of jobs at this time says a lot about the man's practical side. His operas had not swept him up into the Valhalla he would eventually imagine. Was he composer or conductor? Many men whose lives are recalled in this book considered themselves to be both, perhaps not the least of which Mahler and Stravinsky. Wagner came to conducting as an alternative way to pay his bills – always complicated by his need to live beyond his means. Apparently, "the gentle Minna, the cause of his new career, increasingly fascinated him." Evidently, Wagner was happy to stay on with the small Magdeburg opera company in whatever capacity kept him near Frau Planer, as "she tolerated the ardent advances of the little Kapellmeister."[11] Conquest would not be easy. Minna knew that Wagner's prospects were uncertain, and she was not about to again make the same mistake that led to the arrival of her Natalie. For his part, during the painful uncertainties of their courtship, Richard was nervous that other men with better prospects might win her heart, a replay of the tortuous Jenny Pachta experience.

Minna did her all to get Wagner a permanent and somewhat more elevated position with her employer, the Bethmann theater company. Even with his eyes figuratively blinded by Planer's allure, Wagner could see that this was essentially a dead-end deal. He wanted to compose, but first things first: the couple had to have some income to live on. Most of that money came from "loans," from friends and family. Wagner had a bad habit of not repaying anyone. He was better at cajoling money and favors than settling debts. Perhaps if his conducting were to be successful he'd have some breathing room to work on his own music.

Richard's conducting debut of the Mozart opera *Don Giovanni* was nothing short of a fiasco. The performers were unrehearsed; the stage ill-prepared. Graciously, the gifted and highly regarded Wilhelmina Schroder-Devrient agreed to sing for the struggling enterprise. She had agreed to appear only for the second performance, which was to have been the one for Richard's benefit, for his salary. Did she do it for Wagner? The Magdeburg citizens, convinced of a hoax, stayed away, unable to believe that the famous Schröder-Devrient would actually appear in their local musical. She sang to a meager audience, then took a seat in the stalls to listen to the remainder of the programme music conducted by Wagner.[12] Promptly, Wagner quit the company. Minna, of course, could choose to relocate to nearly anywhere in Germany or in Europe, for that matter, anywhere opera was appreciated. She had the cachet her lover only dreamed of earning.

Planer quickly found an assignment in Berlin, much to the chagrin of Wagner. He'd convinced himself that he was in love with her. Maybe he was. "Her absence drove Richard to write frenzied love letters that included a formal marriage proposal. He told her, "Here I accepted the job [in Magdeburg] only for the sake of possessing you." For whatever reason, Minna promptly returned from Berlin. Wagner's impassioned appeals had evidently done the trick. United in some expectation of bliss and passion, they lived together in worry and debt. There was always too little income.

Soon Minna had another prospect, but it would mean undertaking a major relocation. This time it was to Königsberg, in East Prussia; and Wagner, seemingly out of options, had little choice but to follow. Minna championed him for the conductor's post at Königsberg. He got the job, uncertain that he actually wanted it. But that company, too, proved insolvent, and Richard's contract at the Königsberg Theater was terminated. Could more go wrong?

Deeply in debt, Richard persisted in living beyond his means. His free adaptation of Shakespeare's *Measure for Measure*, the year before, which Wagner titled *Das Liebesverbot*, or The Forbidden Love, was a failure. His lack of motivation unclear, whether hiding from creditors or from reviewers, Richard wrote little or nothing for the next six years. Conducting paid some of the bills, but the couple was under enormous strain, neither being satisfied with the decisions they had made. For better or for worse the two were married on 24 November 1836. From the outset it was not an easy alliance. Minna was dutiful, almost painfully so. Richard frittered and borrowed; he gamboled.

Shortly thereafter, Minna ran away to her parent's home in Dresden, "unable to face Wagner's way of life, which entailed continual hiding from creditors. Wagner, thinking she had eloped with a Königsberg merchant named Dietrich, whom he knew to be interested in her, immediately instituted divorce proceedings, but then quickly withdrew them"[13] and eventually the couple reconciled. Richard bought her a dog, content that they had put their marriage back together. He got busy on another opera, *Rienzi*. For a short while Wagner must have thought things were finally coming together. The interlude of peace and productivity was short lived, however, as creditors demanded that obligations be settled, taking Wagner to court. What was there left for him, for the couple, to do?

In the truest sense of the word, the Wagners escaped; Richard's passport had been confiscated. He was now a fugitive. After three stormy weeks at sea they made it to England, then back to the continent where they took up residence in Paris, remaining for two and a half years. At the lowest ebb of fortune, Wagner was forced to spend some weeks in debtor's prison. He was released when his childhood friend Theodor Apel paid the debt from Leipzig. Apparently, some good did come from the harrowing experience of living hand to mouth. Wagner had attempted to write literary criticism, and even some short fiction. More realistically, he sketched a number of ideas for music and poems, to become librettos, for some of his best known operas. In the spring of 1841, while the Wagners were living in a small town near Paris, "a safe distance from his creditors […] he wrote the poem of *The Flying Dutchman* and sketched the entire score in a mere seven weeks."[14] Wagner used Heinrich Heine's poem for the baseline of his story, although the plot line seems to have included a few English legends, as well. The man's talent as a writer of poetry and fiction today goes largely unevaluated and lost in the wake of more compelling musical analysis.

Wagner sold the story for 500 francs, getting a bit of respite from debt, while at the same time his opera *Rienzi* was beginning to show some returns and some long-term potential to earn Wagner a decent income. What role Minna played in all this is somewhat speculative, but we know that she took care of what odds and ends she could to make money, even working on costumes. Her labors allowed Richard to spend time on his work. Wagner had intended the Dutchman to be a one-act curtain raiser for an evening of ballet, and not surprisingly the heroine of this first sketch was named Minna.[15] As *The Flying Dutchman* proved highly successful, it seemed Wagner had largely redeemed himself. The composer adds to the Heine story, however, in one particularly significant fashion; that is, "the possibility of the Dutchman's redemption through the love of a faithful woman. It was surely this which aroused the solipsistic Wagner's creative interest in the Dutchman; for the concept of redemption through love was thereafter to pervade almost every opera he wrote."[16] The *Dutchman* proved wildly successful. The testament to the composer's long suffering wife could not be clearer.

Then more good news arrived, the Dresden Opera was interested in *Rienzi*, apparently at the recommendation of Richard's sometime friend Giacomo Meyerbeer. It would seem that the twenty-nine year old composer was now on the road to respect, and perhaps to some steady income. Richard and Minna settled some lingering Paris debts and decided they must actively champion his work. They would leave France, where he'd had so little success. When he returned it would be under much different circumstances.

"In March 1842 he learned that the Berlin Opera had accepted *Der fliegende Holländer*, on Meyerbeer's suggestion, and to whom, therefore, Wagner was once again indebted. Obviously, the time was ripe for his return to Germany [...] Richard and Minna set off by coach to Dresden.[17] When Berlin relinquished first rights to the *Dutchman*, the Dresden Opera happily picked up the option, and the opera followed *Rienzi* by nearly one year, enjoying its premiere in January, 1843. Early on, the role of Minna, as Wagner's heroine in the play, had been renamed Senta, although the reason for this revision has never been satisfactorily resolved.

Of course, little in Wagner's life then seemed certain or even relatively stable. Offered the post of Dresden Court Kapellmeister, Wagner considered turning it down. Why would he do so? Minna was not happy with that line of thought. After all, this job would mean real income. They quarreled. True, they had often quarreled. Never had their relationship been particularly solid or conventionally comfortable.

Just as Wagner began to realize some success in his work his domestic life fell into even greater disrepair. He was struggling with *Tannhäuser* in the spring of 1845 when the composer's interest in Wilhelmina Schröder-Devrient returned. Perhaps she was never fully out of his mind – this woman to whom he first pledged his goal of achieving artistic merit. We learn that she "provided the decisive stimulus to the final composition of *Tannhäuser*." Wagner writes of his quest for true love, and "a woman I admired only by the most trivial encounters," [...] a love hidden from the urge." We can surmise the nature of the man's urge.[18] While we have no reason to believe that Wagner and this particular Wilhelmina were ever intimate, other women were about to turn his world upside down. Richard, as we know, was ever attuned to anything unconventional. If the women in his life were also unconventional, so much the better.

Wagner was easily taken in by popular social and political causes. As long as they were outré, he was interested. The so-called Dresden Uprising, a microcosm of political unrest in Europe that reached its peak in 1848, gave Wagner a chance to agitate for his own brand of democratic reform. What he really wanted was a fundamental refashioning of the way music was sponsored and supported in Germany. He wanted a German National Theater, and he wrote diatribes and impassioned essays calling for the broadest reforms in German social institutions. What probably tipped him toward active involvement in the affair was the refusal of the Dresden Opera House to stage his *Lohengrin*. Wagner thought he was entitled to more consideration. The German people would support him were it not for the impedimenta of the aristocracy. Central to his problem was the nature of a Court Theater, the favoritism and crony-ism that he was certain worked against him. Wagner felt he was owed more than the Dresden authorities were offering. Was this unrealistic?

The man had every reason to expect that his next opera would be strongly supported by Dresden's music officials. After all, *Tannhäuser* had been a success, although some critics rocked it at first.

He was under pressure. Wagner's debt was becoming unmanageable, and the composer-conductor was looking for assistance and support – vocal and monetary. Actually, Robert Schumann, also living then in Dresden, was ebullient about Wagner's *Tannhäuser* in his letters to Mendelssohn.[19] Wagner had the respect of most of his peers. Further, Wagner the composer had been recognized as a skillful conductor. Being Kapellmeister, however, did not bring him the position and security he felt was his due. What he wanted nearly as much as income was recognition. He craved it, and so he championed a revolution that might create the "republican" conditions for him to realize it. "Only in a totally transformed German society could Wagner see a possibility of realizing his ideals. Artistic reasons, therefore, […] led him into active participation in the *Vaterlandsverein*, an association founded in March 1848 to campaign for the establishment of democracy."[20]

When the revolution failed, Wagner found himself a wanted man, a warrant calling for his arrest. Dragging along a very angry and distraught Minna, Wagner found that once again he had to flee Germany to keep his freedom. Their next several years, often living on the exhausted generosity of friends, would be among their most difficult.

Whether or not he was actively looking for it, Wagner found a number of sources of creative inspiration while in exile. One came to him in books – through his fascination with storytelling; the other came in the form of a young woman. The results led directly to four of his best known operas. We'll return shortly to the role of the extant Norse myth that provides the necessary plot lines.

Richard's revolutionary philosophy also likely worked in his favor, spurred his creativity. Impassioned by perceived injustice to him, he was given to consider what he thought of as human archetypes, plentiful in myth. The Germans love myth. Turning to the legendary *Nibelung*, dating back to about the year 1200, the composer discovered the idea for a four-part operatic saga that would allow him to advance his ideas about heroism and evil. All this, of course, would lead to his celebrated *Ring* cycle, comprised of *Das Rheingold*, *Die Walküre*, *Siegfried*, and *Götterdämmerung*. Not all of this work would come to fruition while Wagner was in exile, but apparently the essential drama upon which it is based did.

Safely away from the Dresden authorities and traveling on a fake, expired passport Wagner managed to get to Paris. The city was uncomfortable, too hot, too sickly, and soon he moved on to Zurich. As soon as he thought it feasible he asked Minna to come join him, which after much protest she agreed to do. "It was painful for Minna to turn her back on her many friends and relatives […] she traveled to Zurich in the last days of August [1849]. She was now forty, her heart condition was well developed, she had aged prematurely and she faced a future of financial uncertainty with fear and foreboding."[21]

Minna had every reason to be leery of what lay ahead, for her husband had made the acquaintance of a couple – he French, she Scots – determined to "care" for Wagner. The composer had given a certain young lady his autograph during a Dresden performance of *Tannhäuser*, and now Jessie Laussot was determined to pay him back in kind.

Wagner was invited to come live with the couple at their home in Bordeaux. He'd live rent free and would have time and opportunity to compose. Not only that, Jessie and others had arranged for Wagner to have a generous stipend to assist him in his work. He needed the financial boon. Did he need the rest of what was tacitly promised? Remember that Wagner craved life at the edge of convention, or just beyond.

Jessie wrote to Minna Wagner and expressly invited her to join them, sensitive to the fact that Minna hated any show of charity. What did Jessie actually want from the arrangement? Ostensibly it was pure philanthropy. Franz Liszt had already paid all the big relocation costs for Richard, and later for Minna. We learn, from Jessie's letter, that her plan would "permit Wagner to create 'in complete accord with the inspiration of his soul,'"[22] She wanted him to be able to think – to write. It's likely that Richard Wagner, obviously attracted to the young woman, also surmised that their relationship could become more complex. In March of 1850 the composer arrived "[i]n Bordeaux [where] Wagner felt as if he had been transported to heaven. The Laussots were devoted to him, Jessie full of sympathy and encouragement for his ideas." Wagner basked in their approbation, but at what cost?

He was totally besotted with the young woman. Suddenly, in Richard's mind, "Minna had no real understanding of him [while …] Jessie seemed to provide everything that Minna lacked – beauty, understanding, and musical talent."[23] Incredibly, Richard and Jessie considered running off together, each leaving a betrayed spouse. Wagner actually wrote a farewell letter to Minna, giving her nothing less than her walking papers, telling her "it must be" – a bizarre reversal on Beethoven's *Es Muss Sein*. Minna was no fool. She knew her husband's flighty temperament.

Shortly, the Wagners patched up the whole misunderstanding, as they agreed to think of it; for even the self-gratifying Wagner realized that his elopement with Jessie was a loony scheme. No one had stood by him as had the long-suffering Minna. Besides which, he was making wonderful progress on his operatic poems and had completed, or nearly completed, significant parts of them upon leaving the Laussot's home. There was still no music, but the plot had to come first. His work, based on Norse legend, would become the basis of the hero's death in *Götterdämmerung*, which would actually be the last of the four operas. Wagner was working backwards, although he likely did not yet know that. More importantly, he now had conceived the superstructure of the entire "Ring." Richard had also written some highly visible and outrageous theoretical tracts, including *Art and Drama*, and his *Judentum in der Musik*, or Judaism in Music,[24] foreshadowing his most appalling anti-Semitic harangues.

When the brief Jessie - Richard fling was spent, about a month later, Wagner also left behind an angry ex-friend – the man threatened to shoot Wagner. For her part, Minna had nearly had all she could take from Richard; now she was willing to try to redeem her repentant husband. Still, how long could she tolerate such disregard for her and her sacrifice? Wagner's fidelity record was not promising. The Jessie Laussot affair weakened a marriage but strengthened a composer's hand.

Jessie apparently lost interest when she found what a cad Richard had been to Minna; then the women began corresponding. In his Autobiography Wagner deliberately underestimated "the importance of this affair and his more pious biographers attempted to ignore it altogether."[25] But Jessie Taylor Laussot had made an enormous difference in Richard's life, and more so in his work. Without the so-called stipend from Jessie and her husband, and from Jessie's mother for that matter; and absent the support for his ideas of capturing the great Norse-German legend, *the Ring* could well have been a much different product, if it would have come together at all. Following this bizarre interlude Wagner turned in earnest to Siegfried, and somewhat less so to Minna. Not surprisingly, the era of the repentant husband was short lived, for Richard was about to meet and fall in love with Mathilde Wesendonck. As we'll see, he wandered a bit before he found her.

Seldom has there been a more powerful Muse in the life of a creative man – not that Mathilde's powers of inspiration were any consolation to the exasperated Frau Wagner. The composer was still an exile, and so therefore was his wife. What did Minna need? Richard, seemingly, didn't much care. Back in Zurich, Wagner was spending more time on political treatises than on music. Robert Schumann published a few of them in his eclectic *Neue Zeitung für Musik*. Wagner also began to spend more time with his Dresden and other German ex-patriot pals than he did with his music. He was stuck. Perhaps he needed, once again, someone to "flatter his mind." He was looking for someone; it was his nature to do so. That someone was near.

Otto Wesendonck was a wealthy industrialist, and a good bit older than his twenty-something wife. The Wesendoncks had attended a performance of Wagner's *Tannhäuser*, in March of 1852, and apparently they became acquainted the following year. The young wife made no secret of her interest in the composer; in fact she had been reading parts of his operatic poems and told Wagner she was fascinated. Soon, the composer had convinced himself that there was also something pretty special in Mathilde. No doubt it was the reflected image of himself as hero.

Why Mathilde came into his life is, once again, a function of how much Richard craved active, physical attention. We can well understand why Minna may not have been up for the job. "No one," Richard complained, "had true sympathy for his ideals and he would be happy to die."[26] This new, young admirer was about to help him to change his mind. Her Christian name had been Agnes, but husband Otto asked her to change it. Perhaps Mathilde's infatuation proved just the spark Richard needed to get going again, after years of languishing with ideas that had struggled to come together.

Soon Wagner was revising his four poems, finding their most viable fit and form, and early in 1853 he put all four dramas into what would be their nearly final structure. He even arranged to have fifty copies of *Der Ring des Nibelungen* printed and made available to friends. This was a wildly extravagant expense, but not at all out of keeping with Wagner's injudicious manner of self-flattery. More significantly, the challenge now was to write the music, which would take the best part of the next decade. So far he had none.

In the spring of 1854, while still suffering for his exile from Germany, Wagner accepted a sixteen-week engagement in London, where he would conduct a range of composers and some of his own work. He tired of repeated performances of *Lohengrin*, the British patrons' favorite, but he did get to meet and become friendly with Hector Berlioz – engaged in a similar sojourn. Berlioz was guest conductor at the New Philharmonic Society. Richard took that poorly. Wagner had to wonder if his journey had been a mistake.

London proved an even greater exile than Richard would have expected. Wagner wrote to Liszt that he felt he was a soul in hell. Work on *the Ring*, specifically on *Die Walküre*, was stalled. He couldn't work. There were less tangible complaints. The Londoners' choice of music was not his own, the weather was lousy, and the pay was not much better. Besides, he really missed Mathilde. For the next few years he plugged away dutifully on the operas before becoming discouraged. It was his habit to become discouraged. The man survived on doses of manic stimuli.

Perhaps Richard needed a respite from all the drama over the lack of money to promote his major and as yet unfinished works, complicated by his philosophical moodiness and romantic uncertainties. He was ready to come home and he needed a refuge. As had so often happened, Richard found one. "For some time Wagner had been interested in finding a quieter, more secluded house in which to live and work." Otto Wesendonck was a generous man, if not especially an observant one. He and Mathilde had just completed a magnificent villa on a lake near Zurich which they called "Green Hills." The property included a small country house, which Otto gave to Wagner. Mathilde dubbed the place "Asyl," a true refuge. "The advantages were overwhelming, not least the enchanting prospect of living only yards from Mathilde [...] His Muse would be virtually at his side: gone would be those somewhat awkward visits to her each day in the late afternoon. With Mathilde to share his creations, and Minna to keep the little Asyl trim and tidy, Wagner envisaged a lifelong refuge of undisturbed bliss and contentment."[27]

Actually, while enjoying all measure of Wesendonck hospitality, Wagner was making real progress on his mythical tetralogy, most of the work going into *Siegfried*, Acts One and Two. *Siegfried* would actually be the third opera. He had already begun to sketch for *Götterdämmerung*. For various reasons, mostly financial, his music publishers, Breitkopf and Härtel, were uncommitted to his *Nibelungen*. Wagner wrote to Liszt in a melancholy tone that he was about to leave Siegfried in the forest solitude. Setting the work aside that summer, he would not return to *the Ring* for another seven years. No doubt he was weary. He needed something entirely different to occupy his genius. It did not take him long to discover such an outlet. Muses have a natural sense of timing.

There were likely two sources of inspiration. His friend Liszt's daughter Cosima and her husband Hans von Bülow arrived to spend some time, actually their honeymoon, at Asyl. Richard was devoted to Liszt and admired his tone poems; their harmonic subtleties are said to have influenced the final texture of the four operas. He was also happy, no doubt, for the infusion of more musicians. Ironically, Cosima, twenty-four years younger than Wagner, would in six years become his lover. But we should not get ahead of the story.

Wagner needed to write some music that would sell, that could be performed. He had been working on what Thomas Mann subsequently described as "something tuneful, lyrical, singable, easy, approachable, and Italianate." In other words it would be in many ways quite the opposite from *the Ring*. It should be something with a small cast and easily produced. Wagner needed the income. Härtel recognized the merit in such a practicable production. The story and score of his efforts, not entirely his, would be *Tristan und Isolde*, the "crystallizing agent [for which] was his hopeless love for Mathilde Wesendonck."[28] The Richard - Mathilde collaboration, which would finally compel Minna Wagner to threaten divorce, was far from being finished.

Between 1857 and '58, and needing to give Frau Wesendonck more of himself, Wagner wrote what we know as the *Wesendonck lieder*, five love songs – for voice and orchestra. The manner in which these songs came to be is a marvelous testament to musedom. Mathilde wrote the poems; her besotted lover set them to music. On New Year's Eve, 1857, "Wagner gave his beloved muse the draft score of *Tristan and Isolde* with a poem dedicated to her: 'Full of joy, empty of pain, pure and free, forever with thee.'"[29] He was recognizing her seminal contributions, for it was her poems, then his music, that had led directly to *Tristan*. In fact, two of the five songs, *Im Treibhaus* and *Träume* were sketches for Tristan, while *Stehe still!* is imbued with the spirit and "secret passion of Richard and Mathilde [...] Wagner orchestrated *Träume* (dreams) and had it played outside the Wesendonck villa on Mathilde's birthday, 23 December."[30]

All of this may have been a bit too much for Minna. She intercepted a note of bold *coloratura*. The affair was out in the open. Again, Minna threatened divorce, and then agreed to try to keep the marriage together. She had more patience and resilience than was good for her. "For a while there was yet another period of calm [...] but Mathilde's intellectual and social superiority was something she could not and would not accept. And so to the final rupture: on 17 August 1858 Minna wrote to Mathilde, starting: 'Before I depart, I want just to say that my heart bleeds that you have succeeded in taking my husband away from me after nearly twenty-two years of married life. I hope this noble achievement will be a comfort to you and make you happy.'"[31] Amazingly, Otto seems to have remained unaffected by most of the drama, until he found his hand forced by Minna Wagner.

The idyll at Asyl came to an end.

By late August they moved out and away from the mess Richard had made. Clearly, his time at the villa, more pointedly his proximity to Mathilde, was a boon to his compositional spirit. While living at Asyl, and before moving on to Venice, briefly to Paris, and eventually back to Bavaria, Wagner also sketched out the three-act musical drama that would become *Parsifal*, his last musical composition. We must credit Mathilde for having created the conditions for, and provided some of the necessary inspiration for, Wagner's greatest successes.

Gradually the relationship with Mathilde, a liaison that for over two years had been intense, became almost formal, and certainly more "proper." The Wesendoncks seemed to have patched up their own rift and moved to Vienna. Mathilde Wesendonck continued to write poetry, work through translations, and to write children's stories, dying at the age of seventy-three, in 1902. Mathilde may have been Wagner's greatest love. Now, with her gone and back once more with an estranged Minna, in Dresden, Wagner was searching for this next comfort. He wrote Minna a letter opining that "… each of us henceforth looks after his own happiness and welfare."[32] Once again, as the saying goes, he was giving the lady her walking papers. His Minna, betrayed, in poor health, and likely in worse temperament, was finally gone. Richard Wagner did not miss a step.

He likely thought that he had found his next flame in Mathilde Maier, a twenty-nine year old woman, bright and well-read, whom he met through his new publishing house, the Schott firm, in Mainz. Franz Schott was interested in Wagner's *Meistersinger*. Ever a master of self-centered need, Richard asked his latest Mathilde to join him in Vienna; wouldn't she like to run his house? He told her he needed someone "to be all that a woman can and must be if I am ever to enjoy life again.'"[33] His affection for her, however, or more importantly hers for him, remained guarded and platonic. Mathilde was happy to be his friend, but she would not go to Vienna. She would not be his maid. Miss Maier later became somewhat closer to the young poetic and passionate Friedrich Nietzsche, suggesting an interesting juxtaposition with Wagner's philosophical hero Arthur Schopenhauer. Actually, Wagner and Nietzsche were to become quite close, each seemingly needing the other's validation. That alliance was still a couple of years away.

Tannhäuser was not successful in Paris. Wagner had spent years trying in vain to make it so. Adding to his misery, *Die Meistersinger* did not pay off as Wagner had hoped and expected. Nevertheless, the composer-conductor again took to overextending his pocketbook. He soon went broke again. His spirits were lifted with his exile. A general amnesty of 1861 permitted Wagner's return to his homeland. A few short years later Wagner arrived in Stuttgart without a wife, without a penny, a man without a future, starring into the abyss. He needed a miracle to keep going, and as he had demonstrated so many times before, he knew how to find one.

This one was a good deal more rich and influential than any of the others. On 3 May 1864, Wagner was summoned to the Munich Court. "Next day, Wagner, fifty-one and the young King [of Bavaria] barely nineteen, confronted each other for the first time. King Ludwig had read the 'Art-Work of the Future' at the age of twelve and attended a performance of

Lohengrin at sixteen. So when he came upon the question, in the foreword to the text of the *Ring*, whether the work would ever enjoy the patronage of some princely Maecenas Ludwig immediately heeded the call."[34] Maecenas, by the way, was a Roman statesman and patron of letters – a sponsor of Virgil and Homer.

How suitable! Wagner wrote to his friend Mathilde Maier that the King had offered him everything. In fact, he gave the strapped composer 20,000 gulden to clear up any debt and get on his feet again. Thereafter they met regularly, planning for the completion of *the Ring*. Their plans even included the funding for a magnificent Festival Theatre, which eventually was built not on the Isar in Munich, but in Bayreuth. Wagner also presumed his pointed political musing and writing, advising the gullible King on such topics as "The State and Religion," as well as resurrected ideas for a German state music school. The young king's homosexuality was likely no real factor in his near-worship of the avuncular Wagner, though there are some who would disagree. Nor should we accept that Wagner contributed to the young monarch's eventual "madness." Rather, "Wagner, and all he stood for, formed part of Ludwig's already nurtured vision of Germany – her heritage, her folk-soul, and his own place as one of her princes."[35] Wagner's music embodied what Ludwig saw for Germany, and the young king was delighted to subsidize its full expression.

Meanwhile, Richard was beginning to think more about Mrs. Cosima von Bülow, whose interest he had again piqued when they fortuitously met up in Berlin. It was a relationship that, over time, went from cool and cautious to one of deep passion. When they first met at his house near Zurich, that is at Otto Wesendonck's house, Cosima von Bülow thought the composer to be self-centered and vulgar.[36] Certainly he was all that. But after all, Cosima was a young woman with strong personality, greatly influenced by other artists and musicians who did not carry on so dramatically. Her refined tastes were influenced, largely in Paris, by the women who raised her. Wagner knew he had made a misstep with her. The composer was annoyed at himself that he had not made a better impression. Wagner wrote to Bülow, "Cosima's reserve toward me really grieves me […and I] truly regret that I let myself go too far in my familiarity." He asked his friend to speak well of him, to help to heal any wounds.[37] Ironically, Bülow, by complying, was setting himself up for the destruction of his own marriage.

Cosima was able to work out the grounds for the rapprochement on her own, gradually coming to see Wagner as truly torn between two women, Minna and Mathilde Wesendonck, for whom she had little respect. Perhaps she was measuring the drama at Asyl against a more gracious and in some ways a more sophisticated relationship between her mother, Marie d'Agoult, and Liszt's long-time second paramour the Princess Carolyne Sayn-Wittgenstein. We should also recognize that Cosima, herself a fine pianist, was more musical than either Minna or Mathilde, and was perhaps naturally more simpatico with Richard. She had also witnessed her father's hopeless slide away from her mother and toward the proverbial "other woman," this when she was only ten years of age, in 1847.

Contributing to her interest in Wagner was a largely unsatisfying marriage to von Bülow. Cosima was disappointed in Bülow's limitations. She, not unlike Richard, wanted to connect to genius; more, she craved the thrill of romance. Cosima also had a fine sense of humor, given to laughing out loud at the silliest things. It was a trait that endeared her to Wagner. Meanwhile, Cosima found husband Hans nervous, given to bursts of temper, and unappealingly full of self-doubt. As for Wagner, "[w]hether she recognized the emotions that were growing in her toward him for what they were or not, there is no doubt that […] the attraction was stirring between them." They both spoke of an opportunity missed when Wagner went off to Venice in 1858. At their next meeting, Cosima told Wagner of her deep affection for him, and he confessed his own for her.

We find "Cosima's reactions were not so mysterious after all. Frustrated in the ardent stirrings of her heart, wanting desperately to love and be loved with totality and abandon, in love with love actually, she was in a state of extreme susceptibility to strong emotional appeal."[38] Not surprisingly, both parties were quick to act on their passions, crushing Bülow and the long, deep friendship of the two men.

Meanwhile, Wagner was also playing to the king's affection. During the time the composer was receiving special favor, money and influence, the two exchanged hundreds of notes, poems, and telegrams. Wagner held King Ludwig in high regard, but his patronage even more so. Injudiciously, he began to try to influence royal governance, and from that moment his troubles soared. Finally, "in December 1865, yielding to pressure from his Cabinet and his family, the King asked Wagner to leave Munich … Wagner complied, having been given another 40,000 gulden a few weeks previously."[39]

Others did not fair as well. Minna, still attempting to make her own way in Dresden, died the next month. She had given Wagner everything, and Richard knew that a major part of his life was gone. He had all but closed it off years before. Now sensing the freedom he had long sought, by March of 1866 he and Cosima were living together in Geneva. They bought a villa on Lake Lucerne, known as Triebschen. Not surprisingly, Ludwig paid for the home, his gift to Wagner to help him to celebrate as the composer turned fifty-three.[40] This was the house Richard and Cosima would occupy together for the next eight of his remaining seventeen years.

Was Cosima a true Muse? It would be hard to say she was not. We can locate plenty of examples of her inspiration.

By 1869, and when Cosima delivered her third child by Wagner, the "completely broken Hans von Bülow divorced her … Now there was nothing to prevent the marriage of Richard and Cosima, which took place five weeks after the woman's divorce."[41] Wagner rejoiced in their official union, which took place on 25 August 1870. She wrote in her diary, "My prayers have been concentrated upon two points: Richard's well being and my hope that I may always be able to promote it."[42] Wagner was both lucky and ruthless in love; Cosima did all she "prayed" to do for him and more.

In only a matter of months, his music again poured forth. Cosima's influence or not, the music Wagner had put aside as too taxing now seemed workable. By the end of the year Richard had finished the instrumental *Siegfried Idyll*, central to his third program opera. He dedicated it to Cosima as a Christmas present. He also offered it to her as a tribute for giving birth to their latest child, whom they named Siegfried. Wagner held off on playing the work until Christmas morning, which was also Cosima's birthday. There could not have been a more propitious start to their late-in-life marriage. We recall that at this time, most of Wagner's mature works were either completed or well sketched.

Wagner was not content to write, to conduct, or even simply to play his music. Richard's next few years were marked by wild polemics and outrageous anti-Semitic tracts, along with the culmination of his Ring cycle. *Das Rheingold* was finally ready by late summer, 1869, and it premiered that September in Munich.

The Ring was complete, but Wagner was often preoccupied with his bizarre political writings and his self-congratulatory autobiographies. "Towards the end of the close period of their relationship, Ludwig had asked Wagner to write a detailed account of his spiritual and physical life, a task which Wagner was only too happy to undertake. He dictated his memoirs to Cosima, but much of what he produced was closer to fiction than autobiography."[43] He realized that he was reversing himself in important ways from his well circulated *Mein Leben* – a memoir that he had worked on for most of his adult life. For Wagner, the possibilities were always greater than the realities.

By 1871, Richard began to wonder if the four operas would ever be staged to his satisfaction. He had always wanted more control of the production of his work and he found that, once again, his benefactor King Ludwig II was the answer. Cosima and Richard made plans for a theatre dedicated to the *Ring of the Nibelung*. No place in or immediately near Munich seemed right. Bayreuth was the answer; this little city would be the ultimate home to Wagnerian music-drama. The couple left Triebschen in 1874 and moved to Bayreuth, occupying yet another magnificent home – Villa Wahnfried, paid for by the whimsy of the King. The Festival Theatre, Wagner's ultimate homage to himself, opened on 13 August 1876. The tetralogy, first conceived twenty-five years earlier, was complete. Now the *Ring* could play, uninterrupted by other program music, or by some potentially discordant conductor or concert master.

Wagner's world was never tidy, but he wanted his music to be so. Without a doubt it was all as visionary as it was often thought to be garish and wildly ornate. Not all of Wagner's contemporaries, including Tchaikovsky, thought so highly of the finished product, the latter pronouncing it "absolute nonsense."[44] Certainly there were also plenty of admirers and even sycophants who thought it was simply pure genius.

Whether or not *the Ring*, with its elaborate, messy repetitions, the obsessive chromatic half-steps, was his greatest work it has surely been his most celebrated. The next year Wagner gave eight concerts in London, but from then on, until his death in Venice in 1883, he stayed pretty close to home. He and Cosima were comfortable in Bayreuth, one further affair, this one with a Judith Gautier, notwithstanding. Cosima essentially ignored it as an untimely diversion, allowing Wagner to come to his senses and back away from the young Parisian on his own terms.

In his final few years, Wagner spent most of his time overseeing his epic work. *Parsifal* was completed in early 1882 and performed for the first time on 26 July at the Festival Theatre, Wagner's theater. He was often a bit uncomfortable about letting others conduct, but realistically he had no choice. On one occasion the perfectionist in Wagner clearly got the upper hand as, at the final performance of *Parsifal,* Richard wrested the baton during the third act and simply took over the remaining work. It was the only time in the Festival Theatre that he did so. What then-conductor Hermann Levi thought of the manner in which he was summarily relieved mid-score is unreported. Arturo Toscanini was one of many eminent conductors to work in that house, fully aware that the first and truest test was to satisfy the spirit of the deceased composer, secondly to satisfy the audience.

After *Parsifal* closed, the Festival year having proven a magnificent success, the Wagners scurried off to Venice for the winter. Richard was in poor health and he tired easily. No doubt, Cosima also needed to get away. They took a large apartment on the Grand Canal, often surrounded by their four children and a horde of visitors. "Liszt was one of them and stayed nearly a month, including [his daughter] Cosima's birthday, for which Wagner had prepared a surprise – the performance of his early symphony."[45] The entire family attended the last evening of the Venice Winter Carnival, on 6 February, but Wagner took a chill and had to retire to his bed for a few days.

The next week, Wagner seemed to sense that his time was limited. He wanted to sleep, he wanted to dream, as he had such wonderful dreams; and Cosima had taken to recording them in her diary. Wagner told her that he frequently dreamt about her, but also about Minna, whom he admitted he had not appreciated. Richard told Cosima that his mother had appeared to him, and he dreamed again of Schröder-Devrient.[46] He also dreamed of composing. Richard said he wanted to write a complement to *Tannhäuser,* but he must have known he never would. He returned, as well, to one more social essay, *Uber das Weibliche im Menschlichen* – On the Feminine in the Human Race. Wagner thought he knew a lot about the subject.

Cosima wrote in her diary that Richard had taken up the score to *Rheingold,* eager to attempt some possible revision. He soon tired. The morning of the 13th, Cosima went to the piano and began to play Schubert's *Lob der Tränen (In Praise of Tears)*, which surprised their son Siegfried, as he had never heard his mother play.[47] Richard heard her, attempted to come to the door, and then rang for his wife to come to him. When she arrived she found him collapsed on the small sofa. Richard Wagner was gone at the age of sixty-nine – dead of heart failure.

Cosima made the arrangement for her husband's body to be returned to Bayreuth, but before the coffin was closed she asked her daughter Isolde to cut some of her mother's long, silver-gold hair, placing it on the embalmed body.

Wagner was buried at Wahnfried, in Bayreuth, five days later. There would be no more essays, no more bold, mythical and heroic compositions, no more preposterous dreams. No more betrayal. There would be no further need to portray the vagaries of redemptive love. Richard was now unable to explain himself, to excuse himself – even to bid a fond *wiedersehen* to the ghosts of his many extraordinary Muses.

Arthur McMaster

CHAPTER TWENTY-ONE

George Frideric Handel (1685 – 1759); German
Domenico Scarlatti (1685 – 1757); Italian
Georg Telemann (1681 – 1767); German
Antonio Vivaldi (1676 – 1741); Italian

This chapter is intended to capture what little we know about the Muse-work in the lives of four eighteenth century musicians. Collectively and conveniently, they form the "other" Baroque and early Classical masters. They would certainly be entitled to the same full chapter treatment given, for example, to J.S. Bach, but they just did not have the requisite romantic inspiration, or if they did we don't know much about it. That said, there were certainly wives and lovers for all of them except George Frideric Handel, who was apparently, privately, and unassumingly gay. He may well have been celibate. In the case of the other three men, however, and unlike Tartini, another early 18th century violin master, these men were not much inspired to write music for a love interest. It just wasn't much done. Antonio Vivaldi, Tartini's countryman, began studying for the priesthood at fifteen, and was ordained at the age of twenty-seven. That is a long time to prepare for Holy Orders, and arguably to be celibate. Still, he did have one special woman in his life. Telemann, married twice, wrote and dedicated music for his favored professional musicians. Domenico Scarlatti offers us a bit more to muse over, albeit not much. We begin with the man who once told King George II, who had asked him about women, that he simply had no time for anything but music.

Musical Muse: Wives and Lovers of the Great Composers

George Frideric Handel

In a moment of unsolicited critical analysis, Ludwig van Beethoven, born eighty-five years after his hero Handel, supposedly said of George Frideric, the ex-patriot Saxon, that he was "the greatest, ablest composer that ever lived." To a great extent, Ludwig based his assessment on the degree to which Handel was successful in multiple music forms. After all, he had in the truest sense of the word pioneered Italian opera in England, before turning to oratorios – easier and cheaper to stage – when the people turned from opera. At this point, and because he was also a businessman, and with his own money tied up in the productions, Handel often found himself nearly destitute for money. He was not down for long. After proving himself in oratorio work, he turned to other dramatic forms, and then to hundreds of instrumental and orchestral compositions. Handel was among the most flexible and diversely-creative of all the great composers.

Born in Halle, born in the same year as Sebastian Bach and Domenico Scarlatti, he did not come to music as a birthright, as did the other two. Actually, most of the men in this volume were blessed with some musical advantage. In this case Handel's father, the town barber-surgeon, said he despised the notion of anyone making a career in music. He not only opposed such a livelihood for his son, but he looked upon music as a "moral weakness." Eventually, the boy's father re-capitulated, but the lad's mother had had to run interference for a few years, bringing George a mock "spinet," and a set of keys, for him to silently practice his drills and scales. Such dedication paid off. And, yes; there was another woman in his music.

The clever way in which the boy exerted his will, gaining his father's reluctant support, is typical of Handel and demonstrated early on that the fellow knew his mind and had the courage of his convictions. When George was seven years old his father took him with him to the ducal court; evidently the elder was called on a medical matter. George Frideric played something on the organ for the Duke, who was so impressed that he gave him money and told Herr Handel that the boy's talent should be encouraged. Rather than displeasing the Duke, his most important patron, and thereby risking his own professional situation in Halle, the father promptly agreed. George was entrusted to F.W. Zachow, organist and the Halle Lutheran church. Herr Zachow worked with the boy for three years and guided young Handel to learn keyboard and the rudiments of composition. Presumably, he could have gotten his first big-time job in professional music, in 1703, had he agreed to marry Diderik Buxtehude's daughter, in Lübeck, upon the old Dane's retirement. Such had been the bizarre condition of appointment as organist at the famous Marienkirche. Buxtehude had done exactly this, marrying the daughter of his predecessor some years before. Handel, eighteen years old and not ready for such a step, understandably demurred, opting instead to move to Hamburg, the locus of German opera, and to learn what he might there learn. Finding the city's music masters down right inhospitable – it seems he made enemies as readily as he made close friends – George decided to make an even more substantial move.

The year 1705 found George Frideric in Italy. Here, he expected to take in the evanescent and exciting people and culture, and more so the music, especially from Corelli. It was all so electrifying. Along the way, Handel became the conduit, of sorts, for Italian opera; first to Hanover and Hamburg, and then on to England where he lived for most of his life. Handel became an English citizen in 1727, though he had been living there, off and on, for almost twenty years. While he lived in Rome he was greatly influenced by the Scarlatti's – Domenico was just George's age. Handel was quick to see that there was much more to music than his countrymen were used to, and he rose to the challenge of building a country of converts. What of the quintessentially human side of the man?

His private life was just that – not only private and largely unrecorded, but protected from the pubic. Letters and even public, written accounts of his life and times give away nothing of his romantic or possible sexual interludes. Perhaps he actually was too busy. Handel worked doggedly, kept largely to himself, and he could be quick to take offense about his size and weight. A number of biographers accept that Handel was a "celibate" homosexual, which could account for his keeping his affairs, or lack of them, private.

Surely, all this makes George Frideric a difficult fit for this volume. But Handel was a prolific and innovative composer, not someone to be ignored, even in a book about Muses. What we come to is that, by all accounts, the great man wrote music for no one – not man or woman. No one tore sufficiently at his heart for the big man to compose something immortal, or even fleetingly engaging. His first biographer, Christopher Mainwaring, wrote that Handel avoided intimacy because he "would not be confined or cramped by particular attachments."[1] Another offers the quaint observation that, "he chose his partners in conviviality with care," and that "his social affections were not strong."[2] Maybe so. His first of many Italian operas, *Rinaldo*, performed in 1711, on the day after Handel's twenty-sixth birthday, was as close as he came to writing anything personal. *Rinaldo* is dedicated to the Queen Anne, thanking Her Majesty for her support. The man was politically astute, if perhaps somewhat socially quiescent. Or maybe he was already laying the ground work to become an Englishman!

Handel's travel, not least of which would include his early Italian sojourns, 1705-1710, had gotten him into an awkward situation with the Hanoverian Court. His trips abroad were expected to be brief, the understanding being that he would return "within a reasonable time." He found it harder still, however, to return to Germany from England, where he had become the ex-officio composer to the Haymarket Theater – the Queen's own. Handel followed up his dedication of *Renaldo* by writing a birthday tune for Anne. The nature of name of the piece is not recorded, but it hardly counts as Muse-inspired.

The royal lady had, of course, done her duty for empire by giving birth to seventeen children, all by husband George of Denmark. None of her children would survive her. Handel does not seem to have been interested in Anne for anything but obvious political and maybe financial reasons. She bequeathed on him the tidy some of 200 £ per annum. When the Hanoverian royal, then George I, succeeded her to the British throne in 1714, and having forgiven Handel for his tardiness from his court in Germany, the monarch doubled the composer's income. Staying in character, Handel wrote his famous *Water Music* for the king, thus assuring his stipend would continue.

Perhaps his greatest work, and arguably his most famous, is the sacred oratorio *Messiah*, which he wrote in Ireland, completing it in just twenty-five days, in 1741. It would not be unfair to offer that the man got his inspiration not from the love of a good man or woman, but from the land. Handel was a great traveler, and he loved to go to new places. This predilection is likely the main reason why he never accepted a significant Kapellmeister position – to do so would tie him down too much.

Some force of genius from the land and people had worked for him in Italy, and now in Dublin he demonstrated again that he was at the height of his creative powers. No one stands close to him in the composition of majestic, powerful oratorios. Frankly, George Frideric Handel demonstrated again and again that he needed no Muse, as most artists, men like Beethoven, Berlioz, Liszt, and Mahler so clearly did.

The last years of his life, George wrote almost entirely oratorios, even though the sonata-symphony form, pioneered by Carl Philip Emanuel Bach, and mastered by Haydn, was becoming more prevalent and popular in the early 1740s and 50s, as the Baroque era began to wane. Handel had made his mark early and was evidently not disposed to take up with new ideas as he approached the end of his long and astonishingly fruitful career. Handel died in 1759, at the robust age of seventy-four. His last major works, following the *Music for the Royal Fireworks,* were oratorios for *Susanna* and *Theodora.* Their name sakes, other than some sense perhaps that they can be said to be biblical, remain obscure, as do oratorios for *Joshua* and *Jephtha*, written in 1752. It would be difficult to demonstrate that Handel, now totally blind and alone, had anyone in mind or in his heart when he titled these last remarkable works. Maybe his Muse was simply not of an earthly realm.

Arthur McMaster

Domenico Scarlatti

A near exact contemporary of Handel, Domenico Scarlatti was born to music, a complete reversal of Handel's youthful experience. His papa was a famous musician. Allesandro Scarlatti, *maestro di capella* to the Spanish viceroy in Naples, was at the age of twenty-five a highly regarded professional musician and artist, totally comfortable in elite social circles. Domenico's destiny as a musician was foreordained. Domenico's mother Antonia (née Anzalone) was descended from a family of musicians as well. We learn "[i]t is doubtful that young Mimo, as Domenico was familiarly called, could ever remember a time when he was not hearing music, or recollect the first occasion on which he himself began to play of sing."[3]

A starker comparison of the two boys, both to become Baroque masters, would be difficult to imagine. The younger Scarlatti met Handel in Venice in 1705 and they became fast friends, not to mention competitors in a staged "harpsichord and organ duel." While they shared much in common, especially a love for staged music and for oratorios, Domenico also became a great keyboard sonata composer, writing over 550 short, luminous masterpieces. We must come back to these works shortly, and consider them in terms of their inspiration and genesis.

Comparisons with the third member, arguably the most celebrated of them all, J.S. Bach – also born in 1685 – offer yet another experience. As we know, Bach stayed close to his teaching and church compositional duties. He traveled little, while the other two men, also performers in their own right, made a career of going somewhere else, and often somewhere that their music would be noticed. Sebastian Bach promoted himself little, Scarlatti did so a great deal, and Handel seemed to be spiritually renewed for his peripatetic ways.

There was also a big difference in the manner in which women impacted Scarlatti's music from that of Handel. While the latter had no women in his life that inspired music, Scarlatti had a few solid ones. He married late, in 1728, at the age of forty-two. His first wife was Catarina Gentili, a sprite of a girl who encouraged him to think like a much younger man. Thinking about music came easily. The Portuguese princess Maria Barbara, who would shortly after Domenico's mid-life wedding become the ruler of Spain, encouraged him at least as much. Domenico wrote the *Te Deum* for her, having already written, if the biographers have not exaggerated the point, all 550 of his harpsichord sonatas for her.[4] What did he write for his little wife? Truly, we do not know.

Scarlatti met the family of his future wife while in Rome for a performance of hisopera *Tolomeo e Alessandro,* in January of 1724; and he met the Gentilis through Rome's elite music circles. The young man did not ask for the hand of Catarina, however, until his opera returned to the city again three years later. Perhaps he truly had to wait for her to become of age. They married the next May; she was all of sixteen years old, her groom a solid and respectable forty-two.

Why were they attracted to each other? The nature of their romantic allure, if there was one, is unrecorded; but music was likely the catalyst. There was another factor, not inconsequential: Domenico may have delayed marriage because he had taken some minor orders in the church. Celibacy, however, was not part of his larger plan.

What do we know is that the fate of the Scarlatti couple was soon tied directly to that of the royals, his employers – Princess Maria Barbara and Crown Prince, the presumptive next King of Portugal and Spain, Fernando VI. The Scarlattis moved to Seville in 1729, where "Mimo" was engaged as the music master to the royal family – just the sinecure he expected and needed. Not to appear ungrateful, Domenico quickly changed his name to Domingo, and his teen-aged wife changed the spelling of hers to Catalina. Meanwhile, Scarlatti continued to give harpsichord lessons to Maria Barbara, no doubt expecting her to master some of those five-hundred plus piano sonatas he was writing for her. Then, just to be sure there was no second-guessing as to where the composer's true allegiance was, he and Catarina cum Catalina named their last born daughter Maria Barbara. When the royal couple moved to Madrid, three years later, the attentive Scarlattis followed. Domenico lived in the capital city for the rest of his life.

Loyalty has its rewards. The royals had already made Scarlatti a Knight of the Order of Santiago. No one knows what his dutiful wife, much taken for granted by all parties, thought of all this affected closeness. We cannot see that she had much of an identity apart from her husband's. With no warning of illness, the young woman passed away suddenly in May of 1739. She was twenty-seven when she died – just half the age of her husband. All the children – their youngest was barely six months old – were entrusted to their maternal grandmother.[5] The children would have a good home with the elders; Domenico still had much work to do.

We know little about Scarlatti's second wife, Anastasia Ximenes, whom he married in 1742. She was a young girl from Cadiz, Spain, and marrying her only furthered Domenico's hispanization. Perhaps that was his purpose. Nevertheless, he must have cared for her deeply. In the last years of his life, his keyboard work largely done, Scarlatti wrote some beautiful songs, at least one of which can be traced to his deep affection for his wife; this is the *Salve Regina*, for soprano, strings and continuo. Having spent most of his life composing music for one woman not his wife, even though we learn that Maria Barbara inspired Scarlatti's imagination as an artist,[6] His final piece seems to have been for the lovely young Anastasia. The composer lived only a short time after its completion.

For her part, and as the composer lay dying, his patroness, student, kindred spirit, and close friend Maria Barbara was also failing. Their thirty-seven years together was remarkable not only for its longevity and productivity, but for their deep affection for each other. We should not assume, however, that Scarlatti's affection for Maria Barbara. or hers for him, in any way lessened the man's devotion to his wife, or wives. Truly, we have little to go on to suggest that the two Mrs. Scarlattis were active Muses to the man, as in some sense, was the Spanish royal. Actually, the lack of music written for or dedicated to these two women is largely a function of the historical records, for "not a single autograph of any of his keyboard works has even been discovered."[7] Only these three women, and of course Scarlatti himself, could now set the record straight. It's not likely they will.

Arthur McMaster

Georg Telemann

Georg Philipp Telemann makes the life of the musical biographer a good deal easier by having left us with extensive autobiographies – three of them, in fact; the key notations were made in 1731 when the composer was fifty years old. Telemann was the longest living of all the major Baroque composers, seeing all of eighty-six years. Bach and Vivaldi were both dead at sixty-five. Telemann had a good twenty more years to make music, and like Sebastian Bach he spent a great deal of his career in the employ of the church. Most composers in those days did. That was where the work was. Along the way, Georg wrote over forty liturgical passions, several sacred oratorios, forty operas, six hundred overtures, and seemingly countless cantatas and psalms. He is perhaps best known and most highly praised for his St. Mark Passion, written in 1759 when he was seventy-eight. Telemann's music career did not get the strongest of starts or endorsements.

Born in Magdeburg in the month of March, four years before his countryman Handel, Georg Philipp Telemann was descended from and closely tied to the Lutheran ministry. His father died in 1685, leaving his mother to care for the three children. She was willing to oversee their music education, but Georg was destined, she was certain, for a career in the church. Maria evidently thought that music was not a proper way of life for her son, that it was somehow a bit tawdry, rather "much on the same level as 'Jugglers, Minstrels, and Merry Andrews.'"[8] Recall that Handel's father had the same reservations. And what if Stravinsky had stayed with his law books!

As the boy's talents became manifest young Georg gradually won over his mother, though she insisted that he continue to study equally his Greek and Latin. By the age of ten he was learning to play, by imitation, the violin and flute. Telemann could not yet read music, but he was about to learn. Georg wrote in his early diary notes that with this knowledge he immediately felt the urge to compose, recalling that "at first I wrote ariettas, followed by motets, [and] instrumental pieces…"[9] This stream of musical precocity dates to the boys pre-teen years, although he did not record it until his first diary of 1718. At twelve years of age he staged his first opera, cadged from an extant production he had seen in Hamburg.

The next year Frau Telemann sent her son to Zellerfeld to study with an old classmate of her husband's. Under this fellow's tutelage, young Telemann advanced his compositional skills and even got in some conducting experience. His exposure to a range of music seems to have triggered a fascination with what was new and different. Telemann, unlike Bach, "swore by everything new and modern. Bach concentrated mainly on perfecting his organ-playing at Lüneberg. Telemann, on the other hand, concerned himself not only with those instruments he had played before – the violin, recorder, and keyboard – but now took up the oboe, the transverse flute, viola da gamba, double bass, trombone, and many others."[10]

Upon completing his prescribed studies he moved to Hanover, considered innovative then, to enjoy and study the prevalent French style of orchestral music. When not pursuing the French – Jean-Baptiste Lully was very popular, as was Couperin, especially so with J. S. Bach – he went to Hildesheim to observe the Italian-style theater. Telemann was determined to take it all in. Along the way, he was preparing for his university studies in Leipzig. Here, Georg met and became life-long friends with Handel. The world seemed to open to Telemann in the city he even began to take parts in operas. Not content only to compose he took singing roles, as well. Could his first Muse be waiting here too?

Yes. Telemann left Leipzig in the spring of 1705, eager to find a court position. The duties of church organist were too limiting and unsatisfying. Besides, there would be more money, and certainly more access to the nobility with a court appointment. Many of the royals and privileged attendants wanted a music education for their children. No sooner had he secured what he thought was such a position with Count Erdmann von Promnitz, at the Silesian town of Sorau (now called Zary, in Poland), but political events worked against him and within the year he was on the move again. What remained, of much greater import, was the love of a young student. Her name was Amalie Louise Juliane Eberlin, lady in waiting to the Countess of Promnitz. Her wealthy father had been an officer in the Papal army and a senior functionary at the Sorau court. Amalie's father was also an amateur composer, and had instilled in his daughter a love for music. Evidently, we know not exactly how, she became Telemann's pupil. His move away from her, he assured her, was only temporary, or at least he would try to stay close. The distance worked to draw them ever closer. They agreed he had to secure the job, and then he could worry about how to make a living, to make a family, with Ms. Eberlin.

Quickly Georg found the position he needed in Eisenach, where he had a full range of court "concert-master" duties, as well as instruction. Here, Telemann met J.S. Bach, and the two had so much respect for each other that Sebastian Bach asked Telemann to be godfather for his son Carl Phillip Emanuel, in 1714. More critical now, however, was his interest in starting his own family. He took a quick leave of absence from Eisenach to return to Sorau and marry Amalie. They were married only fifteen months when she died, shortly after childbirth. Telemann was crushed. He responded in the only way he knew to express his hurt and his love. He wrote a poetic funeral piece for her which, "in spite of all its Baroque imagery, expressed his deepest feelings."[11]

The next year Telemann moved to Frankfurt. Offered the post of Director of Municipal Music, he could not have made a job choice that would keep him busier. He told his friends that he preferred now to stay busy. Frankfurt was a musically vibrant city, and Georg Philipp would do what he could to make it even more so. After all, while his friend Sebastian Bach was writing music for the glorification of God, and perhaps for the edification of his contemporaries, Telemann was taking a more bourgeois road. He did love to work in broader circles than most. It is not that he ignored the church; in fact he served as well as the Kapellmeister at the Church of the Barefoot Friars, writing sacred music as it was needed – working with the church choirs.

While in the Frankfurt municipal post Telemann wrote five cycles of cantatas, oratorios, and other occasional music. In his spare time the man conducted public concerts. Still not sated, he joined one of the city's popular music clubs, the Frauenstein, who promptly offered him the job as director of its musical activities. Telemann was determined to stay busy, possibly as a means of keeping his mind off his deceased young wife and their child. Soon he would find room in his heart, and in his diary, for another woman.

Sometime in 1714 Georg Phillip fell in love again; this time with the sixteen-year old Maria Catharina Textor, daughter of a Frankfurt town clerk. We do not know the circumstances of their meeting, but it must have been powerful. Some music historians have speculated that Telemann's serenade, written the same year as his marriage to the teenager, was autobiographical. The piece is for "*The Virgin Bride and the Noble Groom.*" During the course of their long marriage the couple had eight children, although only two or three survived to adulthood. A committed family man, Telemann was now entering the most prolific time in his professional life.

Added responsibilities inspired the composer to try to bring in more money to pay the bills. Frankfurt was fine while it lasted, but he needed more. He tried another post in nearby Gotha. Finally he got the break he was looking for, and the timing of his next major move could not have been better. In October of 1721, Telemann sought out and was offered the job as Cantor of the Johanneum in Hamburg. What this meant was that Georg Philipp would be responsible for all the music production of the five major churches of the city. As a minimum, Telemann was expected "to provide two cantatas for each Sunday and a new Passion for Lent."[12] He also taught music lessons and worked with the choirs.

Telemann had reached the pinnacle of his career in the city he would frequently travel from, but he would never again truly leave. Hamburg was home for the rest of his life. Undaunted by his massive responsibilities, the composer found time to work in public concerts and to take part in operatic productions. He loved Italian opera and did all he could to champion it in a reluctant northern Germany.[13] The church fathers were not happy with some of Telemann's small and more public musical enterprises, especially so those "operas, comedies, and all manner of entertainments likely to arouse bawdiness even outside the ordained market days…without the consent of this most excellent Council and Citizenry."[14] It is not that they would actually fire him; he was probably too well liked and too capable in his job for that. He shrugged it all off.

While the remonstrations of the city fathers did not appreciably slow him down, neither did his choices bring in the money. One way the composer found to add to his income was to encourage more participation from the city music clubs – the collegiums – where he performed in his own operas. Georg found, as well, that he could actually sell the printed texts of his most popular music, the financial rewards from which grew every year. This composer was entrepreneurial, which brings us to his so called *Tafelmusik*, often expressed in French as *Musique de Table*. Telemann sold subscriptions in the music, and people lined up to buy them.

By the year 1718, when George Philipp was thirty-seven years old, he had written about 200 orchestral suites. The ones that made him some respectable income were the three in his Tafelmusik, composed between 1733 and 1736, when he had some 206 subscribers, "from Germany, France, Denmark, Norway, Spain, Holland, England, and Switzerland."[15] Did the young Frau Telemann have anything to do with this effort? Was she acting here in any inspirational way? Maybe. We have only the analysis that, with Telemann's successful publishing of this music, offered for the layman's enjoyment, such "income was necessary for the raising of his children and the pleasures of his spendthrift second wife, Maria Catharina Textor."[16] Such challenges can be motivational, but might they also be inspirational?

It's estimated that Telemann actually doubled his income with the sale of his "Table Music." In the best sense of the word, Maria was an impetus for, in one sense the big subscriber to the work. Georg was a workaholic. Maria was his time keeper.

Muses are expected to do more than force their men to work long hours to pay bills, however, and that is the main reason why Telemann's remarkable tale is told in chapter twenty of this book, not in the chapter before Verdi, where it otherwise might be found. The good man died, though not from any mundane infirmity. His heart gave out on 25 June 1767. He was eighty-six; the longest lived of the major Baroque masters, and the one who pointed the way ahead. Josef Haydn was a hale thirty-five in the year of Telemann's passing, while C.P.E. Bach was fifty-three. The Classical Era was underway.

Arthur McMaster

Antonio Vivaldi

We conclude the chapter on Baroque masters with the one composer remembered for having written what is arguably the best known piece of music from the entire era – *the Four Seasons* concerti, his moveable feast, his opus 8. He is also the one who may have had the "best Muse," even though he was avowedly celibate – a consequence of his having become, pretty much in name only, a Roman Catholic priest. We'll get to the woman and to the history of that one storied piece of music shortly.

Antonio Vivaldi's life and works are much bigger than one immensely popular concerto. These successes, however, may well strike many music lovers as terribly ironic, because the man died a virtual unknown and in abject poverty. Like Mozart, who would be born just fifteen years after Vivaldi's death, the composer was buried in a pauper's grave outside the city limits. It is possible that he would have remained forever obscure had the ex-patriot American poet Ezra Pound not taken a profound interest in his work, promoting Vivaldi's music at his home in Rapallo, during the 1930s.

Born in Vienna to a musical family, Vivaldi's father was a violinist and operatic arranger. We know next to nothing of the man's mother. While encouraged in his music studies, Antonio trained for the priesthood and was ordained in 1703. His musical tastes and church interests fused, for a while, and a number of his early compositions were written for the Basilica of San Marco, in Venice, where the family worshiped. The church's maestro de cappella, one Giovanni Legrenzi, was Antonio's principal teacher. Sebastian Bach thought highly enough about Vivaldi to write a bit of music known as the *Legrenzi Fugue* (BMV 574). He was also quite an accomplished performer as a teenager, for in 1689, when the lad's father had to be absent from his church duties with the San Marco orchestra, an eager Antonio successfully filled in as violinist.[17]

Be that as it may, the Church was his first calling, and Antonio became a deacon in 1700, when he was twenty-two years old. His was not to be a routine vocation. In what must have been an enormous disappointment to the man, "Father Vivaldi" was forced to leave the active priesthood only a year after his ordination because of poor health, and specifically due to his inability to stand to say the mass. Either that or he was more interested in music than in the sacraments. Biographers are not in accord on this point. If he was sickly, however, it did not take him long to recover his faculties, for the next year he left for Rome to study briefly with Arcangelo Corelli.

Returning to Venice, the young man quickly found gainful employment as a music teacher, again with the church. Still technically a priest, he was hired as violin teacher and master of the girl's choir at the *Ospedale della Pietà*, one of four Venetian charities run by the Catholic

Church "to receive girls who were orphaned for one reason or another," more often than not there was a question of legitimacy.[18] Father Antonio's first known composition was written for these young ladies – it is his *Opus 1*, a set of *trio sonatas for two violins and double bass*, or harpsichord. Corelli's influence in violin technique is clear.

Apparently, there were quite a few girls who became competent musicians at this school and orphanage, and their performances were much in demand. Vivaldi's contract was renewed for the first four years, and he became not only the *maestro de concerti* for the pietà, but for all intents and purposes he was the composer in residence. It was an ideal situation, but such perfect pictures seldom last. Unexpectedly, in 1709, Vivaldi lost favor with a number of the charity's governors and he was dismissed. It was his second major setback in less than ten years. Perhaps he was expected to spend more time composing than traveling? In any event, he did not stay away long; by 1711 he was back at the Pietà. One young student – where have we heard this before? – quickly captured his imagination, and no doubt his heart as well.

Anna Giraud was born, shall we say "without papers," to a French wig-maker living in Venice. The other parent is unknown. While at the Pietà she became a well celebrated contralto, "said to have a delicate figure and pleasant individual features …"

She also had something that strongly attracted Vivaldi, often called "the red priest" because of his flaming red hair. We learn that Vivaldi considered Anna not only a remarkable pupil but looked upon her as his protégé. When the composer moved from church music to opera, he often insisted that she be cast in a key role. Antonio said that "no comparable prima donna is to be found." One biographer tells us that "she performed in an innumerable amount of Vivaldi operas, including *Faranace* and *Ercole Sul Termodonte*.[19]

Certainly there was plenty of second guessing as to the true nature of their relationship, and there were quite a few who suspected an affair of the heart. "Things became especially sticky for Vivaldi when Cardinal Ruffo of the Papal Nuncio forbade him to be 'artistically active… [in his city.]' In response to this, Vivaldi is quoted as saying, 'and this is because I am a priest who does not say mass, and because I have the friendship of the singer Giraud.'"[20] They had something much more than a friendship.

The young lady often used the stage name Girò, the Italianized spelling, while she and Vivaldi were traveling or in production of one of his operas. In his lifetime, Vivaldi claims to have written ninety-four of them. Did he write parts, or entire works, for Anna? He did, and we'll return to the impetus of these works; but by 1723, perhaps earlier, there was a further complication when Anna's older sister Paolina joined them in their travels and productions. This was the year that Vivaldi left the Pietà to concentrate on his own work. The next few years were a time of unsurpassed creativity for the Red Priest.

Vivaldi and the sisters traveled together for fourteen years, visiting and entertaining in many European cities. They were a family in the most avant-garde sense – the three of them. Paolina may have been brought along to act as something of a nurse to the ever-delicate composer. One Italian musicologist asserted in his biography on the Red Priest that Anna was "Vivaldi's legitimate wife." It seems a strange adjective to use – legitimate. Abbé Vivaldi never did actually give up his priesthood; he simply chose not to celebrate the sacraments. Would he marry? It is doubtful. Signor Fantoni could have confused Vivaldi for another man in similar circumstances.[21] In any event, it does not seem likely that their liaison, whatever shape it may have taken over the many years they were together, was so consecrated. Others would have first affirmed and, next, no doubt have decried such a union.

Anna sang and acted the prima donna role in four operas in 1727 and 1728, including Ortona in the marginally successful *Rosilena ed Ortona*, clearly written as a star vehicle for his beguiling Ms. Girò. From time to time Vivaldi acted as the operatic producer and arranger, sort of an impresario, negotiating parts for his beloved Anna from the operas of his contemporaries. Years later, where a part could be altered to favor her style of singing, Antonio wrote and asked for permission to do so – thus often creating a hybrid opera in which Girò might succeed. On one occasion, in 1734, he took an aria from Zeno's *Griselda* and showed the playwright how it could be modified, with care and respect, of course, for his Anna. The other composer was skeptical but willing to try. The surgery worked, and Vivaldi was successful in the outcome; his Anna had become the new and improved Griselda.[22] The work of a Muse can resonate in many manifestations.

Vivaldi returned to the employ of the Pietà in 1735, after agreeing to the same salary he had twelve years before. It was not enough for him to live on. Adding insult to injury it was requested, or perhaps required, that Vivaldi stay put. No more travel. He remained in their narrowly defined employ for the remaining five years of his life. After all, at sixty years of age he'd written an enormous body of music, sacred, instrumental, and operatic. Maybe the abbé was ready to slow down.

It was now ten years since he composed the twelve concerti that would eventually make him one of the world's best known musical artists. Of those original twelve, four have been arranged so as to become "*The Four Seasons.*" Surely he did not know what arrangements posterity would make of the larger effort, but this epochal work did him little financial good at the time.

It seems peculiar that the only piece of music Vivaldi dedicated to his Anna was the opera *Siroe rè di Persia*, in 1739, two years before his death from bronchitis. Ironically, the opera was not a success, and in his last two years Vivaldi's popularity and well as his income sharply declined. We should not take this ignoble ending as the final measure of the man. Antonio created the conditions for another to succeed.

Perhaps the one accomplishment Vivaldi was most proud of and pleased about was his liberation of one young woman from an orphanage whose very purpose, after all, was to develop musical talent. He was singularly successful. Vivaldi had set out on his life's journey knowing he would be a priest and he ended that journey with a transformed woman, Anna Girò, who had instead become his very purpose. The question we might now ponder in this relationship is: who was Muse to whom?

CHAPTER TWENTY-TWO

DVOŘAK, Antonin (1841 – 1904); Czech
MENDELSSOHN, Felix (1809 – 1847); German
RAVEL, Maurice (1875 – 1937); French
SMETANA, Bedřich (1824-1884); Czech

This chapter deals collectively and in brief with the major romantic influences in the lives of one final group of composers. The work of these men is valued none the less than those having their own chapters, but the love lives of these five gents are less well documented, or the facts are confused; or maybe these guys just did not have much energy in that direction. Alphabetically we'll consider "Other Romantics and Early Moderns."

We begin with **Antonin Dvořak.** His father, Frantisek, was an able musician who sang and played the zither, presumably for diversion. His dual occupation was to run a butcher shop, successfully it seems, and to operate a somewhat less successful pub. His mother's family was not musically gifted, but Anna was a good mother and hard worker. Antonin was the first of fourteen children, eight of whom lived to adolescence. They were strong Roman Catholics and much aware of the politics that made Austria their master and German the official language, even throughout their own Bohemia. It was not surprising that the young man was drawn to both strong religious and nationalist aspirations. Dvořak's music frequently reflects such points of view.

Musical Muse: Wives and Lovers of the Great Composers

In the small village school of his home town, Nelahozeves, Antonin was attracted to a number of instruments, including the zither he had heard his father play. He did not get the benevolent, early start in actual instruction so many others did. Still, at eight years of age he convinced the schoolmaster to teach him some violin. He could as well have asked his father, who also played the instrument, but František discouraged his son's music. Papa Dvořak wanted him in the meat trade. After all, meat was a serious family business.

At age fourteen, young Dvořak went to nearby Zlonice to stay with his mother's brother, ostensibly to learn to speak German. There, Antonin found that other ideas interested him more. He was pursuing musical instruction from the schoolmaster, who was also the town choir-conductor. Even the German language teacher, Anton Liehmann, proved to be a decent musician and abetted the lad's music education. Antonin soon added a competency in viola, organ, and piano. Liehmann even gave him some basic instruction in harmony and helped Antonin in simple composition. Soon young Dvořak was composing marches and dances. The uncle he was staying with, supposedly to learn German, saw so much talent in the boy that he paid to have Antonin attend a proper music school, the Organ School in Prague.

Dvořak was influenced by the so-called German Romantics, including Schumann, and he was especially drawn to Schubert's melodizing. Moreover, he wanted to make music for his Czech and Bohemian brethren. With Smetana blazing the way in national opera, Dvořak would give them the chamber music and symphonic works that heralded their beloved homeland.

Dvořak graduated in 1859 from Organ School, which was really a complete conservatory, in spite of the rather self-limiting name. He was now seventeen and ready to strike out on his own. Antonin joined the town orchestra, and soon became the principal viola player for the Prague Provisional Orchestra. He also gave music lessons to supplement his income, a decision that would have unforeseen but agreeable results for Antonin. His first Muse was eager to begin her instruction.

Daughter of the prominent Čermak family, young Josephina needed a tutor. As we have seen happen here so often, the teacher and student were not necessarily looking at the same chords or notes. Dvořak was more interested in romantic possibilities than she, however; so bliss was not immediately ahead. He quickly began writing music for her, in particular the eighteen song cycle *Cypresses*, but Josephina was not buying. This frustration, perhaps actually proved a boon to his "creative aspirations. Dvořak followed up the *symphony in C minor* [he had just completed, *The Bells of Zlonice*], with a *Cello Concerto in A* [1] for Josephina. He never finished it, but her ambivalent coquetry gave him something to concentrate his energies upon. Undeterred, Antonin turned his attention and affections to Josephina's younger sister Anna.

Good father Čermak was not happy. After all, he was a wealthy gold dealer and Antonin was barely making a living wage. In short, Dvořak's music was not fungible. Nevertheless, Antonin managed to date Anna for six years until, with the old man's death, Mrs. Čermakova relented and gave her blessing. The couple was married in 1873. "The fact that their first child was born less than five months after the fact may also have had some bearing on the matter."[2] Theirs was not to be an epic romance.

Anna had a way with the business side of music, working with contracts, agents, and acting as his "*spiritus movens.*"[3] She bore him eight children, the last five of whom lived to adulthood. It is hard to say if they were in love. We have no evidence of Dvořák having dedicated any music to her, but she kept him focused well enough. According to his principal biographer, Dvořák wrote to Anna on 9 December 1884, thanking her and sending her God's blessing for his "great victory" in the performance of his choral masterpiece, the *Stabat Mater*, opus 58, in Worcester, England.[4] This single piece became his stock in trade until 1893 when his better known work premiered. The man's reputation grew and soon he took up the baton, conducting a performance of *Stabat Mater* in London, at the Royal Albert Hall. In his last decade, Dvořák became known and well respected abroad. At the age of fifty-three, he was not finished with travel nor was he done with inspirational women.

One unexpected source must be acknowledged here, although it is not obvious that the lady was a Muse in the traditional way. Antonin Dvořák got quite an impetus to write, teach, and perform in America from Mrs. Jeanette Thurber, a wealthy New York philanthropist who enticed him to go to the New World with a contract that guaranteed him $15,000 per annum. She wanted him to direct the newly founded National Conservatorium of Music, in New York. He and Anna stayed in the United States for three years, spending long summer holidays in Spillville, a Czech-speaking community in Iowa.

Here, Dvořák wrote the best known of his symphonies, the 9th, *From the New World*, in E minor, op 95. If Mrs. Thurber had not convinced him, virtually wooed him, to come to America there would be no *New World Symphony*. Jeanette Thurber gets major Muse credits for this bit of inspiration alone. Dvořák's time in New York continued to be rewarding to his sponsors and his growing legion of supporters, and he wrote four related symphonic poems a few years later. One of them takes for its theme a treacherous female, the water sprite. We'll return to this apparently autobiographical exposition shortly.

Before leaving the U.S. and returning to Prague, there taking up the position of director of the Prague Conservatory, in 1901, Antonin wrote his *String Quartet in F major*, "The American." It also remains one of his best loved works. His last effort was the romantic opera *Rusalka*, which he completed at the age of sixty. In many ways it complements his much revered friend Bedřich Smetana, the father of Czech opera. *Rusalka* was his final piece, his going home opus. In Slavic mythology, Rusalkas appear as beautiful young women who try to lure men into the water, where they will destroy them, actually drown them. We can only surmise to what extent one or more of the Čermak sisters were in his mind when Dvořák completed this final effort.

Let us look in quickly on the complacent genius **Felix Mendelssohn**. His compositional legacy does not fit comfortably in this chapter, since he was a major composer. There are a number of reasons for this analysis, but in the matter of finding and keeping a Muse, Felix

Mendelssohn was dealt a rather short loaf. The man was no more a true Romantic than he was, by and large a master of chamber music; nor for that matter was he expressly a devotee of the true classical period. Many composers learned their art by studying and promoting the work of those that had gone before. They also tended to press ahead and to stake out a clear place on the classical musical spectrum. As did his contemporary, Robert Schumann, Mendelssohn wrote many *lieder*, though truly these songs were not his métier. Felix mastered nearly all genres, frankly owning outright none. Heralded mid-career for his lush symphonies and powerful concertos, in his final years the man chose to return to simple organ music, to sacred music; he even attempted one more opera. He had written only one other and that was at the age of sixteen. Mendelssohn's last completed works were fugues, in homage to Sebastian Bach. Perhaps he was too clever to be expressly one kind of composer. Mendelssohn's choice of musical form is not the only subject in which he leaves us with more questions than answers. What about love? There's not much to report.

Mendelssohn seemed to have no obvious Muse. His wife Cécile was evidently not called to fill such a role, as he dedicated nothing to her, nor did he ever suggest to anyone that she gave him any inspiration for what he wrote. His sister Fanny did, and that leaves us a bit out of phase with the given definition of what constitutes a Muse.   Unquestionably, Fanny Mendelssohn, herself a fine composer, encouraged her younger brother's study and his composition. The young man from Hamburg is rather like the warrant officer of the group – neither fish nor foul.

It would be fair to say that the entire Mendelssohn family was probably more earnest than inspired. Eager to find the most suitable, perhaps the most efficacious path to respect and prosperity, the boy's parents renounced their Jewish heritage in 1805 when the first of the new generation of Mendelssohns was baptized into Protestantism. When Felix was born, four years later, and subsequently was baptized a Lutheran, the family breakthrough was complete. A few years before that, the family had added the Christian name "Bartholdy," no doubt to facilitate their "passing." Felix used the name Bartholdy Mendelssohn for his entire life.

Felix was said to have been a young genius, possibly surpassing even Mozart in being a "quick study." Felix and Fanny took their first music lessons from their mother, Lea. Soon the children moved on to study piano and violin with more professional teachers. The boy gave his first recital at the age of nine, playing the piano in a trio for two horns and piano by Joseph Wölfl. After that, and well into his teen years, Felix worked diligently on composition. He and his supremely gifted sister were both influenced by the study of Bach, and in a broader sense Mendelssohn is credited with "preserving and reviving the most significant work of Germany's musical past," as well as for "laying the ground work of the classical music canon as we know it today."[5] Mendelssohn was also something of a perfectionist. Uncertain of the merit of some of his early songs, the composer was reluctant for them to be published. Felix's first book of songs contains six actually written by his talented sister.[6]

Mendelssohn was nevertheless a prolific composer, often calling upon such literary inspiration as the works of Cervantes, Shakespeare, and especially Goethe's poetry. One of these, the overture to Shakespeare's "A Midsummer Night's Dream," remains one of the young man's best loved works. What makes the piece particularly interesting is that he wrote an overture, "as it were, to an opera that does not exist."[7]

As we have seen repeatedly in this volume the connection of poetry and music remains essential to the compositional work of many men. In this manner, Mendelssohn seems to join a mainstream of composers finding a Muse in the hearths of others. With few exceptions, however, he seemed to have had little need for inspiration from women, or men, or from any archetypal Muse, as we have agreed to use the concept and force of energy for an artist.

OK, so there was no Muse, but perhaps Mary Queen of Scots gave him a boost. On 22 July 1829, Mendelssohn and his lifelong friend Karl Klingemann journeyed from London to Edinburgh. "Soon after their arrival, they visited Holyrood Palace, and the desecrated chapel in which Mary had been crowned queen of Scotland. It was there, as Felix Mendelssohn reported, 'that I found the beginning of my Scottish Symphony;' he would not finish it until 1842." The inspiration, perhaps, took a while to fully take hold.[8]

Before Felix got married, in 1837, one other brief, romantic friendship flashed and was gone. It was on the same trip to the United Kingdom that Mendelssohn met a real woman, not an historical artifact, who, stretching the term, may have served as something of a Muse. "It may not be a complete coincidence that the only piece completed by this freshly minted dandy during his time in England was also dedicated to a young woman, long time Berlin acquaintance Betsy Pistor, in whom Mendelssohn seemed to have taken some romantic interest."[9]

We learn that Felix's friend Karl Klingemann and Felix's sister Fanny "had already taken to referring to Mendelssohn's new *E flat Major Quartet*, op 12, as his 'Quartet in B.P.'"[10] Nothing more came of this liaison. Perhaps Mister Mendelssohn was too busy. Or Miss Pistor was otherwise engaged. It cannot be said that he did not have other romantic interests, perhaps to include the Spanish beauty, London soprano Maria Malibran, whom he met and became infatuated with in 1832. Mendelssohn wrote no music for or about her, either. We hear they did enjoy a few dances together.

When Felix was twenty-six years old, two years before he married Cécile, he moved to Leipzig to become one of the most respected conductors in the land, having served ably as the music director in Düsseldorf. To direct the Leipzig Gewandhaus Orchestra, however, was to reach for the proverbial stars. That Felixachieved such a position at his age was remarkable. Arguably, his duties as director slowed his compositional efforts, and these were relatively lean years, only the St. Paul Oratorio suggests itself for special merit. His work on the great Italian Symphony, his fourth, had long stalled. "After the assumption of his position in Düsseldorf, it would be nine years before he would complete a work, the 'Scottish' Symphony, whose later reception would rival that of his most popular earlier works: the 'Italian,' the Octet [written when he was sixteen years old], or the Rondo capriccioso for piano."[11]

Felix took control of the Leipzig musical world, including the heralded choir of the Thomaskirche, where Johann Sebastian Bach had ruled for three decades, until his death in 1750. For Mendelssohn's first concert, in October of 1835, he conducted his own overture, *Calm Sea, Prosperous Voyage*. Nothing was out of reach for the young man. Before making an ambivalent move to Berlin, supposedly as Kapellmeister, Felix worked for most of the rest of his short life to make the Gewandhaus the best of its kind in Europe. Here, Mendelssohn met Robert Schumann and the two men became close friends. In fact, if not for Mendelssohn, Schumann would have had a more difficult time of finding his audience.

The composer-conductor decided, in 1832, to take a wife. Why? The answer seems to be because he was expected to do so. Cécile Jeanrenaud came from prosperous, serious family of French Huguenots. People thought her bit stiff; "neither extraordinarily clever, brilliantly witty, nor exceptionally accomplished."[12] She had no particular musical talents. She did make Felix happy, and by all accounts they were in love. To what extent his new responsibilities impacted his creativity – Cécile was promptly pregnant – cannot be known, but his productivity took a marked upturn. He returned to choral music (*Psalm 42, op. 42*), a piece of chamber music (the *E-minor String Quartet, op. 44/2*), and wrote three organ preludes and fugues, reconnecting him to the Baroque masters. He had written the superb *St. Paul oratorio* and a piano etude the year before. Mendelssohn was now working once again at *lieder* he had so come to love. His grand, orchestral *D-Minor Piano Concerto*, written in the same year, 1837, suggests that Mendelssohn was nevertheless interested in working in a full range of music.

By the summer of 1838 he had written two more string quartets. Mendelssohn wrote the *Psalm*, or the first draft of it, while on his honeymoon. For whatever reason he decided to push his compositional energy level, we cannot doubt that from the outset of his marriage he was nothing if not doggedly serious. For eleven years he worked steadily on a body of vocal music known as *Songs Without Words*, Books I through VI, all for piano, with the final, unnumbered, written for cello and piano. His final great work, which was nearly his last of any dimension, was the magnificent *Elijah oratorio*, which he did not dedicate at all. He left many of his works undedicated, although he remembered Clara Schumann with his *Songs Without Words,* Book V, in 1844. Perhaps he was too busy writing music to be bothered with such silliness. For many composers, dedications were only another form of handshake. Still, something was keeping him focused.

Cécile's pregnancies – they came quickly and regularly –must have added to Felix's sense of purpose. The couple had five children, the last born in 1845, just two years before Mendelssohn's death. If Cécile was not a Muse, in the standard sense of the word, there is only one woman remaining who may have done such inspirational work for him. Sister Fanny.

We learn that the two women – Cécile was twelve years junior to Fanny – were never especially close. Felix's brilliant sister thought the other woman just a bit dull. There was "little of the intellectual or musical acumen on which her own intense relationship with Felix was founded."[13] Maybe what Fanny thought mattered more than it should have to her sensitive brother. After all, some biographers go so far as to suggest that Felix was in love with his sister.

Felix did write one important piece of music for her. We'll see what that was in a moment. Tragically, Fanny Mendelssohn died unexpectedly on 18 May 1847, having suffering a stroke from which she never regained consciousness. Felix had only just returned home from yet another London trip.

Travel was said to be killing him, but the shock of losing his dear sister, to whom he was closer than to any man or woman, expedited his own end. In the weeks immediately after Fanny's death his own health quickly deteriorated. That summer of despondency, mourning his loss, he visited Switzerland. Surely he was trying to recover his strength while writing one final work for the woman he loved. This was the *String Quartet, No 6, in F minor*, op. 80. The work "was intended as a requiem for his beloved sister Fanny, tap[ping] a vein of emotional intensity Mendelssohn had never located before."[14]

The composer tried to stay engaged in his work, even making plans to return to Berlin to conduct his *Elijah*, but the spirit was gone from him. Mendelssohn suffered a series of strokes in late October, continuing into November, and on the 4th of the month, six months from the passing of Fanny, Felix too was gone.

Maurice Ravel is a study in contrasts. Ravel was one of two great French "impressionist" composers, meaning that he, like Debussy a decade or more before him, developed theories of light and color in music, as had Monet and his fellow painters in the 1870s and early 80s. Ravel was born to an industrious if impoverished railway engineer and his feisty, Basque-born wife in the small French town of Ciboure, on 7 March 1875. The family moved to Paris when the boy was three months old. His mother's influence was strong, emotionally and musically. It was at her knee that Maurice became infatuated with the music of Spain. Mama Marie Ravel was also a freethinker and a real iconoclast, telling her son, "she would prefer to be in hell with her family, than in heaven alone."[15]

Joseph Maurice Ravel's piano lessons, begun at age seven, would prepare him for fame and high regard, both as pianist and composer – mostly for piano. One force in life, however, was scarce. There were nearly no other women in his life besides his mother. While Maurice seems to have been nearly ignored in the Muse department, he did enjoy the company of a few women who were influential in his success, especially so later in his life.

Whatever else one may find to say about Ravel, and he has been described by many biographers and not a few friends as cool and remote, both in personality and in technique – Stravinsky likened him to a watchmaker – he did compose one of the best known paeans to romance ever heard. Ravel wrote the purling *Bolero*, a sixteen minute fantasy for orchestra, in 1928, when he was fifty-three years old. Maurice wrote it expressly for Ida Rubenstein, to whom we must return shortly.

Surely, Ravel's *Bolero* is the quintessential musico-sexual repast of the twentieth-century. The composer confided in his friend Jane Bathori that Ernst "Ansermet finds it very good; I really can't think why."[16] Perhaps the answer rests entirely with Ida, whom Ravel wished to immortalize in music as had Valentin Serov in 1910 in his painting of this Russian ballet dancer. Heightening her allure for Ravel may have been the fact that she was a close comrade of the outrageous, bi-sexual impresario Serge Diaghilev, Igor Stravinsky's running mate.

Back to Maurice: The young man prospered in the expert care of his Paris Conservatoire tutors, and he remained there for six years; but he did not graduate. Ravel won the school's annual piano competition in 1891, but curiously he did less well in the harmony competition. His teachers found Maurice too spirited and emotional. If he was emotional by nature, as was Tchaikovsky, he used it well. Reserved outside, the man nevertheless wrote with his heart.

Ravel decided to leave in 1895, at the age of twenty. With one wonderful exception, his best known and most respected compositions took a while to manifest themselves. When he was twenty-four Ravel wrote the *Pavane pour une Infante défunte*, exposing Chabrier's dance rhythm influence. It was the influence of Mlle Rubenstein, however, the comely and much liberated ballet dancer, not French composers, that adds to the legend of Maurice Ravel.

Maurice asked the violinist Hélène Jourdan-Morhange to marry him, but she declined. His friend Manuel Rosenthal gives us a more detailed account: "[Ravel] liked women very much and was always exquisitely polite and kind to them. His greatest female friend was Ida Rubenstein. He liked her discretion […] she was a very private woman and, with Ravel, she behaved like a little girl, which he adored." Rosenthal adds, "She was so happy to please him and to be able, thanks to her wealth, to procure for Ravel things he couldn't afford, not being well off at all."[17] We know that Ravel frequented prostitutes, but this may say more about his own lack of self-confidence with women than about his moral center. Many of the composers we have considered here were often comforted by the working ladies.

As his music matured, following his stint in WWI as an ambulance driver – reminiscent of Hemingway's teenage service in Italy – Ravel seemed to find his center, writing more sentimental themes. He'd written *Gaspard de la Nuit*, for piano, for his recently deceased father, in 1908, and *Daphnis and Chloe* in 1912 – a work he was particularly fond of; but none was more successful than *Bolero*. Except for a couple of piano concerti, *Bolero* was the last music he ever wrote.

Actually, Maurice had already considered writing another piece of music for Ida, in 1932, this a ballet to be called *Morgaine*, after the famous Arthurian witch, but he seems to have lost interest in the project well before its completion.[18] These two compositions are all we have that could in any way be considered influenced by a woman in his life. Hélène and Ida remained his dear friends for many years. Ravel never married; maybe he waited too long. Maybe he was too inner directed, preoccupied. After attending a performance of his *Daphnis and Chloe*, accompanied by Hélène, he told her that he still had a "great deal of music in his head […] so much more to say."[19] By this time, however, he was also very ill. He probably knew he had little time left.

In his final years he did a lot of travel and some conducting, though no one gave him great marks for his work with the baton. He tired easily while suffering terribly from insomnia. In fact, Ravel had been convinced for years that he had a fatal brain tumor, though no such disease was found after his death in Paris, on 28 December 1937. When Maurice's brother Edouard, who married late in life, also passed away, leaving no descendants, the Ravel family passed quietly into eternity.[20]

Consider the role of the Muse in the life of **Bedřich Smetana.** This composer, called the father of Czech opera, is also said to possess, on a much broader pallet, the musical personality of the Czech peoples. It's a badge he wore honorably.

Smetana may be pardoned for any confusion as to what his own work might have meant to the rest of classical music loving Central Europe. He was raised on Mozart and Haydn, but his early style is strongly reminiscent of Hector Berlioz, whom he greatly admired. In the best sense of the notion, Smetana was open to many influences. It may be this potpourri of musical references, not least folk music, which combined to make Smetana's music so broadly popular in his homeland. More to the point, Czech opera has come to be linked almost entirely to this man. His multivalent nature is easily enough explained.

Bedřich had superb timing. An innovator, he arrived on the Romantic music scene just in time to take advantage of the opportunities to match indigenous art forms with a reforming nation. Bohemia was awakening after hundreds of years of "enlightened despotism." The Czech peoples were ready for something besides Mozart's *Figaro* and *Don Giovanni,* which had dominated the classical stage for forty years when Bedřich was born. Nationalism was alive in the arts, as well as in the taverns.

František, the boy's father, was a master brewer; his mother, František's third wife, was the daughter of a coachman fortunate enough to be in service to a noble family. The Smetanas were reasonably well off and they enjoyed music – papa František even taught himself to play a decent violin. Smetana was born to these hard working, industrious people on Shrove Tuesday, 2 March 1864. It would seem that music might be a natural life's work for the boy, were he to express such an interest. He did just that, but curiously František did not agree, thinking music too frivolous for a career. It's an old story by now – parents of the celebrated early on not trusting music to be a true career. Only when it became evident that Bedřich was a child prodigy did he get the support he would need to study seriously, to devote his young life to music as well as to "normal" studies. It turns out the lad was brilliant.

Little Bedřich was entertaining sophisticated music audiences at six. He was also quick to fall in love, and at age sixteen he was smitten by his cousin Louisa, one year older and presumably wiser. "Smetana wrote two pieces for her. The first, now lost, was a set of eleven short movements for piano, four hands, called *Memories of Nové Město*. The second, which has been preserved, is Louisa's Polka […] a delightful drawing-room dance."[21] The polka became popular and Smetana enjoyed considerable acclimation for the piece. This should not suggest

Musical Muse: Wives and Lovers of the Great Composers

he grew up in Elysian Fields.

Bedřich was a poor student, however, and he and his father had quite a row over his lack of seriousness. So sharp was their argument that young Smetana moved away to Plzen to work on his music and perhaps to resume his studies, perhaps with a more earnest effort. Instead, he fell in love again, and this time the girl was more available, not being a close relative. We'll dig into the good stuff about her in a moment.

In 1842 the young composer, now an excellent pianist, was working in forms close to Beethoven, Mendelssohn, Liszt, and even Slavic folk music – especially dance rhythms. He even wrote some string music. Later that year he tried some Baroque pieces, including a *Minuet,* showing an influence of Boccherini. His interests in women were equally eclectic. In fact, "he was an ardent romantic; a follower of Berlioz, whose temperament and eroticism were close to his own… After Louisa [came] Lida Bradáčova, then he became infatuated with Elizabeth Gollerová, a young beauty for whom he composed *The Elizabeth Waltz*; but Elizabeth proved to be nothing more than a fleeting whim, and her place was taken first by Marie […] to whom he dedicated *The Marina Polka*, then by Kateřina Corinová for whom he wrote *The Kateřina Polka.*"[22] He continued to dedicate music to his young inspirations – Muses every one, though by and large none of them had any staying power. At that point in his life he really didn't care.

All that changed when Smetana fell for Kateřina Kolařová. He wrote in his diary, in April 1842, "when I am not with her I am sitting on hot coals and have no peace."[23] He immediately began to write music for her, the first piece being his *Overtures*, "designed in a four-handed version so that he could become more closely acquainted with Miss Kolařová,"[24] herself quite an accomplished pianist.

We learn that the composer was never in love with that particular body of music, finding the pieces "uneven," but his feelings for Kateřina intensified. He wrote *Two Quadrilles* for her the next year, and these are generally held to be much more capable work. The selection of such music for his new flame is interesting in another sense, as here again Bedřich demonstrated his interest in the broadest range of composition. The quadrille is a form of square dance popular in the court of Napoleon, and then throughout France, some twenty-five years earlier. Soon he wrote for her a bit of music reminiscent of Schubert's piano etudes, this being his piano miniatures called *Songs Without Words*.

When not writing in his diary about Kateřina he told himself: "By the grace of God and with His help I shall one day be a Liszt in technique and a Mozart in composition."[25] What he needed most in order to reach such lofty goals, and to eventually marry Kateřina, was some larger recognition for his compositions, a few paying students to help him retire some debt, and the income that a piano virtuoso might expect to command. He was a gifted pianist, but going it alone, on the open road, as it were, was risky. Prudence intervened in his plans and he opened his own music school in Prague, asking Liszt for a loan and for advice on how to manage such an endeavor. The cautious Liszt sent advice only. Nevertheless, Smetana was now ready to move ahead with the demands and expectations of a householder. One woman would complete the package.

Kateřina Kolařová became the first Mrs. Smetana in 1849, when Bedřich was twenty-five years old; she was twenty-two. Their marriage was a happy one; a couple truly well matched and in much love. In their first four years they had three children, but Kateřina soon became ill with tuberculosis. Perhaps worse, their children, all under the age of nine, became ill and died, one after the next – the eldest of scarlet fever. Devastated, the Smetanas moved to Sweden. Their relocation options were not unlimited.

Bedřich was *persona non grata* in Bohemia because of his revolutionary sympathies. Scandinavia looked like a safe bet. The move looked smart when, in Göteborg, he proved to be successful as conductor, pianist, and teacher. Be that as it may, the loss of the couple's children was enormous. Could they cope?

Smetana attempted to work through his personal tragedies in his compositions, writing a *Piano Trio* for his oldest child, Fritzi, on whom he doted. No doubt the move was to provide a healthier clime for Kateřina; but sadly she, too, passed away ten years later. Bedřich was trying to remain sane, having lost everything that mattered at the age of thirty-five.

He had to work even harder to keep up with his music. He had written a series of *Album Leaves* (in Czech, *Listky do památníku.*) The first was written for Kateřina, three years before they were married, "creating a delicately etched impression of the girl he so much admired." He did not finish the full set of musical notes until 1862, three years after Kateřina's death – two years after his second marriage.

A few years earlier, the composer had been working on some melodies that would become the third act of the opera *The Bartered Bride*, a work intensely morose and gloomy, and not completed until 1866 when the composer was forty-two. Bedřich often kept fragments to use later, as the music seemed to fit. Some fragments showed up in his symphonic poems. The composer, of course, was still learning what he could do, learning how broad and how bold was his pallet? Too, Smetana was much under the spell of Hector Berlioz during these years and more so after the Frenchman's visits to Prague in the mid-1840s. While the revolutionary spirit was high in Bohemia, Smetana attempted to match the fervor of the people with music in kind. One such piece was a revolutionary song on the melodramatic murder of one of the Czech people's greatest heroes and Christian reformers, Jan Hus, was burned at the stake in 1415 for speaking against the abuses of the Roman Catholic Clergy.

Smetana remained interested in such themes even while living in Sweden. But after a decade of a great body of work, much of it would have to be called eclectic, this productivity all but ceased when his wife passed away. Perhaps some tragedies were too big to work through. He may have also been feeling guilty. Some of his work was inspired by a secret source.

Smetana had been involved in a tempestuous affair in the year prior to his wife's death. The woman, a beautiful young Swede, was one of his piano students. We know that countless romances began at the keyboard. This one, however, while producing a temporary Muse, would not end well for anyone concerned. The lady was Fröjde Benecke, a twenty-one year old married woman whose uncle was a famous voice teacher. "She became a medium through which the artist and thinker in him [Bedřich] could pour out the fullness of his soul," We learn "[t]o Smetana there was nothing unusual in being able to exist mentally in two dimensions at once. Kateřina was his wife and affectionate domestic partner, but Fröjde was his Muse and mistress ... and the first piece to reveal his sentiments to her was a transcription of Schubert's *Der Neugierige* (Curious One), the sixth song from Schubert's song cycle *Die Schöne Müllerin.*"[26] We can now surmise that Smetana chose this piece for the essential question posed, demanding a simple yes or no answer. The song asks if the lover agrees and "include(s) the whole world to me?"

Smetana followed this transcription for piano with another called, in English, "*Teardrops.*" The song reveals his feelings for the young woman and the hope that she would grant his wish. Smetana actually wrote a third piece for her – a polka – incorporating into the score the cryptogram on the letters F.E.D.A., built on Fröjda's name. Other composers had done the same thing, most notably Robert Schumann for two of his girl friends – the Countess Pauline Abegg, in 1830, and Ernestine von Fricken, five years later.

These men seemed ever eager to display their infatuations, even if in doing so others would be hurt for such demonstrations. Of course, none of these composers were particularly circumspect in their tireless, if not in fact their selfish, quest for the Muse. Toward the end of 1858, and as Bedřich began to realize how ill his wife was, he broke things off with Mrs. Benecke. Kateřina, failing fast, made it known that she wanted to go back to Bohemia to live, and perhaps to die. Granting her wish to return home was the least Bedřich could do. He would try.

They decided in January to leave, but Smetana had committed to doing three more concerts, which would keep him and Kateřina in Sweden until late March. They finally set out for their return to Prague on April 8th, arriving in Prague, after a short stay in Dresden, on April 19th. Ironically, Kateřina died the same day, never knowing she was again home. Bedřich, guilty and devastated, spent the next few months wandering from one small Czech town to the next, trying to find his way out of the gloom.

In May, Bedřich went to Liszt's home, where he met a circle of musicians that led Smetana to consider opera. He was astonished at how successful Wagner had become in the musical form. He also found the next woman in his life. Kateřina had been dead only three months, but Bedřich's heart was ready to recover. Moreover, as a composer he felt somehow reduced without a woman to support and inspire him. That month he met and promptly fell in love with Barbora (Bettina) Ferdinandová, nineteen-years old, beautiful, and passionate. She was also a gifted painter and singer. Smetana had no chance. They married the next year.

We do not know if the man wrote much music for Betty, other than the *Bettina Polka*, which he composed for her before they married, and which she told him she did not care particularly for. Maybe she wasn't much of a dancer. Smetana wrote it for her "as an affirmation of love [and] a musical portrait of his future wife."[27] It is entirely possible that she had learned of the affair with Fröjde and was none too happy to learn of her widowed husband's indiscretion.

Nevertheless, Smetana was on verge of writing the first of his many successful operas, starting with *The Brandenburgers in Bohemia*. The Smetanas promptly set off for Sweden again; he had become something of a celebrity there. Quickly upon their settling in, Bedřich reopened his music school. It proved a short stay – too many ghosts in the castle.

The newlyweds soon returned to Prague; his operas, his music, would now be central. In the end, he must have decided that his creativity needed a bit of homeland, as well. Had he not returned it is unlikely that the world would have the composer's epic work, *Ma Vlast*, meaning My Homeland. It remains today a kind of second national anthem.

Smetana began to go deaf in 1876 and was forced to give up his job as artistic director of the Czech Theater. He could not properly distinguish the notes. Ironically, this freed him to do his best and most memorable work. He completed *Ma Vlast* as part of a symphonic cycle in 1882. Bedřich had already completed three more operas, including *The Two Widows*, for a total of eight. The cause of his deafness was reportedly syphilis. The composer was never able to determine where he had picked up the dread disease. The reason if not the source should have been evident. There were likely too many possibilities for him to truly be sure. Slowly growing not only deaf but tragically mad, Smetana died in Prague on 12 May 1884, at the age of sixty. In every sense of the word he had left quite a legacy. Absent his beloved wives Kateřina and Bettina, and especially so his interlude with Fröjde, it is doubtful that he would ever have accomplished in music what he did.

Arthur McMaster

AFTERWORD & APPENDIX

We cannot quickly say goodbye to these Muses – by actual count there have been 102 such ladies, along with three men, recognized in this volume – without a further attempt to link them to the music they influenced, music they made together with so many of the world's best known composers.

Many more were only near-Muses, ladies who helped their men to go on, to keep putting down the notes, measure after measure, though they cannot be linked to any original music. I have not counted them. Still, over one-hundred women coaxed, cajoled, cautioned, conspired, and in all manner of means shaped a remarkable outcome from these twenty-eight composers. The appendix below ties these Muses, to just over 180 distinctly identified pieces of music, not including the five-hundred plus sonatas which Domenico Scarlatti wrote for one woman. This tribute, of course, only scratches the surface. Many tunes, themes, and part-songs, and even more variations, and countless Muse-inspired revisions, go unknown and unclaimed.

There were a couple of composers whose work I researched and tried to include here, but I had to abandon them – all deserving chaps. Simply stated, I settled on the ones I did as much for their women as for their genius or celebrity. I wanted to include Mikhail Glinka – the man who nearly single-handedly began the true Russian classical movement. But as I discovered in trying to write Glinka, as well as trying to write Gustav Holst – a deserving modernist if ever there was one – there was just nothing much in the Muse closet for the two. I tried to write a chapter for Dame Ethel Smyth, the British opera composer, and later suffragist, an exact contemporary of another opera genius, Puccini. Smyth shared with Johannes Brahms a love interest in the incredible Lisl von Herzogenberg, but she wrote no music for her. Sorry, no muse for Ethel.

One other whose work and women I attempted to capture here was Niccolò Paganini, but he was actually a virtuoso far more than he was a composer. Given these realities, as well as my own research limitations, we wind up with twenty-eight men and their 100-some Muses; still, they constitute a pretty solid core. Together they exemplify the nature of the Muse over hundreds of years of "classical music," covering every major and most minor forms. Along the way, I trust we have found endearing or alarming vignettes to offer about most of their influential women, as well as a few enchanting men, and that was the purpose, after all. Let's see how the Muses connect graphically to the music:

Arthur McMaster

Appendix

Composer (birth year):	Muse:	Associated w/ Composition
Bach, Johann Sebastian (1685)	Maria Barbara Bach	*D Minor Partita (BWV 1004)*
	Anna Magdalena Wülken	Song: *Bist du bei Mir Anna Magdalena*
Bartók, Béla (1881)	Stefi Geyer	*Second Suite* *Concerto #1 for Violin & Orchestra* *Two Portraits*
	Adila Aranyi	*Violin Sonata*
	Marta Ziegler	*Two Romanian Dances* *Duke Bluebeard's Castle*
	Ditta Pászatory	*Piano Concerto #3*
Beethoven, Ludwig van (1779)	Eleonore (Lorchen) von Breuning	*Schilderung des Mädchens* Songs: *Se vuol Ballare*
	Jeanette d'Honrath	unspecified songs
	Maria Anna v. Westerholt	*Trio in G for Piano*
	Babette von Keglevich	*Piano Sonata in E flat* *Twelve Variations for Piano and Cello, op 66*
	Giulietta Guicciardi	*Piano Sonata #14, C# min (Moonlight Sonata)*
	Josephine Deym	*Léonore overture(s)* *Fidelio*
	Therese Malfatti	Piano bagatelle: *Fur Elise*
	Antonie Brentano	*An die Geliebte*, op 238 *Diabelli Variations on a Waltz*, op 120

Musical Muse: Wives and Lovers of the Great Composers

Berlioz, Hector (1803)	Estelle Deboeuf	*Estelle et Némorin*
	Harriet Smithson	*Symphonie Fantastique* *Harold in Italy* *Roméo et Juliette*
	Camille (Marie) Moke	*fragments*
	Marie Recio	*Beatrice and Benedict*
Bizet, Georges (1838)	Marie Reiter	*The Pearl Fishers* *The Young Maid of Perth*
	Céleste Vénard	*Carmen*
	Geneviève Halévy	opera frags (incl. *Don Rodrique*) *Geneviève de Paris*
Brahms, Johannes (1833)	Lieschen Giesemann	part-songs (lost)
	Clara Schumann	fragments *Four Serious Songs*
	Agatha von Siebold	*String Sextet in G*
	Bertha Porubsky	various songs, poss *Twelve Songs and Romances, op 44.*
	Elisabet v. Herzogenberg	*Four Vocal Quartets*
	Herminie Spies	*Symphony # 3* Numerous songs, incl: *Six Songs and Romance, Op 93a* *Five Songs, op 105-07* *Piano Concert, B Flat*
Chopin, Frédéric (1810)	Titus Woyciechowski	*Introduction and Variations in E Minor*
	Constantia Gladowska	*Adagio to Concerto #2, F min* *Waltz No 10, op 69* Unidentified songs.

Chopin, Frédéric (1810)	Delphina Potocka	Whole of *Concerto #2* *Nocturne in G Minor* *Mazurka in C Mino* *Etude in E Flat Major* *Polonaise in F sharp* *op 44*
	Marie Wodzińska	*Waltz in A flat* *Waltz in E flat, op 9* *Nocturne in B Major op 32.* *No 1*
	Aurore Dupin (George Sand)	poss. *Fantasia in F Minor,* and *Barcarolle* and *Berceuse.* Others
	Jane Stirling	*Two Nocturnes, op 55*
Dvořak, Antonin (1841)	Josephina Čermak	*Cypresses* (song cycle) *Cello Concerto in A*
	Anna Čermak	*Stabat Mater, op 58*
	Jeanette Thurber	*Symphony no 9, in E minor,* *op 95*
Elgar, Edward (1857)	Helen Weaver	*Wind Quintet* Polka: *Helcia* *Enigma Variation XIII*
	Hilda Fitton	*Pastourelle*
	Isobel Fitton	*Enigma Variation # VI*
	Caroline Alice Roberts	piano: *Salud d'Amour* *Enigma Variation # I*
	Alice Stuart-Wortley	*Violin Concerto* Song: *The Angelus* *Symphony No 2* *Cello Concerto*
	Vera Hockman	*Symphony No 3* *The Spanish Lady*
Handel, George Frideric (1685)	None	

Musical Muse: Wives and Lovers of the Great Composers

Haydn, Franz Joseph (1732)	Therese Keller	*Organ Concerto #1*
	(Sister Josepha)	*Salve Regina, in E*
	Maria Anna Keller	not recorded
	Luigia Polzelli	opera: *L'osola disabitata* *Symphonies 63 - 92* *Cello Concerto in D* *Violin Sonata*
	Rebecca Schroter	*Oratorio, the Storm* *Three Trios: Op 82*
	Marianne von Gensinger	sonatas, not further identified
	Brigida Banti	aria: *Non Partir belli'idol mio*
Liszt, Franz (1811)	Caroline de Saint-Circq	*Dante Symphony*
	Valérie Bossier	*Fantasie romantique sur deux melidies suisses*
	Marie d'Agoult	piano fantasies
	Carolyne von Sayn-Wittgenstein	*Twelve symphonic poems*
	Agnes Street	*Liebesträume*
Mahler, Gustav (1860)	Josephine Poisl	*Klagende Lieder*
	Johanna Richter	*Symphony #1* *Blumine(theme) in his 2nd, 4th, 5th and 9th*
	Marion von Weber	song: *In Glucklicher Stunde*
	Anna von Mildenburg	*Symphony #3*
	Selma Kurz	orchestral songs
	Alma Schindler	*Liebst du um Shönheit.* *Symphony # 10*
Mendelssohn, Felix (1809)	Betsy Pistor	*E flat Major Quartet, op 12*
	Fanny Mendelssohn	*String Quartet, No 6 in F Minor, op 80*

Mozart, Wolfgang (1756)	Maria Thekla Mozart	horn concerto
	Aloysia Weber	seven concert arias *Recitative and Aria for Soprano, k 316* *Mia speranza adorata*
	Constanze Weber	*Opera: Abduction from the Seralio* *Mass in C Minor, k 427* *Sonata for Violin and Piano, k 403* *Violin Sonata, k 404*
	Maria Teresa v Paradis	*Piano Concerto No 18, K 456*
	Josephine Auernhammer	Six piano sonatas
	Babette Ployer	Three piano concerti (nos. 14, 17 and 22) *Funeral March*, k453a
	Magdalena Hofdemel	Piano Concerto 27 (k 595 is likely for her)
Puccini, Giacomo (1858)	Elvira Gemignani	unrecorded
	Corinna, Last Name ?	*Madama Butterfly*
	Sybil Seligman	opera: *The Girl of the Golden West*
	Doria Manfredi	opera: *Turandot*
Ravel, Maurice (1875)	Ida Rubenstein	*Bolero*
Scarlatti, Domenico (1685)	Catarina Gentili	unrecorded
	Maria Barbara	*Te Deum* Approx *550* sonatas
	Anastasia Ximenes	song: *Salve Regina*
Schubert, Franz Peter (1797)	Theresa Grob	2 songs; *Gretchen an Spinnnrade;* *Stimme der Leiber* song cycle: *Die Schöne Müllerin*
	Caroline Esterházy	*Fantasy in F Minor*

Musical Muse: Wives and Lovers of the Great Composers

Schumann, Robert (1810)	Pauline Meta Abegg	*Theme & Variation on the Name Abegg*
	Ernestine von Fricken	*Carnaval* (21 piano pieces) *Three Songs by Chamisso, op 31*
	Clara Wieck	*Piano Sonata in F-sharp Minor* *Fantasy in C Major* song cycle: *Dichterliebe Liebesfrühling;* *Arabesque, Blumenstuck* *Concert Allegro for Piano and Orchestra*
Smetana, Bedřich (1824)	Louisa Smetana	11 piano duets *Memories of Nové M̃sto* *Louisa's Polka*
	Elizabeth Gollerová	*The Elizabeth Waltz*
	Katerina Kolařová	piano: *Overtures* *Two Quadrilles* *Songs Without Words* *Autumn Leaves*
	Fröjde Benecke	piano: *Teardrops* polka: *for Fröjde*
	Bettina Ferdinandová	polka: *Bettina*
Strauss, Richard (1864)	Dora Wihan	*Don Juan* opera: *Die Liebe der Danae*
	Pauline de Ahna	opera: *Guntram* *Four Songs* *Ein Heldenleben* *Sinfonia Domestica* opera: *Intermezzo* *Fier Letzte Lieder*

Stravinsky, Igor (1882)	Katya Nosenko	*Storm Cloud* *Faun and Shepherdess* *Serenade in La*
	Zhenya Nikitna	polka
	Vera Sudeikina	*Octet for Wind Instruments* *Violin Concerto* *Perséphone*
Tchaikovsky, Pyotr (1840)	Nadezhda von Meck	*Capriccio Italien* *Symphony no 4*
	Vladimir Shilovsky	*Nocturne in F major*
	Vladimir "Bobyk" Davidov	*Symphony no 6*
Telemann, Georg Philipp (1681)	Amalie Louise Eberlin	*Funeral poem*
	Maria Textor	serenade: *The Virgin Bride and the Noble Groom*
Verdi, Giuseppe (1813)	Margherita Verdi	*Oberto (?)*
	Giuseppina Strepponi	*Nabucco* *Gerusalemme*
	Teresa Stolz	*Don Carlo*
Vivaldi, Antonio (1676)	Anna Giraud (Girò)	opera: *Rosilena ed Ortona* opera: *Sirore re di Persia*
Wagner, Richard (1813)	Jenny Pachta	op. *Die Hochzeit*
	"Minna" Planer Wagner	*Die Fliegende Holländer*
	Jesse Laussot	ideas for *The Ring*
	Mathilde Wesendonck	ideas for *Tristan* ideas for *Parsifal*
	Cosima (v Bülow) Wagner	*Siegfried Idyll*

RESOURCE NOTES

I am indebted to the music scholars whose works are noted below:

Chapter One (Bach)
1. Arnold, Denis. *Bach*. (Oxford: Oxford University Press, 1984). p. vii.
2. Boyd, Malcolm. *Bach*. (Oxford: Oxford University Press, 2000). p. 11.
3. Ibid, p. 19
4. Arnold, p. 5.
5. Wolff, Christoph. *Johann Sebastian Bach, the Learned Musician*. (New York: Norton, 2000). p. 89.
6. Ibid, p. 91.
7. Geiringer, Karl. *The Bach Family*. (New York: Oxford University Press. 1954). p. 132.
8. Wolff, p. 107.
9. Ibid, p. 111.
10. Ibid, p. 114.
11. Ibid, p. 125.
12. Ibid, p. 135.
13. Geiringer, p. 155.
14. Whiting, Christopher. "Agony and Ecstasy," *Strings*, Vol 16:7. 101., April 2002. pp. 30-35. (International Index to Music Periodicals).
15. Geiringer, pp. 160-161.
16. The poem in English is as follows:

    If thou be near, I go rejoicing
    To peace and rest beyond the skies,
    Nor will I fear what may befall me,
    For I will hear thy sweet voice call me,
    They gentle hand will close my eyes.

17. Eidam, Klaus. *The True Life of J.S. Bach*. (Transl. Hoyt Rogers. New York: Basic Books. 2001). p. 143.
18. Geiringer, p. 165.
19. Ibid, p. 171.
20. Pirro, Andre. *J. S. Bach*. (Transl. Mervin Savill. Bonanza Books. 1957). p. 60.

Chapter Two (Bartók)
1. As noted in Suchoff, Benjamin. *Béla Bartók, Life and Work*. (Lanham: Scarecrow Press. 2001) p. 218.
2. Cross, Milton. "Béla Bartók ," *Encyclopedia of the Great Composers and their Music*. Vol. I. (Garden City: Doubleday, 1953).
3. Taken from a press review *(Budapestni Napló)*, as noted in Suchoff, p. 27.
4. Stefi Geyer was born in 1888 and died in 1956.
5. Bela often sent cards to his love interests with original music.
6. Suchoff, p.53.
7. Ibid, p.53.
8. Ibid, p.54.
9. Ibid, p.54.
10. Ibid, p.55.
11. As noted in Somfai, László. *Béla Bartók; Composition, Concepts, and Autograph Sources*. (Berkeley: University of California Press. 1996) p.11.
12. Demeny, János, ed. *Béla Bartók Letters*. (New York: St. Martins' Press. 1971) p.181.
13. Ibid, p.267.
14. Ibid. p.289.

Chapter Three (Beethoven)
1. Bekker, Paul J. *Beethoven*. Translated, M.M.. Bozman. (London: J.M. Dent & Sons, 1939). p. 4.
2. Cooper, Barry. *Beethoven. The Master Musician Series*. (Oxford: Oxford Univ. Press, 2000), p. 5.
3. Jones, David Wyn. *The Life of Beethoven*. (Cambridge: Cambridge University Press, 1998). p. 8.
4. The Nine Variations on a March derive from an original composition by Ernst Dressler.
5. Jones, p.12.
6. His cousin Marie was living in Rotterdam at the time and evidently paid his way, following the loss of her brother Franz Rovantini.
7. Bekker, p. 12.

8. Davenport, Marcia. *Mozart*. (New York: Dorset Press, 1987). p 272.
9. Cooper, p. 21.
10. Bekker, p. 18.
11. Bekker, p. 20.
12. Bekker, p. 21.
13. Cooper, p. 110.
14. Cooper, p. 138.
15. NOTE: History records that Beethoven had horrible handwriting even on his most sober day, in part owing to his lack of formal education and a sense of the flamboyant.
16. See also, Cooper, Barry. *Beethoven and the Creative Process*. (Clarendon: Oxford Press, 1990), p. 50.
17. Solomon, Maynard. *Late Beethoven*. (Berkeley: University of California Press, 2003). p. 19.

Chapter Four (Berlioz)
1. Holoman, D. Kern. *Berlioz*. (Cambridge: Harvard Press, 1989). p. 3.
2. Ibid, p. 2
3. Ibid, p 9.
4. Bloom, Peter. *The Cambridge Companion to Berlioz*. (Cambridge: Cambridge University Press, 2000). p. 12.
5. Holoman, p. 11.
6. Barzun, Jacques. *Berlioz and His Century*. (New York: Meridian, 1959). p. 77.
7. see Berlioz, Hector. *Mémoires*, ed. Cairns, David. (New York: Norton, 1975)
8. Barzun, p. 67.
9. Cairns, David. *Berlioz, The Making of An Artist*. (Berkeley: Univ. of California, 1999). p. 354.
10. Barzun, p. 90.
11. Berlioz, Hector. *Selected Letters of Berlioz*. ed., Mac Donald, Hugh. (New York: Norton, 1995). p. 70.
12. Barzun, p. 111.
13. Holoman, p. 115.
14. Holoman, p. 116.
15. Barzun, p. 134.
16. Holoman, p. 101.
17. Barzun, p. 207.
18. Berlioz, Cairns, p. 372.
19. Taken from Beatrice and Benedict, Barzun, p. 372.
20. Berlioz, Mac Donald, p. 413.
21. Ibid, p. 433.
22. Ibid, p. 435.

"

Musical Muse: Wives and Lovers of the Great Composers

Chapter Five (Bizet)
1. Dean, Winton. *Bizet.* (New York: Collier, 1962). p. 15
2. Parker, Douglas Charles. *Georges Bizet, His Life and Works.* (Freeport: Books for Libraries Press, 1969). p. 19.
3. Ibid, p. 28.
4. Curtiss, Mina. *Bizet and His World.* (New York: Knopf, 1958). p. 90
5. Dean, p. 45.
6. Curtiss, pp. 121-22.
7. Schoenberg, Harold C. *Lives of the Great Composers.* (New York: Norton, 1997). p. 334.
8. Curtiss, p. 122-23.
9. Ibid, p. 126.
10. Ibid, pp. 128-29.
11. Ibid, p. 140.
12. Ivan was finally performed in 1946 in Germany, the score having been ignored or lost for 60 years
13. Dean, p. 68.
14. Ibid, p. 68.
15. McClary, Susan. *Carmen.* (New York: Cambridge University Press, 1998). p. 39.
16. Ibid, p. 39.
17. Dean, p. 78.
18. Ibid, p. 85.
19. Curtiss, p. 265.
20. Dean, p. 105.
21. McClary, p. 42.
22. Ibid.
23. Dean, p. 119.

Chapter Six (Brahms)
1. Mac Donald, Malcolm. *Brahms.* (New York: Schirmer Books, 1990). p.2.
2. Ibid, p. 8.
3. Ibid, p. 8.
4. Latham, Peter. *Brahms.* (New York: Collier Books, 1962). p. 21.
5. Henschel, George. *Personal Recollections of Johannes Brahms.* (Boston: AMS Press, 1978). p. 44.
6. Ibid, p. 48.
7. Mac Donald, p. 34.
8. Swafford, Jan. *Johannes Brahms, A Biography.* (New York: Knopf, 1998) p 137.

9. Ibid, p. 137.
10. Ibid, p. 140.
11. Musgrave, Michael. *A Brahms Reader.* (New Haven: Yale University Press.) p. 52.
12. Clara Schumann, quoted in Musgrave, p. 52.
13. Musgrave, p. 53.
14. Spiegl, Fritz. *Lives, Wives and Loves of the Great Composers.* (London: Marion Boyers, 1997). p. 48.
15. Ibid, p. 48.
16. Swafford, p. 197.
17. Ibid, p. 197.
18. Ibid, p. 201.
19. Ibid, p. 240.
20. Spiegl, p. 48.
21. Musgrave, 297.
22. Mac Donald, p. 237.
23. Ibid, p. 352.
24. Latham, p. 70.
25. Mac Donald, p. 240.
26. Musgrave, p. 54.
27. Mac Donald, p. 296.
28. Ibid, p. 350.

Chapter Seven (Chopin)
1. Schonberg, Harold C. *The Lives of the Great Composers.* (New York: Norton, 1997). p. 184.
2. Holcman, Jan. *The Legacy of Chopin.* (New York: Philosophical Library, 1954). p. 93.
3. Siepmann, Jeremy. *Chopin, The Reluctant Romantic.* (Boston: Northeastern Press, 1995). p. 22.
4. Jordan, Ruth. *Nocturne, A Life of Chopin.* (New York: Taplinger, 1978) p 32.
5. Siepmann, p. 41.
6. Ibid, p. 45.
7. Jordan, p. 58.
8. Ibid, p. 75.
9. Ibid, p. 73
10. Ibid, p. 76.
11. Siepmann, p. 61.
12. Jordan, p. 84.
13. Szulc, Tad. *Chopin in Paris.* (New York: Scribner, 1998) p. 48.

14. Ibid, p. 57.
15. Siepmann, p. 82.
16. Szulc, p. 70.
17. Ibid, p. 81.
18. Ibid, p. 81.
19. Siepmann, p. 117.
20. Jordan, p. 124.
21. Ibid, p. 127.
22. Holcman, p. 71.
23. Siepmann, p. 124.
24. Wright, David C.F. *Frederick Chopin*. A talk given and recorded in October 1972. www.wrightmusic.co.uk/chopin.html
25. Siepmann, pp 124-125.
26. Ibid, p. 125.
27. Wright
28. Wright
29. Siepmann, p. 139.
30. Ibid, p. 150.
31. Szulc, p. 332.
32. Ibid, p. 371.
33. Siepmann, p. 224.
34. Ibid, p. 227.

Chapter Eight (Elgar)
1. Moore, Jerrold Northrop. *Edward Elgar, A Creative Life*. (Oxford: Oxford University Press, 1984). p. 54.
2. Ibid, p. 55.
3. Reilly, Richard R. "Elgar", *Crisis Magazine*. www.malvern.net/attractions/elgar.htm.
4. Moore, p. 31.
5. De-la-Noy, Michael. *Elgar: The Man*. (London: Allan Lane, Penguin, 1983). p. 31.
6. Ibid, p. 27.
7. Ibid, p. 29.
8. Mundy, Simon. *Elgar*. (London: Omnibus Press, 2001). pp. 19-20.
9. Ibid, p. 22.
10. Ibid, p. 26.
11. Ibid, p. 27.
12. Moore, p. 101

13. Kennedy, Michael. *Portrait of Elgar.* (Oxford: Oxford University Press, 1987). p.35.
14. Ibid, p. 36.
15. Ibid, p. 42.
16. Mundy, p. 35.
17. Moore, pp. 150-51.
18. Mundy, p. 47.
19. Kennedy, p. 97.
20. De-la-Noy, p. 74.
21. Mundy, p. 64.
22. Ibid, p. 85.
23. Kennedy, p. 209.
24. Ibid, p. 168.
25. Moore, p. 375.
26. Ibid, p. 561.
27. Kennedy, p. 161.
28. De-la-Noy, p. 105.
29. Mundy, p. 124.
30. Ibid, p. 139.
31. Allen, Kevin. *Elgar in Love.* (Malvern: Aldine Press, 2000). p. 1.
32. Moore, p. 793.
33. Allen, p. v.
34. Ibid, p. 24.
35. Ibid, p. 24.
36. Ibid, p. 72.
37. Moore, p. 809.

Chapter Nine (Haydn)

1. Hughes, Rosemary. *Haydn.* (New York: Collier, 1963) p. 23.
2. Ibid, p. 31.
3. Geiringer, Karl. *Haydn, A Creative Life.* (New York: Norton, 1946). p. 48.
4. Butterworth, Neil. *Haydn, His Life and Times.* (26-27)
5. Geiringer, pp. 68-69.
6. Ibid, p. 70
7. Letter to Luigia Polzelli from Haydn, dated August 4, 1791. *Haydn Letters.* Botstiber-Pohl. (Leipzig: 1927)
8. Geiringer, p. 72.
9. Butterworth, p. 84.
10. Ibid, p. 85.

11. Ibid, p. 96.
12. Geiringer, p. 108.
13. Ibid, p. 113.
14. Ibid, p. 85.
15. Hughes, p. 95.
16. Ibid, p. 102.
17. Geiringer, p.133.
18. Hughes, p. 119.
19. Butterworth, p. 128.

Chapter Ten (Liszt)
1. Czerny, Karl. *Memories of My Life*. (Strassburg, 1968) p.27f.
2. Note: The paternity of Xavier Mozart is somewhat in doubt. He was named after Mozart's student and Constanze Weber Mozart's friend Franz Xaver Süssmayr, who finished the Mozart Requiem (k. 626) for his deceased patron and teacher.
3. Załuski, Iwo and Pamela. *The Young Liszt*. (London: Peter Owen Publishers, 1997). p 35.
4. 1803-1877
5. Załuski, p. 37.
6. Watson, Derek. *Liszt*. (New York: Schirmer, 1989) p. 12.
7. Taylor, Ronald. *Franz Liszt*. (New York: Universe Books. 1986) p.18.
8. Załuski, p.126.
9. Taylor, p. 19.
10. Załuski, p. 142.
11. Ibid, p. 142
12. Ibid, pp.164-165
13. Ibid, p. 169
14. Taylor, p. 41
15. Ibid, p. 41.
16. Ibid, p. 43
17. Liszt, Franz. *An Artist's Journey, Letters, 1835-1841*, Translated by Charles Suttoni. (Chicago: University of Chicago Press. 1989). p. 13.
18. Szulc, Tad. *Chopin in Paris*. (New York: Scribner, 1998). p. 171
19. Sokoloff, Alice H. *Cosima Wagner, Extraordinary Daughter of Franz Liszt*. (New York: Dodd, Mead & Company, 1969). pp. 25-26.
20. Watson, p. 41.
21. d'Agoult, Marie. *Mémoires* 1834-54. ed. Daniel Olliver. (Paris, 1927.) p.168.
22. Watson, p. 74.

23. Ibid, p. 76.
24. Walker, Alan. *Franz Liszt, Vol. II, The Weimar Years.* (New York: Knopf, 1989). p. 3.
25. Watson, p. 76.
26. Ibid, p. 78.
27. Walker, p. 6.
28. Ibid, p. 10.
29. Beckett, Walter. *Liszt.* (London: Farrar, Strauss, and Cudhay, Ltd., 1963). p. 35.
30. Watson, p. 160.

Chapter Eleven (Mahler)

1. Holbrook, David. *Gustav Mahler and the Courage To Be.* (New York: DaCapo Press. 1982) p. 17.
2. Carr, Jonathan. *Mahler, A Biography.* (Woodstock: Overlook Press. 1998) p. 15.
3. Ibid, p. 9.
4. Ibid, p. 16.
5. Ibid, p. 16
6. Gantz, Jeffrey. "*Gustav Mahler's Blumine: A Love Story.*" (www.bostonphoenix.com/pages/boston/mahler.html)
7. Ibid.
8. Carr, pp. 41-42
9. Ibid, p. 42.
10. La Grange, Henry-Louis. *Bibliothèque Gustav Mahler.* (www.andante.com/profiles/Mahler/symph 1.cfm)
11. Ibid.
12. Engle, Gabriel. *Gustav Mahler, Song Symphonist.* (New York: Engle. 1970) p. 58.
13. Carr, p. 45.
14. Ibid, p. 53.
15. Ibid, p. 63.
16. Ibid, p. 64.
17. Ibid, p. 97.
18. See: < http://classicalcdreview.com/kurz.htm>
19. see Mahler, Alma. *Gustav Mahler, Memories and Letters*, ed. D. Mitchell. (John Murray, 1968)
20. The influential German poet was Friedrich Rückert, 1788-1866.
21. Carr, p. 109.
22. Engle, p. 107.
23. Ibid, p. 109.
24. Carr, p. 206.

Chapter Twelve (Mozart)

1. Schoenberg, Harold C. *The Lies of the Great Composers.* (New York: Norton, 1997). p. 95.
2. Ibid, p 96.
3. Einstein, Alfred. *Mozart, His Character, His Work.* (London: Grafton Books, 1986) p. 15.
4. Ibid, p. 15.
5. Rosselli, John. *The Life of Mozart.* (Cambridge: Cambridge, 1998). p. 24.
6. Ibid, p. 24.
7. Solomon, Maynard. *Mozart, A Life.* (New York: Harper Perennial, 1995). p. 11.
8. Schoenberg, p. 100.
9. Carr, Francis. *Mozart & Constanze.* (New York: Avon Books, 1983.) p. 15.
10. Einstein, p. 53.
11. Ibid, p. 53.
12. Carr, p. 17.
13. Solomon, p. 175.
14. Einstein, p. 381
15. Ibid, p. 383.
16. Carr, p. 32.
17. Solomon, p. 219.
18. Bloom, Eric. *Mozart.* (New York: Collier, 1966). p. 100.
19. Ibid, p. 102.
20. Einstein, p. 224.
21. Holmes, Edward. *The Life of Mozart and his Correspondence.* (New York: DaCapo Press, 1979), p. 170.
22. Solomon. p. 10.
23. Emily Anderson, trans. *The Letters of Mozart and His Family*, London, 1985, as edited by Maynard Solomon, *Mozart, A Life.* p256.
24. Spiegl, Fritz. *Lives, Wives and Loves of the Great Composers.* (London: Marion Boyers, 1997). p. 155
25. Solomon, p. 271.
26. Ibid, p. 296.
27. Einstein, p. 241.
28. See Alfred Einstein's treatment of "Mozart and His Contemporaries," pp 140-141, in *Mozart, His Character, His Work.*)
29. Einstein, p. 269.
30. Carr, p. 72.
31. Ibid, p. 73.
32. Ibid, p. 56.

33. Ibid, p. 78.
34. Ibid, p. 87.
35. Ibid, p. 101.
36. Ibid, p. 103.
37. Einstein, p. 194.
38. Carr, p. 107.
39. Ibid, p. 108.
40. Osbourne, Richard. Program Notes, Wolfgang Amadeus Mozart, Klavierkonzerte: Nos 19 & 27. DG Label 449-722-2.
41. Carr, p. 146.
42. Solomon, end note, p 582, n 55.
43. Ibid, p. 481.

Chapter Thirteen (Puccini)

1. Carner, Mosco. Puccini, A Critical Biography. (New York: Holmes and Meier, 1974.) p 248.
2. Ibid, p 16.
3. Ibid, p.17.
4. Weaver, William, and Simonetta Puccini, ed. *The Puccini Companion*. (New York: Norton, 1994). p.10. Hereafter PC.
5. Carner, p. 17
6. Ibid, p. 44.
7. Weaver, William. *Puccini, the Man and His Music*. (New York: Dutton, 1977). p. 15.
8. Ibid, p. 20.
9. Phillips-Matz, Mary Jane. *Puccini, A Biography*. (Boston: Northeastern Press, 2002). p. 78.
10. Spiegl, Fritz. *Lives, Wives and Loves of the Great Composers*. (London: Marion Boyers, 1997). p.161.
11. Ibid, p 162.
12. Phillips-Matz, p. 132.
13. Ibid, p. 86.
14. Weaver, PC, p 112.
15. Ibid, p. 114.
16. Phillips-Matz, p. 142.
17. Carner, p. 148.
18. Ibid, p. 149.
19. Ibid, p. 162.
20. Seligman, Vincent. *Puccini Among Friends*. (London: MacMillan, 1938) p 208.
21. Phillips-Matz, p. 223.
22. At the time of her father's death, Elvira's daughter Fosca was writing to Sybil as a dear friend. See Vincent Seligman, *Puccini Among Friends*.
23. Phillips-Matz, p. 226.

24. Maehder, Jürgen, in Weaver, PC, p 271.
25. Ibid, pp 272 – 273.
26. *Turandot*, finished by Franco Alfano, opened at La Scala on April 25, 1926.

Chapter Fourteen (Schubert)
1. Gibbs, Christopher H. *The Life of Schubert*. (Cambridge: Cambridge University Press. 2000). p.
2. The sketch is by Ferdinand Georg Waldmüller completed in 1827.
3. Reed, John. Schubert. (New York: Prentice Hall, 1997). p.2.
4. edited, Otto Erich Deutsch, *Schubert, Memoirs by His Friends*.(London: 1958), p 50.
5. Reed, p. 5.
6. Newbould, Brian. *Schubert, The Music and the Man*. (Berkeley: University of California Press, 1997). p. 22.
7. Ibid, p. 23.
8. Ibid, p. 35.
9. Reed, p. 17.
10. Grove Encyclopedia of Music, Vol. 22., p 658.
11. Grove, p 658
12. Clive, Peter. *Schubert and His World; A Biographical Dictionary*. (London: Oxford University Press, 1997.) p. 64.
13. Newbould, p. 189.
14. Reed. p. 24.
15. See Maurice J.E. Brown, "The Theresa Grob Collection of Songs by Schubert," *ML*, April 1968, pp 122-34.
16. Gibbs, p. 52.
17. Ibid, p. 53.
18. Ibid, p. 58.
19. Program notes by Clive Brown, Schubert, *Symphony No. 8 in B minor*. Nimbus Records, D 110825. 1991
20. Newbould, p. 218.
21. Ibid, p. 218.
22. See "Schubert a la Mode"; by Rita Steblin, Reply by Charles Rosen, in <u>The New York Review of Books</u>, Volume 41, Number 1, October 20, 1994.
23. Reed, p. 100.
24. Newbould, p. 266.
25. Clive, p. 46
26. Ibid, p. 46.

Chapter Fifteen (Schumann)

1. Schonberg, Harold C., *The Lives of the Great Composers*. (New York: Norton, 1997). p.170.
2. Ostwald, Peter, *Schumann, Inner Voices of a Musical Genius*. (Boston: Northeastern University, 1985). pp. 14-15.
3. Basch, Victor, *Schumann, A Life of Suffering*. (New York: Tutor, 1936) p10.
4. Dowley, Tim, *Schumann*. (London: Omnibus, 1982). p.10.
5. Ostwald, p. 17
6. From Schumann's autobiography, published in part by Schoppe and Nauhaus, the Robert Schumann House, Zwickau, 1973, p.43.)
7. see Robert Schumann, *Tagebücher*, edited by G. Eismann, Leipzig: VEB Deutscher Verlag für Musik, 1971)
8. Dowley. p.13.
9. Ostwald, p.26.
10. *Tagebücher*, ed., Eismann, pp 94, 109. See also Ostwald, p. 28.
11. Jensen, Eric Frederick, *Schumann*. (Oxford: Oxford University, 2001) p. 36.
12. Ostwald, p. 95.
13. Dowley, p. 46.
14. Szulc, Tad, *Chopin in Paris* (New York: Scribner, 1998) p. 64.
15. Ostwald, p. 97.
16. Litzmnann, Berthold, *Clara Schumann, Ein Kunsterleben*, 7th ed., (Leipzig: Breitkopf & Härtel, 1925), pp 83-85.
17. Ostwald, pp 102-103.
18. Spiegl, Fritz. *Lives, Wives and Loves of the Great Composers*. (London: Marion Boyers, 1997). p. 182.
19. Dowley, p. 51.
20. Ibid, p. 51.
21. Jensen, pp. 152-153.
22. Basch, p. 72.
23. Ibid, p 73.
24. Ostwald, p 122.
25. Ibid, p. 125.
26. Steinberg, Michael P., "Schumann's Homelessness," in Todd, R. Larry, ed., *Schumann and His World*. (Princeton: Princeton University, 1994). p 70.
27. Daverio, John, "Schumann's New Genre for the Concert Hall," in Todd, p 129.
28. Ostwald, p. 182.
29. Daverio, p 130
30. Jensen, p. 146.
31. Ostwald, p. 167.

32. Ibid, pp 188-189.
33. Ibid, p. 214.
34. Dowley, p. 87
35. Ostwald, p. 244.
36. Dowley, p. 106.
37. Ibid, p.108.
38. Basch, p. 208.
39. Ostwald, p. 245.
40. Dowley, p. 121.
41. Jensen, pp. 320-31.
42 Spiegl, p. 187.

Chapter Sixteen (Strauss, R)
1. Kennedy, Michael. *Richard Strauss*. (Oxford: Oxford University Press, 1995). p 2.
2. Del Mar, Norman. *Richard Strauss, A Critical Commentary of his Life and Works.* Volume One. (Ithaca: Cornell University Press, 1986) p. 3.
3. Kennedy, p. 5.
4. Ibid, p. 2.
5. Ibid, p. 11.
6. von Bülow, Hans, and Richard Strauss. *Correspondence.* Edited by Willi Schuh and Franz Trenner. (London: Boosey & Hawkes, Ltd., 1955.) pp. 22-23.
7. Del Mar, p. 41.
8. Kennedy, p. 11.
9. Ibid, p. 12.
10. Wilhelm, Kurt. *Richard Strauss, An Intimate Portrait.* (New York: Thames & Hudson, 1984). p. 30
11. Ibid, p. 30.
12. Kennedy, p. 18.
13. Del Mar, p. 64.
14. Ibid, p. 65.
15. Ibid, p. 69.
16. Kennedy, p. 17.
17. von Bülow, p. 82.
18. Kennedy, pp. 18-19.
19. Wilhelm, p. 248.
20. <www.americansymphony.org/dialogues_extensions/99_2000season/000_01/16/leon.html.>
21. Del Mar, p. 65.

22. Kennedy, p. 19.
23. Watson, Derek, *Richard Wagner, A Biography*. (New York: McGraw-Hill, 1979) p.151.
24. Kennedy, p. 21.
25. Ibid, p. 22.
26. Ibid.
27. Del Mar, p. 88.
28. Wilhelm, p. 57.
29. Del Mar, p. 193.
30. Kennedy, p. 75; p. 154.
31. Wilhelm, p. 68.
32. Ibid.
33. Kennedy, p. 195.

Chapter Seventeen (Stravinsky)
1. Schoenberg, Harold C. *The Lives of the Great Composers*. (New York: Norton, 1997.) p. 489.
2. White, Eric Walter. *Stravinsky, A Critical Survey.* (New York: Philosophical Library, 1946) p. 13. Stravinsky, Igor & Robert Craft. *Conversations with Igor Stravinsky*. (Garden City: Doubleday, 1959). Hereafter Conversations.
3. Stravinsky, Igor. *An Autobiography*. (New York: Norton, 1962). p. 6.
4. White, p. 13.
5. Stravinsky, Igor & Robert Craft. *Memories and Commentaries*. (Berkeley: University of California Press, 1981.) p. 25. Hereafter M&C.
6. Ibid.
7. White, p. 14.
8. Stravinsky, *An Autobiography*. p. 6.
9. M&C, p. 21.
10. Walsh, Stephen. *Stravinsky: A Creative Spring*. (New York: Knopf, 1999) p. 38.
11. Ibid, p. 43.
12. Ibid, p. 92.
13 Stravinsky, *An Autobiography*. p.12.
14. Dobrin, Arnold. *Igor Stravinsky, His Life and Times*. (New York: Thomas Y. Crowell, 1970). p. 30
15. Walsh, p. 92.
16. Ibid, p. 93.
17. Stravinsky and Craft, *Conversations*, p. 39.
18. M&C, pp. 57-58.
19. Dobrin, p. 32.

20. White, p. 22.
21. Walsh, p. 134.
22. Ibid, p. 135.
23. White, p. 27.
24. Ibid, p. 30.
25. Dobrin, p. 105.
26. Ibid, p. 60.
27. Joseph, Charles M. *Stravinsky, Inside and Out.* (New Haven: Yale University Press, 2001). p. 73.
28. Ibid.
29. White, p. 76.
30. Joseph, p. 75.
31. Walsh, p. 276.
32. Ibid, p. 313.
33. Ibid, p.319.
34. Dobrin, p. 103.
35. Walsh, p. 319.
36. Ibid, p. 326.
37. Ibid.
38. Stravinsky, Vera & Robert Craft. *Stravinsky in Pictures and Documents* (New York: Simon and Schuster, 1978). p. 236.
39. Ibid, p. 239.
40. "Igor Stravinsky, "from,Wikipedia, the free encyclopedia; <www.en.wikipedia.org.wiki/IgorStravinsky> 12/28/04
41. Stravinsky, *An Autobiography.* p.103.
42. Bratby, R.G. "Octet." <www.musicalnotes.co.uk/notes/stravinsky3.html.> 12/28/04
43. Joseph, p.280, n. 9.
44. Serkin, Peter. Program notes: New World Records, 80344; Piano Works by Igor Stravinsky, Stefan Wolpe, and Peter Lieberson.)
45. Goldbarth, Michael; "Flowers, Valentines, and Ballerina Beauties," National Ballet of Canada – Stravinsky Violin Concerto; November 18, 2004. Hummingbird Centre, Toronto.)
46. White, p. 148.
47. Steinberg, Michael. Program Notes. <www.nehrlich.com/chorus/stravinksyprogramnotes.html.>
48. Craft, Robert, *Chronicle of a Friendship,* (New York: Knopf, 1972) p. 197.
49. Dobrin, p. 167.
50. Ibid, p. 168.
51. Stravinsky, Vera, & Robert Craft, *Stravinsky in Pictures and Documents*, Plate 31.

Chapter Eighteen (Tchaikovsky)
1. Warrack, John, *Tchaikovsky*. (New York: Scribner's, 1973) p. 27.
2. Schonberg, Harold C., *The Lives of the Great Composers*. (New York: Norton, 1997) p. 366.
3. Warrack, p. 53 .
4. Ibid, p. 54.
5. Ibid, p. 110.
6. Ibid, p. 111.
7. Brown, David. *Tchaikovsky Remembered*. (London: Faber and Faber, 1993) p. 61.
8. Osborn, Andrew. Concert Program Notes: <www.gdyo.org/docs/ProgramNotes/3-6-05.pdf.>
9. Warrack, p. 63.

Chapter Nineteen (Verdi)
1. Hemingway, Ernest, to George Plimpton, Interview in The Paris Review, Spring 1958.
2. Walker, Frank, *The Man Verdi*. (Chicago: University of Chicago Press, 1982.) p.5.
3. Phillips-Matz, Mary Jane, *Verdi, A Biography*. (Oxford: Oxford University Press, 1993) p.28.
4. Schonberg, Harold C., *The Lives of the Great Composers*. (New York: Norton, 1997.) p. 249.
5. Oswald, Charles. *Verdi, A Life in the Theatre*. (New York: Knopf, 1987) p. 5.
6. Ibid, p. 6.
7. Phillips-Matz, p. 51.
8. Ibid, p. 52.
9. Walker, p 22.
10. Ibid.
11. Phillips-Matz, p 86.
12. Walker, p. 36.
13. Phillips-Matz, 89.
14. Ibid.
15. Walker, p. 33.
16. Wechsberg, Joseph, *Verdi*. (New York: Putnam's, 1974). p.21.
17. Phillips-Matz, pp.112-113.
18. Walker, pp. 48-49.
19. Ibid, p. 49.
20. Wechsberg, p. 31.
21. Ibid, p. 32.
22. Phillips-Matz, p.151.
23. Ibid, p. 159.
24. Ibid.
25. Wechsberg, p. 33.

26. Oswald, p. 76.
27. Ibid, p. 88.
28. Walker, p.164.
29. Ibid, p. 186.
30. Wechsberg, p. 78.
31. Phillips-Matz, p. 502.
32. Ibid, p. 547.
33. Oswald, p. 206.
34. Phillips-Matz, p. 558.
35. Walker, p. 286.
36. Ibid, p. 288.
37. Phillips-Matz, p. 598.
38. Oswald, pp. 243-244.
39. Phillips-Matz, p. 634.
40. Ibid, p. 635.
41. Ibid, p. 639.
42. Wechsberg, p. 51.
43. Oswald, p. 301.
44, Ibid, p. 302.
45. Wechsberg, p. 170.
46. Program notes, TELARC, CD-80254; Verdi, *Quatro Pezzi Sacri.* 1991.
47. Wechsberg, p. 241.
48. Ibid, p. 28.
49. Oswald, p. 328.

Chapter Twenty (Wagner)
1. Watson. Derek. *Richard Wagner, A Biography.* (New York: McGraw-Hill, 1979.) p. 116
2. Ibid, pp. 20-21.
3. Gutman, Robert W. *Richard Wagner: The Man, His Mind, and His Music.* (New York: Harcourt, Brace & World, 1968.) p. 3.
4. Watson, p. 23.
5. Ibid, p. 24.
6. Glasenapp, C.F., *Life of Richard Wagner.* Translated by William Ashton Ellis. Vol 1, (New York: Da Capo Press, 1977) p. 90.
7. Gutman, p. 8.
8. Watson, p. 29.
9. Panofsky, Walter. *Wagner, a pictorial biography.* (New York: Viking Press, 1963) p. 12.
10. Gal, Hans. *Richard Wagner.* Translated by Hans-Hubert Schönzeler. (New York: Stein and Day, 1976.) p. 17.
11. Gutman, p. 47.

12. Osborne, Charles. *Wagner and his World.* (New York: Scribner's, 1977) p. 17.
13. Ibid, pp 19-20.
14. Watson, p. 68.
15. Ibid, p. 65.
16. Osborne, p. 35.
17. Ibid, p. 27.
18. Panofsky, p. 38.
19. Gal, p. 39.
20. Watson. p. 98.
21. Ibid, p. 110.
22. Gutman, p. 133.
23. Watson, p. 113.
24. Gal, p. 51.
25. Watson, pp. 114 – 115.
26. Ibid, p. 126.
27. Ibid, p. 147.
28. Ritchie, Reginald Steven. Richard Wagner, *Classical Music Midi Page*, May, 2002. <www.classicalmidi.co.uk/wagner.htm>
29. Deutsche Website: < www3.stzh.ch/internet/zuerichkultur/home/instituionen >
30. Watson, p. 152.
31. Panofsky, p. 52.
32. Ibid, p. 61.
33. Ibid.
34. Ibid, p. 65.
35. Watson, p. 198.
36. Ibid, p. 151.
37. Sokoloff, Alice, H. *Cosima Wagner, Extraordinary Daughter of Franz Liszt.* (New York, Dodd,. Mean & Company, 1969). p. 97.
38. Ibid, p. 106.
39. Panofsky, p. 76.
40. Ibid.
41. Osborne, p. 83.
42. Sokoloff, p. 210.
43. Osborne, p. 89.
44. Ibid, p. 102.
45. Sokoloff, p. 264.
46. Watson, p. 314.
47. Sokoloff, p. 265.

Chapter Twenty-one (Baroque and Early Classical)

1. <www.andrejkoymansky.com/liv/fam/bioh1/hand1.html>
2. Burrows, Donald. *Handel.* (New York: Schirmer Books, 1994), p.373.
3. Kirkpatrick, Ralph. *Domenico Scarlatti.* (Princeton: Princeton University Press, 1953). p. 8.
4. Boyd, Malcolm. *Domenico Scarlatti, Master of Music.* (New York: Schirmer Books, 1986). p. 99.
5. Ibid, p. 141.
6. <w3.rz-berlin-mpg.de/cmp/Scarlatti_d.html>
7. Boyd, p. 148.
8. Petzoldt, Richard. *Georg Philipp Telemann.* Trans. by Horace Fitzpatrick. (New York: Oxford University Press, 1974), p. 6.
9. Ibid, p. 10.
10. Ibid, p. 13.
11. Ibid, p. 29.
12. <www.amarcordes.ch/comositeurs/telemann_grove.htm>
13. <www.hoasm.org/XIZ/XIA_Telemann.html>
14. Petzoldt, p. 51.
15. Ibid, p. 74.
16. <www.goldbergweb.com/en/magazine/essays/1999/09/419_2.php>
17. Landon, H.C. Robbins, *Vivaldi, Voice of the Baroque.* (New York: Thames and Hudson, 1993). p.16.
18. Ibid, p. 25.
19. www.vanderbilt.edu/htdoc/Blair/Courses/MUSL243/bacvivwb.htm>
20. Pastorek, Carmen. "Little Orphan Anna," in <www.vanderbilt.edu/htdoc> as above.
21. Landon, p. 100.
22. Ibid, p. 122.

Chapter Twenty-two (Romantic and Early Modern)

1. *Schönzeler, Hans-Hubert. Dvořak.* (London: Marion Boyars Publ., 1984) p. 43.
2. Ibid, p. 55.
3. Ibid, p. 56.
4. Šourek, Otakar. *Antonin Dvořak, Letters and Reminiscences* Transl. Roberta Samsour. (Prague: Artia, 1954). pp. 86-87.
5. Mercer-Taylor, Peter. *The Life of Mendelssohn.* Cambridge: Cambridge University Press, 2000.) p.35. (hereafter, MT)
6. Kaufmann, Schima. *Mendelssohn, a Second Elijah.* (New York: Tutor Publishing Company, 1936) p. 268.
7. MT, p. 56

8. Ibid, pp. 84-85.
9. Ibid, p. 86.
10. Ibid, p. 87.
11. Ibid, p. 131.
12. Ibid, p. 150.
13. Ibid, p. 159.
14. Ibid, p. 202.
15. Ornstein, Arbie. *Ravel; The Man and Musician.* (New York: Columbia University Press, 1975,) p. 9.
16. Nichols, Roger. *Ravel Remembered.* (New York: W.W. Norton, 1987) p. 48.
17. Ibid, p. 36.
18. Ornstein, p. 103.
19. Ibid, p. 108.
20. Ibid, p. 109.
21. Large, Brian. *Smetana.* (New York: Praeger, 1970) pp. 10-11
22. Ibid, pp 16-17.
23. Ibid.
24. Ibid, p.18.
25. Ibid, p. 19.
26. Ibid, pp. 80-81.
27. Ibid, p. 102.

Index

Abegg, Pauline, 160-161, 164, 272(n)
de Ahna, Pauline (see Strauss, wife of)
d'Agoult, Marie, Countess, 101-103, 105, 270(n)
Albrechtsberger, Johann, 27
Aryani, Adila, 15-16, 267(n)
Asyl, 229-230, 232
Auden, W.H., 196
Auernhammer, Josephine, 134, 271(n)
Bach, Johan Sebastian
    compared with Beethoven, 22
    early years, 5-6
    inspiration of, 13
    Leipzig, in, 11
    at the Weimar Court, 9
    wives: Anna Magdalena, 10-13, 267(n)
Maria Barbara, 6-10, 267(n)
Bach, Carl Phillip Emmanuel, 12, 88, 93
Bach, Johann Friedemann, 10
the Bäsle (see Maria Thekla Mozart)
Banti, Brigita, 94, 270(n)
Barezzi, Margherita (see Verdi, wives of)
Baroque (music), 22, 24, 88, 243, 260
Bartók, Béla
    folk (peasant) music, 14, 15, 20
    nationalistic style, 16-17
    youthful travel, 15
    wives: Marta (Ziegler), 17-19, 267(n)
    Ditta (Pásztory), 19-20, 267(n)
Bauer-Lechner, Natalie, 115-116
Beethoven, Ludwig
    and Bach, 22
    and Haydn, 25-26
    and Mozart, 24
    and Schubert, 149
    conversation book, 31
    early music instruction, 23
    eccentricity, 22
    "Immortal Beloved," 22, 29-30, 31
Beethoven, Johanna, 31
Benecke, Fröjde, 261-262, 272(n)
Berlioz, Hector
    conductor (as), 38-39, 42
    early music training, 33
    Mendelssohn (with), 36
    music critic, 34
    wives: Marie Recio, 38-40, 42, 268(n)
Harriet Smithson, 35-38, 268(n)
Bizet, Georges
    early years, 43
    learning Italian, 48
    military service, 48
    traveling in Europe, 45
    Wagner and, 48-49
    wife: Geneviève (Halévy) Bizet, 47-48, 268(n)
de Bosset, Vera (see Stravinsky, wives of)
Boccherini, Luigi, 260
Bossier, Valerie, 100, 270(n)
Brahms, Johannes
    early years, 51-52
    piano playing in brothels, 52
    on Liszt, 52
    with the Schumanns, 53, 55-57
    Brentano, Antonie, 1, 22, 30-31, 267(n)
    von Breuning, Eleonore (Lorchen), 24-25, 27, 267(n)
    von Bülow, Hans, 58, 175, 177, 179
Buxtehude, Diderik, 7, 238
Carus, Agnes, 159
Čermak, Anna (see Dvořak, wives of)
Čermak, Josephina, 252, 269(n)
Chanel, Gabrielle (Coco), 192-193
Chopin, Frédéric
    creativity and passion 67
    early compositions, 62-63
    in Poland, 68
    question of sexuality, 63, 155
Church music, 12, 22, 34, 38, 44, 61, 85, 92, 100, 104, 160, 162, 164, 206, 216, 258
Craft, Robert, 192-193, 195
Czech opera, 253, 258-259
Davidov, Vladimir (Bobyk), 204-205, 273(n)
Deboeuf, Estelle, 34, 41, 268(n)
Debussy, Claude, 187
Delius, Frederick, 86
Deym, Josephine, 28-29, 267(n)
d'Honrath, Jeanette, 25, 267(n)
Diaghilev, Sergei, 188-189, 191
Dickens, Charles, 142, 184
Dostoyevsky, Fyodor, 184
Dupin, Aurore, aka George Sand, 66, 103-104, 269(n)

Dvořák, Antonin
    harmony, (instruction in), 252
    marriage, 90, 254
    New York (in), 253
    wife: Anna (Čermak), 252-254, 269(n)
Eberlin, Amalie, 244, 273(n)
Elgar, Edward
    as poet, 74
    depression, 84
    influence of Handel, 80
    influence of Schumann and Wagner, 76
    religious stigma, 79
    "Variations" explained, 80-82
    wives: Alice Caroline (Roberts),78-79, 80, 84, 269(n)
Elgar, Carice, 79, 86
Endenich, 52, 172
Esterházy, Caroline, 153, 156, 271(n)
Esterházy, Prince Anton, 89-90
Fauré, Gabriel, 49
Fernandinova, Bettina, 262-263, 272(n)
Fitton, Hilda; Isobel, 78, 269(n)
"the Five", 186
Flaubert, Gustave, 184
folk music (various), 16, 20, 42, 61, 140 199, 259-260
von Fricken, Ernestine, 163-164, 272(n)
Gemignani, Elvira (see Puccini, wife of)
von Gensinger, Marianne, 92-93, 270(n)
Gentili, Catarina (See Scarlatti, wife of)
German Opera, 112, 131, 179, 217, 238
German Romantics, 15, 17, 159, 252
Geyer, Stefania (Stefi), 15-17, 267(n), 276(n)
Giesemann, Lieschen, 52, 268(n)
Gireau (Girò) Anna, 248, 273(n)
Gladowska, Constantia, 63, 68, 268(n)
Glinka, Mikhail, 42, 183-184, 265
Gollerová, Elizabeth, 260, 272(n)
Grob, Theresa, 151-153, 155, 271(n)
Guicciardi, Giulietta, 28, 267(n)
Halévy, Geneviève (see Bizet, wife of)
Handel, George Frideric
    Bach (influence of), 13
    England (home in), 239-240
    sexuality, 239
    travel (interest in), 239
Haydn, Franz Josef
    final six symphonies, 94
    London (in), 91-92
    singer (as), 86-87
    meets Beethoven, 93
    wife: Maria Anna (Keller), 89-90, 270(n)
von Herzogenberg, Elisabet, 58-59, 265(n), 267(n)
Hesse, Herman, 182
Hockman, Vera, 85-86, 269(n)
Hofdemel, Magdalena, 133, 137-138, 271(n)
Hofdemel, Franz, 137
Hoffman, E.T.A., 36
Hölderlin, Friedrich, 109
Holst, Gustav, 82, 265
d'Honorath, Jeanette,25, 267(n)
Hummel, Johann Nepomuk, 95
idée fixe, 34, 36, 37
"Immortal Beloved," 22, 29, 30-31
Italian Opera, 142, 146-147, 210, 216, 238, 239, 245
Joseph II, Emperor, 26
von Keglevich, Babette, 27, 267(n)
Keller, Therese, 89, 270(n)
Keller, Maria Anna (see Haydn, wife of)
Klimt, Gustav, 118
Kolařová, Katerina (see Smetana, wives of)
Kurz, Selma, 117-118, 270(n)
Laussot, Jesse, 227-228, 273(n)
Leoncavallo, Ruggerio, 139, 142, 143
Liszt, Franz
    Beethoven's influence, 98
    Chopin (with), 65, 68
    Mozart compared with , 96
    poetry (use of), 98
    political consciousness, 99
    teacher (as), 102
    Wagner (and), 106-107
Ludwig II, King of Bavaria, 232, 234
Mahler, Gustav
    conductor (as), 113, 114
    existentialist interests, 110
    fixated with death, 109
    poet (as) 109-110
    Vienna (in), 116-117
    wife: Alma (Schindler), 118-120, 121-122, 270(n)
Malfatti, Therese, 29, 267(n)
Manfredi, Doria (aka Dora), 144-145, 271(n)
Maria Barbara, Princess of Portugal, 241, 271(n)
Massenet, Jules, 48, 140
von Meck, Nadezhda, 201-203, 273(n)
Mendelssohn, Felix
    choral music (return to), 256

homage to Bach, 254
poetry (use of), 254-255
Mendelssohn, Fannie, 254-256, 270(n)
von Mildenberg, Anna, 115-116, 270(n)
Moke, Camille, 36-37, 100, 268(n)
Mozart, Wolfgang
    death of mother in Paris, 128
    early music training, 124
    father's influence, 124-126
    Masonic connection, 132, 135
    Paris (in), 128-129
    Vienna (in), 125
    wife: Constanze (Weber), 124, 130-134, 136-137, 271(n)
    Mozart, Leopold, 124-126
    Mozart, Maria (Thekla), 125, 271(n)
    Mozart, Nannerl, 133
Mussorgsky, Modest, 42, 185-186, 204
Napoleon, Louis (emperor), 28, 33, 260
Nicolai, Otto, 61
Nikitna, Zhenya, 193, 273(n)
Nosenko, Katya, see (Stravinsky, wives of)
Opera Buffa, 88, 208
Pachelbel, Johann, 5
Pachta, Jenny, 223-225, 273(n)
Paganini, Niccolò, 99-100, 161, 265
von Paradis, Maria Teresa, 133, 271(n)
Pászatory, Ditta (see Bartók, wives of)
Picasso, Pablo, 1, 191-192
Pistor, Betsy, 255, 270(n)
Ployer, Babette, 134, 271(n)
poetry, role of in music comp., iii, 2-3, 44, 73-74, 80, 86, 93, 98, 110, 166, 182, 201, 241, 255
Poisl, Josephine, 111-112, 270(n)
Porubsky, Bertha, 55-56, 268(n)
Polzelli, Luigia, 90-91, 94, 270(n)
Potocka, Delphina, 65-67, 69, 72, 269(n)
Pound, Ezra, 75, 188, 247
Powell, Dora(bella), 81-82
prix de Rome, 37, 44
Pushkin, 185-187
Puccini, Giacomo
    autobiographical compositions, 143
    onset of final illness, 144
    success in London, 146
wife: Elvira (Gemignani), 140-144, 271(n)
Ravel, Maurice
    emotion in music, 258
    preparation as pianist, 257

Recio, Marie (see Berlioz, wives of)
Reiter, Marie, 48-49, 268(n)
Richter, Johanna, 111, 270(n)
Rimsky-Korsakov, Nikolai, 186-188
Rimsky-Korsakov, Vladimir, 186
Roberts, Caroline Alice, (see Elgar, wives of)
Romanticism, 15, 17, 36, 51, 65, 97, 150
Rubenstein, Ida, 257-258, 271(n)
de Saint-Circq, Caroline, 65, 98, 102, 270(n)
Saint-Säens, Camille, 46, 48
Salieri, Antonio, 27, 97, 150
Sand, George; see Dupin, Aurore, 38, 66-68, 269(n)
Sand, Solange, 70-71
von Sayn-Wittgenstein, Carolyne, 41, 104-107, 169, 270(n)
Scarlatti, Alessandro, 243
Scarlatti, Domenico
    commitment from the "royals," 242
    friends and influences, 243
    wives: Catarina (Gentili), 240-241, 271(n)
    Anastasia (Xinenes), 240-241, 271(n)
Schroter, Rebecca, 92, 270(n)
Schindler, Alma (see Mahler, wife of)
Schubert, Franz
    Beethoven influence, 154, 156
    bi-sexual nature, 155
    early music, 149
    influence of poets, 152-153
    intelligentsia (with), 154
Schumann, Robert
    autobiographical compositions, 166
    Brahms (with), 170-172
    Clara's music career, 161, 167, 171
    early music experience, 158
    imaginary friends, 162
    influence of Schubert, 156
    interest in poetry, 157
    mental illness, 168, 170-172,
    Schülverein, 159
wife of: Clara (Wieck), 10, 61, 63-65, 69-70, 160, 164-166, 170-188, 256, 266, 268 (n), 272(n)
Seligman, Sybil, 145, 271(n)
Shakespeare, William, 35, 37-38, 216, 223, 254
Shilovski, Vladimir, 202, 273(n)
von Siebold, Agatha, 54-55, 268(n)
Smetana, Bedřich
    Berlioz (influence of), 259
    Liszt (learning from), 260
    Schubert (influence of), 260, 262

Musical Muse: Wives and Lovers of the Great Composers

    wives: Bettina (Ferdinandová), 262, 272(n)
    Katerina (Kolařová), 260-261, 272(n)
    Louisa Smetana, 259-260, 272(n)
Smithson, Harriett (see Berlioz, wives of)
Smyth, Ethel Mary, 58, 265
Spies, Hermine, 58-59, 268(n)
Stirling, Jane, 71-72, 269(n)
Stolz, Teresa, 213-217, 273(n)
Strauss, Richard
    Italy (in), 175-176
    Mozart, (influence of) 175, 179
    poet (as), 181
    tone poem (and the), 174
    Wagner, champion of, 180
    wife of: Pauline (de Ahna), 176, 179-80, 182, 272(n)
Street, Agnes, 107, 270(n)
Strepponi, Giuseppina see Verdi, wives of)
Stravinsky, Igor
    American jazz (and), 184
    Bizet (influence of), 186
    expatriate (as), 191
    Glinka (influence of), 183
    Russia (return to), 196-197
    USA (in), 195-196
    wives: Catherine/Katya (Nosenko), 185, 187-189, 191, 193, 273(n)
Vera (Sudeikina), 190, 194-195, 196-197, 273(n)
Stuart-Wortley, Alice, 83, 85-86, 269(n)
Süssmayr, Franz Xavier, 97, 136-137
Tafelmusik, 245-246
Tartini, Giuseppe, 2, 3, 237
Tchaikovsky, Pyotr,
    French upbringing, 198-199
    Bizet (and), 50
    Mahler (and), 145
    sexuality, 200, 201
Telemann, Georg
    Bach (friendship), 244
    entrepreneur (as), 245
    Hamburg (in), 245
Textor, Maria Catharina, 245-246, 273(n)
Thurber, Jeanette, 253, 269(n)
Unger, Caroline, 98
Venard, Céleste, 46-47, 268(n)
Verlaine, Paul, 190
Verdi, Giuseppe
    early music training, 205
    theater-oriented (as), 206

travel (love of), 210
    wives of: Giuseppina (Strepponi), 207-209, 212, 214, 273(n)
    Margherita (Barezzi), 205-208, 273(n)
Vivaldi, Antonio
    J.S. Bach (praise from), 247
    orphanage work, 248
    Roman Catholic priest (as), 247
Wagner, Richard
    conductor (as), 222
    in exile, 239
    conductor (as), 222
    in exile, 39, 239
    Judaism (and) 220
    Liszt (with), 107, 174, 231
    poetry (and), 224, 231
    revolutionary ideas, 225-226
    self-taught, 222
    travel (and), 103
    wives of: Cosima (von Bülow), 103-105, 146, 179-181, 230-233, 273(n)
    Minna (Planer), 222-225, 226-227, 231, 273(n)
Weber, Constanze (see Mozart, wife of)
Weber, Aloysia, 127
von Weber, Carl Marie, 221
von Weber, Marion, 113-114
Wesendonck, Mathilde, 230-233, 273(n)
Wieck, Clara (see Schumann, wife of)
Wihan, Dora, 176-177, 178, 272(n)
Wodzinska, Marie, 67, 269(n)
Woyciechowski, Titus, 63-65, 268(n)
Ximenes, Anastasia, (see Scarlatti, Domenico, wives of)
Ziegler, Marta , (see Bartók , wives of)

Arthur McMaster

Author's Biography:

A former student of piano, Arthur McMaster was a member of various choral and acting groups in New York and Virginia. Nominated for a Pushcart Prize in 2006, he has published poetry on Robert Schumann, Leonard Bernstein, and Beethoven in numerous journals, including a prize-winning poem on Mozart in "The Piano Press." His drama "Prisms," won the Florida Stageworks competition in 2000. Mr. McMaster teaches writing and literature courses at Converse College. He is currently at work on a book about the poets' muses.